Congress For Dummies

P9-ECI-272

Cheat Sheet

House Contact Information

The House Web site: www.House.gov

Also: Clerk of the House: www.clerkweb.house.gov

House e-mail addresses consist of the person's first name and last name, separated by a dot, followed by @mail.house.gov. (Be aware that some people use nicknames and middle initials.)

House Offices

- The Capitol (H).
- Cannon (CHOB), 1st St. & Independence Ave. SE, three-digit room numbers, the first digit is the floor number.
- Longworth (LHOB), Independence Ave. & New Jersey Ave. SE, four-digit room numbers starting with 1, the second digit is the floor number.
- Rayburn (RHOB), Independence Ave. & S. Capitol St. SW (Four-digit room numbers starting with 2) In Rayburn, the second digit is the floor number. All of the buildings have maps to help you find individual office numbers. In Rayburn, there are several subcommittee offices on the "B" level (where the cafeteria is also located).
- O'Neill (OHOB), New Jersey Ave. & C St. SE, also called Annex 1. Slated for demolition by the end of 2002.
- Ford (FHOB) 300 D St. SW, also known as Annex 2.

Senate Contact Information

The Senate Web site: www.Senate.gov

Senate e-mail addresses consist of the person's first name and last name, separated by a dot, followed by @[last name of senator].Senate.gov.

Senate Offices

These buildings have conventional room numbers; the first digit of the room number is the floor number.

- The Capitol (S)
- Russell (SR) 1st St. and Constitution Ave. NE (East Corner)
- Dirksen (SD) 1st St. and Constitution Ave. NE (West corner)
- Hart (SH) 2nd and C Streets NE

For Dummies: Bestselling Book Series for Beginners

Congress For Dummies®

Cheat Sheet

Congressional Recesses

Each recess usually lasts a week or two. You can check the current year's calendar for exact dates.

- Presidents Day: February
- Passover/Easter: March or April
- Memorial Day: Last week of May
- Independence Day: First week of July
- August: Full month until Labor Day in September
- First Thursday in October: Target adjournment

Tips for Visiting a Member or Staffer

1. Be prompt, brief, and concise.
2. Know your goals.
3. Prepare the ground.
4. Do your homework.
5. Be courteous and calm.
6. Know your facts.
7. Offer assistance.
8. Provide data on the cost and economic impact of your proposal if you can.
9. Provide helpful written material and offer to answer any questions.
10. Always follow up with a call, e-mail, or note.

Congressional Contact Information

Capitol switchboard

202-224-3121

Congressional database

http://thomas.loc.gov/

Mailing address

Rep. _____

United States House of Representatives

Washington, DC 20510

Sen. _____

United States Senate

Washington, DC 20515

For Dummies: Bestselling Book Series for Beginners

Congress

FOR

DUMMIES®

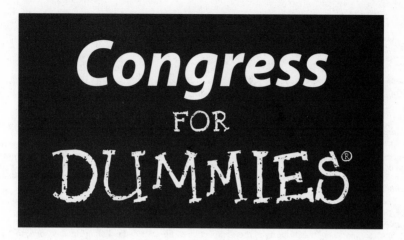

by David Silverberg

**Forewords by Speaker of the House Dennis Hastert and
Senate Majority Leader Tom Daschle**

Wiley Publishing, Inc.

Congress For Dummies®

Published by
Wiley Publishing, Inc.
909 Third Avenue
New York, NY 10022
www.wiley.com

Copyright © 2002 by Wiley Publishing, Inc., Indianapolis, Indiana

Published simultaneously in Canada

For general information on our other products and services or to obtain technical support, please contact our Customer Care Department within the U.S. at 800-762-2974, outside the U.S. at 317-572-3993, or fax 317-572-4002.

Wiley also publishes its books in a variety of electronic formats. Some content that appears in print may not be available in electronic books.

Library of Congress Control Number: 2002110307

ISBN: 0-7645-5421-2

Manufactured in the United States of America

10 9 8 7 6 5 4 3 2 1

About the Author

David Silverberg has covered Congress and congressional politics in one form or another since coming to Washington in 1981.

His first Washington job was as assistant editor of *Near East Report*, a newsletter affiliated with the American Israel Public Affairs Committee, which has been called the most powerful foreign policy lobby in Washington.

As a reporter for weekly newspaper *Defense News* from 1986 to 1993, he covered congressional activity on defense, diplomacy, commerce and trade matters. As editor-at-large for the monthly magazine *Armed Forces Journal International* between 1993 and 1997 he created and wrote two popular features called Congressional Watch and Congressional Darts & Laurels.

In June, 1998 Silverberg began editing and publishing his own quarterly magazine, *The Journal of Information Policy*, the first journal of ideas dedicated to government policymaking in the information age. In May 1999 he sold it to Fed Services Inc.

Today Silverberg is managing editor of *The Hill*, a weekly newspaper covering Congress with the largest circulation of any Capitol Hill publication. He writes three columns for the paper, on defense, technology and globalization. He also oversaw a redesign of the newspaper's Web site and created an electronic e-newsletter on congressional doings called *Omens & Portents*. The site can be accessed at: www.TheHill.com.

Silverberg's writing has appeared in a wide variety of academic and popular publications and he has appeared on a number of national television and radio programs to discuss policy and politics.

Congress For Dummies is his first book.

Silverberg, his wife June Fletcher, a reporter for *The Wall Street Journal,* and their son, Adam, live in Virginia's 10th Congressional District.

Dedication

Most book dedications say a book is *for* someone. They often sound as though the author purchased the book in a store and simply delivered it, dumping it on a desk or the nearest coffee table.

This is my first book and having written it, I now know that writing a book *for* someone means much more than just delivering a manuscript.

Writing a book for someone means keeping before you a vision of the person for whom you're writing – and that vision sustains you through the ordeal of producing the book. But it also means that the person for whom you're writing motivates you to continue through a sometimes long, tedious, and frustrating but ultimately worthwhile process. It means you so want this person to have this product of your labors, and this person so inspires you, that you're willing to endure long hours of writing and research, and forgo beautiful days when you're rather be anywhere than at your desk, and keeps you working through nights when you're dead tired but the deadlines demand extra effort, and make all the sacrifices that a project like this entails. There's an awful lot of meaning in that simple, three-letter word *for*.

And so this book is for June, my lovely wife who deserves so much more than I've given her and who has always been an inspiration and a Muse.

This book is for my son, Adam, who I hope grows up safe, strong, free, and fearless. This is my small effort to improve the world he'll inherit.

This book is for my parents, Sidney and Edna, who gave me a belief in political involvement, in social justice, and in government that serves the people. And it's for my brother Paul, his wife Nancy, and their children.

This book is also for the young reporters at *The Hill* who may not believe it when I cut their copy, or hold their stories, or enforce the deadlines, or tell them that they can't edit on the page proofs, or argue with them about placement, or kick them out of the production room, or discard the dirty dishes they leave in the kitchen sink, but I'm really very fond of them all. Their energy and enthusiasm is invigorating. It was a clear need for a single, simple guide to Congress for people like them that inspired this idea in the first place.

And lastly, this book is for all the people who make the pilgrimage to their Capitol, who I see coming in the thousands to learn about the government of which they're such an integral part. It's for everyone who feels strongly enough to write a letter to register an opinion, or pick up the phone or send an e-mail to the members of the most powerful parliament in the world. It's for everyone who participates and votes. The term "the American people" sounds so trite and overused, but there's nothing nobler or more elevating.

This book is for the American people.

Author's Acknowledgments

This book had a long and difficult gestation and many people helped it along the way.

While this book is dedicated to them, special thanks must expressed to my wife, June Fletcher, without whose understanding and patience and support I never could have completed this project; to my son Adam, who kept me going; and to my parents Sidney and Edna, who encouraged me every step of the way.

My special thanks to Al Eisele, editor of The Hill, who proved that it's possible to be an editor, an agent, and a saint at the same time. I couldn't have done this without him.

My thanks also to Marty Tolchin, editor-in-chief and publisher of The Hill who created and maintains the kind of atmosphere that encourages maximum initiative, experimentation, and creativity. His example of thoughtful inquiry, political interest, and journalistic integrity is a true inspiration.

Special thanks to two women who could see the value of this project and were kind enough to express that support to Wiley Publishing at a crucial time: Cindy McConnell, formerly of the Close Up Foundation, which does wonderful work in bringing young students to Washington; and lobbyist Lydia Borland, who understands the value of people, politics and policy. Thanks too to Dianne Stamm for her warm encouragement and support.

In the two years that we discussed this book I had the opportunity to work with some excellent people at Hungry Minds, now Wiley & Sons. These included Sherry Gomoll, Joyce Pepple, and Susan Decker, all of whose support I appreciated. Very special thanks to Greg Tubach who made sense of so much of the Dummies culture and way of doing things and patiently walked me through it. Thanks to Kathleen Dobie for her editing, suggestions and especially her patience as I painfully learned the Dummies style and how to attach a template. (Bam! I think I've finally got it!). And thanks to Neil for his copy editing even when I disagreed with it.

Thanks too to Jean Gossman, my technical editor. I told her to be ruthless and she was and this book is far better for it. Her knowledge of Congress was invaluable and her patience, persistence, and dedication immeasurably improved this work.

Thanks to intern Matt Dalton for his research and to Frank Meyers, who didn't know what he was scanning, but whose help was so valuable in this endeavor as it is in all others.

My many thanks to the reporters and all the staff at The Hill, from all of whom I've learned so much.

My appreciation to Richard Baker and the staff of the Senate Historian's office, the parliamentary staff of both the House and Senate, and Bruce Milhans of the Architect of the Capitol's office, all of whom put up with my picky questions. And thanks to Brad Fitch and the Congressional Management Service who provide an invaluable service for Congress. Thanks also to John Kornacki, a gentleman and a scholar of the House.

Lastly thanks to all the members and staff of the United States Congress who never knew they were helping to write a book but who add a new chapter each and every day.

Publisher's Acknowledgments

We're proud of this book; please send us your comments through our Dummies online registration form located at www.dummies.com/register/.

Some of the people who helped bring this book to market include the following:

Acquisitions, Editorial, and Media Development

Project Editor: Kathleen A. Dobie

Acquisitions Editors: Greg Tubach, Tracy Boggier

Copy Editor: E. Neil Johnson

Technical Editor: Jean Gossman

Editorial Manager: Christine Meloy Beck

Editorial Assistant: Melissa Bennett

Cover Photos: © Dallas and John Heaton/CORBIS

Cartoons: Rich Tennant www.the5thwave.com

Production

Project Coordinator: Maridee Ennis

Layout and Graphics: Karl Brandt, Amanda Carter, David Bartholomew, Sean Decker, Kelly Hardesty, Joyce Haughey, LeAndra Johnson, Tiffany Muth, Barry Offringa, Jackie Nicholas, Jacqueline Schneider, Julie Trippetti, Jeremey Unger

Proofreaders: David Faust, John Greenough, Carl Pierce, TECHBOOKS Production Services

Indexer: TECHBOOKS Production Services

Publishing and Editorial for Consumer Dummies

Diane Graves Steele, Vice President and Publisher, Consumer Dummies

Joyce Pepple, Acquisitions Director, Consumer Dummies

Kristin A. Cocks, Product Development Director, Consumer Dummies

Michael Spring, Vice President and Publisher, Travel

Brice Gosnell, Publishing Director, Travel

Suzanne Jannetta, Editorial Director, Travel

Publishing for Technology Dummies

Andy Cummings, Acquisitions Director

Composition Services

Gerry Fahey, Vice President of Production Services

Debbie Stailey, Director of Composition Services

Contents at a Glance

Forewords...................................*xxiii and xxv*

Introduction *1*

Part I: Considering the Two Chambers *9*

Chapter 1: Welcome to Congress 11
Chapter 2: Running Your House: The House of Representatives 23
Chapter 3: Scoping Out the Senate 39

Part II: Looking at the Legislative Process.................*53*

Chapter 4: Introducing a Bill 55
Chapter 5: Meeting the Players, Setting the Schedule 75
Chapter 6: Reaching the Floor and Beyond 89

Part III: Following the Money *111*

Chapter 7: Raising Revenues 113
Chapter 8: Budgeting, Authorizing, and Appropriating Government Money 119
Chapter 9: Putting Your Political Contributions to Work 139

Part IV: Lobbying from All Angles *155*

Chapter 10: Looking at Lobbying 157
Chapter 11: Explaining Your Cause 169
Chapter 12: Getting Down to the Nitty-Gritty: Lobbying
Members of Congress 181
Chapter 13: Getting the Job Done: Congressional Staff 199
Chapter 14: Making the Most of the Media 217
Chapter 15: Working with Various Media 251

Part V: Putting the Practical Side to Use *269*

Chapter 16: Making Use of Congressional Services 271
Chapter 17: Visiting Congress 283

Part VI: The Part of Tens *297*

Chapter 18: Ten Tips for Conducting a Lobbying Campaign 299
Chapter 19: The Ten Commandments for Dealing with Congressional Staff 305
Chapter 20: Ten Tips for Dealing with Journalists 309
Chapter 21: Not Even Ten Suggestions for Improving Congress 315

Part VII: The Appendixes 319

Appendix A: Glossary of Congressional and Political Terms 321

Appendix B: Committees of the 107th Congress 333

Index 335

Table of Contents

Forewords ....*xxiii and xxv*

Introduction 1

What this Book Can Help You Do 2
How to Use this Book 2
Conventions Used in this Book 3
    A note on names 3
    Information on icons 4
How this Book Is Organized 5
    Part I: Considering the Two Chambers 5
    Part II: Looking at the Legislative Process 5
    Part III: Following the Money 5
    Part IV: Lobbying from All Angles 5
    Part V: Putting the Practical Side to Use 6
    Part VI: Part of Tens 6
    Part VII: The Appendixes 6
What this Book Is Not 6
A Word to the Wonks Should Be Sufficient — I Hope 7

Part 1: Considering the Two Chambers 9

Chapter 1: Welcome to Congress 11

The Three Branches of Government 12
    The congressional branch 12
    The executive branch 14
    The Supreme Court 15
Congressional Relationships 16
    House-Senate relations 16
    Executive-congressional relations through the years 16
    Congressional-constituent relations 17
Your Role as a Citizen 19
    Voting 20
    Registering your opinion 21

Chapter 2: Running Your House: The House of Representatives 23

Describing the House 24
    Coming up with qualifications 25
    Defining the congressional district 26
Finding a Lawmaker of Your Very Own 29
Doing the Job of Representative 32
    Getting the most from a short-term contract 34
    Diving into the congressional workweek 35

Doing Housework: The Responsibilities of the House 35
    Taxing responsibilities 36
    Considering legislation 36
    Taking care of you, the constituent 37

Chapter 3: Scoping Out the Senate **39**

What It Takes to Be a Senator and How to Find Yours 40
    Qualifying with experience 41
    Setting forth a senator's duties 42
    Finding and contacting your senator 42
Senatorial Responsibilities 44
    Passing legislation 45
    Proceeding to impeachment 48
    Giving advice and consent 49

Part II: Looking at the Legislative Process **53**

Chapter 4: Introducing a Bill **55**

Starting the Process 55
Dealing with the Players 56
    Members of Congress 56
    Staffers 56
    Committee folk 57
Building a Bill 58
    Starting with an idea 59
    Looking at the types of legislation 59
    Introducing a bill 62
    Giving a bill an identity 63
Getting There is Half the Fun: The Legislative Process 64
    Gathering cosponsors 64
    Pushing through the committee jungle 67
    Holding hearings 69
    Making the markup 71

Chapter 5: Meeting the Players, Setting the Schedule **75**

Following the Leaders 75
    Knowing who the leaders are 76
    Putting age before beauty:
      The role of seniority 79
Elbowing into the Huddle: The Role
  of Caucuses and Delegations 80
    Caucuses 81
    Delegations 83
Timing is Everything: Congressional Schedules 83
    The House calendar 83
    The Senate calendar 87

Chapter 6: Reaching the Floor and Beyond **89**

Waiting to Debate 90

Snagging Attention with an Introduction 90

Playing by the Rules: The Role of the Rules Committees 92

Debating on the Floor 94

Speaking in a sedate and timely fashion 95

Timing is everything 96

Adding amendments 97

Voting 98

Struggling toward Yes: The Conference Process 101

Convening a conference 102

Compromising in conference 103

Closing the conference 103

Getting the President's Signature 105

Wielding the veto 107

Overriding a veto 108

Battling after Passage 108

Protecting newly passed legislation 109

Coping with change 110

Part III: Following the Money *111*

Chapter 7: Raising Revenues **113**

Seeing the Sources 113

Acting on Taxes 114

Proposing 114

Disposing 115

Bearing the Burden: Taxation and You 116

**Chapter 8: Budgeting, Authorizing, and Appropriating
Government Money** **119**

Holding the Purse Strings 119

Budgeting 121

Scheduling the money calendar 121

Checking out the players 124

Mandating the type of spending 125

Interpreting the language of the budget 125

Authorizing 128

Appropriating 129

Smoking out the Cardinals and their court 129

Appreciating the appropriations process 131

Being earmarked 133

Inserting Items in Appropriations Bills 135

Chapter 9: Putting Your Political Contributions to Work **139**

Contributing to the Candidate of Your Choice 140
Making an individual contribution 141
Limiting your contributions 142
Giving money early 143
Becoming a PAC-man or PAC-woman 144
Forming and forms of PACs 144
Leveraging your money into influence 146
Distinguishing Hard Money from Soft Money 147
Mastering the Nuts and Bolts of Fundraising 149
Feting candidates with fundraisers 149
Getting professional help 151
Providing Other Campaign Services 153

Part IV: Lobbying from All Angles **155**

Chapter 10: Looking at Lobbying **157**

Explaining the Basics 158
Categorizing Lobbyists 158
Defining and describing 158
Demystifying special interests 159
Getting Your Member's Attention 160
Evaluating Scorecards and Key Votes 162
Determining whether You Need a Professional 163
Choosing a Lobbyist 165
Finding a professional 165
Quantifying the qualifications 166
Working out a plan of action 167
Evaluating your lobbyist 167

Chapter 11: Explaining Your Cause **169**

Knowing What You Want to Achieve 170
Educating Yourself 170
Building Your Case 171
Defining your core issue 171
Practicing the fine art of compromise 171
Knowing Your Issue 172
Doing the research 172
Taking stock of your assets and liabilities 173
Putting together a packet 174
Gathering Support 175
Building coalitions 175
Courting a congressional champion 177
Testifying before Congress 178

Chapter 12: Getting Down to the Nitty-Gritty:
Lobbying Members of Congress 181

Writing to Your Representative and Senators 181
Crafting written communications 182
E-mailing for every issue 183
Sending snail mail 185
Nixing faxing 186
Meeting Face to Face 186
Making an appointment 187
Making the most of face-time 189
Following up 190
Conveying Your Cause 190
Taking a Walk on the Dark Side: Going Negative 191
Giving Gifts, Travel, and Entertainment 193
Gift-giving guidelines 194
Travel 195
Entertainment 195
Keeping the Pressure On 196

Chapter 13: Getting the Job Done: Congressional Staff 199

Making Contact 199
Surveying Congressional Staff 200
Personal staff 201
Staff positions 201
Staff principles 203
Office structure 204
Getting Down to Personalities 206
Acknowledging Committee Staff 207
Committee staff 208
Leadership staff 209
Recognizing Auxiliary Support Staff 210
Congressional Budget Office 210
General Accounting Office 211
Library of Congress and the Congressional Research Service 213
Other support staff and services 214

Chapter 14: Making the Most of the Media 217

Understanding the Relationship between Congress and the Media 217
Getting Your Story Straight 219
Seeing the shades of gray 221
Working the congressional beat 222
Making the News 223
Lobbying the Media 224
Working with editors and producers 224
Working with reporters 225

Writing and Distributing Press Releases 228
    Writing a good press release 229
    Distributing a press release 230
    Following up on your press release 232
Organizing a Press Conference 232
    Booking a venue 233
    Organizing the event 233
Working with Television 236
Broadcasting on Radio 238
Browsing through Internet Media 240
Paying for Space 241
Using Celebrities 242
    Delineating the types of celebrities 242
    Preparing your celebrity 243
    Keeping your celebrity on a tight leash 244
Conducting a Demonstration 244
    The uses of demonstrations 245
    Planning a demonstration 246

Chapter 15: Working with Various Media **251**

Delineating Daily Print Media 252
    The big-three national dailies 252
    USA Today and The Washington Times 254
    Local dailies 255
Cozying Up to Columnists 256
Making the Most of Magazines and Periodicals 256
    The newsweeklies 257
    Ideological periodicals 258
    Regional and city periodicals 258
Courting Capitol Hill Media 259
    Newspapers 259
    Congressional Quarterly 260
    National Journal 261
Burning Up the Wire Services 261
    National services 262
    Specialized, industry, and trade media 262
Trumpeting Broadcast and Cable Television 263
    The broadcast networks 263
    The cable networks 264
    Talk shows 265
Tuning in to Radio 266
Investigating Internet Media 267
Going Abroad with Foreign Media 268

Part V: Putting the Practical Side to Use *269*

Chapter 16: Making Use of Congressional Services 271

Helping Out with the Feds 271
    Intervening with federal agencies 272
    Expediting your passport 273
Intervening in Local Issues 273
Putting in a Good Word 274
    Getting an academy nomination 274
    Serving Congress as a page 277
    Interning in the Capitol 280

Chapter 17: Visiting Congress 283

Visiting the Capitol Campus 283
    Finding out what's where 284
    Touring the Capitol 286
    Adhering to security restrictions 287
    Visiting the Capitol Visitor Center 288
Making Your Way to the House Side 290
    Distinguishing the House office buildings 291
    Making the most of other features 292
Seeing the Senate Side 292
Holding a Function at the Capitol 294
Dining on Capitol Hill 294

Part VI: The Part of Tens *297*

Chapter 18: Ten Tips for Conducting a Lobbying Campaign 299

Knowing Your Core Issues 299
Knowing What You're Trying to Achieve 300
Assessing Your Assets and Liabilities 300
Knowing Whereof You Speak 300
Building Coalitions and Alliances 301
Helping Your Friends and Frustrating Your Enemies 301
Being Open to Compromise 302
Not Expecting Quick Results 303
Finding a Champion 303
Being Patient, Persistent, and Persevering 303

Chapter 19: The Ten Commandments for Dealing with Congressional Staff **305**

Being Prompt 305
Knowing the Goal of the Meeting 305
Preparing the Ground 306
Doing Your Homework 306
Being Courteous and Calm 306
Commanding the Facts 307
Respecting the Staff 307
Being Ready to Offer Assistance 307
Giving them Something to Remember You By 308
Always Following Up 308

Chapter 20: Ten Tips for Dealing with Journalists **309**

Assume the Best 309
Strive for Accuracy 310
Don't Pick a Fight with Anyone who Buys Ink by the Barrel 310
Realize that the Only Bad Question is the One that Isn't Asked 311
You Don't Have to Comment but Never Stonewall 311
Understand the "Public" in Public Figure 312
Avoid Source Remorse 312
Keep Things in Perspective — They'll Wrap Fish in It Tomorrow 313
Don't Fall for "Trust Me, I'm a Journalist" 313
Return Journalists' Phone Calls First 313

Chapter 21: Not Even Ten Suggestions for Improving Congress ... **315**

Get a Toll-Free Number 315
Gather Voting Records Online 316
Post Appropriations Online in a Timely Fashion —
     Like Immediately 316
Hire a Historian for the House 317
Upgrade the House Web Site 317

Part VII: The Appendixes *319*

Appendix A: Glossary of Congressional and Political Terms **321**

Appendix B: Committees of the 107th Congress **333**

Senate Standing Committees 333
Senate Select and Special Committees 334
Joint Committees 334

Index *335*

Foreword

by Speaker of the House Dennis Hastert

*C*ongress For Dummies serves a useful purpose: To inform the people about the duties, responsibilities, and role of the United States Congress. Congress, of course, is not just for dummies. It is for all people who want to participate in their democracy, and play a role in their own futures.

When the founders drew up the United States Constitution in 1787, they specifically outlined a system in which there would be three independent branches of government. All three branches have separate powers and duties that create a system of checks and balances. This system ensures that there is always a watchful eye on the product of the entire institution. While all three branches differ in their responsibilities, they were all formed to protect and promote democratic values and principles on which our nation was founded.

The founders wisely put Congress in the First Article of the Constitution, signifying its unique and extremely vital role in our democracy. Congress makes the laws. Congress holds the power of the purse. Congress affirms treaties and confirms judges. In other words, Congress makes decisions that affect the lives of every American citizen.

But still, many people are confused about the Congress, what its role is and what the differences are between the House and the Senate. The House of Representatives is the "people's House," while the Senate is often called "the world's greatest debating society." It will come as no surprise that as Speaker of the House, I am partial to the House of Representatives. Members of the House face the voters every two years. They are more accountable to the people, and more often reflect the wishes of those who vote. On the other hand, Senators face the voters every six years.

How laws are made is a very interesting, yet complex process. David Silverberg's outline gives readers a simplified and informative view of that process. In this book, he gives a full explanation of the responsibilities, procedures, and makeup of the Legislative branch. Each chapter contributes to the basic understanding of how public policy is formed in our nation's Capitol in Washington, D.C. The author gives explicit examples on the way in which the Constitution sets the standards for how laws are formed and enforced, what strategies Members of Congress use when voting and dealing with outside interest groups, as well as how Congressional Members serve their constituents back home.

It is extremely important that the American people understand how laws are made. This book helps make the process more understandable, which is a good thing. I recommend this book to those who don't understand Congress and want to learn, and to those who think they know Congress, but have more to learn.

Foreword

by Senate Majority Leader Tom Daschle

*T*he title of this book, *Congress For Dummies*, is really a bit of a misnomer. America needs the participation of informed citizens. Our democracy depends on it. Picking up this book doesn't mean admitting you're a dummy. It means you're educating yourself about your government, how it works, and how you can get involved, and there's nothing dumb about that.

Congress can be an imposing institution. I've served here since 1978, and at times I still feel that way. As imposing as Congress is, and as difficult as it may be to understand, the work that goes on here has an impact on the life of every American. Sometimes the work of Congress impacts you in ways you see, like a Social Security check, a new bridge, or our armed forces on parade. Sometimes it impacts you in ways you don't, like laws to keep your air clean to breathe or the water safe to drink.

As the Majority Leader of the United States Senate, I'm pleased that this book explains the workings of the Senate in a simple, clear, easy to follow format.

After all, ours is a government "of the people, by the people, and for the people." This is your government, you elect people to serve you, and you need to keep track of what they're doing.

In his chapter on the Senate, David Silverberg writes "the Senate is the fulcrum that balances the extremes of tyranny and anarchy and makes sure that neither ever tips the scales." Every day, from the opening gavel to adjournment, we work together and walk between those extremes, regardless of our differences.

Congress For Dummies will help you understand how the Senate works, and how it works with the House and the Executive branch to strengthen this great democracy, which depends on all of us to play an important part. Consider this your user's manual.

Introduction

● ●

Come to Washington, D.C. and you're surrounded by enormous, imposing buildings and massive monuments to history, power, and glory. Come to conduct business and you'll be seated in ornate offices or meet people in luxurious restaurants. On the streets people dressed in dark, formal suits rush to and fro, official identification tags dangling around their necks. Occasionally, the air is broken by the sirens of official motorcades taking high officials and foreign visitors to critical appointments. And gleaming atop a hill overlooking the city is the dome of the Capitol building, the home of the United States Congress.

It can all make you feel overwhelmed and very small. But there's no reason for you to feel that way. If you're a citizen and a voter you are the government. *You're* the person in charge. And the government is there to serve *you*.

Nowhere is this truer than in Congress, whose whole purpose is to give you a voice in running the country and to reflect your needs and opinions.

When you have business with Congress, when you're trying to actually get something done, the institution is likely to seem extremely complex and confusing. However, Congress was created by human beings and human beings can figure it out. It's also meant to be responsive to the will of the voters, so any citizen can influence its actions. It just takes persistence, determination, and a lot of patience.

Getting something done also requires a basic knowledge of the institution and that's what *Congress For Dummies* aims to provide. Like all the *For Dummies* books, it's written so that the rest of us can understand this institution that has such power over us — and over which we wield such power.

Congress For Dummies serves no party or ideology. It's neither liberal nor conservative, neither Democrat nor Republican. It has no axe to grind or score to settle, it takes no position on any issue. It uses examples from history, but it endorses no point of view or historical bias. It's entirely written for the citizen who wants to discover more about Congress or work with the institution, and its sole aim is to demystify the institution and provide a simple, practical guide for those who want to get something done — which in this government is no easy task.

My aim is to give you the basic tools you need: What you build is up to you.

What this Book Can Help You Do

This book is written with the citizen advocate in mind. Its most important purpose is to give people who want Congress to do something, or who have to work through the institution of Congress, the tools and knowledge they need to achieve their aims. Accordingly, I spend a great deal of time and effort providing tips and suggestions and insights on how to achieve your objectives. To do that, I go beyond just Congress and provide a guide to working with the institutions that influence congressional behavior, most notably the media. If you're trying to accomplish something in Congress, this book provides the basic tools to get you started.

The most basic of those tools is knowing how the whole system works: The functions of the House of Representatives and its members, the Senate and its members, their duties and how you can make your wishes known to them.

In Congress, the legislative process is as important as the legislation itself, so this book provides a guide to the legislative process. It examines the building blocks of that process and then traces how the process works.

Even if you're not immersed in a cause and aren't working with Congress on a day-to-day basis, there may be times when you feel strongly about the course the country is taking, or you want to register your opinion with the decision makers in Washington, D.C. This book provides some handy guides for contacting your representatives and senators and explains what they do and the institutions in which they serve.

Lastly, the book tries to convey something about working in the overall political and institutional environment. Events and institutions are changing every day, but this book concentrates on those elements that are relatively stable. Every political situation is different and each one involves a different cast of characters, but if you understand the basic processes and the fundamental building blocks, you can place the current information in context and turn it to your advantage.

How to Use this Book

Like all *For Dummies* books, this book is modular — each chapter and section can stand on its own without reference to anything preceding it or following it. If you're interested in finding out about a particular topic, you can consult the Table of Contents or the Index, turn to the appropriate page, and extract the information you need.

The book is also written with the complete novice in mind, someone who has never encountered Washington or Congress or worked with American government. It tries not to assume that you have any previous knowledge of Congress and American government.

Conversely, if you're already on Capitol Hill and work with Congress on a daily basis, you can skip the basics, particularly the early chapters on the institution and the process and find more detailed information.

Lastly, the chapter on visiting Congress is intended for people visiting the Capitol Complex for the first time and it tries to convey some sense of Congress's physical surroundings. The Capitol Grounds are in a period of extensive change and renovation, but history and tradition dictate that certain landmarks remain constant.

Conventions Used in this Book

So that I don't have to repeat myself, and so that you don't have to read the same explanations again and again, I use a few conventions throughout the book. I tell you what they are and describe what the icons mean in the following sections.

A note on names

Throughout this book, I refer to people in Congress as *members*. That's because they're officially *members of Congress*, as though they've been elected to a club. Although the term *member of Congress* can refer to either a member of the House or the Senate, it usually is used to refer to representatives. In this book, however, it means a member of either chamber.

Although people commonly address their representatives in Congress as *congressman* or *congresswoman* when they're speaking, those are not, in fact, official forms of address.

Members of the House are officially *representatives* — they represent the people in their districts. In written correspondence, you can address them as *Representative* (or *Rep.*) or *the Honorable* (or *Hon.*), although the latter is less often used.

Senators are simply that — members of the United States Senate. They're called *senators* and they're usually addressed in writing with the abbreviation *Sen.*

References to specific members in this book are accompanied by their state and party designation: R for Republican, D for Democrat, and I for Independent. Past parties include Whig and Federalist. Living members just get their affiliation and state. If a member is deceased, I give his or her dates of service in the position mentioned (House, Senate, or as Speaker, for example) to give you a general sense of the time when they lived and worked. Whenever their tenure was interrupted by other activities — such as serving in the executive branch — you'll see the designation "interrupted."

If you want more information about any member who served in Congress, I highly recommend Congress's own online biographical service, which you can access at: `http://bioguide.congress.gov/biosearch/biosearch.asp`.

Members encompass both genders but rather than have "his or her" in every third person reference, I alternated chapters. Men get the even chapters and women get the odd ones. There is no deeper meaning to this choice.

Information on icons

Icons are one of my favorite elements in *For Dummies* books. These symbols flag items worthy of special note and make it easier for you to go right to the information you need.

These are anecdotes or historical episodes that cast light on Congress or just prove amusing or enlightening.

Quotations that add perspective or commentary on the subject at hand are marked with this icon. I haven't confined these quotes to members of Congress but have drawn on sayings from every time and place.

A suggestion that can make your lobbying more effective or alert you to a lobbying opportunity.

Whatever you do, don't do this.

Something to keep in mind as you deal with Congress.

Information only a wonk could love.

How this Book Is Organized

This book actually contains two elements: Congress itself and the outside institutions and factors that influence its decision making and behavior. The book helps you work with both.

Part I: Considering the Two Chambers

This part introduces you to Congress, its place in American government as a whole and its elements. I devote a chapter each to describing the House and the Senate.

Part II: Looking at the Legislative Process

In these chapters, I explain the basic legislative process from conception to committee consideration to debate and passage.

Part III: Following the Money

Money is so important to government, Congress, and politics that it gets its own part. This part looks at how Congress raises and spends money and the procedures for doing so. It also looks at how politics are financed and how you can use campaign contributions to further your ends.

Part IV: Lobbying from All Angles

This part introduces you to the elements of influencing Congress directly. It provides hints and tips for making your cause known and memorable, and strategies for convincing your representatives and senators to do what you want. Should you need to hire a professional lobbyist, it provides some basic guidelines for finding, retaining and evaluating a lobbyist.

Because the media plays such an important role in Congress, I devote two chapters to explaining the nature of the beast, how to tame it, and how to make it work for you.

Part V: Putting the Practical Side to Use

The chapters in this part explain what your representative or senator can do for you, and the services you can get from Congress. Chapter 17 provides a brief guide to visiting the Capitol complex.

Part VI: Part of Tens

The famous Part of Tens! Here I provide ten tips for lobbying, ten tips for meeting with a member or staff, and ten tips for dealing with the media.

Part VII: The Appendixes

The appendixes consist of probably the most complete glossary of congressional terms you could hope to find (if I do say so myself), plus a list of the current, permanent House, Senate, and Joint committees.

What this Book Is Not

If you're looking here for tales of congressional scandals you're going to be disappointed. Recounting those sad episodes is not the point of this book. Plenty of books take critical looks at the institution of Congress and its members.

Of course, in 200 years of continuous sessions, plenty of misbehavior on personal and a policy levels has occurred. But, the many scandals are largely anomalies — the vast majority of members serve their country and their constituents to the best of their ability without blemish or reproach.

This book doesn't maintain that Congress is perfect or that improvements can't be made. It does, however, present Congress as it is now and provides a guide to working within the institution. It also accepts as a basic premise that the American form of representational democracy is a pretty good system and that its citizens need to participate in it. As a well-known British Prime Minister once said:

Democracy is the worst form of government except for all those other forms that have been tried from time to time.

— Winston Churchill, House of Commons, November 11, 1947

History suffuses Congress, and the impact of lawmakers long ago still guides congressional actions on a day-to-day basis. However, *Congress For Dummies* is a how-to guide, not a history book, and yet it draws on history for some of its anecdotes and examples. Much excellent and interesting history had to be passed over. I can only hope that what you find here prompts you to delve into the topic and get the full story.

A Word to the Wonks Should Be Sufficient — I Hope

As I wrote this book, I was haunted by premonitions of all the learned members, pundits, commentators, analysts, journalists, lobbyists, critics, and policy wonks — many of whom I know personally — pointing out everything I failed to mention.

My plea to all the inside-the-Beltway experts is this: Have mercy.

Congress For Dummies is intended to reach people who aren't familiar with Congress, to inform them and get them involved. My hope is that it will lead readers to explore Congress and American government on their own.

This book is by no means the last word on Congress. In fact, it's only a beginning. *Congress For Dummies* is an attempt to provide the basics. Every parliamentary procedure discussed here has exceptions, clauses, and sub-clauses that are not mentioned. I know, more than anyone else, how much has gone uncovered.

Throughout this book, I include references to relevant Web sites and to some good books that provide more in-depth information about the topics covered, but by no means are these references an exhaustive bibliography. I hope you'll read them. However, there's so much excellent literature, analysis, and history on the topic of Congress, it can fill a library of its own. If your book wasn't mentioned, please accept my apologies. I hope there will be future editions.

Part I
Considering the Two Chambers

The 5th Wave   By Rich Tennant

"I think Dick Foster should be the one to head up the new Congressional bill. He's got the vision, the drive, and let's face it, that big white hat doesn't hurt either."

In this part . . .

These chapters introduce you to the institution as a whole and give you background and history of each of the chambers.

Chapter 1

Welcome to Congress

• •

In This Chapter

▶ The basic structure of American government

▶ The three branches of government

▶ Your role in the government

▶ Basic forms of participation

• •

*S*tudying American government is incredibly easy. The conquests, dynastic rivalries, clashing clans, and all the rest of the murky history that makes the political science of other countries so difficult is absent here. American government is very rational and logical and proceeds in a straight line from the day it was started. The entire government's functioning is contained in a single document, the Constitution, which can be read in a few minutes.

Unlike so many other countries whose histories began in the dim recesses of time, the United States began on a particular day — July 4, 1776 — when Americans declared their independence from Great Britain. After declaring independence and fighting an eight-year war to establish a separate identity and sovereignty, Americans set out to establish a permanent government.

Initially, the United States was run by a Continental Congress, which, in 1777, adopted the *Articles of Confederation,* a loose system designed to keep the states working together in a confederacy. The Articles served well enough during the War of Independence, but, afterwards, it became clear that the Articles were insufficient to govern the new nation. Delegates from the 13 states gathered in Philadelphia to come up with a new constitution. After working in secret through a hot summer, on September 17, 1787, the Framers of the new system, with George Washington presiding, signed the new Constitution. The Constitution was then submitted to the states for ratification and went into effect in June 1788 when New Hampshire became the ninth state to ratify it.

The Framers wouldn't recognize the country today, but they would certainly recognize the government. For all the changes in the preceding two centuries, and despite 27 amendments to the Constitution, the government they created remains substantially what they conceived.

The Three Branches of Government

Having rebelled against a tyrant, the Framers were leery of any part of the government becoming too powerful. Accordingly, each branch was meant to balance the others, a system known as *checks and balances*. Congress provides a check on the president's powers and initiatives by approving them. The president provides a check on congressional action through a veto. The judicial branch provides a check on both by interpreting the laws and determining whether they're constitutional. No one branch can act alone without the approval of the other two.

Because the fight against Britain was designed to allow the people of America to govern themselves, the Congress was designed to reflect popular will — up to a point. The Framers were very aware of the weaknesses of democracy. Democracies are subject to mass emotionalism, demagogues, mob rule, passing passions, fickleness, and panic. Not only did the Framers draw on the experiences of republics before theirs, they'd been through a revolution and had seen all those things.

Instead of direct democracy, the government created under the Constitution was designed to put in place political institutions that would protect the government from popular passions and allow knowledgeable and experienced people to direct the country's course while still reflecting popular desires. Additionally, the government would reflect the interests and desires of all its citizens while providing a forum to peacefully work out their differences.

The congressional branch

The Framers decided that the American government would be first and foremost a consultative form of government rather than a monarchy or a dictatorship, and that Congress would be its leading institution. The very first provision of the Constitution established Congress and outlined its powers.

All legislative Powers herein granted shall be vested in a Congress of the United States, which shall consist of Senate and a House of Representatives.

> — Article 1, Section 1, The Constitution of the United States.

The Constitution is quite explicit about congressional powers. Congress is empowered to:

- ✔ Establish taxes and other forms of revenue
- ✔ Pay debts and borrow money
- ✔ Provide for the national defense

- ✔ Regulate commerce and bankruptcy
- ✔ Establish laws for citizenship and naturalization
- ✔ Issue money and punish counterfeiters
- ✔ Establish post offices and the means to deliver the mail
- ✔ Promote science and the arts by providing copyrights and patents
- ✔ Establish courts below the Supreme Court
- ✔ Define and punish piracy and felonies committed at sea
- ✔ Declare war
- ✔ Raise and support armies and a navy and regulate them
- ✔ Organize a militia and call it out when necessary
- ✔ Oversee and regulate the capital city
- ✔ Make any other laws necessary

Why we have two chambers

The reason there are two senators for each state is so that one can be the designated driver, according to comedian Jay Leno. Very funny, but not terribly accurate.

Although the Senate doesn't have a great many duties actually spelled out by the Constitution, it plays an important role. The Senate was the creation of something that came to be known as the Great Compromise.

When the Framers met in Philadelphia in 1787, they faced a deep split between the interests of small states and large ones. The small, less populated states would have less clout if representation were proportional (by population). Rhode Island, Connecticut, and Delaware, for example, would always be at a disadvantage because more populous states would have more members of Congress. The small states preferred an equal arrangement in which each state would have an equal number of representatives. The large states, however, wanted their greater population to give them greater clout.

The Framers worked out a compromise: The House of Representatives was given proportional representation so that all elements of the population would be represented, and the Senate would have equal representation with every state represented by two senators. That way all the interests of the states would be represented at the national level. In the same way that the legislative (Congress), judicial, and executive branches of government balance each other, the House and Senate balance each other, because passing legislation requires approval by both houses. As a result, large states can't take advantage of small states and vice versa.

The compromise worked, and it is perhaps one main reason why the Senate, in general, wields a much greater spirit of compromise than does the House.

Congress was also empowered to issue letters of *marque and reprisal,* an eighteenth century practice in which merchant ships were empowered to act as warships and capture enemy ships at sea.

The executive branch

The president, who today is so much the focus of media attention and government activity, was the second thought of the Framers, and his duties are established in Article II. The President

- ✔ Is Commander in Chief of the Army, Navy, and militia
- ✔ Makes treaties
- ✔ Nominates ambassadors, ministers, consuls, Supreme Court justices, and other officials
- ✔ Fills any vacancies that might arise

Even these powers are circumscribed by the Constitution. Two-thirds of the Senate must approve any treaty that the president signs, and the president's nominations are subject to the advice and consent of the Senate.

Despite the constitutional limitations on the executive branch, it's become an enormous and powerful arm of the government. Today, the president of the United States is the most powerful person on earth, commanding an immense nuclear arsenal and the world's strongest military, directing the largest national economy, leading his political party, providing a personal and moral example, and setting the tone and direction of the country and the world. Nonetheless, the president has restraints.

President George Washington was assisted only by secretaries of state, war, and treasury, an attorney general, and a postmaster general. Today, the president presides over 14 cabinet secretaries, each running a department that employs tens of thousands of people. The executive branch also includes more than a hundred independent agencies, bureaus, and commissions. As of 2001, roughly 2.7 million people were employed by the executive branch in a wide variety of capacities. The overall federal budget for fiscal year 2003 is expected to be roughly $1.7 trillion.

While Congress makes the laws and sets national policy, executive branch agencies protect the country, conduct diplomacy, and set rules and standards for commerce and industry. Executive branch agencies monitor the environment, predict the weather, and even establish an official time for the country (which you can access on the Internet at nist.time.gov).

The Supreme Court

Article III of the Constitution establishes a Supreme Court to hold the judicial power of the United States. The Supreme Court has direct jurisdiction over cases involving high officials and the states, but otherwise, it's the court of ultimate appeal.

Although the Constitution makes the Supreme Court a co-equal branch of government, the Senate approves the nominations of Supreme Court justices and determined the duties and responsibilities of all the courts below the Supreme Court when it passed the Judiciary Act in 1789 and subsequent laws that refined that act. Today, the federal court system includes the U.S. Courts of Appeals, divided into 11 circuits, and federal District Courts.

Very early on, in the famous 1803 case of Marbury versus Madison, Supreme Court Justice John Marshall ruled that the Supreme Court has the right and responsibility to determine whether laws passed by Congress are constitutional. Today, the Supreme Court is a powerful branch not because it initiates action but because it reviews congressional legislation and executive actions, and it can nullify what it rules to be unconstitutional.

Amendments to the Constitution

Since it was ratified in 1789, the Constitution has been amended 27 times — although the first ten amendments, known as the Bill of Rights, were drawn up immediately and were ratified as a single group in 1791.

The Bill of Rights establishes ten essential rights that the Framers felt needed to be ensured but hadn't been listed in the Constitution itself, including freedom of speech, religion, the press, assembly, the right to petition government, and the right to bear arms. Subsequent amendments abolished slavery, expanded the right to vote, and made procedural changes. The Eighteenth Amendment, passed in 1919, prohibited the manufacture and sale of alcohol and was repealed by the Twenty-First Amendment in 1933. *Webster's New World American Words of Freedom,* by Stephen F. Rohde (published by Wiley), gives complete text and analysis of the Constitution and amendments to it.

To amend the Constitution, two-thirds of each legislative chamber must approve the proposed amendment, which is then passed on to the states. If the legislatures of three quarters of the states approve the amendment, it becomes part of the Constitution. The states themselves can also amend the Constitution without Congress if two-thirds of the states convene to pass a proposed amendment, and it is then approved by three-quarters of all the states.

The system is designed to ensure that proposed amendments are thoroughly examined, and passing an amendment can take an exceedingly long time. For example, it took more than half a century to pass the Nineteenth Amendment giving women the right to vote. Nonetheless, Congress can impose a time limit on the ratification process.

Congressional Relationships

As part of a balanced, three-branch system, with the American people serving as the big boss who hires them and can fire them at election time, Congress has to maintain working relationships with various bodies and constituencies.

House-Senate relations

Having been set up to provide checks and balances over one another, members of each chamber of Congress tend to get annoyed with each other. Members of the House tend to often get impatient with the Senate's slow deliberation and discussion of legislation, while senators tend to regard representatives as subject to popular whims and passions and lacking the necessary maturity for governance.

But other major differences between the two chambers are in keeping with their origins. In the Senate, everyone is equal, but in the House, the rule is by majority in keeping with the House's representative origins.

You see, in Washington they have these bodies, Senate and the House of Representatives. That's for the convenience of the visitors. If there's nothing funny happening in one, there's sure to be in the other, and in case one body passes a good bill, why, the other can see it in time and kill it.

— Will Rogers, American humorist

Executive-congressional relations through the years

The legislative and executive branches are equal under the Constitution. The Constitution notwithstanding, the relationship among the branches, particularly the executive and legislative, is a constantly shifting one.

Generally, in times of peace and prosperity, Congress has been the more dominant institution. In times of war or danger, the executive branch is the dominant branch.

For much of early American history, the president was relatively powerless, and though not an unimportant figure, was secondary to Congress. From 1820 to 1860, as slavery, states rights, and enormous expansion threatened to tear the country apart, members of the Senate were the ones who kept the nation together with a series of compromises. Executive branch powers increased considerably during the Civil War, as President Abraham Lincoln commanded new resources and sought new authority to keep the union together.

After the Civil War, the relationship continued to change, and some great clashes and momentous events have taken place marking the legislative-executive relationship:

✔ In 1868, Congress passed a measure to prevent the president from removing cabinet officers without its approval. President Andrew Johnson believed that this was unconstitutional, defied the restriction, was impeached, and escaped removal by a single vote. (The president's position was later upheld by the Supreme Court.)

✔ In 1920, the Senate defeated President Woodrow Wilson's bid to have the United States join the League of Nations. The struggle between Wilson and Senator Henry Cabot Lodge (R-Mass., 1893–1924) marked a major shift in the center of gravity to the legislative branch.

✔ In 1933, President Franklin Roosevelt, boosted by Democratic gains in Congress, launched the New Deal to combat the Great Depression. This effort inaugurated a long period of executive branch activism and expansion that continued through World War II and the Cold War of the mid-twentieth century.

✔ In 1994, the overwhelming election of a Republican House and Senate marked a resurgent Congress whose struggle with the executive branch culminated in the 1999 impeachment of President Bill Clinton.

✔ In 2001, terrorist attacks on the United States and the launch of a war against terror inaugurated another period of executive activism at home and abroad.

The relationship between Congress and the executive branch changes every day.

Congressional-constituent relations

For elected officeholders who must provide what people want and reflect what they need, calibrating the popular mood is no easy task. It's part instinct, part empathy, part science, and part reading the newspapers and watching TV.

In addition to your expressions to them, your elected officials and those who would be your elected officials are always polling people to get their opinions on the issues of the day, or else they're holding focus groups to explore peoples' beliefs in depth.

Legislating food

Even food reflects the similarities and differences between the two chambers of Congress. Listen to these tales of soups and puddings:

The Senate's respect for tradition reaches all the way into its dining room. According to legend the Senate serves bean soup because Sen. Fred Dubois (R-Idaho 1891–1907, interrupted), who chaired the committee overseeing Senate restaurants, passed a resolution requiring that bean soup always be on the menu. Sen. Knute Nelson (R-Minn. 1895–1923) also expressed a fondness for it.

In the House, bean soup is on the menu because one steaming summer day in 1904, Speaker Joe Cannon (R-Ill. 1893–1923) came to the dining room and asked for the soup only to be told it wasn't on the menu because of the hot weather. "Thunderation!" he roared. "I had my mouth set for bean soup! From now on, hot or cold, rain, snow, or shine, I want it on the menu every day!"

Similarities in House and Senate tastes for rice pudding, however, had a less happy conclusion.

In 1999, when Sen. Rick Santorum (R-Pa.) tasted the rice pudding in a House dining room, he liked it so much that he asked for the recipe. The House cook, who used a personal family recipe for the pudding, took great umbrage and refused to release it. Even House Administration Committee Chairman Bill Thomas (R-Calif.) got into the act. "Let them eat cake," he said of the Senate attempts to obtain the formula.

No matter how hard Santorum and Senate dining staff tried, they couldn't pry the recipe from the House cook. Ultimately Senate cooks were forced to analyze the House pudding and reverse engineer it to produce a Senate facsimile. Although the new pudding wasn't that good, the Senate had no intention of giving up. "I am confident that as the chef continues to define it, the Senate rice pudding will someday surpass the House rice pudding," Santorum said solemnly.

If you get the chance to visit the Capitol, find out whether your representative or senator can take you to the members' dining rooms where you can dine on bean soup and rice pudding (among many other government culinary delights).

When a federal official or candidate has this information, she has to absorb it and decide how to use it in order to get elected or stay elected. Your opinion is very important in formulating the party platform and the individual candidate's campaign.

Having said that, during the campaign, the candidate will promise you and everyone else the moon and stars to get elected. Most people don't trust campaign promises — and rightfully so. Promises are exaggerated during the campaign and are quickly forgotten as soon as the election is over.

However, a good politician tries to deliver on campaign promises on some level. To do that, though, a politician faces numerous obstacles, including

- ✔ **Opposition from opponents:** Opponents may be from the other party, or they may be people within the candidate's own party who simply don't like another member's proposal.

- ✔ **Institutional drag:** Any organization must go through certain policies and procedures to get anything done, and some organizations take longer than others.

- ✔ **Different leadership priorities:** Party leaders in Congress may have other priorities or different priorities, or they may not support a member's agenda.

- ✔ **Executive branch opposition:** The president or executive branch agencies may oppose a member's efforts.

- ✔ **Distractions:** A member of Congress has to deal with many other priorities.

A member of Congress who delivers on campaign promises is one to be valued, and one who consistently fails to deliver doesn't deserve to stay in office — but a good faith effort and due diligence should count for something, too.

Your Role as a Citizen

Sometimes, as a citizen of the United States, you want to change the way the entire country is operating, or you don't like government policies, or you feel that a specific need isn't being met. The Constitution gives you a route, a mechanism, and a process for making the difference you seek. And the institution through which you work is the United States Congress.

Given the enormity of the country and the complexity of today's society, you may feel as though you don't have a place in government. After all, everything seems to work well enough on its own. A good deal of government activity seems to consist of events reported on the news that you can't do anything about anyway. Furthermore, Americans are very fortunate in that their government intrudes on their lives very little: You have to pay taxes, get a Social Security number, and obtain either a driver's license or an identification card, but otherwise, you can largely live your life without ever coming into contact with your national government, especially Congress.

But although *you* may be able to ignore the federal government, the federal government absolutely cannot ignore you. Your participation determines the government's direction and makes it work — and you're called upon to participate in all three branches.

The people reign in the American political world as the Deity does in the universe. They are the cause and the aim of all things; everything comes from them, and everything is absorbed in them.

— Alexis de Tocqueville, *Democracy in America,* 1835

Looking beyond Congress, your participation is essential for innumerable local, county and state boards, commissions and government bodies that keep your community functioning.

But just because you're called to participated in all three branches doesn't mean that you have to run for office. As an individual citizen, you even have a role to play in the most fundamental building block of the judicial system — as a juror.

Voting

The most fundamental form of participation in government is voting. As a citizen, you're called upon to vote in local, state, and federal elections, and your participation as a voter is critical in all three.

At the local level, you elect officials, such as your mayor, your city or county council, your school board officers, your sheriff, and possibly some judges. Your vote is also critical in deciding various measures, such as issuing local bonds, making procedural changes, and approving local projects.

At the state level, you vote for governor, state representatives or delegates, and state senators. In some states, you also elect judges.

At the federal level, you elect your representative, your senators, and the president and vice president. Congressional elections occur every two years when the entire House of Representatives and a third of the Senate are up for election. Presidential elections occur every four years.

The results of these elections determine the direction of the country, the officials who will administer it, and the people who represent you at different federal levels for the next two, four, and six years.

Voter participation goes way up in presidential election years. Although voters don't often turn out in significant numbers during non-presidential years, political participation spikes during presidential elections. According to the Federal Election Commission, in the 2000 election, 76 percent of eligible voters were registered to vote and 67.5 percent of those registered actually voted. However, only 51 percent of everyone of voting age actually voted.

Furthermore, the effect of presidential elections spreads throughout the political universe. A presidential candidate's popularity carries congressional candidates from his own party into office. A candidate's ability to get into office based on the success of another candidate called *coattails* — the image being that lesser candidates cling to a winner's coattails, as he sweeps into office.

The electric charge that goes through America during a presidential election year is truly amazing to watch. Suddenly, the media, which may have been fairly disinterested in politics during the previous three years, has an intense interest in national politics. Members of Congress who might otherwise be completely ignored are suddenly the focus of attention. Businesses spring up around the election, more political books are published, and the number of internship applications in politically related offices increases.

The entire electoral system is set up to do what the voters want, but if you don't register and vote, you're leaving the country's direction to others. That may seem fine, but it means that your desires and preferences simply won't be taken into account at any level.

At the very least, registering and voting gives you a legitimate right to complain when you don't like what the government does. If you don't even make the effort to register and vote, you essentially have no right to complain.

You can have an even greater impact on the makeup of Congress — and the nature of any election — by voting in party primary elections. These elections to determine the slate of candidates in the general election are often attended only by party activists. Because turnout tends to be low and the elections get relatively little media attention, a vote in a primary election can have a disproportionate effect on the ultimate outcome. In some states or jurisdictions that have overwhelming loyalty to one party or the other, a vote in the primary is frequently tantamount to a vote in the general election itself.

Registering your opinion

Even between elections your opinion matters. No politician can get reelected if he ignores the feelings and beliefs of his constituents. Occasionally, a politician may go against popular opinion — that's part of being a leader, too — but the vast majority of the time, politicians, whether in Congress or in other offices, are trying to carefully calibrate their actions to the popular mood. The whole system is designed to take your desires into account and to give you as many channels as possible to express yourself to your elected officials.

You have some simple and direct ways to reach your representatives and senators:

- ✔ Write a letter.
- ✔ Send an e-mail message.
- ✔ Call on the telephone.
- ✔ Visit your representatives and senators.
- ✔ Speak up at a town meeting.

(Chapter 12 gives you advice on contacting your members of Congress and the Cheat Sheet at the front of the book tells you how to get in touch with them.)

You can register your opinion and then sit back. If things go your way, you'll have the satisfaction of having made a difference. If they don't, you can grumble a bit and either try again another day or complain about the system and politicians in general.

However, if you're willing to put in the time and effort, you can make a significant difference. The system will respond to your efforts — but it won't be easy, and it won't happen fast.

Another easy way to participate in the system is to get involved in a congressional election. Candidates are always hungry for volunteers and money. If you have a cause to push and you want to further it through a candidate, you have numerous avenues. I explain these avenues in Chapter 11, and I discuss contributing money in Chapter 9.

Voting, expressing your opinion, and taking part in the political life of your community are all part of your basic rights and responsibilities as an American citizen.

For in-depth information in how you can be involved in the political process on all levels, pick up a copy of *Politics For Dummies,* 2nd Edition, by Ann DeLaney (published by Wiley).

Chapter 2

Running Your House: The House of Representatives

In This Chapter:

▶ Comparing your house to The House

▶ Tracking down your representative

▶ Discovering what your representative's job is

▶ Realizing the responsibilities of the House of Representatives

▶ Creating House districts

*O*f all federal government institutions, the House of Representatives is the one that's closest to you. It's the body designed to most closely reflect your cares and concerns and the one that's easiest for you to contact. The House is the starting point when you want to register an opinion or get a law passed.

"Such will be the relation between the House of Representatives and their constituents. Duty, gratitude, interest, ambition itself, are the chords by which they will be bound to fidelity and sympathy with the great mass of the people."

— Alexander Hamilton or James Madison writing as "Publius" in "The Federalist No. 57"

Knowing your congressional representative and the district he represents *is* important, because regardless of other identities you may have, you're definitely a constituent of that representative. Although you may not know him personally, or agree with his politics, or even like him, he is your advocate in Washington and representing your interests is his job. If you don't like the way he's doing the job, you have the chance to have him fired (by voting for someone else) every two years.

Describing the House

The House of Representatives consists of 435 representatives, each one representing a congressional district in one of the 50 United States. In addition, four *delegates* represent the U.S. territories of American Samoa, Guam, the Virgin Islands, and the District of Columbia. The territory of Puerto Rico is represented by a *resident commissioner* who serves a four-year term. The delegates and the resident commissioner vote in committees but not on the House floor nor when the House forms a committee of the whole. (For more explanation of these terms, see the Glossary in Appendix A.)

Congressional districts are redrawn every ten years after each census. The first Congress in 1789 was comprised of 100 representatives, each representing approximately 30,000 people within their respective districts. As the country grew, the number of members also grew every ten years until it reached 435 after the 1910 census. Intense debates took place after the 1920 census about equitably increasing the number of members again. With the 1930 census looming, Congress continued to wrangle over the size of the House until it codified the number of seats at 435 with five delegates in 1941. The population has grown since then, of course, but the number of representatives has not. In practical terms, this means that every ten years representatives must speak for more and more people, making it more and more difficult for constituents and representatives to know each other.

Each new year of a Congress is considered a *session*. The first year of a Congress is the *First Session* (these always occur in odd-numbered years); the second year is the *Second Session* (these always occur in even-numbered years). So, you may hear someone say "That bill passed in the first session of the 105th."

Every seat in the House is up for election every two years (with the exception of Puerto Rico's resident commissioner). A *Congress* coincides with the two-year term of members of the House of Representatives. Each Congress since the first in 1789 is numbered sequentially, so that when you hear people discussing the activities of a particular Congress, such as the 106th or the 107th, they're referring to a specific two-year term of the House of Representatives. This short term of office is intended to keep the representatives close to their constituents without allowing power to go to their heads.

The House is run by majority rule and when a majority of members vote to do something in the House, it gets done. The Speaker of the House, who leads the institution, sees to its implementation. Majority rule makes passing legislation relatively efficient, but it also means that the party in the minority has little power to set the agenda or pass any of its proposals. Members of the minority party not only tend to be crushed in the House, but they're also usually humiliated, thwarted at every turn because:

✔ They can't call committee hearings.

✔ They can't get their legislation through the committees.

✔ They're guaranteed to be defeated on the floor if the majority stays together.

The party in power in the House not only likes to outvote its rival, it also likes to rub it in, and members simmer with resentment for years about their treatment.

Coming up with qualifications

The Constitution establishes that representatives must be at least 25 years old and have been a citizen of the United States for at least seven years. A representative must also reside in the state in which he's elected.

Although there's no federal legal requirement that a representative live in or have an address in the district he represents, political common sense dictates that he do so. People electing someone to represent them want to make sure that person knows and understands the district's needs. Getting elected and staying elected if you're not living in the area is well nigh impossible.

Who are to be the electors of the federal representatives? Not the rich, more than the poor; not the learned more than the ignorant; not the haughty heirs of distinguished names, more than the humble sons of obscurity and unpropitious fortune. The electors are to be the great body of the people of the United States. They are to be the same who exercise the right in every State of electing the corresponding branch of the legislature of the state.

Who are to be the objects of popular choice? Every citizen whose merit may recommend him to the esteem and confidence of his country. No qualification of wealth, of birth, of religious faith, or of civil profession is permitted to fetter the judgment or disappoint the inclination of the people.

— Alexander Hamilton or James Madison writing as "Publius" in
"The Federalist No. 57"

Representatives are bound by numerous rules and regulations regarding their actions and behavior. The House Committee on Standards of Official Conduct issues an ethics manual that can be accessed online at the Committee's web site: www.house.gov/ethics. Ethics have been used throughout congressional history for political advantage. A good discussion of ethics and their uses is contained in the book *Glass Houses: Congressional Ethics and the Politics of Venom*, by Martin and Sue Tolchin (Westview Press).

Defining the congressional district

You know that you're a citizen of the United States. You know that you're a citizen of your state. No doubt, you know what county you live in. But how often have you considered what congressional district you live in? Not often — maybe never — if you're like most Americans. Well, if you read these sections, should you choose to think about congressional districts, you will be able to do so from an informed perspective.

Drawing up a district

Your congressional district determines who represents you in Washington, D.C. Every member of the House represents everyone living in a congressional district that is made up of roughly 600,000 people, according to the 2000 Census. (In the original first amendment to the Constitution, the Framers provided that each House member was to represent 30,000 people and that there were at least 100 representatives.)

The *census* (the official count of the population done every ten years in the United States) determines how many people are in each state and whether states have gained or lost population over the preceding decade. Based on the census totals, a determination is made of the number of seats each state has in Congress, which, under the Constitution, must be at least one. When a state has a single House seat, it's called an *at-large* seat.

The state legislatures then draw up the congressional district boundaries. (Usually they draw boundaries for state legislatures, wards, precincts, and other local jurisdictions at the same time. Also, many communities redraw their school district boundaries around this time.)

Redrawing a district: Some call it gerrymandering

Congressional districting is one of the dark arts of democracy. It's a process that's easily abused, subject to much controversy, and usually skewed for political advantage. But it's also crucial if you're going to understand Congress, especially the House of Representatives and your relationship with it. Because congressional districts are redrawn every ten years after census figures become available, you may end up being represented by someone new. The theory behind the redistricting process is that taking a census and then redrawing districts keeps the House representative of the people regardless of changes in population patterns.

The congressional redistricting process is designed to work as follows:

1. **The census is taken in March and April of each decade year (1980, 1990, 2000, and so on).**

2. **When the results are in, the Census Bureau determines which states gained or lost population and apportions the seats in Congress**

according to a mathematical formula. The apportionment is delivered to the president, who delivers it to the Clerk of the House, who in turn sends it to the governors of each state.

3. With the new data in hand, state commissions draw up their congressional districts, each one roughly equal in population, and number the districts.

4. The state legislatures approve the new maps.

5. The governor approves the maps.

In the first election after the census, a new Congress is sent to Washington.

Would that it were so simple!

Political infighting begins in advance of the census as the parties wrangle over the counting method. Arguments erupt over issues such as the fairness of census methods, their accuracy and whether estimates for groups of people who are not precisely counted should be used. Bickering about the results of the census has happened since the first one was taken in 1790. Indeed, Thomas Jefferson so distrusted the official results that he sent a letter to President George Washington with his estimates written in one color and the official results in another — and then Washington vetoed Jefferson's reapportionment scheme!

After the census is taken and states receive the results, the battle begins over how and where to draw the district lines. District maps are crucial and fundamental to determining which party holds political power, so the fighting in state legislatures can become bitter. District lines can be drawn around and through Republican or Democratic areas to provide one party an advantage over the other. Sometimes they're drawn to include or exclude ethnic groups. The resulting maps often turn out so weird or wacky that the more bizarre ones are challenged in court. Each state makes up its own rules and procedures for redrawing congressional districts, and the only uniformity is that which is imposed by the courts.

In fact, an entire book is devoted to the process of redistricting. *Bushmanders & Bullwinkles: How Politicians Manipulate Electronic Maps And Census Data To Win Elections* by Mark Monmonier (The University of Chicago Press, 2001) shows some of the more bizarre maps politicians have concocted.

When the district lines are redrawn, some House members gain new constituents, some are forced to run against close colleagues to see who will survive as a representative, and sometimes members are eased from their jobs when their districts suddenly disappear. It makes the first elections after a census (the ones in years that end with a "2") particularly difficult and important ones.

Elbridge Gerry and the first gerrymander

From the beginning of the United States, politicians understood the crucial role played by redistricting and the games began early on. In 1812, Thomas Jefferson's Democratic-Republican Party controlled the Massachusetts State Legislature. Working off of the results of the 1810 Census, the Democratic-Republicans drew up a congressional district map that Governor Elbridge Gerry reluctantly approved (see the figure in this sidebar).

The new map packed rival Federalists into a few compact districts that left a long, curling Democratic-Republican district that looked vaguely like a lizard. When this shape was pointed out to a Federalist newspaper editor, he shouted: "Salamander! Call it a Gerrymander!" For emphasis, the editor had cartoonist Elkanah Tisdale add wings when he drew the beast in caricature.

Tisdale's cartoon, shown in this sidebar, is one of the most famous political cartoons of all time. Its impact added the word *gerrymander* to our language, meaning manipulation of political boundaries for political gain. (It also led everyone to use the word "gerrymander" with a soft "g" even though Gerry's name actually was pronounced with a hard "g.")

THE GERRY-MANDER.

As an individual you can't do much about the redistricting process; however, if you plan to be involved with Congress, you need to become familiar with the overall results that redistricting can cause. One scenario has some states gaining representatives and becoming more powerful, and other states losing districts and become weaker. When legislation comes up affecting different regions, this changing of the guard is important.

Being aware of the effects of your state's redistricting is even more important, however, because you need to know in which district you end up and who represents you. Keep a close eye on the newspapers for news about redistricting and look at your state Web sites to check out new congressional maps when they are posted.

Finding a Lawmaker of Your Very Own

Quick, without peeking: Who's your representative in Congress?

The very foundation of dealing with Congress is knowing who represents you in the Capitol. When you want to get your cause enacted into law, you must start with your representative to the House of Representatives.

You probably know your representative from his political campaign signs — after all, he has to get reelected every two years. But, if you ignore those signs, you can find out the name and district number of your representative in a couple of ways.

If you have access to the Internet, finding out the name of your representative is easy — just follow these steps:

1. **Go to: www.House.gov, the Web site of the House of Representatives.**

2. **Scroll down to the bottom of the screen.**

3. **Click on the banner that says "Write your representative" in the lower left corner.**

   A new page appears, asking for your state and ZIP code.

4. **Fill in the information requested.**

   The site may also ask for your four-digit ZIP code extension. Fortunately, there's a link right there to a post office site that provides your extension.

5. **Click on the "Contact My Representative" button, and the name of your representative appears, along with a link to the congress member's home page.**

   Your representative's home page lists the number of your congressional district. (For example, I live in Virginia's 10th District.) The district number also is important information, because it provides a basic reference for your dealings with Congress.

   A great link to frequently asked questions about writing to your representative is provided on the "Write your representative" page. I strongly urge you to read through it, because it provides useful information when you're contacting Congress for the first time.

You also can determine the name of your representative by calling the Capitol switchboard at 202-224-3121. The operator will ask for your ZIP code, tell you who your representative is, and then connect you to his or her office.

You also can try local resources such as your local library or city government offices.

Once you discover who represents you, you can visit your representative's Web site, if you have access to the Internet.

On the House Web site, members' Web pages are listed first — presuming you already know the name of your representative. They presume you do know; I presume you don't know, so I'm telling you first how to find out who represents you and then how to visit your representative's page. Follow these steps:

1. **Go to the House home page at** `www.House.gov`.

2. **Click on "Member offices."**

3. **Find your representative in the list and click on it.**

   Remember that you can find your representative by typing in your ZIP code on this page, too. Enter it in the space provided in the bar on the top of the page, and make sure that you enter the name of the state in which you reside.

Congress lags far behind the rest of the world in creating Web pages, but every representative finally has one. Some pages are better than others in terms of information that they convey, and all of them are, of course, full of propaganda that puts each member in the best possible light. At least your member's page gives you a little information about him, his background, his votes, and his stance on some issues. And it provides you with an easy way to contact him.

The House's e-mail addresses are determined by the following formula: The person's first name and last name, separated by a dot followed by the @ sign, and then the word "mail," a dot, the word "house," a dot, and the letters "gov". So an example of a House e-mail address is: `John.Doe@mail.house.gov`.

Knowing this convention is especially useful for contacting House staff members.

The House of Representatives has its own ZIP code: 20515. When writing to your representative, start your letter "Dear Rep. _____" and address the envelope thus:

Rep. _____ (or *The Honorable,* although this is archaic and not often used these days)

United States House of Representatives

Washington, DC 20515

You can also address your letter to your representative's specific office in the Capitol Complex. You can find those addresses by going to the list of representatives at the House Web site mentioned above.

Since the anthrax attacks of October 2001, mail delivery to Capitol Hill has become slow and uncertain, so you may want to use a letter as a follow-up rather than as a primary form of communication. For a full discussion of communicating with members of Congress, see Chapter 12.

Don't forget that each representative has at least one office in the district he represents. Contacting your representative at the local office can save you the cost of a phone call to Washington. You can find the addresses of the district offices by going to your representative's Web site.

Finding out as much about your representative as you can is wise before you start lobbying for him to do something that you want, but I discuss that in Part IV of this book: "Lobbying from All Angles."

House resources

The best resource for getting quick information about the U.S. House of Representatives is the House Web site www.house.gov. Not only can you find out the identity of your representative, but you can also learn about him from his individual Web page, and you can access information about each of the House committees. The site also has links to those House committees, leadership offices, and a variety of other House organizations, and you can see what legislation is being considered, view the various legislative calendars, and access educational links that are useful for schools, when you're planning a trip to the Capitol or need to reach other government offices.

Missing from the site — and from members' individual Web pages — is a bill-by-bill list of members' voting records. In the summer of 2001, a group of summer interns began a letter-writing campaign calling on members to post those records. Such records are not available in easily accessible form on any congressional Web sites. Members argued that the public might misinterpret some of the technical votes, but it seems absurd that publicly taken votes should be so hard to find on the Internet.

Another helpful House Web site belongs to the Clerk of the House, clerkweb.house.gov. It provides a variety of useful links.

Doing the Job of Representative

At its most fundamental, your representative's job is to vote for and against issues before the House. Voting is how decisions are made, and it puts your representative's stance about a given question on the record. Your representative's votes are supposed to reflect the feelings and thoughts that you and other constituents have about national issues.

However, voting is only one small part of a representative's role in Congress.

Your representative wears numerous hats. He:

- ✔ Helps determine national policy
- ✔ Proposes new laws
- ✔ Reviews and votes on proposed legislation
- ✔ Helps constituents deal with the federal government and with personal problems
- ✔ Works on behalf of his local community (his district)
- ✔ Advances the interests of his political party
- ✔ Advocates and supports causes that are important to him
- ✔ Supports and protects the industries and businesses that are important to him and his district

A representative wears these different hats simultaneously and his numerous roles sometimes conflict. What's good for a business in his district may not be good for the country as a whole. Supporting one interest group surely offends a different one. The representative, as is true of anyone in political life, is constantly weighing:

- ✔ The demands of time
- ✔ The political consequences of his actions
- ✔ The directives of his leadership
- ✔ His personal proclivities and principles
- ✔ The campaign promises he made to get elected

Perhaps the best metaphor for a representative is that of a circus performer juggling competing demands while walking a tightrope. If he makes it to the other side of the tightrope, that means he's reelected and then the show starts again. He does it all beneath the glare of TV lights while the crowd critiques — and complains — about his performance. (Some people may add that he's also begging — for votes, for money and for support — while he's performing.) It's a journey that doesn't end until he falls off the tightrope (is defeated for reelection) or opts out of politics altogether.

Former Rep. Romano L. Mazzoli (D-Ky. 1971–1995) added another hat that representatives wear: That of a "communicator, teacher, elucidator and commentator." A representative, out of necessity, must explain Congress and national politics to his constituents and must, likewise, explain his constituents' needs and desires to the rest of Congress.

Because the demands are so numerous and varied and contradictory, representatives tend to specialize and follow one of a number of career courses: He can:

- ✔ Concentrate on casework and make his name with constituent service
- ✔ Concentrate on being active in local issues
- ✔ Champion a particular cause or issue
- ✔ Concentrate on moving up in the party leadership
- ✔ Concentrate on advancing a political ideology
- ✔ Concentrate on legislation or the legislative process

All congressional careers necessarily mix all these activities, but when the member's career is long enough, it tends to fall into one of these categories. Some members consciously choose one of these courses at the outset of their careers; others find themselves naturally tending toward one category or the other.

When you're trying to get something done in Congress, having a sense of your representative's career track helps. When asking for his assistance, you may also be able to offer him assistance in meeting his career goals.

Getting the most from a short-term contract

If you're going to get anything done in Congress you must be acutely aware of congressional timeframes. They determine what you get done, how much you get done, and when you get it done.

Two years may seem like a long time to you, but for a member of the House, it's hardly any time at all. He's barely settled in, hired his staff, organized his office, and learned his way around the Capitol complex before he must run for reelection to keep his seat.

Many forces drive members of Congress, but time looms over everything. Two years is not much time to accomplish anything when you're dealing with something as massive and complex as the United States government. What's more, from virtually the moment members arrive, they're already running for reelection.

Encyclopedias of Congress

Two terrific books published biennially review each member of Congress and provide information about each congressional district. When you're dealing with Congress on any kind of a long-term basis, you must own one or the other — preferably both. One is the *National Journal's Almanac of American Politics*; the other is *Congressional Quarterly's Politics in America*.

The *Almanac* is written by Michael Barone, a senior writer for *U.S. News and World Report* and Grant Ujifusa, president of Ladd-Ujifusa Research Group, his own polling company. It's published by National Journal, which publishes a variety of Congress-related publications. It's issued biennially to cover each new Congress.

Politics in America is published by Congressional Quarterly, another publishing firm producing a variety of publications covering Congress. *Politics* is produced by the staff of Congressional Quarterly and edited by Brian Nutting and H. Amy Stern. It also is produced biennially.

Though my personal preference is the *Almanac*, both books present the members' records, something about each district, and evaluations of each member's performance. Both also are excellent reference works and either one is essential when you're going to be dealing with Congress for any length of time.

Diving into the congressional workweek

Fully appreciating the demands placed on members of Congress is difficult if you're not intimately involved with the institution. Everyone wants a piece of the House members all the time. Representatives are always out on the stump campaigning, or voting, or attending meetings. Frequently, when members retire from Congress, they give maudlin speeches apologizing to their families for missing all the important family events like graduations, birthdays and anniversaries.

During most weeks, Congress is in session on Tuesdays, Wednesdays and Thursdays, which leaves enough time to enable members to travel to and from even the most distant of their home districts and not miss any votes.

Some critics complain that the three-day workweek reduces the amount of work that Congress does — and that's without a doubt true. But if your district is on the West Coast, and traveling back and forth is a five-hour flight both ways, three days in session make sense.

The short workweek doesn't mean that your representative isn't working full time. Members of Congress usually work on Mondays and Fridays — as well as Saturdays and Sundays — talking to constituents, attending events, and working with staff.

If you're going to be talking to a member or working with him in person, you're going to do it on a Tuesday, Wednesday or Thursday if you're in Washington, or on the weekend or Monday or Friday if you're working with the district office.

Just how much of a demand is placed on a representative's time once was brought home to me during a dinner that I had with a member in a Capitol Hill restaurant. The member was carrying two cell phones and wearing two beepers that kept going off during dinner. Finally one of the cell phones rang, and he jumped up from the table to take the call. He came back disgusted: "It was a wrong number," he said. "They thought I was a pizza parlor."

Doing Housework: The Responsibilities of the House

The House often is called "The Peoples' House," because it's intended to be close to you. The two-year terms ensure that members reflect your changing concerns. The fact districts are relatively small means that a member needs to be able to get a feel for everyone in them, and House members deal with local issues more than do members of the "other chamber" as they refer to the Senate.

Taxing responsibilities

At its base, however, the Constitution gives the House one extremely important job not shared by any other part of government: "All Bills for raising Revenue shall originate in the House of Representatives." (That's in Article I, Section 7 of the U.S. Constitution.) In other words, only the House can create any new taxes, and if they're going to do that, you have to agree to be taxed.

The idea behind this role for the House was that only an institution that listened most closely to you should have the power to take away your money — when you agreed to the way it's being spent. The American colonists rebelled against King George of England, because they thought he was taxing them unfairly without their agreement, and the *Framers* — the men who devised our system of government — were determined that would never happen again.

Considering legislation

In addition to taxation, the House routinely considers a wide range of bills affecting virtually every aspect of government and the country during a given session of Congress. In addition to actual laws, the House also passes *Sense of the House* resolutions in which a majority of members register an opinion about a given topic. Although these resolutions do not have the force of law, they carry a certain amount of weight. And yet, critics often make fun of them as empty rhetoric.

Whiskey and rebellion

Just because early Americans were taxed by their own government through the House of Representatives didn't mean that they liked taxation any better than they did when the King did it. In 1794, farmers in western Pennsylvania opposing a tax on whiskey imposed by the new Congress became riotous and ultimately rebellious, attacking federal tax officials and proposing a new country separate from the United States.

When the local militia couldn't put down the rebellion, President Washington himself raised an army of 15,000 men and sent it out against the rebels. The federal army proved so intimidating that the rebellion collapsed without bloodshed. Nowadays people still resent taxes, but they're more likely to express themselves at the ballot box than repeat what history came to know as the Whiskey Rebellion.

Nothing is beyond the reach of Congress. It deals with:

- ✔ Spending government money
- ✔ Regulation of commerce
- ✔ International relations
- ✔ Agriculture and manufacturing
- ✔ The operations of government

And that's just for starters. Congress can weigh in with any subject that it thinks requires federal legislation. Even when legislation isn't necessary, Congress can involve itself through its fact-finding and investigative roles.

Taking care of you, the constituent

Members also work on your individual concerns. This is called *casework* in congressional parlance and many members find it the most rewarding part of the job. A junior member may have little direct effect on national affairs, but he can be a powerful and imposing force in his local community.

Often, just a simple letter from a member can work wonders on your behalf. For example, my father once felt cheated by a real estate developer and wanted to get back a down payment he'd made on a house. He wrote a letter with his complaints to his representative, Rep. Frank Pallone (D-New Jersey). Pallone, in turn, wrote a letter to the developer. The letter didn't make any threats nor really argue with the developer, it merely asked that my father receive proper treatment. Within days my father had received his down payment. This case didn't involve a national law or global policy or even the government, it was just a case where a representative intervened, ensuring that a constituent received fair treatment — and it worked.

Frequently, a representative is most effective in helping you when you're trying to deal with the federal bureaucracy. Such instances may include:

- ✔ Getting benefits from federal agencies like the Veterans Administration
- ✔ Intervening on behalf of contractors or vendors trying to sell or provide services to the federal government
- ✔ Assisting people with immigration or citizenship problems

In order to freely communicate with constituents, members are given *franking* privileges — they're able to mail material to constituents for free. However, franking can only be used for official purposes, not for campaigning and not for personal purposes.

Chapter 3

Scoping Out the Senate

● ●

In This Chapter:

▶ Measuring up to the qualifications of a senator

▶ Getting in touch with your senator

▶ Discovering what a senator does

● ●

*T*he Senate as an institution tends to deal with issues that affect entire states and the nation as a whole. Although House members deal with national and policy issues, their emphasis is on individual constituents and their districts. The Senate places a good deal less emphasis on individual casework than the House does, which is not to say that a senator doesn't take care of individual constituents when they appeal to him. Nevertheless, work in the Senate tends to deal with institutions — states, corporations, and federal agencies — rather than individuals.

Time weighs heavily on members of the Senate, but the pressure is not the same intense kind driven by two-year terms in the House. On the contrary, the pressure on senators has more to do with the Senate achieving a balance between getting things done, while fulfilling its mandate for full and free debate, and its general inclination toward finding consensus.

The issues that come before the Senate are major legislation, nominations, and treaties.

If you want to register an opinion or pass legislation, you must pay as much attention to the Senate as you do the House.

What It Takes to Be a Senator and How to Find Yours

Each state is represented by two senators, so there are 100 senators in all. They speak for the interests of their states.

But more, the Senate is intended to serve as a dual brake: It's a brake on the president, the executive branch, and executive power and prevents the government from excess; and it's a brake on the people when popular enthusiasms threaten to turn to mob rule. Put another way, the Senate is the fulcrum that balances the extremes of tyranny and anarchy and makes sure that neither ever tips the scales.

One story that illuminates the purpose of the Senate may not be literally true, but it is nonetheless enlightening. George Washington was having breakfast with Thomas Jefferson after Jefferson had returned from France where he'd served as minister. Jefferson hadn't been at the Constitutional Convention and asked Washington why he'd agreed to a two-house system including a Senate. Washington observed Jefferson pouring hot tea from his cup into a saucer before drinking it. "Why did you pour your tea into that saucer?" he asked. "To cool it," answered Jefferson. "Just so. We pour the House legislation into the Senatorial saucer to cool it," said Washington.

The Framers of the Constitution intended the Senate to serve as a counterbalance to the House of Representatives: The House is expected to reflect popular passions and passing enthusiasms; the Senate is expected to provide advice to the president and to temper enthusiasm with wisdom and experience.

Preventing tyranny and anarchy

Tyranny and anarchy weren't abstractions to the Framers, they lived through both and stared them in the face. In the first case, they'd endured the oppressive laws and arbitrary rules imposed by King George III, the king of England, until 1776 when they staked their lives, fortunes and sacred honor on a very risky rebellion.

But they'd also seen anarchy when, in 1783, Continental soldiers seeking back pay marched on Independence Hall in Philadelphia where

Congress was meeting. The angry soldiers shouted their demands and stuck their muskets through the windows of the Hall, pointing them at the members. Congress fled to Princeton, New Jersey, and when it formulated the Constitution, it made sure that Congress would run the federal district that would serve as the Capitol (what is today Washington, District of Columbia) to ensure that Congress never again faced such mobs.

The length of a senator's term (six years as opposed to two in the House) is an important difference between the two chambers. Six years can be an eternity in politics, giving senators the luxury of exercising patience as they attempt to achieve their ends. In contrast, a House member is always under pressure to produce results within two years. Only a third of the Senate faces reelection every two years, which means that a certain degree of change keeps the body in touch with popular feeling while it maintains continuity.

The Framers also envisioned senators as ambassadors from sovereign states, so that it was in the Senate that the great debates over states rights were played out. The notion of states as sovereign countries was laid to rest with the Civil War, but the Senate remains the forum for states to pursue their interests through their senators within the national framework.

The smallness of the Senate — there were only 26 senators in the beginning — also established the atmosphere of the Senate: It's very clubby, decorous, and dignified and has a strong sense of identity as a unique institution.

Senators are very fond of a quote calling the U.S. Senate "The world's greatest deliberative body." In researching this book I tried to find the origin of that quotation but had no luck — but I knew I was really stymied when I called the Senate Historian's office and an official historian told me they didn't know its origin either!

Qualifying with experience

The Constitution requires that anyone seeking a seat on the Senate be at least 30 years old, a citizen of the United States for at least nine years and a resident of the state they serve.

The greater experience of senators was reinforced by the way they used to be selected. Until 1913, senators were chosen by their state legislatures rather than popular vote, so they usually were seasoned politicians and legislators.

The propriety of these distinctions [the different requirements for members of the House and Senate] are explained by the nature of the senatorial trust, which, requiring greater extent of information and stability of character, requires at the same time that the senator should have reached a period of life most likely to supply these advantages; and which, participating immediately in transactions with foreign nations, ought to be exercised by none who are not thoroughly weaned from the prepossessions and habits incident to foreign birth and education."

— Alexander Hamilton or James Madison writing as "Publius"
in "Federalist Paper number 62, The Senate"

Setting forth a senator's duties

A senator ensures, above all, that her state's interests are served. The senator must:

- ✔ Advocate and support causes important to her
- ✔ Help determine national policy
- ✔ Promote her state's economic, political, and cultural interests
- ✔ Propose new laws
- ✔ Review and vote on proposed legislation
- ✔ Stop legislation that can harm the state

Senators (as well as representatives) also work for the good of their party.

Finding and contacting your senator

If you don't know your senators, go to www.Senate.gov on the Internet, where you'll find a listing of senators by state. You can also call the Capitol switchboard at 202-224-3121, and the operator will connect you to your senator's office and tell you how to get in touch directly.

Letting the people in

Opening up the Senate to the people was a long, sometimes painful process. Until 1913, with the passage of the 17th Amendment to the Constitution, senators were elected only by the state legislatures, not by the voters of each state. In contrast to the House, starting in 1789, all Senate deliberations were secret. Not until 1794 was the public admitted to some debates, and when the Senate moved from its meeting places in New York and Philadelphia to Washington, D.C., in 1800, its new chamber featured a public gallery.

Although the Senate grew in numbers when new states were admitted to the union, it maintained a clubby, inbred atmosphere with the small numbers of senators smoking cigars, spitting tobacco, and trading favors during votes that often were closed to the public. Many Senate deliberations were kept secret until 1929 when the rules were changed to make all deliberations public, unless a majority of senators voted to close the session. Since then, the Senate has closed its sessions when considering grave matters such as impeachment, national security, or treaties.

The first woman didn't sit in the Senate until 1922, and that was an appointed seat filled by Rebecca Latimer Felton, who served only a single day. Jeannette Rankin (R-Mont. 1917–1919) was the first woman elected to the House in 1916, and in 1932, Hattie Caraway (D-Ark.), became the first woman elected to the Senate.

The Senate Web site is very user-friendly and designed to assist you in contacting your senator. It has instructions for doing so right on the opening screen.

To send an e-mail to your senator from the Senate Web site:

1. **Go to** www.Senate.gov.
2. **Click on "Contacting the Senate" in the top navigation bar.**

   You see a list of senators, their Web site addresses, and e-mail addresses. (More information about contacting the Senate is in the Communication navigation bar on the right side of the page.)

You can find your senator's direct phone number through the Senate Web site, so that you can call without going through the congressional switchboard.

The Senate's e-mail addresses follow this formula: The person's first name and last name, separated by a period followed by the @ sign, the last name of the senator followed by a period, then the word "senate," a period, and then "gov." So a Senate e-mail address is: Jane.Doe@*senator's last name*.senate.gov.

So, if you want to send an e-mail to a senate staffer, you need to know the staffer's first and last names and the last name of the senator he or she works for.

The Senate has its own Zip code: 20510. When writing to your senator, address your letter to "Dear Sen. _____. Then address the envelope:

Senator _____ (or "The Honorable," but this is an older, not-often-used form of address)

United States Senate

Washington, DC 20510

You can also address your letter to your senator's specific office in the Capitol Complex. You can find those addresses by going to the list of senators at the Senate Web site mentioned previously.

Since the anthrax attacks of October 2001, mail delivery to Capitol Hill has become slow and uncertain, so you may want to use a letter as a follow-up rather than as a primary form of communication. For a full discussion of communicating with members of Congress, see Chapter 12.

Don't forget that each senator has offices in the state she represents. Calling a local office can save you the cost of a phone call to Washington. You can find the addresses of the state offices by going to your senator's Web site.

Senatorial Responsibilities

If you think of your representative as your lawyer in Washington, by comparison, your senators act as lawyers for your state in Washington.

Only three duties of the Senate are mentioned in the Constitution

- Passing legislation and making laws in concert with the House. All bills must be approved by both chambers in order to become law.

- Impeaching high officials: The Senate presides over impeachments of the president or other high officials and can remove them by a two-thirds vote.

- Giving advice and consent: The Senate advises the president and approves:

  - Treaties, which it has to approve by a two-thirds vote

  - Nominations of "Ambassadors, other public Ministers and Consuls, Judges of the Supreme Court, and all other Officers of the United States, whose appointments are not otherwise provided for, and which shall be established by Law . . . "

    Since the Constitution was written, *Officers of the United States* has come to mean certain high executive branch officials whose position requires Senate confirmation. This includes cabinet secretaries, generals, and other officials, usually to about the level of assistant secretary.

That's it.

Passing legislation

Like their counterparts in the House, senators can initiate legislation on any subject except new taxes, and they must approve legislation already passed in the House if it's to become law.

Deliberating: Considering all sides

In the Senate's early days, senators saw their duty as refining legislation passed in the House by amending it. Amendments are key instruments in the Senate. Its rules reflect that fact — in contrast to the House where rules are set up governing each piece of legislation and amendments can be limited.

In the Senate, the amendment remains a key function for refining legislation sent by the House. However, senators also initiate legislation in their chamber.

Reading more about the Senate

On March 21, 1980, the granddaughter of Sen. Robert Byrd (D-W.Va.) and her fifth-grade class were sitting in the Senate gallery. It was a quiet Friday afternoon with little business being conducted and Byrd thought, "It might be well if they had something to go back to school and talk about." So Byrd launched into a speech on the history of the Senate.

Such was the modest beginning of what turned into a series of speeches that, when collected, became a four-volume history of the United States Senate. It's a comprehensive examination and explanation of the institution by a man widely regarded as its leading defender and exponent. The speeches were gathered together into a two-volume, illustrated set and published by the Senate in time for its 1989 bicentennial.

The Byrd speeches are available from the Government Printing Office and can be ordered through its online bookstore: bookstore. gpo.gov.

In 1955, then Senator John F. Kennedy (D-Mass. 1953–1961) authored the Pulitzer Prize-winning book, *Profiles in Courage,* a series of portraits of senators who took tough or principled stands on controversial issues of the day.

The fame of its author and allegations that it was ghostwritten for him (an allegation he always denied) have unfortunately overshadowed its substance because it's a very good, readable and informative book with a great deal of insight into the Senate and the people who have served it. A 2000 edition is published by Harper Perennial, New York, and Caroline Kennedy produced an updated version, *Profiles in Courage for Our Time* (Hyperion Books).

Another excellent discussion of Senate history is contained in the book *The Years of Lyndon Johnson: Master of the Senate* by Robert A. Caro (Alfred A. Knopf). This is the third volume of a biography of President Lyndon Johnson, but it contains a lyrical description of the Senate as an institution and colorfully portrays it during the years from 1955 to 1961 when Johnson was majority leader.

For quick glimpses of Senate history, you can't do better than Senate Historical Minutes, short essays written by Richard Baker, the Senate historian. Each of these little gems illuminates an episode from Senate history. They can be accessed by going to the "Learn About the Senate" link on the Senate Web site at www.senate.gov.

Because the Senate was envisioned as a rein on the more passionate House, Senate deliberations were expected to be more considered and analytical, and its members were to take more of a national perspective than the House members, who were closer to the people.

The Senate also provided an answer to a vexing problem the Framers encountered: How can a democracy operated by majority rule ever be able to safeguard the rights of the minority? By placing great emphasis on the equality of different points of view and unlimited debate when discussing them, the

Senate became a haven for the minority points of view. Issues are not so much resolved as they are considered, but, at some point, there has to be closure and a vote must be taken.

As a result of its mandate to consider all sides of the issues of the day, the Senate has been likened to a debating society. Because of its more stringent requirements for admission, the Senate also is compared to a gentleman's club and it, indeed, has a clubby feel to it, moving at a slower pace than the House of Representatives and even working in more ornate rooms at the Capitol. Institutionally, the Senate, as a whole, is conscious of its dignity and treasures protocol, ceremony, and seniority.

"[It is a] Senate of equals, of men of individual honor and personal character, and of absolute independence. We know no masters, we acknowledge no dictators."

— Senator Daniel Webster (Whig 1827–1841)

In the Senate, every member has an equal say in deliberations and more of an effort is made toward reaching consensus, compromise, and accommodation, and yet the Senate can be plenty partisan too. Nonetheless, the Senate takes its protection of the minority point of view seriously.

The Senate's reverence for full debate has given rise to an elaborate set of parliamentary rules designed to promote as full and free a debate as possible while still bringing down the curtain on an issue.

The deliberate road to civil rights

Deference to all viewpoints can also bottle up legislation very effectively. After the South was reincorporated into the union after the Civil War, southern senators effectively used their senatorial prerogatives, their seniority, and parliamentary procedure to stave off any movement on civil rights legislation.

It was the Supreme Court, led by Chief Justice Earl Warren, that eventually circumvented the Senate's refusal to move on the issue. And it was Sen. Lyndon Johnson (D-Texas 1949–1961 [when he became vice president]) who eventually got the Senate to move civil rights legislation, though it didn't actually pass until he used his position as president to continue slain President Kennedy's work on civil rights.

Filibustering: Talking yourself silly

Protection of the minority point of view makes possible the peculiar Senate institution known as the *filibuster,* wherein a senator takes as much time to debate an issue as possible, preventing a measure from being brought to a vote and allowing no other business to transpire. Filibustering senators have done everything from read names from telephone books and chapters of the Bible to preserve their time on the floor. All the while they're talking, their friends and allies are trying to put together deals to find some resolution to whatever issue caused the filibuster in the first place.

A filibuster can be closed by a *cloture vote* of three-fifths of the entire Senate, but that's difficult to arrange. Frequently, a cloture vote is just another way of voting on the issue at hand. When opponents of a filibuster fail to reach their three-fifths majority, the filibusterer has won the day. Technically, a cloture vote limits debate on a measure to only another 30 hours.

Amending: Tacking on tidbits and taking on riders

I was present at a conversation between a House staffer and a Senate staffer in which the House staffer complained that senators attached the most unrelated measures to bills. He said that Senators can stick anything onto any bill, no matter how irrelevant, and that no such actions were allowed in the House. The Senate staffer laughed: "The only rule in the Senate is that there are no rules."

Filibusters of note

The longest single Senate speech since 1900 was made by Sen. Strom Thurmond of South Carolina, then a Democrat, when he filibustered against the 1957 Civil Rights bill. Thurmond spoke continuously for 24 hours and 18 minutes.

Another famous filibuster was one by Senator Huey Long (D-La. 1932–1935) who in 1935 wanted to have appointees to the National Recovery Administration confirmed by the Senate despite President Franklin Roosevelt's opposition. Long spoke for 15 hours, 30 minutes, spending his time reading and analyzing the Constitution, which he claimed Roosevelt had forgotten. With only a few senators in the chamber (most of whom were sleeping at their desks), Long proposed to Vice President John Nance Garner, who was presiding, that all senators be forced to attend the session. Garner refused, saying: "That would be cruel and unusual punishment under the Bill of Rights." Finished with the Constitution, Long said he would answer any question from any senator. Then he answered questions from members of the press gallery who passed him notes. When he ran out of those, he provided Louisiana recipes for fried oysters and potlickers (pan drippings).

Not until 4 a.m. did Long stop talking so that he could take a break that could no longer be put off. Once he was out of the room, his bill was swiftly defeated.

Okay, so that's overstating things slightly, but it does convey a kernel of truth: In the Senate bills tend to be viewed and referred to as *vehicles*, rolling bandwagons that anyone can jump on with anything on their minds.

Proceeding to impeachment

The gravest responsibility of the Senate is sitting judgment on the president and other high officials.

The Constitution sets out three grounds for impeachment in its explanation of the president's duties:

The President, Vice President and all civil Officers of the United States shall be removed from Office on Impeachment for, and Conviction of, Treason, Bribery, or Other High Crimes and Misdemeanors."

— United States Constitution, Article II, Section 4

Treason and bribery are pretty straightforward crimes, but while it was easy for the Framers to write "high crimes and misdemeanors," interpreting precisely what that means has led to a lot of controversy over the years. Each impeachment proceeding has reinterpreted the meaning of that phrase.

The process

Impeachment is a process, not a verdict. *Impeachment* is the process of accusing a high official of a crime and trying him or her. The formal accusations against an official are called *articles of impeachment*. A grave crime that could lead to the impeachment process is called an *impeachable offense*.

Under the Constitution, in case of an impeachment, the House acts as a grand jury, deciding whether an official should be impeached. The House weighs the evidence and decides whether a full-fledged trial is necessary.

If the House believes trial is merited, it sends the indictment — the articles of impeachment — to the Senate, which then forms itself into a jury.

If the official accused is below the level of the president, the vice president acts as the presiding officer of the impeachment. But if the official being impeached is the president, the chief justice of the Supreme Court presides over the Senate proceedings since the vice president would be judging her boss and the person she'd succeed.

If two-thirds of the Senate find the official guilty, that official is removed from office and can never hold office again. He or she is then subject to the regular penalties of law.

The instances

Impeachment is such a serious undertaking that only 62 impeachments have occurred since 1789, and of those, only 17 were federal officials. Two presidents, Andrew Johnson and Bill Clinton, were impeached, but both were acquitted.

Andrew Johnson's impeachment was particularly bitter, because it was widely seen as a purely political action taken by his opponents. With 36 votes needed for removal, Johnson scraped by with a 35-to-19 vote. Bill Clinton also was acquitted when his opponents failed to muster the necessary two-thirds vote.

President Bill Clinton was impeached on two counts. The House voted 228 to 206 that he was guilty of grand jury perjury and voted 221 to 212 that he was guilty of obstructing justice. On February 12, 1999, the Senate found him not guilty of perjury by a vote of 55 to 45, but split 50-50 on the obstruction of justice charge, which was nowhere near the two-thirds required to remove him from office.

The House Judiciary Committee approved three articles of impeachment of President Richard Nixon in 1974 for abuses of executive power, but he resigned before the articles were voted on by the full House or sent to the Senate.

Giving advice and consent

The Senate's other great responsibility is what is called by the Constitution *advice and consent,* and it applies to two functions: approving treaties and approving high officers. Both of these functions are important restrictions on the power of presidents. (Interestingly, the advice and consent function is not mentioned in the Constitution's section on the Senate [Article I, Section 3] but in the executive branch section [Article II, Section 2, Paragraph 2]).

Approving treaties

In the age of kings, monarchs could decide to go to war without consulting anyone other than — possibly — their close advisors or generals. The American colonists suffered because of this, losing people during the French and Indian Wars without having any voice in the decision to go to war.

To prevent a recurrence, the Framers gave Congress the authority to declare war and gave the Senate the power to approve the conclusion of peace. In the eighteenth century this was an extraordinary power to vest in the people.

Even so, the Framers wanted to ensure that treaties were examined with wisdom and knowledge and so they gave this power to the Senate. The executive branch had to have the latitude to negotiate treaties, but ultimately the Senate, as representatives of the people, would have final say on whether the agreement was approved.

So significant was the approval of treaties that the Constitution provides that a two-thirds majority of senators present must vote to approve them.

Today, the Senate advises and consents on hundreds of agreements covering a broad range of topics ranging from trade to arms control to military alliances.

Confirming nominees

In the case of executive and judicial branch nominees for high office, *advice and consent* means examining and approving a nominee's qualifications for the designated office.

As with advice and consent to treaties, this is an important check on the power of the executive and a stark contrast with the monarchical governments of the eighteenth century where the king simply appointed whomever he liked.

Approving nominations is one of the most contentious, sensitive, and difficult tasks facing the Senate. Because the Senate is considering the past and future of a human being rather than some abstract issue or a document like a treaty, passions — political and personal — often run high. There has always been debate over the degree to which a person's personal life is fair game for senatorial inquiry and is likely to affect performance of his duties. Moreover, because a nomination isn't bound by rules of evidence or restrictions of any kind, anything is fair game for inquiry.

As the country and government have grown, hundreds of positions have opened up in the executive branch, the judiciary, and the military that require Senate approval. Usually these are routine and many appointments — for example, lower-ranking generals or lower-level judges — are approved in a group without much discussion.

However, nominations tend to get a great deal of media attention when the Senate considers very high-level officials in sensitive and powerful positions or Supreme Court nominees. Justices serve for life and they, and other high-profile officials, can have a profound effect on the country for years.

These kinds of nominations become national issues when the nominees have taken controversial positions or political arguments arise over their appointments.

CAPITOL CASE

Controversial nominations

Three of the most contentious nominations of recent times were the 1989 nomination of former Senator John Tower (R-Texas 1961–1985) to be secretary of defense, the 1991 nomination of Clarence Thomas to the Supreme Court, and the 2001 nomination of former Senator John Ashcroft (R-Mo. 1995–2001) to be attorney general.

✔ In the case of Tower, allegations of excessive drinking and relations with defense contractors became a factor in consideration of his nomination and it was ultimately defeated by a vote of 53 to 47.

✔ In the case of Thomas, accusations of sexual harassment by a former employee, Anita Hill, prompted nationally televised hearings. Though the allegations nearly stopped his nomination, it was ultimately approved by a vote of 52 to 48.

✔ In the case of Ashcroft, his religious fundamentalism and conservatism raised fears that he wouldn't administer the law fairly. His nomination was ultimately approved by a vote of 58 to 42.

Part II
Looking at the Legislative Process

The 5th Wave   By Rich Tennant

"You're going to try to stop the filibuster, aren't you?"

In this part . . .

*E*verything you need to know about how laws get made at the national level.

Chapter 4

Introducing a Bill

In This Chapter

▶ Understanding the nature of legislation

▶ Getting to know the people

▶ Assembling legislation

▶ Reviewing the legislative process

A merican democracy is a dynamic process designed to do two things:

- ✔ Enable new ideas to become the law of the land
- ✔ Provide everyone with a say in the final product

In this chapter, I show you the process, its elements, and how it's designed to work.

Starting the Process

Turning an idea into legislation is neither swift nor easy. Fisher Ames, a Revolutionary War soldier and representative from Massachusetts (1789–1797), noted when looking at differences between monarchies and republics that: "A monarchy is a merchantman (a ship) which sails well, but will sometimes strike on a rock, and go to the bottom; a republic is a raft which will never sink, but then your feet are always in the water."

When you're dealing with Congress, you'll really feel like you're riding on a raft: Not only are your feet always wet, but you're also navigating without rudder and often drifting with the wind.

Dealing with the Players

Literally thousands of personal, district, and committee staff members help the 535 members of Congress get the job done. The following sections fill you in on who works where and does what.

Members of Congress

The kind of person who gets elected to Congress knows how to motivate large numbers of people, get them organized, convince them to do his bidding, and lead them toward a common goal without appearing too ruthless or egotistical. After all, that's how these people get to Congress in the first place: They put themselves before the voters, organize campaigns and win elections. As a result, Congress is full of gregarious, intelligent, charming, and intensely competitive individuals.

The politicking doesn't end when these charmers reach the Capitol. Indeed, it gets ratcheted up another notch. They're all politicking each other, flattering each other, maneuvering to get what they want, whether it's scrambling to get a bill passed, jostling for a leadership position, or bucking for a committee assignment.

Walk into any congressional dining room or Capitol Hill restaurant with a member and all the members greet each other like long-lost brothers or sisters — when, in fact, they've all been laboring shoulder-to-shoulder for months in the same building, often on the same issues, and often in conflict with each other. Serving in Congress is a world of politicking, ambition, and cheerful human relations. On its darker side are backstabbing betrayals, white-hot ambition, and sometimes fanatical commitment to a cause or an ideology. Imagine high school on a global stage.

You're entering this world to get something done. Fortunately, the strength of following a well-established procedure first outlined in the Constitution, and refined during the centuries since, enables all these people, with their different agendas and goals and personalities, to work together, resolving their differences and contributing to the growth and strength of the country. Ultimately, however, they must respond to you, the voter who put them where they are in the first place. You're going to be part of this amazing process, and you're going to succeed at it.

Staffers

Each chamber of Congress has permanent staff, or officers, who help keep the institution running.

In the House, the officers are the:

- ✔ **Clerk of the House:** Keeps track of all the House business, including legislation.
- ✔ **Chief Administrative Officer:** Responsible for administering House business.
- ✔ **Sergeant-at-arms:** Maintains order in the House.
- ✔ **Postmaster:** Administers the mail.
- ✔ **Parliamentarian:** Tracks and administers parliamentary rules.
- ✔ **Chaplain:** Opens House sessions and counsels members, staff and family.

In the Senate, the officers are the:

- ✔ **Secretary of the Senate:** As chief legislative officer, the secretary is nominated by the majority-party conference, elected by the Senate, and is responsible for ensuring the accuracy of the text of bills and signing the measures the Senate passes. He also supervises the preparation and printing of bills and reports, *The Congressional Record,* and other printed and written materials.
- ✔ **Sergeant-at-arms:** The Senate's chief security officer is responsible for keeping order.
- ✔ **Majority and Minority secretaries:** These party secretaries are responsible for scheduling and coordinating the flow of information between the senators and the political leaders of the different parties.
- ✔ **Parliamentarian:** This officer interprets rules and procedures and assigns bills to committees on behalf of the senator presiding over the chamber.
- ✔ **Chaplain:** This member of the clergy opens the Senate with a daily prayer and advises the senators, their families, and Senate employees on spiritual matters.

Committee folk

Committee assignments arguably are the most crucial decisions facing new members of both houses of Congress. A plum committee assignment can make or break a representative's career. Committee assignments are inside baseball — matters determined purely by the congressional membership, so there are few things you can do as a citizen to help your representative. A member can request a particular committee assignment when he first arrives in Congress, but those decisions are made by the majority leaders. In the 107th Congress, House Republican assignments were made by a Republican Committee on Committees, which interviewed the members and determined chairmanships.

The committee and subcommittee chairmen play an important and powerful role. Chairmen:

- ✔ Lead the committee
- ✔ Preside over committee meetings
- ✔ Determine whether any hearings take place
- ✔ Refer bills to subcommittee
- ✔ Set the committee calendar

Setting the committee calendar is particularly important, because that determines which legislation is considered and when. A committee chairman can simply kill a bill by leaving it off the calendar for that session.

Committee chairmen are powerful, in general, for other reasons as well as their direct influence on legislation. They:

- ✔ Control the committee budget
- ✔ Have more staff than other committee members
- ✔ Name conferees to the House-Senate conferences
- ✔ Are subject to greater media visibility as spokesmen for the committee
- ✔ Get first crack at sponsoring and cosponsoring legislation

The second most powerful person on the committee is called the *ranking member.* This is the most senior member from the other party based on length of service.

Building a Bill

As soon as you start working with Congress, you begin hearing about this bill or that bill. It's as if someone named Bill is everywhere in Washington. In the congressional context, a *bill* is simply a proposal, an idea, that's written up in legislation and presented to the Congress.

Starting with an idea

It all starts with an idea, a simple concept. You take that idea to your representative or senator because you see a need, you have a cause, and you want it to become a law.

Remember that only members of Congress can propose resolutions that are considered by the entire body. Your task comes down to convincing a member to actually want to introduce your idea. (The chapters in Part IV guide you through this lobbying process.)

Anyone can write up, or draft a bill, but only a member of Congress can introduce it. However, the more work that you do for members, the easier it is for them to work on your behalf. When you have a bill that you want Congress to consider, writing it up in legal language and presenting it to your representative or senator as a draft is a good idea. Lobbyists routinely draft legislative proposals.

Figuring out how to write a bill is easy. Just look up an existing bill on the congressional Web site at www.Thomas.gov and follow that format to compose your proposal. Although your representative may make a few changes, he and the staff won't have to do as much work creating the bill by themselves. (For more about lobbying, see Chapter 10.)

Looking at the types of legislation

Several kinds of bills can be introduced and each one has a special designation.

Bill

The *bill* is the most common form of legislation. It's an idea, a proposal and in the House it receives the designation *H.R.* for House of Representatives (not House Resolution as many people think). In the Senate it gets *S.* for Senate. A bill becomes law when it's approved by both the House and Senate and reaches the president's desk for signature. After it's signed by the president, it's no longer called a bill, but becomes an "Act."

Resolution

A *resolution* is much the same as a bill, except that it's usually concerned with the operation of the House or Senate. In other words, it's about something that concerns only the institution and doesn't need to be signed by the president. In the House, such a resolution is designated H. Res. and gets a number, and in the Senate, it becomes S. Res.

Joint resolution

A *joint resolution* is virtually identical to a bill. Contrary to what one would expect given the name, it can be proposed in either the House or the Senate and it goes through the same procedures as a bill and must be signed into law by the president.

One slight difference between a bill and a joint resolution is that a joint resolution frequently has a preamble, a paragraph explaining the justification for the bill with all the "Whereas" resolving clauses that are a feature of legislative language. Joint resolutions are also used to amend bills already under consideration. A joint resolution gets the designation H.J.Res. in the House and S.J.Res. in the Senate.

The only time a joint resolution differs in its procedure for consideration is when it's an amendment to the Constitution. Then it has to be approved by two-thirds of both houses to pass, and it's also sent to the states for ratification rather than being signed (or not) by the president.

Concurrent resolutions

A *concurrent resolution* can be introduced in either house and doesn't go to the president for signature. It isn't a bill and doesn't create any law. Usually, concurrent resolutions are used to express facts, principles, and opinions of the two houses. After being passed by both houses, concurrent resolutions are transmitted to the U.S. archivist rather than the president. In the House, they are designated H.Con.Res. and in the Senate, S.Con.Res.

Many people dismiss concurrent resolutions as having no teeth because a "sense of resolution" has no power behind it. It's merely an expression of opinion and usually reflects the lowest common denominator: For example, "It is the sense of the House and Senate that all Americans should support Motherhood and Apple Pie."

One example in the 107th Congress was S. Con.Res. 44, resolving that, in light of the Japanese attack on Pearl Harbor in 1941, the House and Senate paid tribute to those who died and those who survived the attack. This resolution didn't enact a law, but it expressed a congressional sentiment.

However, dismissing the role that concurrent resolutions can play would be a mistake, especially as part of an overall lobbying campaign. When effectively used to show the sentiments of the Congress where a particular cause or measure is concerned, concurrent resolutions can lead to real legislation, can warn opponents of the strength behind a measure, and can encourage supporters inside and outside Congress.

Private bills

While many people look to Congress for help with personal problems, sometimes such assistance must be approved by the entire Congress in the form of a bill. Your representative or lawyer can tell you whether that will be the case with any proposal you may make.

The use of private bills has declined considerably. For example, in the 96th Congress (from 1979–1981), 123 private bills were passed, but by the 104th Congress (from 1995–1997), the number had dropped to only 4.

Members are leery of private bills because they have the potential for creating trouble for the member if it turns out that the beneficiary doesn't have the cleanest record

In the past, private bills were mostly used to assist people who had a grievance or demand on the executive branch. Moreover, the need for them has declined because today there are more ways to appeal to executive agencies than there were in the past.

Nonetheless, private bills are an option that usually fall into the following categories and go to the following House committees:

- ✔ Armed services decorations issues are handled by the National Security Committee.

- ✔ Civil service issues go to the Government Reform and Oversight Committee.

- ✔ Claims against the government. Domestic claims go to the Judiciary Committee; foreign claims go to the International Relations Committee.

- ✔ Immigration issues (for example, naturalization, residency status, and visa classification) go to the Judiciary Committee.

- ✔ Medical issues (for example, Food and Drug Administration approvals and health maintenance organization enrollment requirements) go to the Commerce Committee.

- ✔ Patents and copyright questions go to the Judiciary Committee.

- ✔ Public land issues (for example, sales, claims, exchanges, and mineral leases) go to the Resources Committee.

- ✔ Taxation issues (for example, income tax liabilities and tariff exemptions) go to the Ways and Means Committee.

> ✔ Vessel documentation issues go to the Transportation and Infrastructure Committee.
>
> ✔ Veterans' benefit issues go to the Veterans' Affairs Committee.

Private bills almost always are introduced only in the House since they deal with individuals and the House is the direct representative of the people (as opposed to the Senate, which represents states). If they get through subcommittee and committee consideration, they then move to the floor where all the private bills are considered together on the first and third Tuesdays of each month (although the House can decide to call them up at any other time when everyone agrees).

Private bills usually go sailing through and routinely are approved by a voice vote. However, whenever two members object to a private bill, it goes back to the committee for reconsideration or is held for further consideration until the next batch of private bills comes up.

Introducing a bill

The introduction process works differently in the two chambers of Congress.

In the House, the steps for introducing a bill are

1. **A member fills out and signs a form available from the Clerk of the House.**

   The signatures of the member and any other sponsors of the bill ensure that everyone whose name appears on the bill as an original sponsor.

2. **The sponsor drops the form in a wooden box called the *hopper*.**

   This is the origin of the phrase "dropping in" a bill, which means that it's been introduced. Likewise, the sponsor of the bill usually makes a speech announcing the introduction of the bill.

When a bill is introduced it's called a *bill* but when it's passed it's called an *act*. Nonetheless, when members give it a formal name, they give it the name it's going to have on final passage, so the formal name — what's technically called the *long title* — describes it as an act.

In the Senate, there's just one step for introducing a bill:

1. **A senator presents his bill to a clerk at the presiding officer's desk.**

   That senator can make this presentation without comment or make a speech to mark the introduction of the bill. When reading the

Congressional Record, you can find many speeches that begin something like, "Mr. President, I rise today to introduce the 'This is Going to Make America Great and Get Me Re-Elected Act.'"

Once in a great while in the Senate someone objects to an introduction of a bill for any reason or no reason. In that case, it's put aside for a day. The following day, if no one objects, the bill is read by title and introduced.

Giving a bill an identity

Now that a tangible piece of legislation exists for members to consider, the fun begins.

When a bill is put in formal form, the Clerk of the House or the bill clerk of the Senate gives it a formal title and a short title and — this is important — a number. This numbering system helps legislators track the proposals they're considering. The number is the designation that absolutely everyone on Capitol Hill understands immediately.

The titles can make a bill an attractive piece of legislation to the other members, so names are chosen carefully. Some bills like the annual appropriations bills simply get utilitarian titles: for example, "Appropriations For Fiscal Year 2003 For The Department Of Defense." However, names that make a bill sound attractive and desirable naturally are more favored. The best recent example of an attractive-sounding bill was the Provide Appropriate Tools Required to Intercept and Obstruct Terrorism (PATRIOT) Act of 2001.

Because Congress considers so many pieces of legislation, the numbers bills are given are important too.

Often, the president's chief campaign pledge is turned into bill number one and submitted with great fanfare at the beginning of the session.

A bill is known by many different names and references:

- ✔ As one of the hundreds of pieces of proposed legislation that come before Congress every year, a bill is known by its number.

- ✔ Bills also are known by their short titles. (For example, the Patriot Act.)

- ✔ Informally, bills frequently are known by the names of their sponsors. (For example, Tauzin-Dingell, or Gramm-Rudman.) This nomenclature often is used when a bill becomes more widely known and covered in the media.

> ✔ Bills also can be informally referred to after special people. (For example, the Brady bill, which was named for wounded presidential press secretary James Brady.)

Getting There is Half the Fun: The Legislative Process

Back when you were in civics class, you discovered the process by which a bill becomes a law. Okay, so you probably don't remember it, but the process actually is quite simple and direct. Figure 4-1 shows you how it works.

All the factors that civics books don't tell you about — the politics, the opposition, the delays, and the outside forces — make the process even more complex. So, a more accurate chart of the process actually looks something like Figure 4-2.

Don't despair. You'll work through this process and make your idea become real.

Gathering cosponsors

The member who introduces the bill is called its *sponsor.* More than one member can introduce a bill, but all the members who sign the original bill are counted as sponsors. After the bill is introduced, other members supporting it become *cosponsors,* though after a bill is reported out of its final committee, no more cosponsors can sign on.

Any member who introduces a bill must garner the support of all his colleagues, so he usually sends out a letter that explains the proposal and why it's important. This is called a *Dear colleague letter* and it's an important letter. While working with Congress, you'll often hear references to these letters, as in: "He sent out a 'Dear colleague' this morning," or, "There's a 'Dear colleague' making the rounds." These are letters sent out among the members soliciting support for the bill, or just notifying members about important information.

The best way to drop in a bill is not to simply do it without warning or support, but to build up as much support as possible before it's even introduced. To that end, members try to enlist other members to offer support from the very beginning.

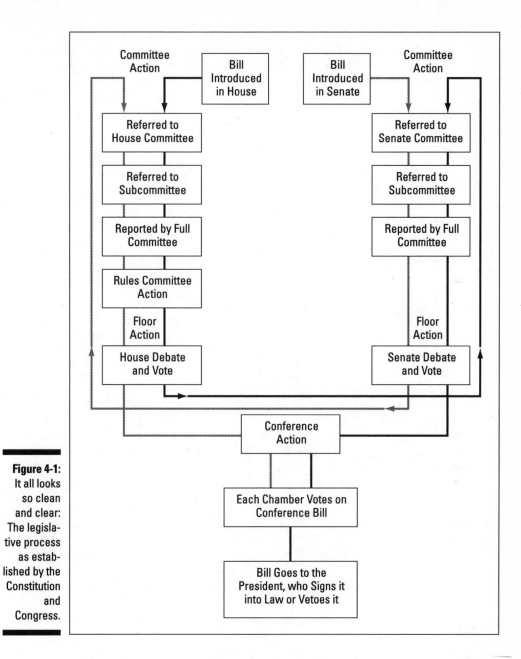

Sponsorship of bills is critical at the early stages of an idea's journey through the legislative process. The sponsor or sponsors of a bill are the members who actually introduce it. The number of sponsors is limited only by the number of members in the particular chamber in which it is introduced (House = 435, Senate = 100). Sponsorship of a bill by powerful or popular members can virtually assure its passage.

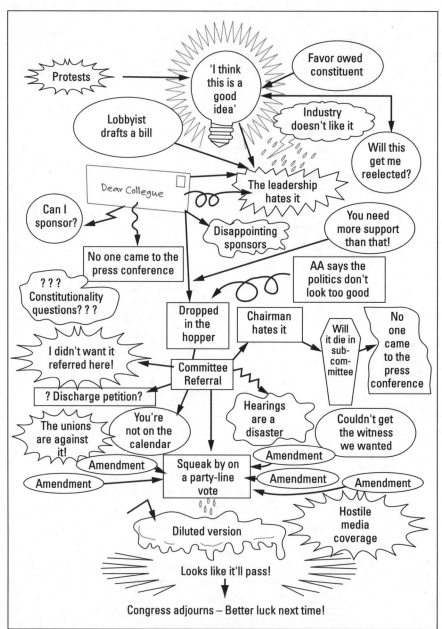

Figure 4-2: The reality of the legislative process is much different when you actually start working with Congress.

The number and quality of cosponsors also are important factors. Cosponsors are members who associate themselves with the bill.

Before a bill is introduced and when the member you're working with is sending out his "Dear colleague" letters, you can help by sending letters to or contacting as many members as possible and urging them to sponsor or cosponsor the bill. If the "Dear colleague" letter isn't out yet, tell them to expect its arrival. If it has been sent, urge them to sign it. A big push by you at this early stage can go a long way toward helping a bill become law. If you have a good idea about which committee the bill will go to, you can also concentrate your efforts on members of that committee.

Members always want to join a bandwagon that's going somewhere, and they're more likely to sponsor a piece of legislation when it:

✔ Has a good chance of passage

✔ Is popular with the public

✔ Will bring credit (and recognition) to its sponsors

When members consider legislation, they carefully look at its list of sponsors and cosponsors, asking:

✔ Do the numbers of sponsors and cosponsors ensure passage of the bill? (If a majority of members sign on, its passage is certain.)

✔ Are key committee chairmen and members signed on as sponsors or cosponsors? (If committee chairmen sign on, it means the bill will sail through the committees.)

Much of the work aimed at passing a bill is done in these early stages, and successful cosponsorships go a long way toward ensuring success.

Pushing through the committee jungle

Sometimes listening to media coverage of Congress sounds like: "It was announced today that the subcommittee on bran flakes of the White Bread Committee recommended to the Senate Select Baking Committee that more yeast be put in the mix, a proposal defeated by the House, which voted as a committee of the whole."

Congress is made up of committees for just about every area that government covers, and government covers everything (see Appendix B for a complete list of congressional committees). It seems like a jungle of committees, sub-committees, select committees, joint committees, and permanent committees. However, if you're ever going to get anything done, you must find your way through this thicket. Actually, it isn't that hard.

Appendix B lists the Standing and Joint Committees of the House and Senate during the 107th Congress.

Classifying your committee

Committees that are relatively permanent and deal with passing legislation are called *standing committees*. They cover most of Congress's committees. However, other kinds of committees include:

- ✔ **Joint committees:** These committees are comprised of members from the House and the Senate. Examples are the Joint Economic Committee and the Joint Taxation Committee.

- ✔ **Select or special committees:** These committees don't pass legislation. They may be formed to oversee one particular subject and thus may be dissolved after only a short period of time. For example, prior to the year 2000, the Senate established the Senate Special Committee on the Year 2000 Technology Problem.

Being referred

After a bill is introduced, it is assigned or *referred* to a committee. In the House, the Speaker of the House refers bills to committee, usually on recommendation by his staff or by the House parliamentarian. In the Senate, bills are referred by the presiding officer, although here, too, such decisions also are made by the parliamentarian. When a bill is referred it is said to be "committed."

When a bill reaches its assigned committee, the committee chairman may assign it to a subcommittee, if he feels it necessary for the bill's proper consideration.

Determining which committee gets what bill can be contentious. Some bills are self-evident — they deal with matters clearly falling within a particular committee's jurisdiction. Bills can also be assigned to several committees. Sometimes committee chairmen argue over jurisdiction of a bill. At that time, determining which committee gets to consider a bill is up to the Senate's presiding officer or the House Speaker. The House Speaker, in particular, can set time limits for committee consideration of a bill.

When a bill goes to several committees, the three ways of referring them are

- ✔ **Concurrent referral:** Two or more committees work on the bill at the same time.

- ✔ **Sequential referral:** The bill is considered first by one committee, then by a second, and then by however many more are assigned by the presiding officer of the House or Senate.

✔ **Split referral:** Some portions of a bill go to one committee, other portions go to as many other committees as appropriate.

Watching a committee work

After a bill is introduced, the committee portion of the legislative process is where:

✔ **Information regarding the legislation and its effects is gathered and researched.**

The committee calls witnesses, examines testimony, reads literature on the issue, and studies staff reports.

✔ **The legislation is altered.**

Committee members alter the wording and substance of the bill to meet their concerns and those of constituents.

✔ **A vote is taken or recommendation is made to the entire chamber on whether or not the legislation should pass.**

A committee can vote down a bill or — if there's especially strong support for a bill that the committee doesn't like — simply pass it on to the entire chamber without a recommendation. Usually, the committee vote determines the ultimate fate of the bill.

Legislation often is killed, sometimes without even a vote. The committee chairman may decide that he so dislikes a bill that he won't even bring it up for consideration — which is his privilege. A bill may also be brought up before the committee and the committee may vote against it and it doesn't proceed any further.

Bottling up legislation in committee is a time-honored and common legislative tactic. It's a way of killing bills without actually having to submit them to a vote by an entire chamber or committee. Sometimes, a committee chairman simply doesn't schedule a bill for consideration by his committee. A *discharge petition* is a way of freeing pigeonholed legislation. A member, usually the sponsor, has the option of circulating a petition that calls for the entire House or Senate to consider a bill without having it pass through committee first. However, a majority of the chamber must sign the petition for it to take effect and that isn't easily accomplished.

Holding hearings

When a subcommittee or committee is considering a bill, it conducts *hearings,* which are simply meetings of a committee or subcommittee to collect information.

Most of what you know about congressional hearing probably is based on what you've seen on TV or in the movies: enormous hearing rooms, jostling photographers, screaming reporters, and hostile representatives or senators.

Actually, most hearings are fairly routine affairs conducted to gather information. Attendance at the more obscure hearings often is limited to the interested committee members and the witnesses. The chairman of the committee presides and perhaps the next most-senior member from the other party attends. Members come and go during the hearing and most of the testimony is directed to the record rather than at the members on the podium.

So many bills come before congressional committees that many of them don't get a hearing, and many that don't get a hearing die in committee.

A presidential bill gets a hearing and budget-related bills get hearings, but otherwise it's up to the committee chairman to decide whether he wants to go through the time and trouble of assembling witnesses and listening to testimony.

Types and purposes

There are three types of hearings:

- ✔ **Legislative hearings** address current or pending legislation.
- ✔ **Oversight hearings** consider the implementation of existing law. These hearings are often the ones used to investigate executive branch agencies.
- ✔ **Investigative hearings** examine allegations of wrongdoing at the public or private level, or determine the facts of a major crisis or disaster.

  Perhaps the most famous investigative hearings were those concerning the impeachment of presidents Richard Nixon and Bill Clinton.

Politically, hearings can be used a number of ways. They can be used to

- ✔ Get expert opinion
- ✔ Release information to the public
- ✔ Criticize administration policies
- ✔ Investigate wrongdoing
- ✔ Embarrass the other party
- ✔ Establish the committee members' positions on an issue
- ✔ Allow individuals or organizations with a stake in legislation to present their positions

Hearing hearsay

In some cases, hearings can be used almost like a trial, enabling members to level accusations at people and institutions. Unlike a judicial proceeding, however, a hearing provides no defending attorneys, no rules of evidence, and no judge.

Sen. Joseph McCarthy (R-Wis. 1947–1957) set the worst example for abusing the powers of hearings. He leveled accusations at witnesses and made charges that couldn't be verified at the hearing or subsequently. In 1954, the Senate censured McCarthy for his conduct.

In a different light, around the same time, Sen. Estes Kefauver (D-Tenn. 1948–1963) conducted hearings that brought the existence of the mafia to the light of day and exposed organized crime for the first time.

Format

Hearings almost always follow the same format. The committee chairman makes a statement setting out his position on the matter and explaining the purpose of the hearing. He's followed by the ranking member. Then each member of the panel makes a statement in order of seniority.

When the members are finished — and it can take a while, depending on how many attend the hearing — the witnesses make their statements. When they're finished, the members begin asking questions, again going in order of seniority starting with the chairman. Each member is usually given about five minutes to ask questions.

In most hearings, the important questions are the first ones asked. As the hearing wears on, the questions frequently get repetitious and the members simply start posturing and speaking for the record. Also, members can use their question time to make statements; they don't have to ask questions.

Making the markup

After members of the subcommittee and committee have conducted hearings on a bill, they may *mark up* a bill, or go through it line by line, altering particular words and making whatever changes the committee members deem appropriate. A bill can become substantially altered after a *markup,* or it may go through without any markup at all.

Resources on the legislative process

When it comes to the legislative process, nothing is more authoritative than Congress's own materials.

The congressional Web sites have short, excellent descriptions of the process.

✔ For the House version, go to: `www.house.gov/house/Tying_it_all.html`.

✔ For the Senate version, go to: `www.senate.gov/learning/learn_process.html`.

Neither site gives you lobbying tips like *Congress For Dummies* (see Part IV), but each serves as a good basic primer. The House version provides a variety of links to current bills and floor action. The Senate version provides a fuller description of the process that includes explanations of unique Senate features.

The best book I know for an explanation of the legislative process is *How Congress Works* by Congressional Quarterly. This has a fuller description of the legislative process than Congress itself provides, and it recounts much of the underlying history while going deep into parliamentary details.

The big drawback to *How Congress Works* is the fact that it hasn't been updated since 1998 and it has limited distribution, although it can be ordered over the Internet. However, at $37.50 it's outrageously overpriced.

I strongly urge you to take a look at the Web sites of the individual House and Senate committees. These have good explanations of each committee's role and list upcoming activities like hearings. The committee sites can be accessed through the main House and Senate Web sites.

Another excellent online resource for information about Congress is C-SPAN's Web site, `www.CSPAN.org`, which has a favorite feature of mine called Capitol Questions `www.cspan.org/questions/congress.asp`. You can ask C-SPAN any question you like about an aspect of Congress. Unfortunately, the site never identifies the author of the answers, but that author is knowledgeable — and entertaining.

When markup is finished, the resulting version is called *the chairman's mark*. The committee then votes on the bill and *orders it reported*. At this stage, the committee can:

✔ Recommend that the entire chamber pass the bill. This is called *reporting out*. With positive recommendation it's called *reporting out favorably*.

✔ Report out the bill without a recommendation. This action is taken when the committee doesn't like legislation but thinks that the entire Congress needs to vote on it because the bill has strong political support.

✔ Kill the bill altogether.

Once its work is complete, the committee also issues a report that explains what it did to the legislation and why. The report may also explain the *legislative intent* of the committee — what it was attempting to accomplish and what effect it wants the legislation to have. This may be important later on when the courts look at the law. Committees almost never take the time or make the effort to issue a report on legislation they voted down — although there's always the possibility one could. In the vast majority of cases, however, a report only accompanies legislation the committee approves.

These reports are given a number and sometimes become as important as the bills themselves. Members who disagree with the committee's actions may file *minority reports* that are included with the report.

If your legislation makes it out of committee, it's ready to be considered by the entire chamber.

Chapter 5

Meeting the Players, Setting the Schedule

· ·

In This Chapter

▶ Casting the roles of congressional leadership

▶ Powering up the seniority system

▶ Playing party politics through caucuses and delegations

▶ Setting the congressional calendar

· ·

Although the legislative process is very well defined by the Constitution and law, the infrastructure that supports it has grown up over time in a much more informal way. Committees, caucuses, and delegations are all like building blocks that members of Congress use to erect their legislative structures.

The congressional calendar provides the framework against which all legislation passes. Understanding the calendar is essential to getting anything done in Congress.

If your cause to succeed, you must use the congressional structure and calendar to further your goals — or at the very least, understand their roles and how they're used.

Following the Leaders

Congress is an extremely hierarchical institution and great deference is paid to senior members and party and chamber leaders. A freshman representative may be a big deal in her local community but becomes small potatoes upon arriving at the Capitol — and more experienced members make sure that the new member knows it.

When you go to work with your representative, you'll discover that more powerful members of Congress determine many — or perhaps even all — of her actions. Sometimes your representative must ignore you or vote contrary to your interests because she has been instructed to do so by those more powerful lawmakers.

Newer members aren't the only ones expected to toe the party line. Members of the House and Senate have long been expected to do as their party leaders tell them: "To get along, go along," is an old congressional axiom and a favorite saying of House Speaker Sam Rayburn (D-Texas 1940–1961). In other words, for a member to get something done, she must go along with the party leaders and vote the way they tell her to. After all, the thinking goes, the political party helped put the new member in office. Now she's expected to return the favor by voting the party line.

In recent years, however, this party discipline has broken down and increasing numbers of members have voted in defiance of their leaders on certain issues. So, although leaders may not be as powerful as they once were, they can retaliate against straying members or coax those errant members back into the fold in a number of ways. They can:

- Kill the member's bills
- Withhold key assignments
- Cripple a member's career within the party
- Block appropriations favorable to the member's state or district
- Deny the member political support in the next election
- Withhold public credit for the member's legislative achievements

Knowing who the leaders are

Knowing the leadership structure of the House and Senate is important, because the people who occupy those positions determine so much of what Congress does.

House leadership

In many ways, the House leaders are more powerful within their chamber than the Senate leadership. Decision making in the House is weighted toward the majority party, so, as long as party discipline holds, much of the leadership's agenda is enacted.

The majority party determines the legislative agenda, and if the leadership decides there's no time to consider a bill during a given session, that bill is effectively dead.

The leaders, in order of seniority, are:

- **Speaker of the House:** The presiding officer is elected by a majority vote of the entire membership of the House. Although theoretically any member can be elected Speaker (in fact, the Speaker doesn't have to be a member of the majority party), in practical fact, the person filling this role almost always is a member of the majority party. A truly powerful person, the Speaker is able to set the legislative calendar and assign bills to different committees.

- **Majority Leader:** The leader of the party that holds the majority of seats in the House is elected by that party's representatives. Another powerful position, the Majority Leader has a great deal of say in setting the legislative agenda.

- **Majority Whip:** Elected by House members whose party is in the majority, the whip serves as the assistant leader of the majority party, so-named because this person's job is to whip members into toeing the party line whenever necessary. Historically, the Majority Whip has been an important position but that has been especially true in recent years. The Whip is the leader closest to the members and serves as a liaison between members and the leadership, communicating messages back and forth. As a result, whips usually know members of the party personally, including their needs and desires, the politics in their districts, and the pressures they face. At the same time, the whip's job is to ensure that members vote the way the leadership wants them to.

- **Minority Leader:** Head of and elected by members of the minority party, the Minority Leader leads the minority, determining its agenda and its stand on the issues that come up before the House. It's the same job as the Majority Leader — only the Minority Leader doesn't hold the votes to impose an agenda on the House.

- **Minority Whip:** Keeps minority members in line, elected by the members of his party.

The Whip positions have become prominent in recent years, and you see frequent media references to the members holding the Majority and Minority Whip positions. Tom DeLay (R-Texas) turned the Majority Whip position into one of real power and influence — he essentially whipped the House into impeaching Bill Clinton. And Nancy Pelosi (D-Cal.) was elected as the first female Minority Whip in October 2001.

- **Republican Conference Chairman:** The person in this position leads the House Republicans. However, in contrast to the majority leader, who's preoccupied with congressional matters, the conference chairman is more concerned with party politics, developing party positions and getting the party's message out to the public.

✔ **Democratic Caucus Chairman:** Leader of the House Democrats, the caucus chairman presides over caucus meetings, oversees the development of Democratic policy positions, and conducts a conference about political issues at least once a year.

Senate leadership

The power of the Senate leadership resides largely in its control of the Senate schedule, which is made up by the Majority Leader. Senate rules prevent the kind of majority dominance that exists in the House — in the Senate there's more deference for minority viewpoints. One of the most important aspects of Senate leadership is the national platform it provides for its holder — sometimes serving as a potential springboard to the presidency.

✔ **President:** The Vice President of the United States also serves as the president of the Senate. Although this position is constitutionally mandated, it nevertheless is largely ceremonial, and the vice president generally attends only when needed to break a tie (the only time the vice president ever casts a vote).

Senators address the vice president and whichever senator fills in for him as "Mr. President" or "Madame President" when a female senator presides, when they speak from the floor of the Senate. The presiding officer — whoever it is — keeps order, recognizes senators who wish to speak, and enforces parliamentary procedure.

✔ **President Pro Tempore:** Elected by the entire Senate, the President Pro Tempore is the official presiding officer of the Senate when the vice president is absent. The President Pro Tempore also designates senators to stand in during the residing officer's absence, so you often see different senators presiding over the chamber. This is a largely ceremonial position and often goes to the most senior senator in the entire chamber.

✔ **Majority Leader:** The true, practical leader of the Senate is the Majority Leader, who is elected by the Senators who are members of the majority party. The majority leader sets the calendar, adjudicates disputes among members, and leads his party and the Senate as a whole.

✔ **Majority Whip:** As is true in the House, the whip is in charge of keeping senators voting the way the leadership wants and coordinating their positions on legislative business.

✔ **Minority Leader:** The leader of the minority party.

✔ **Minority Whip:** The person in charge of ensuring that senators from the minority party vote the way the minority leadership decides.

✔ **Conference Chairmen:** The Democratic or Republican senators who hold this position oversee their parties' support organizations. The conferences provide communications services to the senators and gets the party message out to the media and public.

✔ **Policy Committee Chairmen:** The Democratic and Republican senators in this position are in charge of formulating their parties' approach to national policy issues.

Putting age before beauty: The role of seniority

As you thread your way through Congress, you'll come across the importance of seniority at every turn. *Seniority* is a system wherein simply by hanging in there and getting re-elected over and over, members of Congress accumulate power — the longer they're in office, the more powerful they become. The seniority system permeates both chambers and though it has eroded somewhat, it still remains strong.

The longer members remain in their chambers, the more power they accumulate, the higher they rise within the institution, and the more they attain positions of power like committee chairmanships or leadership positions. And those are the formal benefits of seniority — the intangible benefits include a wider circle of contacts, accumulation of favors owed, and broader recognition among colleagues, lobbyists, and the public. Seniority also brings deference, respect, and media coverage — and that brings a greater ability to work one's will.

Seniority has always played an important role in the Senate — it being by design that the senior chamber and its qualifications require older and more experienced members than the House. The downside of seniority is that it makes change more difficult and entrenched interests become ever more entrenched with time.

In the House, the seniority system was broken up to a degree as a result of the Republican takeover of the House in the 1994 elections. Determined not to have all-powerful committee chairmen sitting in office forever, Republicans changed the system. Whereas before, committee chairmen could serve unlimited terms, under the new rules, they are limited to serving no more than three terms and chairmanships are determined by a process of interviews with the leadership rather than strictly by seniority.

The breakup of the seniority system in the House means that even if the chairman of the committee considering a bill opposes it, and it doesn't make it through the committee the first time, the same bill may have a better chance during the next Congress or when the chairmanship changes and a new and more sympathetic chairman takes office.

CAPITOL CASE

Swaying the balance of power

After the 2000 elections, the Senate was evenly split, 50–50. Because the vice president was a Republican, that party was considered to have the majority and took the leadership and the committee chairmanships.

However, on May 24, 2001, Sen. Jim Jeffords of Vermont announced that, because of disagreements with the president and the Senate leadership, he was leaving the Republican Party and becoming an Independent.

Because he'd vote with the Democrats on Senate organizational matters, his switch changed the entire control of the Senate and Democrats took over the leadership as well as all the committee chairmanships.

Loss of chairmanships was among the many appeals Republicans made to Jeffords to convince him not to switch. "They would lose the power some of them had acquired only a few months prior," Jeffords writes of his colleagues. "And while the power of a chairmanship in an evenly divided Senate is far from absolute, it is still considerable. With it they had hoped to advance the causes and dreams that were as important to them as mine were to me."

Jeffords' decision was a wrenching one and he explains it at length in his book *My Declaration of Independence* (Simon & Schuster).

In the Senate, seniority still holds strong sway but in 1995, the system crumbled when the Republican caucus voted to limit committee chairmanships to six years. In 2002 that was extended to include ranking member positions as well since the Republicans were in the minority (in other words, a senator can only serve as the most senior committee member from the minority for six years). This change, along with the change of one third of the Senate every two years (after elections) means that there is unprecedented fluidity in the Senate leadership.

REMEMBER

Whenever a different political party attains the majority, the entire leadership changes, also. The majority party always rules.

Elbowing into the Huddle: The Role of Caucuses and Delegations

Congress has organized itself to the nth degree with informal overlapping groups intended to address particular concerns. These organizations are known as caucuses and delegations.

Caucuses

The origins of the term *caucus* are obscure, although one theory has it that it's a Native American term. Usually used in a political context, it means simply a meeting. As a verb, it means to meet to make a decision. As a noun it means a private gathering of members to make decisions, often before a general, open meeting.

Congressional caucuses play important roles, bringing together like-minded members for a variety of purposes. Caucuses are the basic political units that determine whether anything gets done in Congress. Caucuses enable congressional members who might otherwise be competing with each other politically or ideologically to work together on matters of common concern. Because they're not mandated by the Constitution or either chamber's rules, they're considered *informal* organizations.

The largest caucuses are the two party caucuses, which respectively encompass all the members of the Democratic Party and the Republican Party. The party caucuses are so important they have permanent formal offices. Unlike the Democratic and Republican caucuses, whose leadership is formalized with full-time staffing, other caucuses tend to be informal organizations. The caucuses are administered out of the caucus chairman's office and make use his regular office staff on caucus business.

The best listing of informal caucuses usually is found in the *Congressional Yellow Book*, a directory of members of Congress and organizations published by Leadership Directories, Inc. Another source is the biennial *Congressional Staff Directory* published by Congressional Quarterly. (For more details of these books see Chapter 12.)

Ethnic caucuses also meet regularly. They include the congressional Black, Hispanic and Native American caucuses.

Besides ethnicity, caucuses also represent ideological concerns of members who have a particular approach to issues. These caucuses have the best names, including:

✔ **Blue Dogs:** Members of this caucus are conservative Democrats who often vote with Republicans on economic or fiscal issues.

The name has several origins: It's a takeoff from an old term *Yellow Dog Democrats* that referred to Southern Democrats who were so anti-Republican as a result of the Civil War that they were said to be willing to vote for a mangy yellow dog as long as it was a Democrat. The more immediate origin of the modern name were pictures of a blue dog by a Cajun artist that hung in the offices of two Louisiana members who played host to meetings of the caucus. Blue Dogs also claim that they've had their necks wrung so much by extremists on both sides of the political spectrum, they've turned blue.

✔ **Congressional Progressive Caucus:** This caucus is comprised of Liberal members who take a common position on social justice and economic issues.

✔ **Log Cabin Republicans:** Gay Republicans make up this caucus. They vote the same way on sexual preference issues.

The mission of Log Cabin Republicans is to work within the Republican Party for the equal rights for all Americans, including gay men and women.

✔ **The Centrist Coalition:** Senators who take middle-of-the-road positions on social and economic issues belong to this caucus.

Industry caucuses consist of members concerned about the issues pertaining to particular industries and they range from auto to steel caucuses in the Senate to bikes to bearings in the House. A 1998 study found 173 of these caucuses.

Many more caucuses attract members of Congress and the makeup of these caucuses and directions they take are ever-changing as new members are elected and new concerns and common interests develop.

When building support for your cause, see whether you can enlist caucuses relevant to your issue on your behalf. Getting an endorsement from a caucus or two can be a powerful lobbying tool and can even help convince undecided or hostile members to change their minds, or at least not to oppose you.

Definitions and labels

In your everyday activities, you may not define yourself as a Democrat or Republican or liberal or conservative, but as you work with your representative and senators and you penetrate more deeply into the heart of what Congress is doing, these labels become increasingly important because they define a member and, more important, they're the way members define themselves.

When someone calls himself a conservative Democrat, or a liberal Republican, or is part of a

particular ideological caucus, that person is telling the world that he or she will behave and vote in a certain, predictable way and stand for the principles of that caucus. These labels also help members define their identities and guide their policy positions. Even more important, they define the members and their political positions to the voters who elect them.

As you work with members, be aware of how the members define themselves so that you can tailor your approach accordingly.

Delegations

All the senators and representatives from a particular state form that state's delegation. The senior member of the delegation is its recognized leader. Regardless of what ideological proclivities its members may have, the delegation works together on issues of common concern to the state.

If your issue affects different states, rallying support for it is possible by appealing to members on a state basis. Remember that you can also block unfavorable legislation the same way.

Timing is Everything:
Congressional Schedules

Whoever wrote the Book of Ecclesiastes in the Bible must have had Congress in mind: "To everything there is a season and a time to every purpose under heaven." Certainly in Congress there's a season and a time for every purpose. Although understanding the nature of the pressures placed on members and the timing of legislation are important, you also must be aware of the legislative calendar, which I go through in the following sections.

The House calendar

The House calendar follows a predictable pattern — just like the year itself — and spending considerations drive it. After all, determining how revenue for government is raised and spent is Congress's role. Because budgeting is the key driver in congressional deliberations, all other legislative work, whether budget-related or not, tends to organize itself around the budget process.

Whenever you seek passage of new legislation, introducing it at the beginning of a first session of Congress always is best. Doing so gives your proposal time to make its way through the committee process so that it might even be considered by the entire chamber before it adjourns.

A representative's activities take place in the two-year time frame between election cycles for House members. I clue you in to the cycle in the following subsections.

Each two-year term of the House of Representatives is called a *Congress*. Each year of the Congress is called a *session*.

The First Session, odd-numbered years

Congressional elections occur on the first Tuesday after the first Monday in November. Congress begins its work as early in the new year as possible.

January: Under the Constitution, members begin their terms at noon on January 3, unless Congress has previously passed a law designating a different day. On the first day they're sworn in and take care of organizational matters such as electing a Speaker of the House and a Majority Leader in the Senate. However, most substantive legislative work doesn't really start until the president gives the State of the Union address, usually around January 20, except after a presidential election in which case the inaugural address takes its place. The speech is a blueprint for what the president intends to do and what he'll be asking of Congress. Congress observes Martin Luther King Jr.'s birthday on the third Monday in January.

February: On the first Monday in February, the president sends a detailed budget to Congress. The House and Senate budget committees have six weeks to develop their own budget in response and this work takes up all of February. Congress determines how much money the country is likely to raise through taxes and how much can be spent. Hearings begin on the president's budget. Many bills are introduced around this time for Congress to consider throughout the year. Congress recesses for the Presidents Day holiday on the third Monday of the month, usually for the entire week.

March: In this month the House and Senate budget committees are required to finish their version of the budget. This is the budget within which the rest of Congress will work out how to spend tax dollars for the rest of the year. But besides the budget, March in the first session is a time for hearings and committee work. Even worse, there are no holidays in March, so Congress has to meet all month!

April: Regular work continues. (See Chapters 2 and 3 for the responsibilities of the House and Senate, respectively.) At least in April there's a weeklong Passover/Easter recess based on the dates that the holidays fall.

May: By now bills should be finished and authorizing committees should be making recommendations on the nature and content of government programs. At the end of the month, Congress recesses for a week for Memorial Day.

June: Appropriations committees begin their work of actually appropriating money based on the authorizing committees' recommendations. (Chapter 8 explains the budgeting and appropriating processes.)

July: A busy month as bills are whipped into final shape and move from the committees to the floor, but with a week's recess for July 4. By now the appropriating committees should be in full swing.

August: Month-long recess! Time for members to head home for barbeques, reintroduce themselves to constituents, hold town meetings, and even get some vacation. Many members also use August to take trips overseas to investigate government programs, visit troops, and do some shopping.

September: The House and Senate should have each passed appropriations bills by now. House-Senate conference committees meet to reconcile the differences. The adjournment target is usually the first Thursday in October.

October: Congress traditionally targets the beginning of the new fiscal year, October 1, for adjournment, either on that date or the nearest Thursday, so that members can go home to enjoy well-deserved time with their families and friends and get back in touch with their constituents. Unfortunately, the House rarely hits that target date.

November–December: Home time.

The way it really works: Because Congress sets its own deadlines; it can change them or violate them any way it wants. It almost never meets the deadlines it sets for itself. The budget committees sometimes struggle over the numbers well past March and the authorizing and appropriating committees sometimes start their work without waiting for a budget resolution — unless an extremely strong Speaker who orders them not to and forces them to wait for the budget so there's budget discipline in their deliberations. Then, the deliberations of the authorizing committees usually drag out. And I've never seen the appropriators meet their deadline of October 1. Instead, the debating and arguing drag on and on and members start looking at their watches and their calendars, desperate to leave town. But at least in the first session, they don't have an election hanging over their heads. That changes in the second session.

The Second Session, even-numbered years

The second session is much like the first (see the previous section), with three exceptions:

- ✓ At the start of the second session in January, there's a backlog of legislation from the first session.

- ✓ Every House member who chooses to run again faces an election at the end of the second session, so members are driven in a way that they aren't in the first session. All their activities are under scrutiny, all their votes subject to criticism from potential challengers. There's much more posturing and grandstanding. Often bills are introduced or voted on for purely political reasons — to make members of one party look good or members of the other party look bad. But, by the same token, there's much more pressure to actually achieve results.

✔ By the end of September, beginning of October of the second session everyone is desperate to get out of town. All the House members and a third of the Senators need to run home to campaign. The pressure grows to wrap up work and end the session as early as possible.

This can become a very complicated and frustrating time for members. The Senate, which doesn't have quite the same time pressures as the House because only a third of their members are up for reelection, may drag its heels on completing legislation. Older House members with safe seats don't need to campaign as heavily as less-established members and can take their time with bills, making members straining to hit the campaign trail squirm.

If you need something done on a local level, a very good time to approach your representative is in June, July, and August of the second session (even-numbered years), which some people refer to as the "silly season." Your representative's campaign is getting into high gear so the member needs political campaign contributions, volunteers and endorsements and she'll be very willing to accommodate constituent requests.

So that she gets reelected, she'll also want to show voters that she's a can-do type who gets things done in Washington. "Silly season" is when your representative is most vulnerable, most receptive and most driven to meet your needs. Use the time wisely!

In a presidential election year

The first six months of a new presidential administration and a new Congress are six months of confusion as everyone sorts everything out. It's just like going to school for the first time. As a pupil, you have to get used to a new teacher, new subjects, and new classrooms. It's the same for Congress, which has to

✔ Get used to a new administration and learn to work with it

✔ Confirm the new president's appointments to cabinet departments and the rest of the executive branch

✔ Organize itself and elect new officers

✔ Deal with legislation left over from the previous Congress

✔ Appoint new committee chairmen and staff, as necessary.

Furthermore, if the administration is completely new or if the majority party in either house or both houses has changed, Congress's organizational work is that much more difficult.

In a nonpresidential year

A new session is much less complicated if there isn't a new president in the White House as well. Traditionally, the president loses support in his first mid-term election so much of such a first session is dominated by the executive and legislative branches defining their relationship and the parties jockeying for political advantage. Nonetheless, the adjustment is not as great as the one with a new administration.

Adjournment: Getting out of town

It's amazing how hard these guys work to get into Washington and then how hard they work to get out of Washington once they're there.

A first session is more likely to drag out because the members are not up for reelection that year and can afford a lengthy session. Usually, a first session ends sometime between mid-October and mid-November.

Whether it's a presidential election year or not, the second session of a Congress is overwhelmingly dominated by the need for House members to get reelected, so members are in a hurry to pass the bills they're required to — the appropriations bills. While members are always acutely conscious of how their votes and statements and actions will be perceived by voters, they become increasingly conscious of it as the session wears on.

In different years, the pressure of the impending election can either spur the Congress on to heights of achievement or paralyze it in partisan bickering and political fear. It's impossible to tell which is more likely, but it depends on the president and his relationship with Congress, the agenda and outside events.

The Senate calendar

The Senate is also under time pressure, but it's of a different source than the two-year terms of the House. There are three sources of time pressure:

- ✔ **Passing appropriations bills to keep the government running:** Appropriations bills funding the different government departments must be passed every year and no matter what else the Senate does it must pass those. These can be big, unwieldy bills with all sorts of other measures tacked on. (See Chapter 8.)

- ✔ **The six-year term of a senator:** Even though senators have more time than House members or even the president to pursue an agenda, it's still not that long given the difficulty of changing something as enormous as the country. Getting major legislation or reforms passed can take ten years or more.

✔ **The two-year change in the composition of the Senate:** Senators have to look to their own reelection and they must deal with the nature of the Senate, a third of which changes every two years. There is pressure on senators to take action if they want to work with particular colleagues who might be ousted in the next election.

The Senate works according to the same budgetary calendar as the House. While it has some of the same pressure points as the House, overall it moves at a much more stately pace and has fewer opportunities for pressure and citizen input.

CAPITOL CASE

Arriving with an agenda

Though it happens very rarely, if a president or a dominant political figure arrives in Congress with a well thought out agenda, it's possible for Congress to move very fast and accomplish a great deal in the first days of a session. Indeed, smart politicians are very well aware of this and forge ahead quickly while Congress is still organizing — or put another way, before their opposition can coalesce.

There are two famous examples of this. In 1933, President Franklin Delano Roosevelt was inaugurated and immediately launched The New Deal. A desperate population seeking some relief from the Great Depression had elected him with an overwhelming majority — and elected a Democratic House and Senate as well. In the first 100 days of his administration, Roosevelt created, and Congress approved, dozens of new federal agencies and programs to deal with the economic collapse that followed the stock market crash of 1929. Most of the thinking about these measures had already occurred outside of government in the preceding years. That gave Roosevelt and a supportive Congress the theoretical framework to proceed.

In 1994 a similar situation occurred, only this time the Republicans were the beneficiaries.

During the first two years of President Bill Clinton's administration there was growing frustration in the country with the Democratic Congress and Clinton's policies. Rep. Newt Gingrich (R-Ga. 1978–1999) used this discontent to implement a conservative agenda. Gingrich formulated the Contract with America consisting of 10 measures and had all the Republican House candidates pledge to implement it. In the 1994 elections the Republicans won majorities in the House and Senate and, taking a leaf from Roosevelt's book, Gingrich led a 100-day legislative blitzkrieg. He didn't pass all the provisions of the Contract, but he did radically restructure the government and he achieved much of what he set out to do.

In both these cases, these rapid revolutions were the result of unique personalities and circumstances. They were also the result of well thought out and carefully conceived ideological agendas and overwhelming electoral mandates. In the future, politicians will likely try to create these kinds of revolutions again. Usually, though, the experience of an opening congressional session is one of confusion and disorientation and slow adjustment as the legislative and executive branches learn to work together.

Chapter 6

Reaching the Floor and Beyond

. . . .

In This Part

▶ Following legislation that reaches the entire chamber

▶ Knowing the rules for considering legislation on the floor

▶ Getting down to the nature of floor debates

▶ Considering legislation from both sides — House-Senate conferences

▶ Signing or not — the role and effect of the president

▶ Monitoring implementation of your law

▶ Revisiting issues that never seem to be resolved

. . . .

*T*hanks to C-SPAN, the cable television network dedicated to covering Congress, millions of people are more familiar with congressional proceedings. And, the funny thing is, people still are surprised by what they see. Debates in either house aren't usually what you expect, based on what you've seen in movies, with all the members sitting in rapt attention at their desks in the Senate or in their seats in the House.

Instead, proceedings in both houses often are confusing, because many times a single speaker in the chamber is seen passionately orating to what amounts to an empty room, spotted with a few members seated at far-flung desks. Even during major debates, people enter and leave the chambers and members confer with each other in small groups. Making out exactly what's going on is difficult.

Debate is, indeed, taking place, but you need to realize that not all members have to be present all the time during the debate. Usually members are putting their positions on the record when they speak, rather than trying to win other members over to their points of view. By the time a bill reaches the floor, members usually have established their positions on an issue. But, when a vote is close or the results are in doubt, floor activity can be intense: Party leaders and advocates pro and con urgently lobby members who haven't declared their positions or who genuinely are undecided.

By the way, when you hear the word *floor* used in reference to Congress — and you hear it a lot — it doesn't refer to any old floor under your feet. *The floor* refers to the place where all the members of the entire chamber — House or Senate — debate and ultimately cast their votes on the great issues of the day. The floor is where issues are decided — the ultimate destination of all legislation.

Waiting to Debate

Waiting for a debate and vote is like waiting for a pizza delivery: They may give you a range, say within 30 minutes, but you don't really know when it's going to arrive until it gets there. The same is true of legislation. Some legislation may take longer to pass than expected, because other events interfere. A bill's sponsor may pull legislation whenever he thinks it will lose a vote, which saves the sponsor from defeat and humiliation but throws the legislative agenda into confusion.

At the end of sessions and before recesses, when members are anxious to go home, they can work late into the night or even into the next morning, and votes can come in rapid succession with little advance notice.

The leadership of each chamber of Congress determines their respective calendars. *Whip notices* provide the most authoritative indications to representatives and senators of pending debates and votes. These notices, delivered in print or by e-mail, tell members when legislation is expected to come up and how members of the Whip's party should vote. Only people professionally involved in congressional affairs, such as members, staff, and the media, receive these notices. (Chapter 5 explains the various leadership positions.)

Snagging Attention with an Introduction

Often, the first time the public becomes aware of a particular piece of legislation is when it reaches the floor. That's when a bill receives the most media coverage. However, from a lobbying point of view, almost all the work shaping the legislation is done before it ever makes it to the floor.

The public isn't the only entity unaware of legislation before it reaches the floor. For many members of Congress the first scent of pending legislation doesn't waft their way until it reaches this stage. Of course, members of the committee considering the legislation are (or at least should be) familiar with bills coming up, but, unless the legislation is highly publicized, the majority of members and their staffs have been too busy working on other issues to know about everything that reaches the floor. They may be unfamiliar with your bill and even surprised by its arrival. Under these circumstances, members look to their staffs, constituents, the legislation's sponsor, the party leadership, and the committee members who handled the legislation for guidance on how to vote.

Resources for the floor

Two handy, pocket-sized guides are full of helpful information for keeping track of representatives and senators, especially when you're watching floor debates.

One is called *Congress at Your Fingertips,* published by Capitol Advantage Publishing. The other is called *U.S. Congress Handbook,* published by Votenet Solutions, Inc.

Both books have pictures of the members and a variety of useful information including names of committee members, maps, phone numbers, Web sites, and so on. If you deal with Congress for any length of time, you'll end up getting one or the other — and the longer you use them, the stronger your preferences grow for one or the other.

Personally, I prefer *Congress at Your Fingertips;* it's the one I've always used. I particularly like the alphabetical listing of senators and representatives and their phone numbers located in the front of the book.

Both companies publish handbooks with customized covers, so you can put your organization's logo there and hand them out as mementos to members, volunteers, and anyone else you choose.

Capitol Advantage can be reached at; Capitol Advantage, P.O. Box 2018, Merrifield, VA 22116-2018; phone 703-550-9500; Web site `www.capitoladvantage.com`. Votenet Solutions can be reached at: Votenet Solutions, Inc., 11th and G Streets NW, 11th Floor, Washington, DC 20001; phone 800-868-3638; Web site `www.Votenet.com`.

For information about bills and their status, nothing beats Thomas, the Library of Congress's Web site for tracking legislation. Thomas can be accessed at `thomas.loc.gov`. You can find out the status of bills, their text, their sponsors, and their numbers by using keywords, titles, or numbers.

For just sheer fun reading, I highly recommend *Congressional Anecdotes* by Paul F. Boller, published by Oxford University Press (1992). It's a wonderful, readable book full of stories that illuminate congressional history and the foibles and frailties of the people who have filled it and continue to fill it.

Bills go through three *readings* — literally, reading the text of the bill. The term is a holdover from the days when some lawmakers were illiterate and a bill literally had to be read to them. Today, it just means a presentation of the text of the bill in printed form or a reading of its title — although a member can demand that it be read in full.

- The **first reading** in both the House and Senate is when the bill is introduced.

- The **second reading** in the House is when the bill is presented for debate and opened up for amendments. In the Senate, the second reading occurs when the bill is referred to a committee for consideration.

- The **third reading** in both the House and Senate occurs when the bill is presented for final passage.

The floor portion of the legislative process is one of the most dangerous that your cause confronts, because members can offer amendments that substantially change the substance and intent of your bill (see the "Adding amendments" section later in this chapter).

And, of course, your bill can be stopped, ice cold, on the floor and voted down.

Playing by the Rules: The Role of the Rules Committees

Differences between the two chambers really become evident when it comes to their respective floor debates.

The Senate values unlimited debate and exhaustive consideration of legislation. Amendments are an important means of refining legislation in the Senate, so few restrictions are placed on them and members can offer amendments on virtually any subject regardless of whether it's germane to the legislation at hand.

The House also values discussion but is governed by the majority and puts a higher premium on efficiency.

The Rules Committee was the first committee ever formed in the House of Representatives in 1789. After all, the first thing that members of Congress had to do was set their terms of debate.

Although the Senate Rules and Administration Committee governs all the internal rules of the Senate, its jurisdiction extends to almost everything internal to the Senate: running the Senate side of the Capitol and overseeing the Senate's rules of conduct, credentials, elections of Senate officers, and so on. This committee's role in governing legislation, however, is relatively limited.

By comparison, the House Rules Committee plays a much more important role in governing legislation.

Two types of rules apply to legislation in the House are

✔ **Standing rules:** These rules for the normal business of the House and its committees. At the beginning of each Congress, the entire House and all the committees establish their standing rules, analogous to by-laws established by any organization from a high school student council to a school board. Members usually just approve rules from the previous Congress, but occasionally make alterations. Standing rules usually cover

   • **Duties of officers:** what each officer is expected to do

   • **Code of conduct:** How each member is supposed to behave

   • **Order of business:** How bills or other business are to be raised before the chamber

   • **Admission to the floor:** Who can come to the floor

   • **Parliamentary procedures:** The procedures for conducting business.

✔ **Special rules:** Special rules apply to specific pieces of legislation and usually are established by the rules committee.

The House Rules Committee comes into its own when it applies special rules to specific legislation. It can determine the rules by which legislation can be debated, and that goes a long way toward determining whether legislation passes.

Almost all House legislation goes through the Rules Committee. The chairman of a committee that reports a bill asks the Rules Committee for and almost always proposes the specific kind of rule that is desired. The committee listens to the committee chairman and any members who prefer a different rule, and then votes to favor one of the following:

   • **An open rule:** This permits any *amendments* (changes or alterations to the bill) — although in the House amendments must be *germane*, in other words, related to the topic or intent of the legislation.

   • **A modified open rule:** This rule means that some parts of the bill can be amended, some can't.

- **A closed rule:** No amendments are allowed. The House must vote on the legislation as it is reported out of committee.

- **A modified closed rule:** Again, some parts are amendable, some parts aren't. The difference between a modified closed rule and a modified open rule is that the former is presumed closed except for the parts that are specifically open, while the opposite is true of the latter.

Before debate begins on the substance of a bill, a majority of the House must approve the Rules Committee's rule. Often the rule becomes a substitute for the bill itself. Whenever a bill is controversial, and members don't want to vote for it but are under public pressure to do so, they'll vote against the rule. Doing so effectively kills the legislation, and members don't have to cast an unpopular vote against the actual bill. And yet, they nevertheless have stopped the legislation.

Debating on the Floor

Politics are a passionate profession. In early days, Congress, at times, was a stormy and violent place, with members toting guns and starting fistfights about political issues.

Fortunately, Congress of today is much more sedate. Of course, the institution is much more mature now, and the importance of parliamentary procedure is one of the reasons. Much of the purpose behind the use of *parliamentary procedure* — a system of rules for meetings and debate — is taming and controlling political emotions that arise so that everyone has a fair chance to speak.

Debates are restricted: only members and their staffs are allowed on the floor and only representatives or senators can speak. This form of debate is representative government at work: The representatives and senators are supposed to stand between the population and the government, using their wisdom, experience, and expertise shaping the best legislation possible, and at the same time reflecting popular desires.

When you attend a congressional session in either the House or Senate, you'll hear elaborate courtesies and titles, deference to rank, and extreme politeness as members yield floor time to each other, all of which is part of an effort to soothe raw feelings and keep the discussion polite and rational.

Even so, members can become excited.

Addressing Congress with ideals at stake

Most congressional speeches are fairly routine, but debate can become exciting when momentous issues are at stake and outcomes are uncertain.

Senator Robert Byrd (D-W.Va.) is famous for wearing a red vest when he's giving a speech that he considers particularly important. This serves as a clear and clever signal to other senators and the media to pay attention to his words.

During the impeachment of President Bill Clinton, an eloquent speech by his supporter,

Senator Dale Bumpers (D-Ark. 1975–1999), is credited with helping convince the Senate to acquit the president.

Perhaps the most famous congressional speech — certainly the most famous Senate speech — was delivered by Senator Daniel Webster (Whig-Mass. 1827–1841) on Jan. 26, 1830. Called "The Second Reply to Haynes," referring to the senator he was refuting, Webster convinced the Senate that states didn't have the right to nullify federal laws that they didn't like.

Speaking in a sedate and timely fashion

Incidents of violence in the Congress (see the "Fighting words" sidebar) led to elaborate rules of decorum that are followed under ordinary circumstances:

✔ Members must address all their remarks to the presiding officer. That's why they always begin by saying "Mr. Speaker" in the House, or "Mr. President" in the Senate (where they're addressing the vice president or the person standing in for the vice president). Whoever is speaking is not supposed to address other members or people in the gallery directly. And, when addressing the Speaker, the president, the vice president, or any other presiding officer, members are supposed to be respectful.

✔ Members are required to address other members by the state they represent, not by name. This form of address also is designed to soothe passions and is why members are always saying things like, "Will the gentleman from South Carolina yield for a question?" rather than simply naming the representative or senator. It puts one more layer of protection between individuals.

Members of one chamber do not mention the name of other chamber (House or Senate) by name. They, instead, refer to the other chamber as "the other body." This is intended to maintain the independence of each chamber and prevent friction between them. Indeed, Thomas Jefferson wanted both chambers to be so independent of each other that he wanted each to pretend the other wasn't there.

✔ Members are not supposed to question each other's motives, personalities, or conduct unless that conduct is the focus of congressional scrutiny. A member is not supposed to take the floor and say, "Rep. X got drunk last night and jumped in the Tidal Basin," even if everyone knows that Rep. X got drunk and jumped in the Tidal Basin. This demeanor is an outgrowth of Sen. Charles Sumner's attack on Sen. Stephen Butler (see the "Fighting words" sidebar).

✔ Members are not supposed to use profanity, obscenity, or vulgarity.

✔ Members are not supposed to walk in *The Well,* the area in front of the dais where the presiding officer and clerks sit when another member is speaking.

✔ Members are not supposed to eat, drink, smoke, make telephone calls, or use laptop computers on the floor.

✔ Members are not permitted to bring hats or coats onto the floor and are expected to dress appropriately to preserve the decorum and appearance of the chamber. (It wouldn't look very dignified with hats and coats strewn about. Besides, that's why the members have cloakrooms just off the floor.)

Timing is everything

Maybe you've watched C-SPAN or read the *Congressional Record* and observed the elaborate dance that occurs as members of Congress go about their daily activities. The splendid dialogue often sounds like this:

Senator A: How much time do I have left?

Presiding senator: Proponents of the bill have 50 minutes left.

Senator A: I yield myself 15 minutes.

Senator B: Will the distinguished gentleman yield 10 seconds to reply to his earlier question?

Senator A: I yield the distinguished senator such time as he may need.

Senator B: Thank you, my answer is "Maybe," and I yield back my remaining five seconds.

Senator A: I thank the distinguished Senator.

What's going on in this example is that time is so precious on the floor of the Senate and the House that members trade minutes of floor time. Admittedly, sorting things out to the last second is a bit of an exaggeration but not that much. At one point during the campaign finance reform debate in March 2001, Sen. John McCain (R-Ariz.) asked Sen. Chuck Hagel (R-Neb.): "If the senator will yield for a 10-second comment?"

Much of the job of the presiding officer is spent determining and allotting time to the various members to speak. In a major debate the floor leaders of each party will be given a block of time — for example, 60 minutes, the usual time allotted for a debate — and then divide it up among the members of their caucus so that each one who wishes to can make a speech. In the House, members are limited to speaking for five minutes for each amendment.

In fact, debates can be very long because the clock only counts the time the member is actually speaking — not the time eaten up by side dialogues, parliamentary business and conferences between the members managing the debate.

Adding amendments

One of the most confusing and at the same time most important aspects of floor activity is the amendment process. Whenever you're tracking the fate of legislation, you must keep track of amendments and amendments to amendments.

Among the several types of amendments used in both the House and Senate are:

- **First-degree amendments:** They are amendments to the bill itself.
- **Second-degree amendments:** They are amendments to amendments.
- **Substitute amendments:** This kind of amendment can replace the entirety of an original amendment.
- **Amendment to a substitute:** An amendment to a substitute changes the substitute.
- **Amendment in the nature of a substitute:** An amendment in the nature of a substitute replaces the entire bill with a new text.
- **En bloc amendment:** An en bloc amendment brings many amendments together into a single amendment.

The House is much tougher on amendments than the Senate. The House prohibits *third-degree amendments* (amendments to amendments to amendments). House amendments must be *germane,* or have relevance to the substance or intent of the bill. In the Senate, the definition of *germaneness* is so broad it that allows just about any kind of amendment to be tacked onto any bill.

The House has a clever device called an *amendment tree* that graphically shows the types and order of amendments. Amendments to the main amendment (second-degree amendments) are voted on first, followed by amendments to a substitute amendment, followed by the substitute amendment to the main amendment, followed by the main (first-degree amendment). See? It's a piece of cake.

In the House, debate on an amendment is supposed to take only five minutes for each side; however, members can prolong the debate by using a variety of tactics such as changing a single word and calling it a new amendment just to get an additional five minutes debate time.

Senate rules governing amendments are more flexible, and as a result, more confusing. In its early days, the Senate saw its role as refining legislation that the House had crafted, so amendments became enshrined as a primary way of doing business. Nowadays, the Senate still loves its amendments. Furthermore, because all tax legislation originates in the House, and the Senate can't create any new tax measures, amendments are the only way that the Senate can shape tax legislation.

One of the most time-consuming activities during a floor debate is voting on the amendments tacked onto original pieces of legislation.

Keeping track of amendments and their variations during a floor debate is difficult, unless you're actually present. The parliamentarians in both chambers track which amendment is being voted on. When you watch the debate on television and lose track of what's going on, you can try to obtain information about the amendments from your representative's office, the office of one of the sponsors of the legislation, or the office of the floor manager, the member overseeing passage of the bill on the floor. However, the amendment process is so complex, you can have little effect on it in real time as a citizen.

Don't feel too badly when the amendment process confuses you; members also become confused. Frequently, members vote *for* amendments they oppose or *against* the ones they favor. In the *Congressional Record*, members frequently submit notices changing their votes. They make these changes to clarify their positions and set the record straight, but they also make them because the legislative process can be confusing. By the time a bill takes its final shape, legislators usually know what they're doing. (One hopes!)

Voting

Few things are more impressive than watching a roll-call vote on a momentous congressional issue, especially in the Senate. Members file into the chamber, taking their places and responding when their names are called.

CAPITOL CASE

Fighting words

The two major political parties in England's House of Commons are kept at sword's length from each other by a large table. That way, duels can't break out during heated political debates. In America, we don't have that system, and at times, political debates have become so heated that violence has erupted on the floors of the House and Senate.

The favorite altercation these days is tie-grabbing. In September 1995, Rep. Sam Gibbons (D-Fla. 1963–1997) was arguing with Rep. Bill Thomas (R-Calif.), chairman of the Ways and Means Committee, in a Capitol hallway. Although most of the altercation involved angry name-calling, a tie was grabbed. Nowadays an event like the tie-grabbing receives plenty of news coverage. Dubbed "the brawl in the hall," the Gibbons-Thomas tiff was a delicious gossip for weeks in Washington.

In 1859, antislavery Senator David Broderick (D-Calif. 1857–1859) was killed at Lake Merced near San Francisco in a duel with proslavery California Chief Justice David Terry. Terry accused Broderick of following the "wrong Douglas," meaning black leader Frederick Douglass rather than Democratic Leader Sen. Stephen Douglas. Broderick called Terry a dishonest judge and a "miserable wretch." Terry killed Broderick and later served the confederacy when the Civil War broke out in 1860. He was killed in 1899 when he threatened the life of a Supreme Court justice.

Walking canes, which prevailed as a fashion accessory in the 1800s, exerted a magnetic pull on members, especially southerners, to settle their disputes with sticks and there were numerous battles with canes. The worst violence between members occurred May 22, 1856. The altercation had all the elements: personal honor, North versus South, House versus Senate, slavery, and — surprise of surprises — a walking cane. Three days before the clash, which was sparked by the debate whether to admit Kansas to the union as a free or slave state, Sen. Charles Sumner (R-Mass. 1851–1874) delivered a blistering speech — "Crime Against Kansas." No mere off-the-cuff remarks, Sumner's commentary went on for two days and took up 112 pages in the *Congressional Record.*

Sumner's wrath was focused on proslavery Sen. Andrew Butler (D-S.C. 1846–1857) and Democratic Leader Sen. Stephen Douglas (D-Ill. 1847–1861). Sumner compared them to Don Quixote and Sancho Panza, equating Butler's defense of slavery to Don Quixote's defense of Dulcinea in terms so nasty and crude they're still offensive more than a hundred years later.

Three days later Butler's cousin, Rep. Preston Brooks (D-S.C. 1853–1857), entered Senate chambers after the day's adjournment, carrying a cane. He found Sumner working at his desk and told him that the speech, which he had read twice, had insulted his state and his kinsman, Brooks ferociously thrashed Sumner, who at first tried to escape. So desperate was Sumner that he yanked his desk from its moorings, but he soon collapsed under the blows.

Having beaten Sumner unconscious, Brooks did what any self-respecting politician would do: He held a press conference. "I gave him about 30 first-rate stripes," he boasted. "Towards the last he bellowed like a calf. I wore my cane out completely but saved the head — which is gold." Brooks also defended his actions in a speech to the House, which was unable to pass a condemnation. Nonetheless, Brooks resigned his seat but was immediately reelected. Admirers from across the South sent him new canes. He died the following year.

Sumner took three years to recover, but he returned to serve 18 more years in the Senate. The Brooks-Sumner altercation puts a little modern-day tie-grabbing into perspective.

The chamber is tense and hushed; the members and gallery strain to hear each "yea" or "nay." No noise is permitted in the galleries or on the floor while everyone tallies votes. The presiding officer announces the result.

Despite the solemnity, however, congressional votes usually seem as chaotic as congressional debates do.

After voting, representatives and senators go to the press galleries to attend press conferences where they explain their actions, like athletes after a big game.

Being carded in the House

With 435 members who can vote on the floor of the House (delegates and the Resident Commissioner of Puerto Rico vote only in committee), voting can be an elaborate and time-consuming process. Often, on noncontroversial items, the presiding officer will simply say, "Without objection, so ordered" — in other words, if no member objects or demands a more detailed vote, the measure or proposal passes.

The House — and only the House — has the ability of forming itself into a Committee of the Whole, acting as a single big committee where the rules for doing business are less stringent than on the floor. Fewer members are needed to form a *quorum* — the minimum number of members required to be present in order to conduct official business — (218 under normal circumstances, 100 in a Committee of the Whole) and procedures are expedited.

Standing and sitting

The House and Senate follow different seating systems on the floor. By custom, Republicans sit to the left of the presiding officer's chair and Democrats to the right. An Independent must decide on which side of the aisle he wishes to place himself.

The House doesn't have assigned seating. The Senate, on the other hand, does, and provides each senator with a small, mahogany desk. (For more information on the history of the Senate desks and seating arrangements, go to the Senate Web site at www.senate.gov/learning/artf_desks.html.)

Members addressing the House for formal speeches go to one of two podiums in the Well and speak from there. During debates, however, members address informal remarks — those dealing with the amount of time available or procedural questions — to the presiding officer from their seats.

Because the House floor has more seats, its chamber is used for joint sessions of Congress and the State of the Union speech.

There are four kinds of votes in the House:

- ✔ **Voice vote:** All the members say "Aye" or "Nay" in unison and the presiding officer determines the tally from that.

- ✔ **Division vote:** Members stand to register their votes. It's not as quick as a voice vote, but it's more exact. However, it's not so exact that there's a public record of how each member voted.

- ✔ **Yea-and-nay vote:** This is the dreaded roll call vote where a clerk calls each member's name and records the vote, whether "Aye," "Nay", or "Present," (which is the same as abstaining or is used simply to constitute a quorum). Any member can call for this kind of vote and this procedure can be used to also determine if a quorum is present. This is very rarely used nowadays.

- ✔ **Recorded vote:** This vote is just as accurate but much quicker than a roll call. It's done by "electronic device" and it has been employed since 1974.

  Members enter the chamber in no particular order, insert electronic cards into 44 machines strategically situated around the room, registering their presence and then vote "yea," "nay," or "present." An electronic tote board registers the voting results, and after 15 minutes, the presiding officer announces the results. Any member can demand a recorded vote.

Singing out and signaling in the Senate

Because there are only 100 senators, taking a vote is less cumbersome than in the House, and the Senate does not use electronic devices to record its votes. Senators have three types of votes:

- ✔ **Voice vote:** Where they call out yeas or nays in unison.

- ✔ **Roll call:** Where the clerk calls each senator's name.

- ✔ **Yea-and-nay vote:** This is more than a voice vote but less than a roll call. Each senator tells the clerk her vote. In fact a yea-and-nay vote in the Senate can appear quite cryptic, with senators signaling thumbs up to the clerk or strolling past the presiding officer's platform registering her vote with the clerks. However, each senator's vote is recorded.

Struggling toward Yes: The Conference Process

If a bill reaches the conference stage, its supporters have demonstrated stamina, strength, and perseverance.

Both chambers of Congress must pass a bill for it to become a law. And, even when that happens, the two bodies usually pass different versions. They can take a number of routes to get to a final version that is exactly the same in both chambers:

- ✔ One chamber can yield to the other, using the other chamber's version of the bill.
- ✔ The two chambers can send the bill back and forth until they reach a common position.
- ✔ They can call a conference committee to work out any differences.

This last procedure holds the greatest potential for substantially altering for a piece of legislation. Check out the next section to see why.

Convening a conference

Either chamber can call for a conference but the other chamber first must agree to the call, and then both chambers must vote in favor of going to conference to resolve the differences in each chamber's version of the bill.

Once both chambers agree to a conference, conferees must be appointed. In the House, responsibility for picking conferees rests with the Speaker. In the Senate, the entire body elects the conferees.

Although each chamber has different procedures for appointing conferees, in reality, both usually follow recommendations by the chairman of the committee that handles the original legislation.

Choosing members to serve on a conference committee is one of the most delicate and important steps in the legislative process, because representatives and senators who are appointed have a great deal of influence on the final shape of the legislation.

Conferees usually consist of the committee chairman, the ranking member, and members of the committee or relevant subcommittee that handled the legislation in the first place. When the legislation is particularly technical or intricate committee members with particular expertise also will be appointed.

The number of conferees is not limited, but the majority of conferees hail from the party that holds the majority of seats in the chamber. Conferences can be quite large, especially when a number of committees have been involved with the legislation under consideration.

Compromising in conference

The conferees from each chamber fight for their respective chamber's version of the bill. Conferees act as ambassadors, trying to negotiate a treaty — both sides must exercise some give and take to reach an agreement.

A chamber sometimes tries to ensure that its version of a bill is supported in conference by formulating instructions for the conferees, telling them how far they can compromise on provisions of the bill, what they can discard, and what they must retain. This is often the case when members want to ensure that a particular provision within their version of the bill is not eliminated or diluted. Additionally, members who are not serving on the conference but who fought hard to include provisions in a bill often try pressuring conferees into keeping their provisions, because they don't want to see them wiped away in conference.

The wide latitude conferees are given in shaping legislation is the subject of a great deal of controversy, because conferees can go as far as completely rewriting the bills they're entrusted to reconcile. Members, having labored and sweated over the bills to get them passed the first time don't want their handiwork to be wiped out with a few strokes of the pen in conference. By the same token, the whole point of a conference is to find a common ground with the other chamber, so members realize that some compromise is inescapable. Instructions to the conferees presumably ensure that the core elements of a bill remain despite the conference — but not necessarily.

Closing the conference

The vast majority of conferences end with some kind of compromise. However, the House has rules to terminate the conference if the conferees have gone 20 calendar days from their appointment and failed to reach a compromise, or *make a report,* in legislative language. In such a case the House can either discharge the old conferees and appoint new ones or give the current conferees new instructions.

If the House has set an adjournment date and is within six days of reaching it, representatives can speed up the process by giving conferees just 36 hours to reach an agreement before the chamber discharges them, appoints new conferees, or issues new instructions. In practice, this almost never happens.

The Senate doesn't have the same kind of formal limits on conferences. If things are dragging on too long, it can vote to instruct the conferees — as far as it goes in ending the conference.

Conferees also can declare their deliberations at a hopeless deadlock. In that case, the legislation is dead and the entire process must begin again in the next session, that is, if proponents of the legislation have the stomach for it.

In general, a compromise usually is hammered out, because no one wants to go through the ordeal of the legislative process again.

The conference committee votes on the final bill, and if a majority approves, it moves out of the conference committee and back to both chambers for another vote. The conference usually drafts a report that explains what it has done, which often is a clearer explanation of the shape and nature of the resulting bill than the original text of bill. Minority members usually add their comments and criticisms at the end of the report.

The bill and the report then are sent to the respective chambers to be approved again. Because this is the *third reading* of the bill, no amendments are permitted. (For more about the different readings, see "Snagging Attention with an Introduction" in the beginning of this chapter.)

The chamber that acts first on the conference bill can do three things:

- ✔ Approve the report and bill
- ✔ Reject it
- ✔ Recommit it to the conference committee for further consideration under the chamber's rules

After either chamber votes in favor of the bill, the conference committee is dissolved and the bill cannot be sent back to that committee.

When the bill comes out of conference or one chamber has passed it and the onus is on the one that hasn't, conferees make speeches to their colleagues justifying their actions and putting their compromises in a positive light. "This is an honest bill," is probably the most often-heard cliché as the conferees try to soothe the wounds of members who didn't get what they wanted, calm unhappy constituents, and sell their handiwork to their chambers.

In the vast majority of cases, the bill and report are simply approved by both houses. Everyone has done so much work, so much time has passed, and, because conference reports usually come out toward the end of the session, everyone wants to go home.

When the final version of the bill is passed by both chambers, it's *enrolled,* meaning that it's printed on high quality paper, certified by the Clerk of the House and the Secretary of the Senate, signed by the Speaker of the House and the presiding officer of the Senate — in that order, no matter where it was proposed — and presented to the president.

Getting the President's Signature

After Congress passes a bill, it doesn't become law without the president's signature, and if he vetoes it, it may not be enacted at all (although Congress has the option of overriding the veto). Thus, the president is an immensely powerful presence throughout the legislative process despite his small constitutional role.

The president's role in legislation begins while legislation is being formed. "There's no lobby more powerful than the President of the United States," a powerful lobbyist once said. That lobbyist is right. In our system of government, the president can't command, because the president must go to Congress like anyone else and convince the members to do what he wants. Congress can accept or reject the president's recommendations.

Having said that, remember that the president is unlike any other lobbyist. The major difference, of course, is that the president is the highest elected official of the land, leads the executive branch of the government, oversees the economy, and serves as commander-in-chief of the armed forces, making him responsible for the defense of the nation. A majority of the people gave him a mandate to govern, and, as a result, he speaks for the entire nation at home and abroad. When he speaks, he can talk to the entire country at once, if he so desires.

The president has a team of legislative liaisons, political advisors and policy specialists constantly monitoring congressional activity. They stay in touch with the congressional leadership of both chambers, helping to shape legislation as it moves through Congress.

The White House can't monitor all bills, but it pays close attention to those that it thinks are important, and if it wants changes, it often gets them, especially when the president's party is in power in one or both of the chambers. All that it takes is a word to the leadership or the appropriate legislator.

When the opposing party is in power in one of the chambers, the president has a much tougher job because lobbying has to be much more active, especially when Congress seems bent on passing legislation the president doesn't like.

The president's lobbying efforts are just like yours (see Chapter 10): It takes salesmanship. The president and his officials have to convince a majority of Congress to go along with his desires. However, three differences exist between you and the president when it comes to lobbying Congress:

  ✔ He's the president and you're not.

  ✔ He has many more tools at his disposal to convince members of Congress to do what he wants.

  ✔ He has a veto.

CAPITOL CASE

Making the most of the situation

President Ronald Reagan used the White House to great effect during his administration. When he was fighting with the Senate to sell advanced aircraft to Saudi Arabia in 1982, he brought opposing senators to the White House one by one for quiet chats in his personal living room. Reagan appealed for their support on the basis of personal loyalty and the national need.

For many, this visit was all it took to change their minds. But, not taking any chances, after the senators left the president, they were brought downstairs for a tough political talking-to full of political threats.

One senator in particular changed his vote on the basis of this second conversation. "We stood him in front of an open grave," gloated one of the assistants after the administration won the vote.

When the president wants something, he can draw on a wide variety of instruments to convince members to accede to his desires. He can

- Promise them federal benefits like public works projects in their states or districts
- Aid their pet projects and programs
- Campaign for them at election time
- Mobilize the entire country on behalf of his agenda or against his opponents
- Command more media attention than any other official
- Raise more money than any other public figure on behalf of his supporters
- Place friends, constituents, and relatives of supportive members in official positions
- Propose all sorts of honors and awards for friends and allies
- Appeal to members' sense of duty and patriotism

One of the president's most effective tools is the official hospitality of the White House. Having members over for breakfast or lunch or inviting them to a state dinner replete with glamorous celebrities produces an extraordinary effect even with veteran lawmakers accustomed to public attention. The White House actually is a rather modest building, but it exerts a hypnotic effect on its invited guests.

Passing 'em back

President Harry Truman probably had the most contentious relationship with Congress of recent times. During the 80th Congress (from 1947 to 1949), Truman vetoed 75 bills, 33 of them by pocket veto.

The House and Senate, dominated by Republicans, attempted eight overrides and succeeded six times. This Congress was the famous — or infamous (depending where your allegiance lies) — group that Truman called the "do-nothing Congress." One would think that the relationship would have improved during the next Congress, which included a Democratic majority in both chambers. On the contrary, that Congress witnessed 79 presidential vetoes. Five overrides were attempted, and three succeeded. No other president since then has come close to his record.

Given the president's power, knowledge and influence, by the time a bill reaches his desk, it's usually shaped to his liking, especially when he's working with a friendly Congress.

However, when Congress is in unfriendly hands, it may pass legislation that the president doesn't like and the president, therefore, may have to use the ultimate constitutional tool: *the veto.*

Wielding the veto

After Congress sends the president a final bill, he has 10 days to act on it in one of two ways:

✔ **Sign it into law.** If he doesn't want to sign it but doesn't want to veto it, he can simply ignore it and it becomes law in ten days (excepting Sundays) while Congress is in session.

✔ **Veto it.** The word "veto" literally means "I refuse" in Latin, and the president has the constitutional power to stop a piece of legislation in its tracks, even after it's been through the entire legislative process. It's the Constitution's ultimate executive check on legislation.

The president can veto a bill in two ways:

 • **The return veto:** The *return veto* mechanism is a straightforward provision in the Constitution. The president simply refuses to sign the legislation into law and sends it back to Congress with a message explaining why the legislation wasn't signed.

 • **The pocket veto:** In a *pocket veto,* the president neither vetoes a bill nor signs it — but if Congress adjourns during the 10-day period when the president has the bill, the bill doesn't become law. In other words, the president puts the bill in his pocket, waits out the Congress, and nothing happens.

Overriding a veto

When the president vetoes a bill, the legislation is dead unless Congress takes action.

Congress can override the veto, and in doing so, passes the bill over the president's formal objection. Overriding a presidential veto requires a two-thirds majority vote of the members present and voting (in other words, those who are actually in the chamber rather than two-thirds of the total) in each chamber.

An override vote is a momentous step and difficult to win. In recent years the mere threat of a veto has been enough to convince members not to proceed with provisions that the president doesn't like.

Battling after Passage

In Congress, Yogi Berra's famous line, "It ain't over 'til it's over," takes on a maddening connotation: No issue is ever truly resolved, it just keeps coming back again and again and again.

Celebrating and signing success

When the White House decides to make a bill signing a big deal, it can become a very big deal.

If the weather is good, the president may decide to move the ceremony outside, perhaps in the famous Rose Garden. When it's inside, he may sign the bill in the East Room.

Everyone gathers, including the president, sponsors, leadership of the House and Senate, selected guests with an interest in the legislation. The White House media attend, usually bored with another signing ceremony and cracking jokes. An official White House photographer also takes pictures.

All the principal movers and shakers give speeches, usually praising each other's role in passing the legislation and lauding what the new law will do.

Then the president sits down with about a dozen pens. All members crowd around, arranging themselves so that they're included in the photograph of the signing, which they all plan to send to constituents, claiming credit for passage of the bill. The president symbolically signs the bill, likely using a different pen for every letter of his name so that pens can be given to the bill's sponsors as souvenirs.

The legislative story usually ends when the president signs a bill into law. However, legislation often is diluted or negated in subsequent years. The bill's opponents may try to either upend your law through the courts or pass legislation that negates the law just passed.

The assault usually begins shortly after your bill is signed into law.

Opponents will likely take one of several courses of action, either individually, in combination, or in concert with one another:

- They may announce that they'll introduce counterlegislation to revoke or significantly alter the law.

- They may mount an immediate court challenge to the law.

- If the legislation comes up for renewal after a fixed period of time — known as reauthorization — they may try to kill it or substantially alter it at that time.

- Regardless of whether they go to court or Congress, they will likely:

  - Start studies saying that the law just passed isn't working. These studies may take a year or more to compile, but they're full of statistics that explain why the law needs to be refined further and then the groups that commission the studies will try to refine it to death.

  - Find sympathetic academics and commentators to attack the law and predict doom now that it's law. (These people probably opposed the law all along.)

Protecting newly passed legislation

Advocates and supporters of the law need to be awake, aware, and alert to opponents' activities and ready to counter them. Citizen lobbyists must continue working with representatives and senators who helped you get the law passed.

Some things advocates can do are:

- Watch the media for stories about the law in action and keep files of those stories, regardless of whether they're favorable.

- Maintain files of stories from individuals with testimonials about the law's positive effects in their lives. Favorable stories can be widely publicized.

- Just because a bill passed doesn't mean that all alliances automatically dissolve. Supporters should stay in touch and share information on the law, its effect and developments concerning it. They may have to mobilize again.

✔ When opponents' studies say a law isn't working, supporters can prepare counterstudies and press releases proving that the opposite is true. It's very helpful to have supportive facts handy and readily accessible for the media. (See Chapters 11 and 14.)

✔ Opponents' activities can be tracked by:

- • Subscribing to and reading their publications. They'll usually announce any initiatives aimed at overturning legislation.

- • Checking opponents' Web sites frequently to find out what's being said about the law, its supporters, and their own activities.

Coping with change

Legislation is a dynamic process, but a sense that nothing ever gets finished pervades Washington, D.C. Here's why:

✔ Each new law creates new challenges that then must be handled through further legislation.

✔ Laws have loopholes that sometimes are deliberate and sometimes are inadvertent. Loopholes must either be closed or further defined.

✔ Courts hand down judgments that alter how laws are implemented. They may declare the law unconstitutional, in which case a new law has to be passed that achieves the same goal but meets the constitutional standard. Court challenges and appeals can take years.

✔ Opponents of laws always are challenging them in the legislative arena or in the courts.

✔ Executive agencies and state governments charged with implementing and enforcing the law may not be doing the job properly.

✔ People who are adversely affected by laws appeal to Congress and tell their stories in the media, which creates more legislative activity.

One of America's greatest strengths is that it forever is changing to meet new circumstances. Its legal and political system is designed to be flexible and accommodate those circumstances. America's political system also is designed to allow maximum citizen input. Individual citizens can suggest new laws and support proposals being considered by Congress. The process isn't fast, and it certainly isn't easy, but it has worked for more than 200 years.

It's true: Nothing ever ends in Washington. "It ain't over 'til it's over" and *it ain't ever over.* Maybe that's a good thing.

Part III
Following the Money

The 5th Wave   By Rich Tennant

"That? That's Schedule LVES-1
We've never had to use it. But,
if anyone actually discovers how
to grow money on trees, Uncle
Sam's got a form to get his
fair share of the leaves."

In this part . . .

As it does for the world, money makes Congress go 'round. These chapters trace the role of money in the congressional processes — from raising it to spending it — for the country and for individual members.

Chapter 7

Raising Revenues

· ·

In This Chapter
▶ Dealing with money matters
▶ Taxing the citizenry

· ·

*F*ounding Father Benjamin Franklin said in 1798, "Our Constitution is in actual operation; everything appears to promise that it will last; but in this world nothing is certain but death and taxes." His words are still true more than 200 years later.

How to approve appropriate taxes that raise revenues effectively and fairly has vexed governments and the governed since the dawn of recorded history As John Marshall, chief justice of the United States Supreme Court (1801– 1835), said: "The power to tax involves the power to destroy." Governments struggle with obtaining revenues they need; people struggle with avoiding taxes as best they can.

In this chapter, I take you through the method Congress uses to raise revenue and then spend it.

Seeing the Sources

The government gets money — *revenue* — to run its operations from many sources:

- ✔ It imposes tariffs and customs duties on foreign goods coming into the United States.
- ✔ It charges duties and fees for a wide variety of services, for example, charging people entering national parks or ranchers who graze their cattle on federal lands.
- ✔ It borrows money and issues bonds.
- ✔ It levies fines and collects penalties for wrongdoing.

But by far the largest source of revenue is from *taxation,* a proportion of income taken by the government from individuals, businesses, and corporations.

Not all revenue-related measures are contained in tax legislation. Frequently nontax bills, such as bills covering energy, education, or housing policies, include tax provisions. These measures usually include *tax credits* — a reduction in the amount of taxes owed (technically, a direct reduction in tax liability) — or *tax cuts* — a reduction in the rate of taxation.

A huge industry is built around lobbying, interpreting, and implementing tax law. Legions of lobbyists, lawyers, and accountants constantly dissect, analyze, and create new revenue-related measures. For a tax-related measure to go unnoticed by at least some member of the public is next to impossible, given this high level of scrutiny.

Acting on Taxes

Procedurally, proposed tax legislation is processed the same as any other bills. Bills that raise or lower taxes are not produced annually like appropriations bills, nor is there any set number of them. Years can go by without new tax bills, or a number of them can be proposed in any given year.

Nonetheless, taxation is so contentious and momentous that tax legislation receives very special attention, and more than one tax bill being considered in a legislative year is extraordinary.

Other than a constitutional restriction that tax bills must come from the House, bills go through committee, floor consideration, conference, reconciliation, second reading, and presidential signature just like any other pieces of legislation. But, unlike most other bills, revenue bills tend to generate much more interest and lobbying efforts, because they generally affect so many people and businesses so profoundly.

Proposing

Most new taxes — or major tax cuts — virtually always originate with the executive branch. A member of the House can propose a new tax on the floor, but doing so is an extraordinary event and can be a career-ending move. The process of raising new taxes usually starts with the administration discovering that it needs new revenues and proposing methods for raising the funds. Occasionally, the president decides that existing taxes are unnecessary and proposes that they be ended, lowered, or phased out. One example of this was the hotly debated tax cut proposed by President George W. Bush in 2001.

The president usually presents his tax proposals to Congress in the annual State of the Union address.

Although the president can propose more than one new proposal related to taxes in a year, doing so is an extremely rare event.

Disposing

Under the Constitution, any new revenue-raising legislation must come from the House of Representatives, so new tax bills are proposed there. The leading House member from the president's party usually introduces a measure that contains the president's proposal at the very beginning of a congressional session.

Like any other bill considered in the House of Representatives, a tax proposal is introduced in the House, referred to a committee, considered by the committee, reported out, and sent to the Senate.

Reaching the Ways and Means Committee

Revenue-generating measures always are referred to the House Ways and Means Committee. This committee was one of the first established back in 1787. Its jurisdiction covers

- ✔ All measures related to taxation or which raise revenue
- ✔ Bills that concern foreign trade and the imposition of tariffs on imported goods
- ✔ The government's borrowing and the level of debt permitted by law, known as the *national debt ceiling*
- ✔ The Social Security program
- ✔ Assistance to needy families and welfare programs
- ✔ Compensation for unemployment
- ✔ Mandatory and entitlement programs like Medicare, pensions to veterans and other qualified recipients, aid to the disabled, and survivors insurance

When the Ways and Means committee receives a revenue bill, it conducts hearings and marks up the legislation the way it would any other bill.

Sitting pretty in the Senate

Although the Senate doesn't have the same constitutional role as the House in generating tax bills, the Senate Finance Committee — the Senate's counterpart to the House Ways and Means Committee — can have significant influence on tax bills, after they're passed by the House. The Senate can alter and amend tax bills as they can any other bill.

Examining the Joint Taxation Committee

Anyone who worked out her taxes — and that should mean every American citizen — appreciates the complexity of the tax code. If paying taxes is complex, writing tax law is even more complex.

Knowing that to be true, Congress created the Joint Committee on Internal Revenue Taxation in 1926. The name later was shorted to Joint Taxation Committee. The committee:

✔ Prepares tax materials for the rest of Congress

✔ Helps draft tax legislation

✔ Analyzes proposed legislation

✔ Helps members with tax-related constituent cases

✔ Estimates the financial impact of tax legislation

✔ Reviews proposed refunds

✔ Investigates tax-related matters

The committee deals only with taxes, and though it includes representatives from both chambers, its staff strives to provide purely independent, non-partisan objective services to members of Congress who come to it for technical advice in drafting tax legislation and understanding the implications of tax measures.

Bearing the Burden: Taxation and You

Few things get people more riled up than new taxes. Taxation affects everyone, everyone has an opinion, and every opinion counts. And, because everyone pays close attention to them, new tax proposals receive a great deal of publicity, which makes following them through the legislative process fairly easy.

Familiarizing themselves with the latest changes in tax law and passing that information on to you is the job of tax lawyers and accountants. But if you want to be a savvy taxpayer, keep an eye out for tax- and revenue-related measures introduced in Congress, especially during the early days of a congressional session. You can make sure that you're up to date on tax-related matters by regularly checking the media and searching congressional databases by using Thomas (http://thomas.loc.gov), the Library of Congress's search engine using key words like "taxes," "taxation," or "revenue."

Every taxpayer is familiar with the Internal Revenue Service (IRS) and many people think that tax policy originates with the IRS. However, the IRS is an enforcement and collection agency. It doesn't make tax policy; it merely implements the laws that Congress passes, makes sure everyone pays their taxes, and gathers the returns at tax time.

The IRS and the Treasury Department issue tax *regulations* — executive branch rules (as opposed to laws passed by Congress and signed by the president) with broad implications for the average citizen, but Congress determines who is taxed, what is taxed, and the rate of tax that is levied. Whenever you want to register a complaint about tax policies, go to Congress, not the IRS.

As an individual citizen, the best way that you can influence tax legislation is simply by expressing your opinion to your representative and senators.

If you're a member of an industry or trade association affected by a tax measure, register your opinion with the association. By the same token, let an association representative know when you see a tax measure with implications for your industry.

If you'd like to testify when a measure is considered, contact the Ways and Means Committee or the subcommittee handling the legislation. Be aware, however, that association presidents usually testify only about tax measures that affect their industries.

Taxing resources

Innumerable books have been written about taxation, not least of which is *Taxes For Dummies 2002,* written by Eric Tyson and David Silverman and published by Wiley. *Taxes For Dummies* provides detailed analyses of the latest changes in tax laws and what those changes mean to you when you fill out your forms. (Look for periodic updates for the most recent information.)

I must confess that curling up with a book about taxes isn't really my idea of a good time, but an exception is *For Good and Evil: The Impact of Taxes on the Course of Civilization, 2nd edition,* by Charles Adams, published in 1999 by Madison Books, Lanham, Maryland. This comprehensive, surprisingly readable, history of taxation is told in a penetrating and — believe it or not — entertaining way. If you're looking for background information on taxes and why they are the way they are, I highly recommend this book.

Chapter 8

Budgeting, Authorizing, and Appropriating Government Money

• •

In This Chapter

▶ Preparing the budget

▶ Winding its way through Congress: The budget process

▶ Distributing government money

• •

Money matters prompt many Americans to contact their congressional representatives and senators. Communities, states, and individuals call on Congress for assistance with meeting their needs — police equipment, improvements to sewage treatment plants, and city parks, for example — and representatives and senators do their best to oblige.

Every citizen pays taxes; however, what you get back for those taxes can vary widely and depend on many factors, not least of which is politics.

Think of the government budget as a pie — not the kind you bake, the kind that appears in newspapers and government reports — a pie chart.

Your and your neighbors' taxes are the ingredients that make the pie possible. If you're going to get your piece of the final product, you need to know exactly what ingredients go into it, how it's baked, and how the pieces are divvied up. In this chapter, I give you a rudimentary understanding of what goes into the pie and how and who slices it up.

Holding the Purse Strings

Essentially, the budgeting, authorizing, and appropriating process is one of slicing the budget pie into smaller, finer pieces. Budgeters initially cut the pie into big, broad chunks, which they then hand off to appropriators who carve it into smaller slices that were approved by the authorizers.

Money is a major element of congressional deliberations, taking up the bulk of congressional time and effort and following its own special rules and timetable. The budgeting and appropriations process determines the pace and timing of congressional activity.

Granting money and/or withholding it are methods Congress uses in controlling the executive branch. But, it's a weapon that can backfire: In 1995, Congress refused to provide the funding that the Clinton administration needed to operate, and the government shut down for 22 days. Ultimately, members of Congress suffered more political damage than the president, and Congress hasn't exercised its constitutional right to make that decision since.

Every year, Congress must approve a budget and then provide the means for government agencies to operate, or *appropriate,* the money to meet the budget. Congress makes these provisions in 13 different appropriations bills. (The bills correspond to the appropriations subcommittees, which are listed in the "Appropriations subcommittees and bills" sidebar in this chapter.) The first appropriation bill in 1789 doled out $639,000 for 13 individual expenditures. In 1794, the Army was given its own appropriations bill, followed by the Navy in 1799. Over the years the number of separate bills increased until it reached 13 in 1997. With the emphasis on homeland security since September 11, 2001, it's likely to increase again. These bills may not receive as much media attention as other measures that Congress considers, but they are by far most important.

Of all the bills that Congress considers and passes, the appropriations bills are the only ones that absolutely must be passed each year without fail.

Talk of converting to a biennial budget process — setting two-year budgets — has long been a topic in congressional circles. Changing to a biennial process would be more efficient and may save money, but Congress retains so much control over the government by reviewing the budget every single year that it's very unlikely to surrender that much control.

Money and taxation was a major preoccupation of the Framers when they crafted the Constitution. Keeping taxation close to the people meant deciding that all tax bills had to originate in the House of Representatives. The Framers were also quite specific in regulating how money would be spent, as the following quote illustrates.

No money shall be drawn from the treasury, but in consequence of appropriations made by law; and a regular statement and account of receipts and expenditures of all public money shall be published from time to time.

— U.S. Constitution, Article I, Section 9

Many were the causes of the American Revolution, but a big one was money: Colonists didn't like being taxed by the government in Britain without first being consulted, and it was a prime cause for one of the many complaints in the Declaration of Independence.

For imposing Taxes on us without our Consent: . . .

— Declaration of Independence, explaining the
reasons for the break with Great Britain

Budgeting

The operations of the United States government begin with a budget proposed by the president. The president's budget actually is prepared by the
Office of Management and Budget (OMB), which examines budget requests
made by all executive agencies and decides which requests to present to
Congress and in what amounts.

The president traditionally goes before a *joint session of Congress* — the
House and Senate meeting together — on or about January 20 every year to
deliver the *State of the Union* address — except in years following a presidential election, in which case the inaugural address takes its place.

The State of the Union Address isn't an ordinary speech. This address is
important from a budgetary point of view, because the president explains to
Congress what's important to him and why, giving his congressional supporters and the party faithful arguments on behalf of his program in Congress and
at the grass-roots level. It explains the broad thinking behind the detailed
budget he is going to present.

In most cases, the president's budget proposal with all the detailed dollar
amounts is submitted to Congress, the media, and the public on the first
Monday in February — a week or so after the State of the Union Address.
Some variation may exist in this process, but usually not much. Immediately
after the budget proposal is submitted, you can find long articles in the media,
analyzing the budget and telling you what it means for your community.

TECHNICAL STUFF

The government deals in *fiscal years* and *calendar years.* The federal *fiscal
year* (12-month accounting cycle) runs from October 1 through September 30.
The calendar year runs from January 1 through December 31. When Congress
is considering the budget, it's working on the *next* fiscal year. For example, in
February 2002, Congress received the president's proposal for fiscal year
2003 (often written as FY 2003). Whenever you follow the congressional
budget and appropriations debates in the media, remember that they're
almost always struggling with the budget for the coming fiscal year.

Scheduling the money calendar

Money follows its own timetable in Congress. Although some key dates are
written into law (shown in bold-faced type in the list that follows) most are

target dates, and regardless of how hard Congress tries, slippage, overlap, and delays usually occur before a budget is finalized. Figure 8-1 gives you an overview of the whole process. The calendar-year budget schedule normally adheres to the following order:

- **First Monday in February:** Deadline for submission of president's budget.

- **February 15:** Deadline for submission of Congressional Budget Office report on projected spending for the forthcoming fiscal year. This examines the assumptions underlying the president's budget (for example, is the president expecting too much in revenues?) and its likely economic impact (for example, will the budget help or hurt the economy?).

- **Six weeks after the president's submission:** Deadlines for the congressional standing committees to submit their own views of the president's budget to the House and Senate Budget committees.

- **March:** House and Senate budget committees develop separate budget resolutions. These are concurrent resolutions and don't have to be signed by the president. The House Budget Committee reports in March, and the full House votes on the budget resolution roughly one week later.

- **April 1:** Deadline for Senate Budget Committee to report its budget resolution. The full Senate acts on its budget resolution roughly one week later.

- **April 1–15:** House-Senate conferees develop a conference report on a budget resolution, and each chamber votes on the resolution conference report.

- **April 15:** Congress completes action on the concurrent resolution, generally referred to as the *budget resolution,* on the budget.

- **April 15–May:** It's very important that all congressional activity involving money stay within the framework of the congressional budget, so Congress has developed an elaborate process for keeping all its legislation within that framework. Committees overseeing government programs (known as *authorizing* committees, which are explained more fully in the following "Authorizing" section) develop *reconciliation legislation* — legislation that makes their bills identical and keeps their bills in line with the budget resolution.

    This reconciliation legislation is extremely important in the budget process because programs can be created by it. (For example, the legislation providing health insurance coverage for people who lose their jobs, known as COBRA coverage, was named for the 1986 Consolidated Omnibus Budget Reconciliation Act.) These bills are then reported to the budget committees. The Budget committees take this legislation and send it to the floors of their respective chambers. After the reconciled bills are passed in each chamber, House-Senate conferees develop a conference report on reconciliation and take it to the floors of their respective chambers for final passage.

- **May 15:** The target date for the House to begin considering annual appropriations bills.

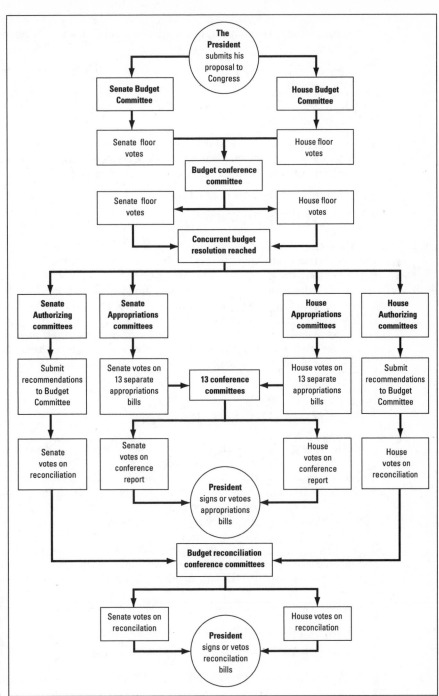

Figure 8-1:
The congressional budget process.

- ✔ **June 10:** The House Appropriations Committee is supposed to report out, approve, and send to the floor, the last of its annual appropriations bills.

- ✔ **June 15:** The target date for Congress to complete action on reconciliation legislation (if necessary).

- ✔ **June 30:** The target date for the House to complete action on House appropriations bills.

- ✔ **July 1–September 30:** Senate completes action on Senate appropriations bills. House-Senate conferees complete action on appropriations conference reports and bring them to the floors their respective chambers.

- ✔ **September 30:** Fiscal year ends.

- ✔ **October 1:** New fiscal year begins.

The Congressional Budget and Impoundment Control Act of 1974 forms the basis of the current congressional budget process. Until this act was passed, President Richard Nixon had been using presidential power to *impound,* or hold back, congressionally appropriated funds, stopping what he thought was excessive spending on specific items. Lower courts found his actions illegal (although the Supreme Court never ruled on the issue) and the Democratic Congress resented his actions. As a result, Congress adopted procedures that still are in use today to stop the impoundments and reform the budget process, providing the clearly-defined system in use today.

Checking out the players

From a congressional standpoint, submission of the budget begins a six-week period of intense scrutiny of the president's proposal. Although the president proposes a budget, Congress actually formulates and approves the budget. And although the Office of Management and Budget (OMB) analyzes the budget for its economic impact, Congress needs its own analysis, so the Congressional Budget Office (CBO) begins picking the proposal apart.

At the same time, House and Senate budget committees begin hearings with testimony from cabinet secretaries, the director of the OMB, and other high-level administration officials. Among the questions they try to answer are

- ✔ Are the economic assumptions made by the president's budget sound?

- ✔ What is the likely state of the economy in the coming year?

- ✔ Are the anticipated amounts of tax revenue realistic?

- ✔ Does the budget meet the country's needs?

- ✔ Are the costs of the president's programs realistically estimated?

Mandating the type of spending

Congress grapples with two kinds of government spending: *Mandatory* or direct spending and *discretionary* spending.

- ✔ **Mandatory** or **direct spending** is money that must be spent either by law or because of the nature of the program. For example, the government must pay interest on the national debt, Medicare, and Social Security, so Congress must accommodate these amounts and cannot really alter them in the budget.

  Much of this spending goes to *entitlements* — programs to which people or businesses are entitled because they meet certain federal eligibility criteria. For example, citizens 65 years of age or older are entitled to Social Security payments upon retirement.

- ✔ **Discretionary spending** is spending that Congress can control. Most of the congressional budget activity is directed at calibrating this kind of spending.

Although Congress can control it to a certain extent by determining the qualifications or *eligibility* for receiving the funds, direct spending must be spent. Discretionary spending, however, can be divided up any way Congress deems fit.

The mandatory spending portion of the budget has grown through the years because of increasing entitlements. About two-thirds of the national budget consists of mandatory spending.

Two terms essential to understanding the budget process are *budget authority* and *outlays*. You see these terms used repeatedly in budget discussions:

- ✔ **Budget authority** is the power, or authority, to spend money. This term usually is used in the sense that a committee is empowered to spend up to a certain amount. It's been compared to the limit on a credit card.

- ✔ **Outlays** are monies that actually are spent. Just as you may not spend all the money available to you on your credit card, many programs don't spend their full budget authority during a given fiscal year.

Interpreting the language of the budget

After examining the budget for six weeks, House and Senate budget committees produce budget resolutions that sort the budget into 20 *functions,* or spending categories, and set amounts that can be spent for each function. Although these amounts are called *allocations,* you'll also frequently hear them referred to as the *top line.*

Operations codes

All government operations come under one of the budgetary functions in the following lists:

Function	Operation
050	National Defense
150	International Affairs
250	General Science, Space, and Technology
270	Energy
300	Natural Resources and Environment
350	Agriculture
370	Commerce and Housing Credit
400	Transportation
450	Community and Regional Development
500	Education, Training, Employment, and Social Services
550	Health
570	Medicare
600	Income Security
650	Social Security
700	Veterans Benefits and Services
750	Administration of Justice
800	General Government
900	Net Interest
920	Allowances
950	Undistributed Offsetting Receipts

Discretionary allocations are provided for under Section 302(a) of the Budget Act and often are referred to as *302(a)s.* This money goes to the House and Senate appropriations committees, which then hand it out to their respective and various subcommittees, where the allocations are referred to as *302(b)s.*

The Budget committees give a second round of allocations to what are called the *authorizing committees,* which deal with the policy implications of the spending. (See the section about "Authorizing," later in this chapter.)

Having completed the allocations, leading members of both budget committees then get together, working out differences in House and Senate budget resolutions and producing a conference report, which is usually adopted in April or May. The conference report is Congress's budgetary blueprint for the remainder of the year.

The budget resolution produced by the budget committees isn't binding, but instead, is a concurrent resolution that expresses the sense that Congress believes the contents of the resolution indicate what the budget ought to be. The resolution doesn't require the president's signature. The budget nevertheless is enforced through a variety of other measures.

Breaking budget allocations is tempting for members because no one is ever happy with the amounts he is allocated. Nonetheless, some form of fiscal discipline must be maintained. Congress has two means of accomplishing that:

- ✔ **Procedural:** Nothing can be allowed outside of established congressional procedure.
- ✔ **Statutory:** These prohibitions are written into law.

Under procedural restraints (cited in parentheses following each listing that follows) in the Budget Act:

- ✔ Legislation that exceeds a committee's allocation is not allowed. (Section 302(f))
- ✔ Taxing and spending legislation can't be considered before the budget resolution is passed (although this doesn't apply after May 15 in appropriations bills). (Section 303(a))
- ✔ Exceeding the ceiling on budget authority and outlays and considering legislation that reduces revenues below the budget floor are prohibited. (Section 311(a)(1))
- ✔ Borrowing money, contracting, or opening lines of credit in legislation that isn't subject to appropriations is prohibited. (Section 401(a))
- ✔ Creating new entitlement authority in the fiscal year preceding the budget year. (Section 401(b))

Statutory controls include:

- ✔ **Discretionary spending caps:** These are limits — *caps* — that can be put on discretionary spending and not exceeded. If caps are exceeded, funds may be *sequestered,* or held back.
- ✔ **Pay-as-you-go (PAYGO):** This control requires that whenever legislation is passed that increases spending or reduces revenues, money must be taken out of certain mandatory spending programs, such as Medicare, Medicaid, income assistance, civilian retirement, and student loans. Exceptions are, for example, in a national emergency when these limits are lifted. However, essentially, whenever Congress spends more money, or takes in less, adjustments must made elsewhere to balance increased spending or reduced revenues. Given how people depend on these programs and the political consequences of meddling with them, PAYGO is a powerful incentive to stay within the budget.

The House Budget Committee Web site at `www.house.gov/budget/budget-process-brf.pdf` includes a good discussion of the entire budget process in all its detail.

Balancing the budget so that expenditures equal revenues has long been one of the great political quests of the U.S. Congress and serves as the basis for much of the political debate in the United States. In 1969, President Lyndon Johnson's last budget was balanced, but after that America began experiencing deficit spending — where more money is spent than is taken in. Arguments about the reasons for deficits and who was to blame have filled numerous books already. For decades, Congress and presidents struggled to balance the budget. Doing so became particularly acute in the 1980s and 1990s when deficits ballooned. A series of reform measures were undertaken in Congress to control the deficit, which finally was wiped out in the late 1990s by a booming economy and growing *surpluses* — more money was taken in than was spent. Whatever other issues Congress tackles, expect it always to struggle with walking the line between deficits and surpluses.

Sometimes the government discovers that it needs additional discretionary money that it didn't anticipate in the annual budget. In that case, the administration requests a *supplemental appropriation,* and Congress can appropriate the money outside the usual budget calendar.

Authorizing

In the same way that you can't build a building without a foundation, Congress can't spend money without authorization from the committees that have jurisdiction over the various policy areas. If the budget committees provide the blueprint for government spending, the authorizing committees lay the foundation on which the appropriators build.

The authorizing committees also are Congress's standing committees (see Appendix B for a list of standing and all other committees). Between April and May these committees conduct hearings on government programs within their jurisdictions. They examine these programs to see whether they need to be altered to receive more or less funding and to ensure that the money they've already received is being properly spent.

At the conclusion of their deliberations, each committee passes a law called an *authorization act,* which sets up the terms and conditions for operating the executive branch departments, offices, agencies and programs under their jurisdiction, allows money to be spent on them, and specifies how that money will be spent. Sometimes these committees provide authorization for a single year, other times it's provided for multiple years.

When you're concerned about a particular program, the authorization process is important to you, because the authorizing committees determine the shape and size of your program. Your quest for government money is much stronger when an authorizing committee approves the program.

Appropriating

The real power within Congress resides in appropriations. When Congress passes the budget resolutions and reports, the work of the budget committees is done. The authorizing committees can alter government programs, but the appropriations committees actually dole out the money for them.

House and Senate appropriations committees arguably are the most powerful in Congress, and their chairmen are the most powerful members. Indeed, appropriations committees have been called a "mini-Congress," because their memberships are large and reflect all the divisions and rivalries within the Congress as a whole. Each appropriations committee — like all congressional committees — is divided into subcommittees. (For a list of appropriations subcommittees, see the nearby sidebar titled, "Appropriations subcommittees and bills.")

Smoking out the Cardinals and their court

A seat on an appropriations committee is a desirable position for a member. Members serving on such committees are in a position to appropriate money for their home districts or states. The more federal money that flows home, the more credit the member receives — and the more likely the member is to be reelected.

In addition, a rank-and-file member of Congress must go to a member of the appropriations committee to get an appropriation — putting these members in a politically powerful position of being able to collect political debts, making them even more powerful within the institution. Seats on the House and Senate appropriations committees don't go to just any member. (Check out Chapter 5 for information about how members are assigned to committees.) Although neither committee has formal rules stating that experience is necessary, seats on the House or Senate appropriation committees tend to go to more experienced members who have served at least two terms. However, there have been some exceptions. For example, in the Senate, Sen. Robert Byrd (D-W.Va.) was named to the panel in his first term, and in 1981, so many Republican freshmen were elected to Congress that some not only got seats on the committee, they even received subcommittee chairmanships.

In the same way that the chairmen of the House and Senate appropriations committees are some of the most powerful members of Congress, the appropriations subcommittee chairmen also are powerful. Indeed, they're so powerful that they're referred to as *Cardinals* — equating them to the College of Cardinals of the Roman Catholic Church, which elects the Pope.

Appropriations subcommittees and bills

The appropriations subcommittees are the same for the House and Senate, and each corresponds with one of the appropriations bills.

✔ **Agriculture, Rural Development, Food and Drug Administration, and Related Agencies:** All the appropriations related to the Agriculture Department, farming, and food, with assistance to rural areas thrown in for good measure.

✔ **Commerce, Justice, State, and the Judiciary:** This committee corresponds to four key cabinet departments: Commerce oversees and regulates commerce and includes a variety of agencies including the Bureau of the Census. Justice includes the Justice Department and the Federal Bureau of Investigation. The State Department conducts foreign affairs.

✔ **Defense:** The Army, Navy, Air Force, Marines, and all defense-related spending.

✔ **District of Columbia:** Support and maintain the city of Washington, D.C.

✔ **Energy and Water Development:** The Energy Department, the nation's energy supply, nuclear matters, and development of rivers, shorelines, and the water supply.

✔ **Foreign Operations, Export Financing, and Related Programs:** Expenditures overseas including foreign aid, military assistance, and support for U.S. exports.

✔ **Interior:** Appropriations for the Department of the interior and national parks.

✔ **Labor, Health and Human Services, and Education:** Appropriations for these three major cabinet departments and their programs.

✔ **Legislative:** Appropriations for Congress itself and all legislative branch activities.

✔ **Military Construction:** Essentially, this appropriation covers most federal construction, both military and civilian, and is kept separate because of the number and complexity of the construction projects and because many take place in members' states and districts.

✔ **Transportation and Related Agencies:** The Transportation Department and anything having to do with transportation including agencies such as the Federal Aviation Administration and the National Transportation Safety Board.

✔ **Treasury, Postal Service, and General Government:** The Treasury Department, the Postal Service, and a variety of independent agencies such as the Federal Election Commission and the General Services Administration (which does the buying for the civilian side of the federal government). Included in this appropriations bill is the funding for the White House, including the president's $400,000 annual salary.

✔ **Veterans Affairs, Housing and Urban Development, and Independent Agencies:** Two cabinet departments and a number of independent agencies such as the Environmental Protection Agency and the Consumer Products Protection Agency.

For all their power, appropriations committee chairmen are under tremendous pressure:

✔ From each subcommittee chairman who wants that subcommittee's priorities fully funded.

✔ From individual members and others who want to include *unauthorized* appropriations — money that hasn't been cleared by an authorizing committee. Often unauthorized appropriations are requests by individual members trying to channel money to their home states or districts without going through the entire process.

✔ From *riders* — additional provisions — and amendments to appropriations bills. Riders often alter spending priorities or insert policy provisions the committees never intended to include. Riders almost always are inserted in the Senate, where the rules are much more lax about attaching nongermane provisions to a bill.

✔ From party leadership in the House and Senate who want certain programs funded or not funded for political reasons.

Appreciating the appropriations process

When the appropriations committees receive their allocations from the budget committee, the allocations are divided among the subcommittees. The subcommittees then begin conducting hearings to examine the different government programs under their jurisdiction. These hearings are important because they determine how much funding government agencies receive for the coming year. Cabinet secretaries and high level officials frequently testify at them. (For more about allocations, see "Interpreting the language of the budget" earlier in this chapter.)

When subcommittees finish their hearings, they prepare a draft bill for members of the subcommittee to mark up, or revise. These markups can be either open or closed to the public, but they're frequently closed to enable members to have frank discussions about programs they're funding and to enable them to wheel and deal in private. Committees that deal with defense and foreign affairs usually close their markups on the basis of concern for national security. (For more about markups, check out Chapter 4.)

When the markup is complete, the bill is sent to the entire committee, where the chairman puts all subcommittee bills together and sends the entire bill to the full chamber.

Appropriations power

Appropriations committees have considerable latitude in deciding what to fund and what not to fund. They can't create new programs because only authorizing committees can. However, the appropriations committees can:

- ✔ Decide not to fund a program that's already been authorized.

- ✔ Fund a program for which authorization already has expired. (This frequently happens when authorizing committees haven't been able to reauthorize a program because of political disputes or a lack of time, and the appropriators want to keep the program going.)

- ✔ Provide funds for unauthorized programs.

Including an unauthorized program in an appropriations bill always is dangerous, because doing so can be challenged by any member with a *point of order* merely pointing out that such an action violates established procedure. Unauthorized programs also have an additional disadvantage of fitting almost everyone's definition of wasteful spending. However, occasionally the House Rules Committee grants an appropriations bill a waiver from points of order against unauthorized appropriations.

Appropriations timing in the House and Senate

In the House, appropriations bills are considered *privileged* bills and go straight to the floor without review by the Rules Committee. House rules against nongermane legislation usually protect House appropriations bills from too many extraneous provisions or amendments.

The House appropriations process usually takes place between the middle of May and early June, and the entire House usually votes on the bills by the end of June.

With completion of House action, the Senate usually begins considering appropriations bills in July.

The Senate appropriation process is much the same as the House process with one important exception: Because Senate rules are much friendlier to amendments and riders, virtually anyone can stick nongermane provisions onto appropriations bills. And because appropriations bills absolutely must be passed, they are favorite vehicles for almost any kind of notion, appropriation, or policy provision regardless of how distant it may be from the subject matter of the bill itself.

Whenever Senate appropriations bills haven't been completed before the end of July, the Senate appropriations staff generally works through the August recess preparing for the final sprint in September, when the Senate is likely to vote on completed appropriations bills.

Following completion of the appropriations bills in both chambers, the appropriators meet in conference to reconcile the differences between the House and Senate versions of the bills. A great many differences usually exist between the two, and they must be worked out in negotiations.

The goal is to pass, conference, and reconcile all 13 appropriations bills in both chambers and then pass the final versions in the House and Senate in time for the October 1 start of the new fiscal year. The bills come through the process at different rates for a variety of reasons. For example, a bill may have a controversial provision that causes a great deal of debate that eats up a lot of time, so it limps to the finish line while bills without controversial provisions sail through. Emergencies and unexpected funding requests also can slow down individual bills.

Although Congress rarely meets its deadline, more pressure to finish on time is exerted in election years. And even then, appropriations battles can rage on into November or sometimes even into December.

When the House and Senate don't finish their jobs by October 1, they can pass a *continuing resolution,* usually referred to as a *CR,* to continue funding affected agencies at their existing levels. Continuing resolutions can apply for however long Congress decides, but keeping them short and then renewing them as needed is the preferred course of action. When numerous agencies will otherwise be left unfunded, all the outstanding appropriations are swept into one enormous bill called an *omnibus continuing resolution.*

When all the appropriations bills are finished, they're sent to the president for his signature. He provides the final control on the bills (see Chapter 4). Ultimately, the bills need to reflect — however imperfectly — the full national consensus about how the nation's money is spent.

Being earmarked

Nothing drives the president, executive branch officials, and government spending reformers crazier than earmarks. An *earmark* is a congressional set-aside, specifying that a specific sum be spent for a specific purpose within a larger appropriation bill. For example, in a military construction appropriation of $100 million for building a new Army barracks, an earmark specifies that "$10 million of this sum must go for construction of a 200-room facility of three floors and six doors on the corner of West and Maple streets in Podunk, Anywhere, USA." Furthermore, an earmark may set a spending floor: "Not less than $10 million will be spent on this project."

Whenever a member is trying to obtain federal money for a project, his best bet is trying to receive it through an earmark, which must be made by an appropriations committee member. He can apply for money through the normal appropriations process, but an earmark guarantees that he's going to get the money.

Members can really bring home the bacon by earmarking all sorts of home-state and home-district projects. In fact, having the ability to earmark is what gives appropriations committee members so much of their power: They can produce projects that usually have their names emblazoned them, which helps them get reelected again and again.

Naturally, all this earmarking adds up to hundreds of millions — sometimes billions — of dollars.

A million here, a million there, and pretty soon you're talking about real money.

— attributed to Sen. Everett Dirksen (R-Ill., 1951-1969)

From an executive-branch perspective, earmarks vastly reduce the administration's spending flexibility. Earmarks are binding whenever they are

✔ Included in the text of appropriations bills

✔ Amendments offered on the floor

✔ In conference reports that accompany appropriations bills

When the president signs bills to which they're attached, the earmarks become law.

The majority of earmarks, however, are stuffed into reports that the House and Senate appropriations committees issue when they report out their bills. And, they're often in statements issued by committee chairmen when they introduce their bills to their respective chambers. Although these earmarks don't have the force of law, they nevertheless express congressional intent and are treated as if they're binding. Furthermore, for all the discontent they have toward earmarks, executive branch officials know that they must go before Congress again the next year and their budgets may suffer whenever they challenge earmarks.

In addition to earmarks, members can impose *limitations* on spending by restricting the use of appropriated funds or by setting a ceiling on the amount that can be spent. Although these rules don't apply in the Senate, in the House, limitations

✔ Can't change existing law

✔ Create new law

✔ Don't apply to bills other than the one in which they're inserted

✔ Apply only to the current fiscal year

For a good discussion of earmarks and limitations, see the 1999 Congressional Research Report, *Earmarks and Limitations in Appropriations Bills* by Sandy Streeter, available online at www.house.gov/rules/98-518.htm.

Officials in the administration of President George W. Bush have joined many previous administrations in calling for *merit-based reviews* of spending, which is a purely rational system of reviewing the appropriations process.

Picking out the pork

Wasteful government spending is derisively known as *pork,* a turn of phrase that has bothered the pork industry for years. What constitutes pork and what constitutes legitimate government spending usually is in the eyes of the beholder — or the recipient. An old saying states that "Pork is always in the other guy's district."

Reformers usually find pork spending among the innumerable earmarks lodged within appropriations bills. Sen. William Proxmire (D-Wis., 1957–89) was famous for handing out an annual "Golden Fleece Award" to programs he found most absurd or wasteful. Sen. John McCain (R-Ariz.) frequently names what he thinks are wasteful programs and points out their sponsors, much to the dismay of his colleagues.

The origins of the term pork in denoting wasteful spending go back to America's agricultural roots. In the autumn, after hogs were slaughtered, farmers lined barrels with alternating layers of salt and pork and then dipped into the barrel through the winter whenever they needed meat. When used as a term for doling out, pork has its origins in the practice of doling out salted pork to slaves on southern plantations.

As a political term, pork is a shortened version of *pork barrel,* which gained currency throughout the nineteenth century as a reference to a government handout. In 1913, Sen. Robert La Follette (R-Wis. 1906–1925) referred to a *pork barrel bill* in his autobiography, and the term has stuck ever since.

There doesn't seem to be a perfect method for distributing government money. Distributing the nation's resources in a purely democratic way probably is impossible, especially given the short time frames in which a budget must be formulated and approved. The system that has emerged is one where institutional power, seniority, and political adeptness play a very large part in how the nation's wealth is distributed.

When it comes to your project, you simply have to trust that your representative or senator is strong, senior, and savvy enough to push through your request. It's not a bad thing to remind your member of your need around the time the House does its appropriations bills (May–June) or when the Senate takes up its bills (July–August–September). Be sure to monitor the progress of your appropriation and stay in touch with your members to offer whatever assistance you can with facts and data.

Inserting Items in Appropriations Bills

Whenever necessity calls for a project to be attached to an appropriations bill for funding from the federal government, be sure to contact your representatives and senator first, explaining why the government needs to back such a project. (See the Cheat Sheet for information about how to contact your representatives in Congress.)

A tale of two appropriations

In 1991, sheriff's deputies in Ashland County, Wisconsin, watched helplessly while Daniel Bochler froze to death in the icy waters of Lake Superior. Bochler, 16, was snowmobiling on the ice when he fell through, and authorities had no way of reaching him.

To prevent future recurrences, local authorities sought an Ice Angel windsled, a propeller-driven, shallow-draft craft that would give them access to frozen surfaces of lakes and ponds.

For several years, the county fire department tried to obtain the necessary money from the Federal Emergency Management Agency (FEMA) but without any luck. Finally, County Sheriff John Kovach called his representative, Rep. David Obey (D-Wis.), who happened to be the ranking member on the House Appropriations Committee, and asked if he could secure money for the windsled.

Obey, a fiscal conservative, has been vocal in attacking unnecessary spending — particularly the kind obtained through earmarks, special congressional set-asides. At first, his staff was unenthusiastic. But several months after contacting him, Obey returned Kovach's call and told him he'd obtained the money.

The $70,000 for the Ice Angel consisted of earmarked Community Development Block Grant funds in the fiscal 2002 Veterans Affairs, Housing and Urban Development and Independent Agencies appropriations bill.

In 2002, administration officials singled out the Ice Angel as an example of unrestrained and irresponsible earmarking. But Obey's staffers noted that Congress has the right to make such earmarks.

When your representative or senators have this information, they apply to the relevant appropriations subcommittee for funding. House members can make these applications through the House Appropriations Committee Web site at www.house.gov/appropriations/welcome.html. Each subcommittee has different requirements and forms to fill out, but for the most part, at a minimum, they ask members who want to apply:

- **Details of the request:** How will the money be used?

- **The amount required:** How much?

- **The recipient:** What project, improvement, or organization will receive the money and be responsible for managing it?

- **Previous funding:** Has the recipient ever received federal funds before?

- **National implications:** Will this appropriation have a national impact? Why is it important to the entire country?

In the Senate, the process is much more informal because there are fewer senators. The senators simply write letters requesting earmarks to the chairmen and ranking members of the appropriations subcommittees.

Whenever a representative or senator sits on an appropriations committee, the task of getting the appropriation becomes much easier because he can work on his own appropriation request through the committee. Otherwise, members who do not sit on appropriations committees must lobby appropriations committee members just like anyone else and hope that their request gets funded.

In the same way that the appropriations committees are a kind of mini-Congress, anyone submitting a new item for consideration needs a sort of mini-champion among members of the appropriations committees.

Inevitably, there's an enormous amount of horse-trading and politicking in pursuing appropriations requests. Members support each others' requests and then trade favors, they lobby the subcommittee chairmen, and they seek special consideration of their requests in order to show constituents (who they hope will reelect them) that they're working for their district or state in Washington, D.C. Appropriations is one of the most intensely political processes within the overall political process.

In addition to all the activity by the members, an entire corps of specialized lobbyists helps different causes receive appropriations. Many of these lobbyists served on appropriations committees at one point or another.

Chapter 9

Putting Your Political Contributions to Work

In This Chapter

▶ Contributing to congressional election campaigns

▶ Forming a political action committee

▶ Separating hard money from soft

▶ Having fun with fundraisers

▶ Giving nonfinancial services to political campaigns

*T*he saying that "Money is the mother's milk of politics" is true. Getting elected as a candidate for federal office means raising enormous sums of money. Buying time to reach the 600,000 people that House members represent can be expensive. Statewide senatorial races are even more expensive.

In the 2000 elections, congressional candidates spent a total of $3 billion on their campaigns. Sen. Jon Corzine (D-N.J.) reached an all-time record when he spent an estimated $64 million to win his Senate seat that year.

Explaining where this money comes from and how it's raised, spent, and regulated takes up an inordinate amount of legislators' lives.

Your citizenship gives you the right to participate in the political life of the nation and of Congress. Your vote is the minimum means of making a difference. If, however, you're trying to do more, you can leverage your money into a higher degree of influence in a perfectly legal, legitimate, and surprisingly inexpensive way.

If you're going to become involved with Congress, you need to play the campaign finance game, because contributing to election campaigns is a prime means of influencing and gaining access to lawmakers. The game isn't hard and you don't have to be rich. Indeed, laws passed during the past 30 years have increasingly made becoming an important player in political campaigns easier for the small contributor. Remember, candidates appreciate every dime that people send them.

Contributing to the Candidate of Your Choice

The ability to financially participate in politics isn't limited to the rich. Any citizen can contribute to a candidate she likes, and during a tight race, five and ten dollar contributions coming in the mail can mean a great deal to a candidate seeking office. For generations, Americans have participated in "bean-feeds," picnics, and bake sales to raise money for their candidates. A series of reforms after 1974 opened up the gates to political participation even wider. (See "Becoming a PAC-man or PAC-woman," later in the chapter.)

Contributors can donate to a variety of recipients:

- ✔ Individual candidates
- ✔ Political parties
- ✔ Political action committees
- ✔ Associations, unions, and lobbies

I go into detail about all of these possible contribution recipients in the following section.

Citizens of foreign countries and firms that are awarded contracts by the federal government are prohibited from making political contributions.

Whenever you contribute to a congressional candidate, you:

- ✔ Help determine the overall makeup of Congress by electing a candidate or candidates who believe as you do
- ✔ Support someone you expect to assist you and advance your beliefs
- ✔ Ensure that you'll always have access to that person when you need it
- ✔ Ensure that your interests will be taken into account when decisions are made
- ✔ Collect favors that you can cash in when you need something done

Members of Congress know very well who contributes to their campaigns and how much. As a result, they're dutifully attentive when contributors call.

Money isn't the only means of gaining access. Any constituent can set up an appointment, write a letter, or make a phone call. Not realizing that money helps in opening political doors is, however, naïve.

Caesar seeks "crass" contributions

The role of money in electoral politics dates back a long time. Perhaps the most famous political contributor of the ancient world was the Roman, Marcus Licinius Crassus, who was enormously rich and so tasteless that his name gives us the word *crass,* meaning crudely materialistic. He provided financial support to a young, up-and-coming politician named Julius Caesar, who in return, dutifully furthered Crassus's interests.

Ultimately, in 53 B.C., Crassus was named to command an army marching on Parthia (Persia). The Parthians, however, unimpressed with his riches, defeated his army, and killed him.

Making an individual contribution

The easiest way to make a contribution also is the most direct: Write out a check to the candidate's campaign committee and mail it in. Whenever you want some credit in the flesh, personally deliver it to the campaign committee. Many people make contributions at fundraisers, or you can play host to a fundraiser yourself. (See the "Feting candidacies with fundraisers" section later in this chapter.)

You're always contributing to a *candidate for office,* never to a member as a sitting official. After all, sending money in return for a specific action constitutes bribery, so all your contributions are made for the purpose of winning an election. Accordingly, your contributions are best made to the member's campaign committee.

Campaigns may also ask for donations after an election in order to retire a campaign debt, but the donation goes to the campaign, not the individual, and it is illegal for the money to be used for anything other than the stated purpose.

The Federal Election Commission (FEC) regulates donations and political giving, and the FEC's Web site is an excellent place to find the latest news about the electoral process, read the regulations, and research details of the law. You can access it at www.FEC.gov. You can write to the FEC at 999 E St. NW, Washington, D.C. 20463, and call them at 800-424-9530 or 202-694-1100.

Contributing versus bribing

Some people can see little difference between campaign contributions to a candidate who supports their positions on issues and outright bribery — but there are strong and important distinctions.

Bribery is a specific payment in return for a specific action. For example, if you tell Rep. Jane Doe that you'll pay her $1,000 in exchange for introducing a private bill, that is bribery.

Contributing is a way of supporting a candidate whose broad positions and ideals reflect yours and whom you want to see in office. Contributions serve as a form of political influence and political participation, but they are not the same as buying a specific, traceable, legislative action on a specific legislative measure.

A campaign contribution is directed only to electing a candidate whom you believe should be in office. If you strongly believe that the Mom & Apple Pie Party will bring peace on earth and you want as many members of that party in Congress as possible, then you contribute to your local Mom & Apple Pie Party candidate.

Your contribution brings with it certain benefits if the candidate wins. You win her gratitude for your support. If you call her up and ask for an appointment and she remembers your contribution, she will likely make time to see you. If she's from another party, but received money from the Mom & Apple Pie PAC, she'll know that the members of the PAC supported her because they think that she believes in the ideals of Mom and apple pie and that she should always vote for Mom and apple pie whenever it comes up — or else she'll face their wrath in the next election.

Limiting your contributions

The Bipartisan Campaign Reform Act of 2002 (BCRA) passed and signed in March 2002 limits individual donors to contributions of no more than $2,000 to a federal candidate *per election*. In this context, primaries, runoffs, and general elections are each considered separate elections, so your contribution limit may be as high as $6,000, if your candidate faces a runoff (although the more likely level is $4,000 since runoffs are very infrequent). You can contribute a total of $95,000 to federal elections during a two-year election cycle. An *election cycle* runs from January 1 in an odd-numbered year to December 31 in an even-numbered year. (See the section about "Distinguishing Hard Money from Soft Money" later in this chapter.) Of that $95,000, only $37,500 can be contributed directly to candidates (as opposed to parties) during the two-year cycle.

Contribution limits also apply to people who are *testing the waters* — people who are examining whether to become a candidate. You can contribute up to $1,000 to such a candidate. If that person decides to run, her campaign counts your contribution as a campaign contribution. Of course, if you back a water-tester who backs out, your contribution is money down the drain.

A very good explanation of the limits and provisions of the BCRA is contained on the Web site of the Campaign Finance Institute at www.CFInst.org.

Donors are not allowed to contribute more than $100 in cash, and if you don't want to stay anonymous as a campaign contributor, you can only give $50 in cash. Any contributions of more than $100 must be made in the form of a check, money order, or "other written instrument," as the FEC puts it.

If you've already contributed your limit, don't think that you can get around political contribution limits by giving money to another person to make a contribution or by making a contribution in your child's name. Both practices are illegal. You may think that no one will know the difference, but if a problem occurs with the campaign or the election and people and records are subpoenaed, odds are you'll be caught.

Political contributions are *not* tax-deductible.

Giving money early

Giving money to a candidate at an early stage — even before she's decided to run — is very effective, because at this stage, the potential candidate:

- Doesn't usually have much support
- Isn't usually well recognized
- Needs money for activities like polling
- Considers an early donation as a great vote of confidence that is long remembered

A famous political action committee called EMILY's List (Early Money Is Like Yeast — it makes the dough rise) specializes in contributing to pro-choice, Democratic, women candidates who haven't run for office before. An early contribution has a way of attracting more money later on because it demonstrates that people have confidence in the candidate and her chances of winning.

After a campaign, any leftover money should be used to liquidate expenses and pay off debts, returned to the donors, or contributed to other political groups with the donors' permission — but there's almost never any money left over.

After you contribute, you'll be on the candidate's list for future donations — and the fact that you donated may be shared with other party candidates. You'll get plenty of invitations to fundraising events and future solicitations. Be aware that a donation is an invitation to be dunned for further contributions. However, also remember that you're doing this to further your impact in Congress.

Becoming a PAC-man or PAC-woman

Contributions are much more effective and go much farther when a group of people gets together and pools its resources. When a group of people raises and spends more than $1,000 in political contributions in a calendar year, it becomes — hold onto your hat — a *political action committee* or *PAC.*

PACs are usually organized around a particular issue or to further a particular cause or can be affiliated with a corporation, association, or union.

So much criticism is directed at PACs and their influence that it seems ironic that PACs are the result of campaign finance reforms. In 1971, Congress passed the Federal Election Campaign Act (FECA), which consolidated a number of reform proposals. The Act further was reformed in 1974, 1976, and 1979, in the process creating the Federal Election Commission. One of the glaring problems revealed by the Watergate investigations into political crimes committed by President Richard Nixon was the enormous amount of political money raised from only a few wealthy donors without any accountability or oversight.

The PAC system was instituted to make the entire campaign finance system more public, more accountable, and more accessible. In fact, the PAC system succeeded to a remarkable degree. Political contribution data is now accessible and can be sliced, diced, and cross-referenced to reveal detailed patterns of giving and influence.

PACs are not something that other people participate in just to have a nefarious influence on politics. PAC members are your friends and neighbors getting together about issues that concern them, putting their money where their mouths are, and making the political arena work for them. Nothing is mysterious or evil about anything to do with PACs at all. And when you're serious about having influence in Congress, you need to participate too.

I once belonged to a PAC, but the politics were just a cover for the group's real purpose — enabling singles to mingle. We nicknamed it PartyPAC. Members were young and didn't have much money, so a $200 contribution put the person making it on the board of directors. Much to my wife's annoyance, I received mailings from the group for years after I left. As a matter of fact, PACs are a great way to mix business, politics, and socializing.

Forming and forms of PACs

Under FEC definitions, PACs come in two varieties:

✔ **Nonconnected committees:** These are PACs that have no relationship to a larger organization like a corporation, union, candidate, or party. They're purely independent.

✔ **Separate segregated funds (SSF):** These are political action committees formed by corporations or unions that make contributions to candidates.

Both are generally called PACs, but legal differences exist.

Nonconnected committees

Because the intent of PACs is to enable people to become involved in the political process, forming the nonconnected variety is extremely simple:

1. **Bring together people you know who care about your cause or issue.**

   Ask each of them to make a contribution. You can register your PAC with the FEC at any time, but you won't normally want to do it until you've actually raised the legal threshold of $1,000 at which point you have to register with the FEC.

2. **Give your PAC a name.**

   The only prohibition is that you can't use the name of a candidate. For a list of existing PAC names, check the FEC's Pacronym Web site at `www.fec.gov/pages/pacronym.htm`.

3. **Elect officers.**

   The FEC requires only that you have a treasurer. You're also likely to want (or need) a president, vice-president, and secretary. (You can name these positions anything you want.) A board of directors also is a good idea. Eligibility for becoming an officer or director can be linked to the size of the members' contributions to the PAC if you want.

4. **Within ten days after you've raised (or spent) your $1,000 (whichever comes first), the treasurer must file Form 1 with the FEC.**

   This form is available online at `www.fec.gov/reporting.html` or by writing to the FEC at Federal Election Commission, 999 E Street NW, Washington, D.C. 20463. Once filed, the FEC assigns the PAC an identification number.

Bam! You have a PAC.

In the PAC system, the treasurer (having an assistant treasurer or two isn't a bad idea) has plenty of work to do. He or she:

✔ Files all the forms with the FEC

✔ Signs all reports and statements

✔ Must deposit all the contributions in the PAC's bank account within 10 days of receiving them

✔ Authorizes expenditures

✔ Monitors compliance with election law

✔ Keeps records of receipts and disbursements

The treasurer also bears the liability if the FEC brings an enforcement action against the PAC.

Because the whole purpose of PACs is to make the political contribution process as transparent as possible, when you contribute $200 or more to a PAC, your name becomes part of the FEC's public records. So, contributing to political campaigns isn't a way to remain anonymous. Anyone can look up PAC contributions simply by typing a ZIP code into a database. To try it, go to www.opensecrets.org/states/index.asp. You may be surprised by what your neighbors are contributing.

Separate segregated funds

Many companies and unions form PACs, or SSFs, as the FEC prefers to call them. In generic terms, these groups often are called *corporate PACs.*

SSFs differ from unconnected committees, because the sponsoring organization can provide as much money to the SSF as it wants and those amounts don't have to be revealed in the same way that unconnected committees must reveal theirs. The PAC makes itself known by its candidate contributions, and the connection between the corporation and the SSF is obvious at the outset.

Although unconnected PACs can accept anyone as a member, membership in an SSF is limited to people who have a relationship with the sponsoring organization, for example employees, stockholders, or members of the organization. Corporations are allowed neither to reimburse employees for political contributions nor to make direct contributions. They can make contributions only through their SSF.

Leveraging your money into influence

When your PAC is established, you must examine the records of members of Congress (or any politicians) and decide which ones you want your PAC's money to support for election or reelection.

One of the wonderful things about membership in a PAC is the chance that it gives you to meet face to face with the elected officials or candidates. Would you like to meet someone for whom you have questions, locally and in person? Have the PAC invite the candidate to a coffee or PAC gathering. Candidates are likely to respond favorably to an invitation from a PAC in their quest for campaign contributions.

After your PAC examines the records of candidates, it decides which ones to support. The PAC makes its decisions any way it wants, either through a vote, consensus, or whatever rules it establishes.

Being a member of a PAC also enables you to make a larger contribution than as an individual: You can give $5,000 per calendar year to a PAC.

But most important of all, your PAC tells candidates to whom it contributes that you and your fellow PAC members are concerned about an issue and that you support the actions and positions of the candidate.

Distinguishing Hard Money from Soft Money

In 2000, Sen. John McCain (R-Ariz.) made loopholes in campaign finance laws the center of his campaign for the presidency, and Americans heard a lot of discussion of *hard money* versus *soft money.*

- **Hard money** is regulated, limited, reported political contributions to candidates and campaigns that fall under FEC regulations and the FECA.

- **Soft Money** is unregulated, unlimited, unreported contributions that fall outside FEC and FECA restrictions. These expenditures are *independent* and are not linked to any election campaign.

Under campaign finance law, anyone is allowed to contribute or spend as much money as she likes and doesn't have to report it to the FEC as long as the expenditure is independent of an individual political campaign. You can take out an ad for or against a candidate or engage in other kinds of *electioneering* — which is different than campaigning, because it isn't directed by or at a particular campaign — as long as you do it on your own. You can also make these kinds of contributions to national political parties and special interest groups.

Sen. McCain, who was joined in 1995 by Sen. Russ Feingold (D-Wis.) and later by Reps. Chris Shays (R-Conn.) and Martin Meehan (D-Mass.) as cosponsors, argued that unregulated soft money corrupts American politics because it favors the rich, the well-connected, and corporate interests. Furthermore, McCain and his cosponsors argued that although independent expenditures were supposed to be about broad issues beyond individual campaigns, they were, in fact, used to influence specific elections; moreover, big contributors put pressure on lawmakers by influencing the national parties.

Efforts to reform soft money contributions began in the mid-1980s, picked up steam in 1992, and McCain made them a central priority of his efforts as senator.

In his fight to enact his reforms, McCain faced numerous obstacles, frequent defeats, and presidential vetoes. Strong arguments were made about the measure, and at one point, House Speaker Dennis Hastert (R-Ill.) warned that the House version of the bill amounted to "Armageddon" for members.

After nine years of effort, the reform bill, known as the Bipartisan Campaign Reform Act of 2002, passed both chambers and was signed into law March 27, 2002, by President George W. Bush. As part of the compromise in the final version, hard money limits were raised to permit more contributions, while limits were imposed on soft money. Some of the provisions of the final version of the McCain-Feingold bill are

- ✔ A ban on soft money contributions to national political parties. The parties can't accept soft money contributions after November 6, 2002, and they have to dispose of all soft money in their accounts by December 31, 2002.

- ✔ A mandate that noncorporate or nonunion organizations that spend more than $10,000 per year on electioneering must report their spending to the FEC.

- ✔ An increase in individual contributions to $2,000 per candidate per election.

- ✔ An increase in individual contributions to national party committees from $20,000 to $25,000 per year.

- ✔ An increase in individual contributions to local or state parties from $5,000 to $10,000 per year.

- ✔ An increase of the total individual contributions to $95,000 for every two-year election cycle (the cycle starts January 1 of odd-numbered years and extends to December 31 of even-numbered years), but only $37,500 can be spent on candidates during that cycle.

Throughout the consideration of McCain-Feingold, numerous arguments were heard about its impact on politics. Those arguments continue even after its passage.

Opponents of McCain-Feingold maintain that the act limits free speech and is unconstitutional. They immediately launched a lawsuit against the measure. The Supreme Court will ultimately determine whether it remains in force.

Mastering the Nuts and Bolts of Fundraising

Much of the art of fundraising lies in knowing who to call for large donations and getting those people to contact their friends. The means of fundraising is limited only by the law and your own imagination.

Sure, political fundraising policy is the subject of plenty of discussions, but how do you actually go about raising funds for a candidate, a PAC, or a cause?

Among the numerous ways are

- **Direct appeal:** You simply ask people for money in person.

- **Direct mail:** You mail out appeals. The disadvantage of direct mail is in the cost of printing and mailing and perhaps buying or renting a mailing list, but using this method can also bring in considerable amounts of money if it's done well. A 3 percent return on a direct mail appeal is considered a very good result.

- **Phone banks:** You gather volunteers together to make calls to solicit donations.

- **Sales:** This method includes everything from bake sales to benefit auctions that are usually conducted by volunteers and bring in small amounts of cash.

Feting candidates with fundraisers

The best — and most common — means for raising political money is a fundraising event, usually referred to as a *fundraiser*.

Fundraisers come in all shapes, sizes, and levels of sophistication, from home coffees to thousand-dollar-a-plate, black-tie dinners for hundreds of people.

But candidates want money, whether it comes from a woman wearing a ball gown or a T-shirt, so don't be intimidated. Think of a fundraiser as just a party where friends will gather to eat, drink, share some good times, and advance their particular cause.

If you can throw a party, you can throw a fundraiser. If you don't want to serve as host to the fundraiser, find someone else to do it for you.

At the most basic, grass-roots level, fundraisers consist of calling people you know who share a common interest in a candidate or a cause and inviting them to get together.

When the fundraiser is for a candidate, you need to coordinate it with the candidate's campaign committee and scheduler so that the candidate knows where to be, what audience she's addressing, and how to include it in her campaign calculations. You must tell campaign officials what you plan to do, how many people will attend, and how much money you expect to raise.

The people you're inviting must know that the get-together they're attending is a fundraiser and that they'll be asked to contribute money. Invitations frequently include a suggested minimum donation or a per-seat, per-plate, or per-table charge.

Speakers usually provide the attraction for people to attend fundraisers. A typical fundraiser invitation looks like the one in Figure 9-1.

Figure 9-1:
Your
invitation to
a fictional
fundraiser.

> *Harry and Louise Anyone are pleased to invite you*
> *to support the reelection of Rep. Jane Doe*
> *At their home*
> *1234 Anywhere Lane*
> *Saturday, May 4 at 2:00 PM*
> *Rep. Doe will discuss the vital issues facing our community*
> *and answer your questions*
> *Suggested contribution: $$$*
> *Coffee and doughnuts will be served*
> *RSVP by April 15*

Your friends and contributors gather round, drink their coffee, and eat their doughnuts. Rep. Doe arrives and speaks about the great things she's done in Washington and what she hopes to do if — excuse me, when — she's reelected.

At the end of the speech and a question and answer period, the host or the person who organized the fundraiser stands up and says something like, "Representative Doe, what you've said is so inspiring that I want to show my support for the fine job you're doing in Washington, and I'd like to present you with this check for (whatever amount of money)." The initial contribution is the signal for other members of the audience to express their appreciation by handing over their checks or making pledges. At some fundraisers people announce how much they're giving, which puts pressure on everyone else to contribute as much or more. The right technique depends on the event and the audience.

When you're serving as host, making the amount that you name a big one isn't a bad idea. It gives everyone else an idea of the high end for that particular fundraiser, which inspires them to do their best. The host going first and giving the largest contribution usually is best.

The check needs to be handed to the campaign manager or whoever has accompanied the candidate rather than the candidate who is prohibited by law from handling the funds herself.

The campaign worker and the fundraising host should total the amount of money raised so that both sides are clear and in agreement on the numbers to prevent any cheating and to have two independent records. When the event is PAC-related, the PAC's treasurer must record the total and report it to the FEC.

Some people pass a hat so that people can contribute cash, but remember, you want to avoid cash whenever possible for all the reasons I cover in the "Limiting your contributions" section earlier in this chapter.

Getting professional help

From the simple coffee or cocktail party, the complexity of fundraising events grows broader and higher.

As you proceed higher up the ladder of fundraising efforts, you encounter professional political fundraisers. These people can be helpful, and unlike lobbyists, you'll know when you're getting your money's worth by the amount of money they're able to raise for your candidate. They coordinate events, work the lists of possible donors, put together speakers, and may even come up with new and creative ways of drumming up resources for your cause. Of course, they must be paid either a flat fee or a percentage of the take.

A young friend of mine once approached a presidential campaign and told campaign workers that he wanted to serve as a fundraiser for them. The workers didn't take him seriously. "Okay," the campaign manager said, "raise $10,000, and you're hired." My friend had worked as a youth coordinator for a national organization. He called the ten richest young people he knew, telling each one: "If you contribute $1,000 to this campaign, I'll guarantee you a seat on the floor of the national presidential convention" — a coveted ticket among political activists and hard to get. The next day he went back to the campaign with $10,000. He was hired on the spot — but his candidate later dropped out of the race. I don't know whether his contributors ever received their seats at the convention.

Additionally, you can coordinate your fundraising efforts with the national parties. Each party has congressional campaign committees:

✔ In addition to the Democratic National Committee (www.DNC.org), which oversees the entire Democratic organization and effort, the Democrats have the Democratic Congressional Campaign Committee (www.DCCC.org) to coordinate their House campaigns and the Democratic Senate Campaign Committee (www.DSCC.org) to coordinate their Senate races.

✔ In addition to the Republican National Committee (www.RNC.org), the Republicans have the National Republican Campaign Committee (www.NRCC.org) to coordinate their House election effort and the National Republican Senatorial Committee (www.NRSC.org) to coordinate their Senate campaigns.

✔ Other parties raise funds as well. Visit their Web sites to find out how to contribute.

Parties also raise money directly over the Internet through their Web sites, and you can contribute using a credit card.

All parties provide ways of becoming involved in the political process and are delighted to hear from volunteers, activists, and contributors.

Maximizing your influence with candidates so that they further your cause and assist what you're trying to do politically is the point of fundraising through political contributions.

Providing Other Campaign Services

Campaigns always are looking for volunteers and a wide variety of services. You can leverage nonmonetary contributions into political influence on behalf of your cause.

You can offer your home for campaign events, and as long as your costs are less than $1,000 per election (or $2,000 when you're working on behalf of a party), they're not counted as campaign contributions.

Other services you can offer campaigns include:

- Volunteering for campaign work
- Gathering other volunteers for a campaign
- Posting signs and distributing literature
- Organizing events like fundraisers and rallies
- Helping generate positive publicity for the campaign

After they're elected, candidates remember all these contributions, but when you need to talk to a representative or senator after she's elected to Congress, reminding her about all the wonderful things you did for her way back when she was a struggling unknown, never hurts.

Discovering contribution resources

When it comes to learning about the role of political contributions in Congress, the Center for Responsive Politics in Washington, D.C., is an unparalleled resource. This nonprofit center does nothing but track political money and analyze data from the Federal Election Commission (FEC) in just about every imaginable way. It also issues periodic reports about which members receive the most money, which PACs and industries contribute the most money, and what effect money has on the political process. The center's Web site, www.Opensecrets.org, is a truly awesome compendium of data and databases that enable you to track money throughout Congress and the rest of the political system.

For official news and information, plus forms and general helpful electoral information, go to the FEC's Web site, www.FEC.gov, which is one of the better government sites and is full of useful data.

The Campaign Finance Institute is a good resource for following campaign finance laws and their reform. Find its Web site at www.CFInst.org.

Fundraising is an entire science unto itself, and for a complete treatment of it, you can do no better than *Fundraising For Dummies* by Katherine Murray and John Mutz, published in 2000 by Wiley.

Part IV
Lobbying from All Angles

"We appreciate your personal and financial backing of this bill, however, Congress is reluctant to name it after you. I'm sure you can understand, Mr. Hairbrane."

In this part . . .

I offer tried-and-true methods for making your voice heard and your concerns known to your members of Congress and to the media. I help you strategize, explain, persuade, and publicize your issue and your interests.

Chapter 10

Looking at Lobbying

In This Chapter

▶ Sorting through the different types of lobbyists

▶ Recognizing the nature of special interests

▶ Getting to know a member of Congress

▶ Hiring and evaluating a professional

A s soon as you become involved with Congress, you begin hearing about lobbies, lobbying, and lobbyists. Lobby is a word that has taken on a pejorative meaning, implying sleaziness and manipulation. Basically, however, *lobbying* is just arguing your case with lawmakers and trying to talk them into doing what you want, regardless of whether that means introducing a bill, voting a particular way, or taking a particular action. Nothing is mysterious or inherently evil about it. In the nonpolitical world it's usually known as salesmanship.

Indeed, not only is nothing mysterious about lobbying, you have a Constitutional right to do it: The first amendment to the Constitution states: "Congress shall make no law . . . abridging . . . the right of the people to peaceably to assemble and to petition the Government for a redress of grievances." Lobbying is a form of petitioning, so your right to lobby is guaranteed by the First Amendment.

Know this, however: Lobbying in favor of a particular act of Congress takes time. Don't expect any quick action from Congress — on anything. The wheels of Congress may grind fine, but they also grind very, very slowly. A good guideline: Expect efforts that require passage of a stand-alone bill to take at least three to five years. Congress is so overwhelmed with other issues, routine annual work of authorization and appropriations, and politics that it may take several sessions over a period of years before it can consider your cause. When you're working on a major issue, it can take even longer. Sometimes you may be surprised by getting something passed quickly, but usually not.

Although the political system is open to you, getting your way isn't easy, and that's exactly how the Framers of the Constitution intended it.

Explaining the Basics

Just as there are many kinds of salesmanship, there are many kinds of lobbying and lobbying campaigns, but they break down into a few main types:

- **Association:** Usually done by trade associations and membership organizations. It tends to focus on very technical or legal provisions in specific bills that affect the association's membership, whether those members are companies, other organizations, or individuals.

- **Corporate:** Done by a company or industry on its own behalf, corporate lobbying campaigns tend to focus on issues or provisions of law that affect a specific company or industry.

- **Grass roots:** This is lobbying on a mass basis that relies on large numbers of people expressing the same opinion to as many lawmakers as possible.

- **Individual:** Lobbying by an individual without organizational ties on behalf of an individual cause.

- **Nonprofit:** Lobbying on behalf of ideas or causes that don't involve commerce or business, usually for humanitarian or idealistic reasons.

Lobbying campaigns — lobbying coalitions — often use a mixture of lobbying types. For example, nonprofit lobbying campaigns often involve considerable grass-roots lobbying, with people demonstrating and going in large numbers to Capitol Hill. But most lobbying activity tends to fall within these broad categories.

Categorizing Lobbyists

Usually when people refer lobbyists, they're talking about professionals, people who hire themselves out to clients to work on their behalf. Frequently, lobbyists started their careers either as members of Congress or as congressional staffers, leaving government service and then using their contacts on behalf of their clients. Some lobbyists base their business on a long-standing relationship with a single, powerful member of the House or Senate.

Defining and describing

Full-time lobbyists spend their days influencing lawmakers and members of the executive branch to pursue particular courses of action or introduce, shape or alter pieces of legislation. The different kinds of lobbyists include

- ✔ **Association lobbyists** represent industry and trade associations.

- ✔ **Corporate lobbyists** work on behalf of individual companies. Usually these people have titles like Vice President for congressional relations.

- ✔ **Foreign agents** lobby for foreign governments and businesses and are registered with the United States government.

- ✔ **Nonprofit and public-interest lobbyists** work on behalf of various causes and voluntary organizations.

- ✔ **Professional lobbyists** work on behalf of the clients who hire them.

All full-time professional lobbyists must register with Congress.

If you're simply on Capitol Hill on behalf of your own cause, you don't have to worry about registering, and you're completely free to talk to any representative or senator who wants to talk to you. Registration is necessary only when you accept payment from clients for whom you have lobbied.

Demystifying special interests

One thing that you, the lobbyist for your cause in Congress, will have to get over is all the pejorative talk about special interests running the country and not having the good of the country as a whole in mind. After all, what is a special interest but you? The term *special interest* usually describes any person or group of people who pursues their own interests. That means you and the cause that you plan to take up with your representative in Congress. In practice, however, a special interest usually is the other guy who's pursuing his particular interest in conflict with your particular interest.

How lobbying got its name

The origin of the terms lobby, lobbyist and lobbying as they relate to legislative power-brokering tends to be disputed, but one of the better explanations — or at least one of the more colorful ones — suggests that the definitions sprang from the lobby of the old Willard Hotel, which for years was one of Washington, D.C.'s fanciest establishments and has hosted every president as a guest or for a social function from Franklin Pierce in 1853 to today. It still proudly displays Abraham Lincoln's bill when he stayed there before being sworn in as president as well as the menu for his inaugural banquet.

The story is told that when Ulysses S. Grant was president (1869–1876), he liked to go for a drink at the Willard bar. People looking for all kinds of favors would gather in the hotel lobby to talk to him as he was leaving. Grant, it is said, coined the term "lobbyists" in describing these people. The lobby in question faces Pennsylvania Avenue and is close to the White House.

If you go to Washington, you can still visit the Willard, a magnificently opulent building, which was renovated in 1983 and today is again one of the city's premier gathering places.

Registering as a lobbyist

When circumstances make it necessary for you to register as a professional lobbyist, you must do so within 45 days of making a lobbying contact or being retained to lobby for a client. To actually register, all that you do is fill out Form LD-1 and file one copy with the Secretary of the Senate and one with the Clerk of the House of Representatives. To obtain the form and all the instructions about registering, check out this page on the Senate's Web site: www.senate. gov/contacting/contact_lobby_ld1. html.

As soon as you begin pursuing your particular cause, you become a special interest.

If you've come to Congress to get your particular idea or cause adopted, you're going to have to petition the government more effectively than your opponents. That's why effective lobbying is so important.

The country's founders assumed that conflict would occur among and between special interests, or *factions,* as they were referred to in the *Federalist Papers*. The Framers' idea was to have all the interests competing in a free and open marketplace of ideas. They also thought that sensible people would choose the best ideas among them. In a system that made the right to petition government one of its fundamental precepts, there could be no other result.

> *By a faction, I understand a number of citizens, whether amounting to a majority or minority of the whole, who are united and actuated by some common impulse of passion, or of interest, adverse to the rights of other citizens, or to the permanent and aggregate interests of the community.*
>
> — James Madison, writing as "Publius" in *Federalist* No. 10, appearing Nov. 23, 1787, in *The New York Packet.*

As James Madison noted, people always divide into factions for a wide variety of reasons. Because the causes of factionalism cannot be prevented, the only thing the government can do is control its effects and make sure that factionalism never becomes destructive.

Getting Your Member's Attention

If you're going to do any work with Congress, you need to get to know your representative or senator personally and to get him to know you. Letters and e-mails are fine, but nothing can substitute for meeting with and getting to know your members of congress face-to-face.

Becoming acquainted with your House or Senate members should be easy, because they're public people who are supposed to be accessible. They need to know as many people as possible, and they need as many people as possible to know them. Besides, lest you forget, the kinds of people who go into politics usually are "people people." They enjoy being around other people, meeting new people, and doing things for and with people. Some, but not many, shrinking violets have entered politics — it isn't a profession for introverts.

Among the numerous ways that you can get to know your representative or senator are

- ✓ **Contributing to or volunteering in his campaign:** When you want to make a real impression, nothing beats making a political contribution or working on a campaign. Successful members keep good lists of contributors and volunteers. They know where the money and help come from regardless of whether they keep those lists on paper or in their heads. And, they often make extra efforts when a well-known supporter requests a favor. Big campaign contributors obviously carry more weight, but even a token contribution can gain you access to a member when you need him — just be sure when you get in touch by mail, e-mail, or phone that you remind him that you're a contributor. For more about political fundraising and using it, see Chapter 9.

- ✓ **Playing host to coffees or teas:** Around election time you can do your House or Senate member a favor by organizing coffees or teas so that he can meet you, your neighbors, or the members of your organization.

- ✓ **Organizing or attending fundraisers.**

- ✓ **Going to town meetings.**

- ✓ **Visiting the district office and introducing yourself:** Many members make a point of going out into the community, meeting people in supermarkets or at fairs and festivals, getting know them, and hearing their concerns. Some use mobile or satellite offices to do constituent work at shopping centers or other places where people congregate. Whenever you see your representative or senator at a public event, shaking hands and introducing himself to people, make a point of introducing yourself.

You may also want to make a member aware of your works when you're involved in community activities. Whenever the local newspaper publishes an article about you or your organization, clip it and send it to your representative's office. You may not be asking for a particular favor, but you'll definitely be starting the process of alerting the member to your efforts. That way, if you need a favor later on, your representative or senator at least will be aware of you.

Evaluating Scorecards and Key Votes

How to vote on a particular issue is entirely up to the member — after, all making that kind of judgment is what he was elected to do. However, you're equally entitled to your opinion of his actions.

You can judge a member on many levels and for many different things, but in the American political process, the way a member votes is what puts his position on the record for the entire world to see.

And, because everything in Congress is decided by voting, members vote on issues large and small, absurd and momentous, technical and cosmic.

What counts for you is how the member votes on your issue or your bill. Many lobbies determine that certain votes are considered key markers in their judgment of members' positions. These votes usually are known, not surprisingly, as *key votes*. When used as a verb — "We're going to *key-vote* this one." — it means that the lobbyist is using a particular vote for establishing an attitude toward a member or that the vote is considered an important factor in establishing a politician's position on a particular issue.

Some lobbies also issue *scorecards*, or lists of every member of the House and Senate — like report cards — that actually grade each member's position on a particular issue.

The *Almanac of American Politics* (See Chapter 2) uses scorecards, or *ratings* as they term them, to determine a member's ideological orientation. The *Almanac* cites the scorecards of 11 different groups:

- ✔ American Civil Liberties Union (www.aclu.org)
- ✔ American Conservative Union (www.acu.org)
- ✔ American Federation of State, County, and Municipal Employees (www.afscme.org)
- ✔ Americans for Democratic Action (www.adaction.org)
- ✔ Chamber of Commerce (uschamber.org)
- ✔ Christian Coalition (www.cc.org)
- ✔ Concord Coalition (concordcoalition.org)
- ✔ Information Technology Industry Council (www.itic.org)
- ✔ League of Conservation Voters (www.lcv.org)
- ✔ National Tax-Limitation Committee (www.limittaxes.org)
- ✔ National Taxpayers Union (www.ntu.org)

Scorecards are useful for permanent, long-term lobbies, because they can grade members over the course of many sessions. They're also useful for telling voters where politicians stand and for telling the legislators whether they're doing well or badly in the eyes of the lobby.

Members who receive high scores on a lobby's issue may be rewarded with campaign contributions, willing campaign workers, plaques, endorsements, and praise from the lobby. By the same token, bad scores can intimidate legislators into toeing the lobby's line.

However, scorecards also are double-edged swords. Giving members bad grades can anger them, and many often think they've been unfairly graded — just like students who don't like the marks they receive.

Scorecards need to be used judiciously after serious thought and only when a determination is made that the advantages of issuing the scorecard far outweigh its disadvantages.

Determining whether You Need a Professional

Odds are you already have a professional lobbyist working on your behalf — though not necessarily for you as an individual. If you're a member of a trade association or a union, lobbyists represent you in Congress. Of course, they're not working directly for you as an individual, but they are working on behalf of your industry, your union, or your interests. For example, one of the biggest associations and most powerful lobbies in Washington, D.C., is the American Association of Retired Persons (AARP), represents 30 million members. You may think of this organization primarily as a social or consumer organization, but if you're retired and a member, lobbyists are walking the halls of Congress speaking for you.

Don't make the mistake of assuming that you need a professional lobbyist to gain access to lawmakers. Although some lobbyists foster the impression that you can't get a meeting with a member of Congress without one of them arranging it for you, that is utter nonsense. Anyone can (and should feel free to) contact his or her representative or senator, and anyone can get a meeting, if and when time permits.

Frankly, I regard hiring a lobbyist as a last resort, but sometimes, you just can't accomplish your mission by yourself. At that point you need to get a professional lobbyist. When do you go pro? It's a judgment call. Some of the signs that point to the need for hiring a professional lobbyist are:

- ✔ The complexity or technical nature of an issue requires the expertise of someone who knows the field well. Business issues, bills directed at one particular company, or complex regulatory questions may be better handled by a professional.

- ✔ You simply can't devote the time and effort required. You think that you need someone in Washington full time to monitor the issue, and you don't have an office there or can't be present yourself.

- ✔ You need to launch and coordinate a broad-based, elaborate political effort.

- ✔ You're trying to get money. Appropriations issues often are best handled by a professional. These money issues require a thorough knowledge of the appropriations process, the small number of congressional players involved, and federal funding processes. Often a professional lobbyist's services are particularly valuable in this field. For info about the appropriations process, turn to Chapter 8.

Professional lobbyists bring with them three advantages:

- ✔ **Established connections:** Lobbyists have usually worked with the lawmakers and regulators who are working on your issues. In most cases, you can presume that the lobbyist has good relations with these people and is trusted by them. When a lobbyist calls, lawmakers will pick up the phone or give the lobbyist an appointment and truly listen to his counsel.

- ✔ **Experience:** Lobbyists have experience dealing with members of Congress and other representatives of the federal government who are handling or have handled your issue. They know the institution and its procedures.

- ✔ **Knowledge:** Lobbyists generally know your issue's current situation and the players, politics, and history surrounding it. They also have an idea how to achieve your ends. This knowledge is the kind that comes only from dealing directly with these people and being immersed in congressional politics.

A good lobbyist needs to be able to provide you with a broad strategy for achieving your aims and to map out a plan for you to sell your cause to the entire country, work with the media, and talk to federal regulators in the executive branch. He should be able to influence anyone and everyone who may have a say on your issue.

Turning to a pro

Many times I've heard this story: A business executive is peacefully sitting at his desk when his boss walks in and says, "We've got a problem that has to be solved by Congress. You were on the school board (or volunteered for a political campaign, or carried a sign in a rally, or were in the Army), take care of it." The executive panics — he's completely unqualified.

Another story: At a neighborhood gathering one of my neighbors wants all the local homeowners to chip in a thousand dollars each to hire a lobbyist to get our Zip code changed to a more prestigious one. It hasn't occurred to him to simply write a letter to our representative.

(Besides, ZIP codes belong exclusively within the realm of the United States Postal Service and are outside the purview of Congress.) Usually, as soon as someone hears that he must deal with Congress, his first reaction is that he must hire a professional lobbyist at an exorbitant sum to get anything done.

Obviously, I don't agree with that philosophy, given that this book explains how you can lobby for yourself or your company or organization. Remember that Congress is there for you. Your representative or senator is your chief lobbyist and you have many ways to approach him.

Choosing a Lobbyist

A common technique used by lobbyists seeking business is warning you of the dire consequences that pending legislation may have unless you hire him to head it off. Don't be intimidated into hiring a lobbyist. Check out the claims. Do some research. Get some other opinions. What the lobbyist is saying may actually turn out to be true, but you need to double-check for yourself.

You must register as a professional lobbying organization whenever you hire one or more professional lobbyists — including contractors or freelance lobbyists. If you're part of a firm that doesn't receive — or at least doesn't expect to receive — more than $5,000 for lobbying during a six-month period, you don't have to register. You also don't have to register whenever your organization has full-time professional lobbyists in-house but doesn't spend more than $22,500 during any given six-month period on its lobbying efforts.

Finding a professional

TIP

Big lobbying firms have institutional names and a roster of distinguished partners, but if you're a fairly small account, they're going to foist the real work off on some associate and you'll never see or hear the Big Name. A small firm may lack the name recognition of a bigger one but often brings greater energy and attention to your issue.

Perhaps the best models for choosing a lobbyist are the ones that you use for choosing any other professional, including:

- **Paying attention to word of mouth:** Referrals are the most common means. Someone may already be well known in your particular field. In the same way that law firms hire big legal names as *rainmakers,* lobbying firms hire big names — former members of Congress, former executive branch officials — to drive their businesses.

- **Seeking out recommendations:** Asking your representative, senator, or members of their staffs for the names of lobbyists who are sympathetic to your issue is not unreasonable. They know who is active in the field and who has the best reputations. A recommendation does not necessarily mean a referral, but at least it can get you started in the right direction.

- **Researching your needs:** You can also pick up names from publications that cover your subject. When you see someone repeatedly mentioned as a spokesman for a particular position on an issue, especially one involving commercial interests, that person often is a professional lobbyist. You can try reaching that person through his or her affiliated organization.

- **Hiring Washington, D.C., law and public relations firms:** Washington D.C., is full of law firms and public relations firms whose chief purpose is to lobby government. Washington lawyers are different than most — many tend not to deal with law in the courtroom sense. Rather, many are former members of Congress, officials, and staffers who know particular issues and can represent you. The same applies to public relations and strategic services professionals.

As is true when hiring a lawyer, be skeptical of boastful claims by prospective lobbyists. Determining the validity of a lobbyist's boasts is difficult, given the amorphous nature of lobbying and the often-arbitrary methods used when assigning credit for legislative achievement. Legislation passes through so many hands and so many people and institutions claim credit for success when it passes that you must dig deep to get a true sense of who accomplished what.

Quantifying the qualifications

Ultimately you have to go with your gut, but looking at the following attributes can to help in the selection process:

- **Familiarity with your issue:** Does the prospective lobbyist know the topic well?

- **Shared goals:** A hired gun takes on any client, but when a lobbyist has a real affinity for what you're doing, he will be a better lobbyist on your behalf.

✔ **Cost:** Washington lobbyists currently charge between $300 and $600 per hour. Smaller or newer lobbying firms charge on the lower end of that range. Additional charges can include entertainment, travel, and incidental expenses.

✔ **References:** Ask the person or firm for references. Call the references and ask whether they were satisfied with the service they received. Whenever the lobbyist worked for a current or retired member of Congress (which they usually have), call that member and ask about the lobbyist.

✔ **History:** What issues has the lobbyist worked on before? What do other individuals and the media say about this lobbyist? Conduct an Internet search about the particular lobbyist or lobbying firm.

✔ **Compatibility:** Do you get along with the person handling your issue? Although this factor is an intangible, it nevertheless is important. An affinity with your lobbyist helps you feel that your issue is getting the attention it deserves.

Working out a plan of action

Don't expect miracles or instant gratification just because you hired a lobbyist. He may have many connections and be very capable, but he must maneuver through a cumbersome system against many obstacles. Nonetheless, you don't have endless time or money. When the lobbyist is first trying to gain your business, he needs give you some kind of rough idea of what he will do for you and how long it will take.

When you've selected a lobbyist, sit down with him and work out a plan of action together. This plan needs to cover:

✔ Your lobbying goals: What are you trying to achieve together? The more specific you are the more effective your lobbying effort.

✔ A timetable for achieving these goals.

✔ Milestones so that you can gauge progress toward your goals.

✔ A budget: Don't leave this open-ended unless you have very deep pockets. Professional lobbying can become a very expensive proposition very quickly.

✔ The terms of payment: Most lobbyists, like lawyers, work on a retainer plus hourly charges, including travel, expenses, and entertainment.

Evaluating your lobbyist

After you hire a lobbyist, be sure to check up on his activities. Don't just assume that your lobbyist is busily at work on your issue. Make sure that he sends you regular reports on his activities on your behalf — and don't settle for a few clipped articles from a couple of newspapers, which some lobbyists churn out and refer to as client reports. You want real information showing some thought and care and attention to your issue.

Follow up on the reports and get information on the progress of your issue from as many sources like congressional staff, publications specializing in Congress (see Chapter 15 for info on the different media) and any other sources of information as possible. The occasional phone call just to remind your lobbyist that you're alive never hurts, either.

And, as always, nothing can substitute for being well informed. Stay on top of your issue through every available means. See whether your lobbyist is mentioned in the news. When she is, send her a note letting her know that you're watching.

Remember, your lobbyist works for you, and because you're the one whose paying him, you should get your money's worth.

Chapter 11

Explaining Your Cause

. . . .

In This Chapter

▶ Determining your goals and what's most important to you

▶ Getting a clear idea of the tools you can use

▶ Building a coalition and finding a champion

▶ Speaking at a hearing

. . . .

So, how are you going to convince what often is perceived as an unruly, untamed, and nearly ungovernable group of people — also known as the U.S. Congress — to do what you want? Remember that you must convince a majority of them.

You can try just strolling into a congressional office and talking about what you want to do. The staffers will be polite but probably a bit distant, listening to you and taking notes. Maybe they'll even offer you tickets to the gallery so that you can see the entire House or Senate in action. Then a senior staffer will come by and courteously escort you out of the office. Everyone will go back to work and forget you were ever there.

Another scenario is the warm greeting without a follow-up. I can't tell you how many times I've heard this story: A constituent drops by unannounced to see a representative or senator and is treated like royalty. The legislator listens closely and sympathetically to the constituent's complaints, nodding in agreement. The member emphatically states that something must be done, vows to do it, and gives orders to her staff members, who then scurry off to do her bidding. She proposes a course of action and promises that the job will be done. The constituent leaves the office feeling important, gratified, and convinced that something is, in fact, being done. Days that go by without a word from the member turn into weeks. The weeks turn into months. The constituent never hears back from the legislator or staff. The issue is forgotten and nothing is done.

Merely dropping in and getting warm and fuzzy promises from your legislator isn't the way you get the job done in Washington. If you're going to be effective, two things must govern your actions if your cause is going to succeed: planning and follow-up. These are the issues I talk about in this chapter.

Knowing What You Want to Achieve

In the same way that a salesman is better and more effective when his sales strategy is carefully thought out, your lobbying campaign will turn out better when it's carefully planned and conceived. So, you must ask yourself some important questions at the outset of your campaign:

✔ What do I want to achieve?

✔ What is most important to me; what's my core issue?

✔ What do I want the members of Congress to do?

✔ What *don't* I want the members of Congress to do?

If you're going through the lengthy struggle of trying to convince Congress to pass the legislation you've proposed or simply to do what you want, *you* must know precisely what you want in real terms. Your goal can't be something broad or vague like world peace. Everyone wants world peace, but getting it is beyond the scope of any congressional legislation. However, a concrete action, such as ratifying a treaty banning the use of land mines, for example, stands a better chance of succeeding.

When you're clear about your goals, you'll also be clear about the obstacles you face and the assistance you're likely to get, and as a result, you'll have a much clearer idea of what you need to do.

Educating Yourself

Knowing all you can about the members and legislation under consideration is important to the success of your lobbying campaign. Fortunately, Congress has provided an excellent means of looking up legislation. It's called Thomas, after Thomas Jefferson. To get there:

1. **Go to** www.House.gov.

2. **Go to the bottom of the Web page to the Thomas icon and click on either the icon or the word "THOMAS."**

3. **You're presented with the option of looking up a bill by its number or by a pertinent word or phrase.**

4. **Fill in the fields, and you should be able to find the legislation you want.**

Building Your Case

To be effective, you have to be committed to your *core issue,* the basic goal you're working toward and on which you will not compromise. At the same time, you have to be pragmatic and flexible. You need to be willing to compromise on less important issues to further your efforts on your core issue.

Defining your core issue

Your *core issue* is the essence of what you're trying to achieve, the absolute, rock-bottom minimum, or the issue on which you won't compromise under any circumstances. It's what means the most to you and establishes a filter through which you judge everything and everyone.

Establishing your core issue gives you a foundation to build upon during the long struggle ahead and the inner strength to face the disappointments, distractions, and diversions you'll confront when addressing your issue before Congress. You're going to face opposition and find that you have to make sacrifices and compromises. You're going to be shaken, rattled, and rolled, so you'd better know exactly what you want.

You can't always get what you want, but if you try sometimes [and your goals are clear] you just might find, you get what you need.

— Mick Jagger & Keith Richards, lyrics to
You Can't Always Get What You Want

Practicing the fine art of compromise

Believe me, by the time that you reach your goal — if you happen to get that far — you'll no doubt already have compromised on just about everything under the sun. If you want to succeed, you must be clear on what you're after and why you're after it.

Every situation is different, but by the time you reach your final goal, your legislation is likely to look substantially different than it did at the outset in order to appeal to the broad numbers of people necessary to pass it.

CAPITOL CASE

Sticking with an IDEA

In the spring of 2001, Sen. Jim Jeffords of Vermont had qualms about a tax cut proposed by the president and was worried about Social Security and Medicare. But as a Republican, he went along with the party program.

However, one program was very important to him: the Individuals with Disabilities Education Act (IDEA), which sets guidelines for educating disabled students. Originally, the cost of meeting the guidelines fell on states and localities. Jeffords wanted to shift that burden to the federal government and guarantee IDEA's funding. It was an idea he vigorously promoted in the Senate.

As time went on and Jefford's differences with his leadership grew, getting full funding for IDEA became his core issue and something on which he would not compromise. When Democrats promised to be more accommodating on IDEA, Jeffords overthrew the political allegiance of a lifetime and declared himself an Independent.

Jeffords is a practical politician and he'd made many compromises in the course of a career that started with his election to the House in 1974. But IDEA was so central to what he wanted to do as a legislator that he severed close political ties, broke friendships with his Republican Senate colleagues, put the Senate in the hands of the Democrats, and changed the political balance of the country to achieve it.

Knowing Your Issue

When you're ready to start lobbying, you must clear your mind of any misconceptions about what is and isn't real so that you have a clear, objective, and unemotional view of your situation.

Doing the research

You must read and absorb everything you can lay your hands on about your cause or issues. You can never be too well informed.

Your research needs to give you a sense, pro and con, of who the major congressional players are with regard to your issue, who you'll need to work with — or against — and what forces you'll be dealing with. You should have a strong sense of your opponents' arguments on the issue.

Also, try to think through all the possible implications of the legislation you're seeking, especially its economic impact. No impact is too remote or implication too distant to be considered — and then research these possible effects.

By the time you're ready to launch a campaign in Congress you must know your issue, inside and out. You should have read the most important books on the issue, visited the Web sites of the players and organizations involved, and familiarized yourself with the media covering it. That means you must know

- ✔ The current situation concerning your cause.

- ✔ Why the law you're proposing needs to be passed or the action you're pursuing needs to be taken and precisely what changes need to be made.

- ✔ Why and where the current law falls short.

- ✔ The history of your issue.

- ✔ Which members and organizations support the status quo and who is likely to support a change like the one you're proposing. The easiest and fastest way to do this is by doing an Internet search that includes the name of an organization or member and a few key words identifying your issue.

For extra credit, discover your weaknesses by pretending that you're an opponent of the legislation you want enacted. Make a list of all the reasons why your idea is a bad one and your cause should never succeed. You can then better prepare to answer your critics, and arguments against your cause or issue won't catch you by surprise.

Taking stock of your assets and liabilities

Sit down and make a list of the assets and liabilities of your cause. *Assets* are factors you can present that enable you to prevail during the battle. Typical assets are

- ✔ Willing volunteers to write letters to their senators and representatives and make calls on behalf of your cause when necessary

- ✔ Sympathetic local lawmakers or officials who publicly endorse your cause and who write or visit representatives or senators

- ✔ Supportive businesses that make an effort on your behalf

- ✔ Concerned unions who mobilize their members on your cause's behalf

- ✔ Compelling stories that garner publicity and make readers or viewers sympathetic to your cause

- ✔ Favorable publicity that puts your cause in a good light

- ✔ Ample funds to use for mailings, paid advertisements, or professional support
- ✔ Supportive celebrities who will draw publicity to your cause

Typical *liabilities* are obstacles you face or factors that don't advance your cause. Examples are

- ✔ Determined opposition trying to stop you from achieving your ends
- ✔ Public indifference to your cause
- ✔ Lack of time to devote to your cause
- ✔ Lack of volunteers or workers to do the work required for a significant lobbying effort
- ✔ Lack of publicity or negative publicity that puts you or your cause in an unfavorable light
- ✔ Lack of funds preventing you from spending money on necessary items
- ✔ Absence of a network involved with your cause to give you the support for tackling the tasks required for advancing your issue

You may have all of these assets or liabilities, only some of them, or none at all — every situation is different. However, after you compile your lists and you begin lobbying, you'll be better equipped to take maximum advantage of your assets, and you'll be more likely to know exactly what you have in your toolkit.

Putting together a packet

When you visit a lawmaker, you should leave him or her with a packet of information that helps the lawmaker advance your cause. The more work that you do for the lawmaker and his or her staff, the more weight your point of view is likely to carry. A binder sporting the logo of your cause serves as a great cover for your packet, which should include:

- ✔ **An introductory letter:** You may have already introduced yourself or written to the member before, but that doesn't matter. An introductory letter not only reacquaints the member with you, but it introduces you and your cause and provides your contact information to anyone else who may come into contact with your packet.
- ✔ **Talking points:** At least ten arguments in favor of your cause or the bill you're trying to get passed. Make them short, simple, and clear to help the member in discussions with other members. Ten, of course, is an arbitrary number, but it's also a good one: Any fewer and it seems you don't have the arguments, any more and they're likely to be forgotten.

- ✔ **The legislation or action:** You need to supply the lawmaker with a copy of the bill already introduced or a draft of the bill you'd like to see passed or the action you'd like to see taken.

- ✔ **A one-minute speech:** This is a short speech of about 300 words that the member can make on the floor during the time at the beginning of the legislative day in the House when members give very brief speeches on any topics of their choosing.

- ✔ **A long speech:** You can go on as long as you want in the long speech. The member can use this speech in Congress or when talking to civic groups or constituents. The important thing is that you supply the material in case the member needs it.

- ✔ **Background material:** Besides a brief history, the background about your issue needs to discuss the current situation and why the member should do what you want.

- ✔ **A press release:** This document describes your cause and announces the member's support for it. The member can submit it to the media or you can send it to the media with the member's permission.

If you're planning to see more than one member, you must tailor the speeches and press releases to each member's needs. It's embarrassing, to say the least, if two or more members enter the same speech (written by you) into the *Congressional Record*. If your packet includes speeches and a press release, each and every one must be different.

Gathering Support

As an individual citizen you can do much — but even the most energetic and committed individual can't do everything it takes to get legislation passed or change the political system.

Democracy is built on numbers, so you have to mobilize numbers of people to support you and your cause if you're going to be successful. You can do this by building coalitions with like-minded groups. But you also need assistance from within Congress as well — from what I call a *champion*.

Building coalitions

No man — or woman — is an island and that's especially true in the legislative process. You have to form alliances with people and organizations that share some of your goals. The more people and organizations that you can persuade to pursue your agenda — regardless of how fractured their unity in your favor may seem — the more powerful your voice is in Congress. Only by forming alliances — assisting other organizations and groups in pursuing their goals — can you ensure their cooperation in pursuit of your goals.

When planning your lobbying campaign, make a list of the organizations with which you can form alliances. After you start lobbying, and especially after you receive media coverage, you can expect other organizations to approach you. Listen to them carefully so that you can make judicious decisions about including them in your growing army. The stronger your army — the larger your forces — the more likely your victory.

As you research your cause, you should become aware of existing groups and organizations that share your interests. A very fast way of conducting this research is by doing an Internet search using your issue as the keyword. Numerous Web sites should pop up.

Write to these organizations (you can contact many through their Web sites) stating your goals and soliciting their support for your cause. You should treat your communications with these groups the same way you treat your communications with your representative and senators and state:

- Who you are
- Who you represent
- What you want to do
- Why this issue is important in general
- Why the issue is important to the organization
- What you would like the organization to do
- Why doing this is in the organization's interest

Whenever feasible, you can also make a list of people in the districts or states of other key representatives or senators who favor your cause, with whom you can form alliances, and with whom you expect to work. When your campaign takes off, you can encourage these people to contact their legislators on behalf of your cause.

If you've never sought help from constituents in the districts of congressional representatives other than your own, you will have to develop the contacts. There's no easy way to do this, and often it just takes time as you widen your circle of contacts, your cause gets more publicity, and your supporters become more active and reach out to other like-minded people. You should also monitor the media and contact people mentioned who may prove helpful.

Courting a congressional champion

Every piece of legislation or initiative in Congress has its champion, meaning a representative or senator who leads the way. In a purely legal sense, the *sponsor* of legislation is the member who introduces it to the chamber. Sponsors and champions are not necessarily the same, although ideally, they are.

A champion does more than merely sponsor legislation. A *champion* is someone who understands the issue the same way you do and is committed to pursuing it. A committed champion lobbies fellow members, sells the legislation to the media, and genuinely works hard to get the legislation passed. Getting your cause or bill passed means that you must find a champion in Congress. (In the past such a person was called a *horse,* or someone who pulls the cart, but I haven't heard that term used in a long time.)

Sometimes, a champion comes to you. A member may believe in your cause or see some political advantage in advancing it. More often, however, finding a champion is your job.

One of the first places to look for a champion is right in your own hometown — or at least in your congressional district. There's nothing wrong with asking your own congressional representatives for help first. However, if the legislation you want passed doesn't fall into her area of expertise or scope of authority, your representative or senator may recommend another member who more closely identifies with your cause and is willing to make the legislative effort.

There's no protocol or procedure for finding a champion. If your own representative isn't interested in championing your cause, the best you can do is approach other members who feel the way you do or persuade a member that championing your cause will help her politically. Here again your research into the issue can help you identify a member who shares your interests you're likely to hear or read about her in the coverage of your issue.

A delicious dilemma to be in is when multiple members bid to sponsor your cause. You may have a choice of champions — up to a point. If you find yourself in this happy position, you should go with the member who is most senior, has the greatest clout in Congress, or otherwise appears in the best position to achieve your ends.

Each member is an independent lawmaker entirely capable of taking action on her own without consulting you.

Less enthralling but just as much a problem is finding a champion when your cause is less popular or prominent. If that's the case, then you must find your champion on your own, perhaps offering some kind of incentive to the member to promote your cause. Providing financial support in the form of campaign contributions is one incentive (Chapter 9 talks about campaign contributions).

If your financial resources are sparse, you can:

- ✔ Help find grass-roots workers for your champion's next campaign
- ✔ Garner favorable mention about your champion in the press
- ✔ Provide some other form of inducement to attract your champion's support for your cause

Use whatever inducements you have because without a champion your legislation is down for the count.

Testifying before Congress

If your issue reaches the point of being heard by a committee or subcommittee, you may be called upon to testify, or more likely, you may volunteer to testify.

If you do want to testify, call, e-mail, or write to the office of the committee holding the hearing, your representative or senator, or the chairman of the committee. Tell the staff:

- ✔ Who you are and who you represent
- ✔ The hearing at which you want to testify
- ✔ Why you want to testify and your qualifications as a witness (for example, any special expertise you have on the subject or if you're the head of an organization with a stake in the issue)
- ✔ The points you want to make or the information you want to convey

You may also want to suggest someone else as a witness. Your congressional champion — the member promoting your cause — also needs to be in touch with the committee and able to put your name forward as a witness.

When it looks like the committee is not going to conduct a hearing on your bill, and you want one, you can offer to do the work of putting together a witness list. Taking some of the burden of organizing a hearing from the committee staff may help you get a hearing.

Don't assume that a hearing is a hostile interrogation. Look at it as an excellent opportunity to put your case before Congress, the press, and the public. You should be able to get through a hearing in fine style, and when it goes in your favor, it can be a powerful boost to your cause.

You'll know whether your testimony is successful from the media coverage of the hearing and from the reactions of the members themselves.

I've seen many people testify before Congress, and the witnesses who do it best are the ones who are well prepared and try to engage the members, treating them as collaborators rather than adversaries.

Like any good farmer will tell you, before planting the seeds of your cause in Congress, you have to prepare the ground first. Much of your work takes place before the hearing. Pay courtesy calls to all the members of the panel or their staffs, even the ones who oppose you. You may be surprised at the decency and helpfulness that even your opponents can exhibit. Usually, no one wants surprises. The members want to know what you're going to say, and you should feel free to try to find out what they're going to ask. You can also provide members with questions (either of you, your opponents, or other witnesses) that you believe need to be asked at the hearing. And you need to provide likely answers to those questions. Doing so enables members to follow up on answers either from you or your opponents.

Asking a sympathetic committee member or staff member to help you get ready for your particular hearing is a good idea. Be sure to ask members and staffers: "Is there anything in particular I need to know or prepare for this hearing?"

Before you testify, have friends help you prepare by asking questions that you're likely to hear.

When you testify:

- **Relax:** Yes, you're going to be in a big public forum, but being nervous isn't going to help. Likely as not, you've been dealing with this subject for a long time, and you thoroughly know your material. Enter a hearing feeling well rested, confident, and well prepared.

- **Have a good prepared statement:** In fact, have two versions of your statement:

  - A long version that has all the facts that you want to present. You furnish a copy of it to the panel beforehand, and it becomes part of the record of the hearing and provides information about your cause over a long time.

  - A shorter version that takes no more than ten minutes to read. You present this version orally to the committee.

Make numerous copies of the long statement — at least a hundred or so, depending on the likely size of the audience for the hearing — to give to each of the members, the press, and members of the public who attend the hearing. You can never have too many copies.

✔ **Stay calm and cool:** Never get riled, never lose your temper, don't take anything personally, and never insult the members even if they insult you or are being particularly dense or stupid. Polite firmness and respect are the order of the day.

Try making the hearing a collaborative effort with the members. You're trying to help them understand your cause and win them over to your point of view. Approach them as a collaborator:

✔ Take the attitude that you want them to have all the information they need to make an informed decision.

✔ Be as candid as possible. And remember that you're under oath, so any lies will be treated as perjury and prosecuted.

✔ Don't fudge information or try to evade questions. If you can't remember a fact, simply say so. If you don't know the answer to a question, simply say, "I don't know the answer to that, but I'll look into it and get the answer to you as soon as I can." And then do it — preferably in writing and preferably within a week (sooner if possible).

✔ Feel free to elaborate or put your answers in context. A hearing is not like a trial where someone is going to object to a question or a prosecutor insists on a "yes" or "no" answer. Feel free to speak as much as you think necessary — but don't bore the members.

Chapter 12

Getting Down to the Nitty-Gritty: Lobbying Members of Congress

• •

In This Chapter

▶ Finding the best way to get in touch with your representative and senators

▶ Preparing your testimony for Congress

▶ Lobbying negatively — when you must

▶ Using gifts and entertainment

• •

*Y*ou're informed. You know your strengths and weaknesses. You know what you want to achieve. You're psyched, you're pumped, and you're going to change the world. Now what?

Getting in touch with your representative and senators comes next. In this chapter, I'll presume that you've neither met nor had any prior contact with your representative. I'll go over the nitty-gritty details of contacting your elected officials in Congress and provide some tips for effective lobbying.

Writing to Your Representative and Senators

The time-honored way to reach a representative or senator to introduce yourself and your cause is to write a letter. Hand-written letters are how voters reached their representatives in Ben Franklin's day and they are pretty much the way most Americans — and members of Congress — expected to be reached. But that ended October 15, 2001, the day a letter laced with anthrax was opened in the office of Sen. Tom Daschle (D-S.D.), the Senate Majority Leader. Suddenly, mail was potentially poisonous, and from that point on, communication changed.

Writing to your congressman was fine when you were sure that your letter would get through and mail delivery was the essence of representative government. Because mail was such an important method of communication, the Capitol Hill mail system was one of the best. But once the anthrax-infected letters began arriving, that system became uncertain. In some cases, whether to burn bags of mail that was feared tainted was debated, and some letters never reached members.

Today, you either have to introduce yourself in person or start your lobbying campaign by e-mail and follow up with regular mail.

Crafting written communications

The degree of care congressional staff gives your cause reflects the amount of care you put into your written communications, whether electronic or paper. Therefore, make sure that your information is accurate and that your letter has no typos (run a spell-check program before sending e-mail and proofread — or have someone else proofread — a paper letter before mailing it).

If you're writing about your cause, explain it clearly and directly. Tell the member:

- Who you are
- Why you're concerned
- Why he should be concerned
- Why he should act
- What you want him to do

The information is the most important part of your message.

Do you want him either to support or oppose a piece of legislation? Be sure to include the bill name and number. Explaining, if you can, who the sponsor and cosponsors are also is helpful. Chapter 4 has info about sponsors. Do you want him to support something? Tell him what kind of support you want: Should he give speeches, make an endorsement, write a letter on your behalf? Do you want your senator to support or oppose a nominee? Make sure to state whom. And if you want him to initiate a bill, tell him that too and give him details about the kind of bill you'd like to see introduced.

A member can do all these things, but you have to tell him what it is you want. Be sure to include supporting documents or articles.

Explaining how the member benefits from taking the action you're proposing is worthwhile. What advantages does the member gain if he does what you ask? Tell him whether doing what you ask will help him to get re-elected, encourage donors to contribute to his campaign, benefit his district, or bring him favorable publicity. Try to list as many advantages as you can.

You may also be writing with a negative message complaining about an action he's taken. Going negative under any circumstances has to be done with delicacy and discretion. See the "Taking a Walk on the Dark Side: Going Negative" section.

E-mailing for every issue

Web-based communication, including e-mail, has been growing as a means of communication between Congress and the public through the 1990s and continues to grow in the 21st century. In 1998, Congress received about 20 million e-mails; in 2000, that number rose to 48 million.

Before December 1998, when constituents started e-mailing opinions about the impeachment of President Bill Clinton, congressional offices received only a few dozen e-mails per week, and Senate offices only a few hundred. Most offices preferred to respond to e-mails by regular mail. Members preferred this system because:

- They were familiar with paper methods and had always done it that way.

- They were fearful that if they responded by e-mail, their words would be altered and thereby send false messages to constituents over their signatures.

When e-mail volumes were low, office staffers read the e-mails and responded to them fairly easily. However, in January 1999, when the impeachment process hit its peak, House offices began receiving up to a thousand e-mails a day and Senate offices up to ten thousand. Individuals sent much e-mail to all members of Congress.

After Clinton's impeachment proceedings, e-mail volumes subsided, but they never returned to their earlier, lower levels. Then, in 2001, even before anthrax-laden letters were mailed to House and Senate offices, e-mail suddenly became the primary way of communicating with members. On September 11, 2001, the day of the terrorist attacks on the Pentagon and New York City, calls jammed Washington's telephone system and cell phones wouldn't work, but e-mail stayed up. In October, when anthrax was found in the mail, e-mail quickly moved from being a nice toy that many members didn't take terribly seriously to the primary means of communication on Capitol Hill — and the volume of e-mail increased by 400 percent over previous levels.

Research shows that thoughtful, well-conceived e-mails receive as much time and attention from staff members as paper letters, so think carefully about what you want to say in them.

You want to have an e-mail dialogue with the member and his staff, but you also want to avoid becoming a pen pal. In this context, a *pen pal* is a bad thing, someone who has (or tries to have) endless dialogues with the staff, which is tempting to do with e-mail. Keep your correspondence businesslike and as brief and to the point as possible. Members and their staffs are there to help you, but they're not psychiatrists; they have to serve many people, and they have only so much time in the day to do it.

It is imperative that you provide your full name and mailing address in your e-mail so that members and staff can get in touch with you.

Filtering and ranking and sorting (oh my!)

Congressional offices have been struggling to cope with the recent flood of e-mail. Staffers in nearly every office I've contacted stoutly maintain that all e-mails are read and considered.

Offices generally rank incoming e-mails from least important to most important by using the following classifications:

- ✔ **Spam:** Spam is the least important kind of e-mail, including messages that are irrelevant to Congress or to the member, press releases, or commercial come-ons, basically the kind of stuff that you'd trash, too.

- ✔ **Mass-mailings:** Next come messages that deal with issues before Congress but are merely generated en masse for members of Congress by a lobby or organization. These are cookie-cutter messages, each one exactly the same for every member, even though they may come from different senders. When you've read one, you've read them all. Most are trashed.

- ✔ **Original messages:** The important e-mails are original messages that come directly from constituents. These are serious e-mails and the staff either responds directly or takes the messages to the member for review. The most important of these messages come from state or district constituents.

- ✔ **Crucial information:** Even more important are messages coming from individuals whom the member knows and containing crucial information the member has to have.

- ✔ **Expected responses:** At the top of the heap are messages that the member expects or anticipates are responses to e-mails the member has sent out.

Congressional staff members live in fear of missing crucial e-mails. When an important e-mail isn't forwarded/flagged, someone's head may wind up on the chopping block.

Figuring out who should sort through e-mails is a tremendous problem. The job can't be entrusted to an intern who may not know the names of individuals who are important to the member, and yet it takes more time than a senior staffer has to devote to the task.

Your introduction to a member at the outset of your lobbying campaign will likely be through written communication. However, you must use a different mix of written messages today than was used before October 15, 2001.

Finding out where to send your e-mail

To send an e-mail to a member of Congress, follow these steps:

1. **Go to the House of Representatives Web site:** www.House.gov.

2. **Scroll down to the bottom of the page where it says "Write your representative" and click on the link.**

3. **Select the state and fill in the ZIP code field.**

4. **Fill in the resulting form.**

5. **Write your message and submit it.**

Congratulations, you've taken the first step!

Your e-mail is now out there, but I'd suggest following up with a paper letter. Doing so reinforces the message in your e-mail and creates a paper trail that can be kept in files.

Sending snail mail

You say you haven't joined the technological mainstream yet. When you write a letter, you use good, old-fashioned paper and pen. Wait, you say you use a manual typewriter!? Well, regardless of whether you use real or virtual ink, what you say and how you say it remain pretty much the same; nevertheless, I have a couple letter-specific tips to share.

I strongly suggest that you send a letter on high-quality, heavyweight paper, preferably with a letterhead. It sounds ridiculous, but it's true: The quality of your paper conveys how much care and attention you devoted to the subject you're writing about. Upholding this kind of reflection also means that your letter shouldn't have any typos or grammatical errors.

Paper letters are important if you're not a constituent of the member. Because congressional offices ignore or delete nonconstituent e-mail, paper may be the only way that you can get through to a representative or senator who isn't from your district or state.

The House has its own Zip code: 20515. When writing to your representative, address your letter to Rep. _____ (or, an older form of address is *The Honorable* XXXXX), United States House of Representatives, Washington, DC 20515. Start the letter with "Dear Rep. _____."

You can also address your letter to your representative's specific office in the Capitol complex.

The Senate also has its own Zip code: 20510. Address your senator as "Dear Sen. _____" and mail your letter to Sen. _____, United States Senate, Washington, DC 20510 or to the specific office.

Nixing faxing

Faxes are not the best way to communicate with members. Most staffers with whom I've discussed this method say that they're slow and expensive, and unless a member or staffer specifically requests that something be faxed, faxes are more trouble than they're worth. Congressional offices are bombarded with *broadcast faxes* — the same document faxed to hundreds if not thousands of recipients — from dozens of sources and frequently find them burdensome.

Meeting Face to Face

My favorite moment in any movie dealing with Washington is when the hero makes a phone call to a member of Congress and barks into the phone, "Let me speak to the senator!" After a second's pause, the hero continues, "Hello, Senator?" It cracks me up every time. No one ever gets a member of Congress on the first try, not even the president, although maybe he's been lucky from time to time.

A face-to-face meeting, *face-time* in Washington lingo, is something that needs to be set up with care. Sure, running into a representative or senator on the campaign trail or at a party and making your pitch is possible, but when you're trying to schedule a serious meeting, you need a little more time and planning.

A lobbying success story

One of the best examples of grass-roots lobbying is a case of the Memory Plaque Project.

John Keath Coder died in July 1992 of complications from exposure to Agent Orange while serving in the military in Vietnam. His sister, Ruth Coder Fitzgerald, thought a plaque on the Mall in Washington would be an appropriate honor for veterans who died from the effects and aftereffects of the war.

Fitzgerald wrote to government agencies like the National Park Service, the Vietnam Veterans Memorial Fund, and veterans groups, and after two years, found sufficient interest to incorporate an organization, start a Web page, and expand her letter writing to 40 members of Congress, the news media, and veterans groups that endorsed the project.

But Fitzgerald couldn't find any members of Congress willing to sponsor the plaque, and in August 1999, she grew discouraged and considered abandoning her efforts until a letter written by Fitzgerald's neighbor prompted someone to write to Rep. Elton Gallegly (R-Calif.), whose aide, Brian Clifford, discussed the project with Fitzgerald and convinced Gallegly to take up the cause.

Fitzgerald found her champion, and from there, Gallegly introduced H.R. 3293 on November 10, the eve of Veterans Day, and quickly rounded up 104 cosponsors. The proposal received significant media attention and reached the floor of the House on May 9, 2000, with 290 cosponsors and passed by a unanimous vote. Sen. Ben Nighthorse Campbell (R-Colo.) introduced his own version of the bill (S. 1921), and more veterans' organizations endorsed the idea. There, it passed by unanimous consent.

On June 15, 2000, President Bill Clinton signed Public Law 106-214, and the memorial plaque became a reality.

Making an appointment

Having a mutual friend introduce you to the member or speak to the member on your behalf always are good ideas. But when you don't know the member and he doesn't know you, and neither of you has met under any circumstances, paving the way with written communications is best. An e-mail or letter can serve as an icebreaker, so that the member and the member's staff have at least some familiarity with you and your issue. (The preceding "Writing Your Representative" section gives tips on making the initial contact.)

After you break the ice, you can ask for an appointment either in writing or by telephone, using the following techniques:

✔ If you write an e-mail or letter to set up an appointment, explain that you want to have a face-to-face meeting and what you want to discuss at that time. Whenever possible, provide a range of dates when you'd like to meet, noting when you'll be in Washington or when you'd like to visit with the member at a district office. Remember that you don't have to see him in Washington and that meeting the member in the home district or state sometimes is more effective.

✔ If you call the member's office on the telephone, you'll probably reach a staff member. Tell the staffer:

- Who you are (if you're a constituent, be sure to mention that fact)

- What you want to discuss

- How long you expect your discussion to take

- When you'd like to meet

- Where you'd like to meet

- Why a face-to-face meeting is necessary

If you've already communicated with the office in person, by e-mail, or by mail, refer to your previous correspondence.

You'll likely get an appointment, but you have to be flexible, given the complexity of the member's schedule. If you're in Washington for only a few days, the member may not be able to accommodate your schedule. Be patient and keep trying to schedule a meeting in the state or district office or on another occasion in Washington. The member has to serve constituents so sooner or later you should get your appointment.

If the member is not available, you may be able to see a staffer. Don't be offended or put off because you're not seeing the member. Seeing a staffer, no matter where he is in the office hierarchy, is an opportunity for you to lobby on behalf of your cause. Having the right staffer on your side can be the key to a successful lobbying campaign. In fact, staffers are so important that I wrote a separate chapter on them — see Chapter 13.

In all your discussions, be sure to be courteous and reasonable. No matter how obstructive or dense they may seem, screaming at staffers, insulting members, and getting angry or argumentative won't advance your cause.

By the same token, don't allow a member to browbeat or intimidate you. You know what you're pursuing and you know why. A member may challenge you or ask what may seem like hostile questions, but you always need to be respectful but firm and ready to handle skepticism or opposition.

When lobbying, especially on a particularly emotional issue, people often falsely assume that the righteousness of their cause clearly shines through and will carry the day. Remember that lawmakers constantly deal with people who think their causes are as just and compelling as you know your cause is. Members have to balance a number of often conflicting factors in making their decisions, weighing what they believe is the right thing to do with what's best for the country, what's best for their constituents, what's politically expedient, what's best for groups and individuals to whom they're beholden, and with what their political party and leadership demands that they do — not necessarily in that order. Losing objectivity and being unable to appreciate the points of your opponents or uncommitted people is easy when you're an advocate, but losing your perspective makes you a less effective advocate.

Making the most of face-time

Regardless of whether it's debates, chores, answering mail, or just going to the bathroom, time drives all things on Capitol Hill. What does this mean to you as a lobbyist? It means that you have to be time conscious also.

Members are torn by many demands, and you don't want to add to their burdens. They will try to accommodate you, especially when you're a constituent, but you have to do your part. Every second is precious, so adhere to two guidelines to make the face-time that you have with the member count for as much as possible.

- Show up a little early for your appointment.
- Get down to business quickly: A few minutes of small talk to get started is fine, but remember that the member may be called away at any moment, so make your main points early in the meeting.

Although you're expected to be punctual, members often are delayed, have to beg off, or are called away to vote. Don't be offended; this is just the nature of doing business in Congress. If your meeting is disrupted for some reason, make another appointment if you can.

Many people assume that members are high and mighty beings, existing way above the normal realm of people like you and me, but they're not. They have a great many responsibilities, and they're always in the public eye, and they're pretty unusual in the sense that they're extremely friendly and more articulate than many of us. The point is that lawmakers are approachable and can be talked to like human beings rather than gods. Indeed, if they're expecting to be reelected, they better be extremely approachable and, out of necessity, must be on hand at state fairs, Rotary International breakfasts, high school commencements, and anywhere else people gather. All you have to do is be in the same place at the same time as the member.

Following up

Events, appointments, letters, and e-mails all are well and good, but unless you continue the process and implant yourself and your cause in the member's mind, you won't accomplish anything.

The work that you do after every event, every encounter, and every discussion with a lawmaker is called *follow-up*, and it's extremely important. If you're invited to a dinner or a party by a lawmaker, send a thank-you note after the event, or a sincere regrets letter if you can't make it for some reason. Meetings with lawmakers need to be followed up with a note, or a letter, or a memo summarizing what was said and a thanks for taking the time to meet. Following up with the staff members you're dealing with doesn't hurt, either.

Remember what you're doing: The lawmaker and his staff are dealing with numerous issues, a multitude of constituents, and conflicting demands. You need to be noticed, and your concerns need to be addressed. Getting that done takes persistence.

One tale circulates around Washington that former President George H. Bush had always written thank-you notes throughout his life (probably still does). The tale concludes that his diligence is responsible for his career in government and is what got him elected president. Maybe it's true and maybe it isn't — but it certainly is a good example of follow-up.

Conveying Your Cause

Your lobbying will be most effective if you're well informed about your topic, when you discuss your issue calmly and dispassionately, and when you remain open to other ideas and even arguments against your beliefs.

Quality information has no substitute. Follow as many sources of information about your area of interest as possible. Read about it in newspapers, in magazines, and on the Internet. Know your subject area thoroughly. Remember that people in Congress have a constant hunger for information but are bombarded with it from all sides.

Lobbying days

Many organizations sponsor conventions in Washington or send organization members to what are called *lobbying days.* These are days when members of a particular organization fan out through Congress, lobbying on issues that are important to the organization.

Lobbying days can be great fun and they can relieve you of much of the work involved in setting up individual appointments. The organization usually sets up appointments for you and matches you with your representative and senators. The members, for their part, know that they'll be meeting many of their constituents, so they set aside time for the meetings.

In addition, many organizations also set up briefings, receptions, and dinners where you can socialize with your senators and representatives and hear them speak on your issue.

However, even when you're meeting with a member in a group on a lobbying day, the same rules apply for this meeting that apply for a meeting that you set up yourself. The organization's lobbyists need to inform you about their lobbying goals (the issues pro and con), the bills, and bill numbers that you're there to push for or against. Even so, you need to read up on those issues so that you're ready to discuss them from the moment you walk into the members' offices. Your can make your presentation much more effective by relating the issue to your personal life and providing unique examples and anecdotes.

When it comes to Congress, repetition is no sin. You must explain your cause in exactly the same terms to what may ultimately amount to hundreds of people, and yet each of them expects — unrealistically — your explanation to be unique and exclusive. Politicians face this predicament all the time. They give exactly the same speeches again and again, and each repetition must be delivered with the same vigor and enthusiasm as the first. However, if you believe in what you're doing, the knowledge that you're advancing your cause just a bit further with each recitation makes dealing with this plight more palatable.

When you're lobbying on a specific measure be sure that you know exactly what it is. That means knowing the name of the bill, its sponsors, and its number. Members keep track of legislation that way, so if you want to have a substantive discussion, be sure you know precisely what you're talking about.

Taking a Walk on the Dark Side: Going Negative

Although I believe in a positive but persistent approach over a long period of time and regard every relationship as a potentially long-term one, only in extreme cases do I burn bridges. My personal belief is that it's better to be noticed and remembered in a positive way by a lawmaker; however, some people think that the only way to be noticed by their representative or senator is being so obnoxious and annoying that the member or his staff deal with the issue just to get rid of it. That is certainly an approach, but not a good one, especially if you are embarking on a long-term effort.

That said, sometimes being nice and polite just doesn't get you anywhere. For example, when a member advocates a platform that runs counter to your beliefs and refuses to help you under any circumstances, you may decide that using a negative approach is your only option.

You can apply negative pressure on a member by:

- Endorsing, supporting, or raising money for the member's opponent
- Mobilizing other lobbies or special interest groups against him
- Joining or contributing to coalitions opposed to him or what he stands for
- Approaching local or national media with your complaints against him
- Taking out ads opposing him

Try not to make threats, but if you must, make sure you can back them up because, likely as not, bluffs will be called.

One lobby had a problem with a member of the House who consistently thwarted its aims. The lobby searched the member's district to find a candidate from the same party to oppose the member, convinced this individual to run against the member in a primary election, and supported his candidacy. Opposition in the primary vastly weakened the member; he had to spend time, money, and effort defeating his opponent. After the member won the contested primary, the lobby switched sides and supported the member's opponent from the other party in the general election and successfully defeated him. Although professional lobbyists usually use this sophisticated approach, you can conduct a similar campaign on a smaller scale by supporting opponents of the lawmaker you oppose in primary and general elections.

Taking a negative approach makes it much harder — if not impossible — to deal with the member in the future. Although bridges sometimes can be rebuilt, once burned, most never are reconstructed.

Don't let the contest become personal, if you can help it. Working against a member is business, and should be kept on a business footing. Politicians expect opposition as part of the rough and tumble of politics (although many don't like it and some have surprisingly thin skins), but you can express opposition without attacking the member personally. And don't ever drag a member's family or friends into the fray.

Knowing precisely what you want and what constitutes *right* or *good* actions versus *wrong* or *bad* actions by a member is essential. This secret is arguably what fuels the two most effective lobbies in Washington: the American Israel Public Affairs Committee (AIPAC) and the National Rifle Association (NRA).

Although these lobbies have different agendas, they often get their way for these simple reasons:

- ✔ They know what they want.
- ✔ They help their friends and hurt their enemies.
- ✔ Everyone knows what they favor and what they oppose.

While the views of these lobbies may sometimes appear extreme, and their positions simplistic, this simple approach to lobbying is effective.

If you plan to imitate their approach:

- ✔ Know what you want.
- ✔ Know what you want the member to do and make sure the member knows what it is, too.
- ✔ Have a simple test for determining whether the member's doing what you want and let the member know that you're monitoring his or her actions.

Informing a member that you disapprove of an action that he has taken (or plans to take) through e-mails or letters is not a bad thing; however, don't send the member only criticism. When a member does something that you think is right, let him know that too. You want the member and staff never to be entirely sure whether a message from you is praise or condemnation — you just want them to open the message.

Giving Gifts, Travel, and Entertainment

Gift-giving, wining, dining, and travel have been used for currying favor throughout history, and these amenities certainly are no strangers to Congress.

However, so much abuse has occurred through the years and so many ethical issues have been raised by gifts from lobbyists and constituents that Congress has developed an elaborate set of rules and restrictions covering gift-giving, travel, and entertainment. In the House, gift-giving and travel are regulated by the Committee on Official Standards of Conduct (also referred to as the Ethics

Committee). In the Senate, the Rules Committee handles rules on gifts. Check out these Web sites to find out more about gift-giving and the Congress:

- The House rules on gifts and travel can be accessed on the Web at `www.house.gov/ethics/Gifts_and_Travel_Chapter.htm`.
- "Highlights of House Ethics Rules" are available at `www.house.gov/ethics/Highlights2002.htm`.
- Senate gift rules are available at `http://rules.senate.gov/senaterules/rule35.htm`.

Although not identical, in their most important aspects, the House and Senate rules essentially are the same.

In a nutshell, both chambers simply prohibit all gifts — any gifts that can be accepted are actually exceptions to the rules.

As a lobbyist, you must exercise extreme care when offering gifts. A member is absolutely prohibited from soliciting a gift, and a member or staffer accepting a gift in exchange for a particular action is illegal. (That's bribery, folks.)

Having said that, gifts nevertheless are a way of life on Capitol Hill and many people want to give gifts to their friends in Congress or provide tokens of their esteem. Plaques, baseball hats, or T-shirts are customary ways to help members remember your organization or cause. Plaques are especially good because members love to decorate their offices with them.

Surprise gifts may be well and good for your friends and acquaintances, but they can mean big problems on the Hill. When you want to give a gift, call the member's office first and make sure that doing so is okay with the member. That way you won't embarrass the member, who might otherwise have to turn down the gift. Likewise, you'll save yourself the expense of an item that might have to be junked.

Don't think of giving a gift in Congress as the intimate act that it is at home: Giving gifts in Congress is a stylized ritual with a specific political purpose that is governed by strict laws. Similarly, whenever you want to have a meal with a member, be aware that the member has to pay for any one-on-one meal. Travel also is restricted.

Gift-giving guidelines

Acceptable gifts that fall under the exceptions are judged by their monetary value.

Members can accept gifts that are

- ✔ Worth less than $50 (plaques, hats, pens, and T-shirts are good examples).

- ✔ From relatives, other members, and employees.

- ✔ From personal friends. However, when the gift is worth more than $250, the House Committee on Official Standards must rule on its permissibility.

- ✔ From foreign governments, provided they're not worth more than $260.

Members cannot accept:

- ✔ Gifts worth more than $50.

- ✔ More than $100 worth of gifts from a single source in a calendar year. Gifts valued at less than $10 don't count toward that total; however, members aren't permitted to engage in *buydowns* — a practice by which the member pays only a fraction of the value for a gift. For example, the member pays $6 but gets a gift worth $55.

Perishable gifts like fruit, pastry, flowers, or plants are subject to the same rules as all other gifts. When you send an office a Christmas fruit basket worth more than $50, the staff has to either donate it to charity or dump it.

Travel

A member can accept necessary food, transportation, and lodging from a private sponsor whenever the member is traveling to a meeting, speaking engagement, or a fact-finding event in connection with his official duties.

However, the number of days that members can receive such hospitality is limited by the following factors:

- ✔ If the travel is domestic, the member can receive four days worth of hospitality.
- ✔ If the travel is foreign, the member can receive seven days worth of hospitality.

The member must approve all staff travel in advance in writing.

Entertainment

Food not only powers our bodies, it's also the fuel of politics. But, you guessed it; a legacy of lavish dining has led to myriad rules governing the kinds of dining that members and staff can and cannot accept.

A member can

- ✔ Accept the hospitality of a private home — unless the host is a registered lobbyist.
- ✔ Attend charity, political, or official duty-related events when they're *widely attended* (in other words, no intimate little high-priced get-togethers or personal movie screenings). Some degree of public participation must occur.
- ✔ Attend receptions.
- ✔ Attend any events paid for by federal, state, or local governments.

Unless he pays the market value, a member cannot

- ✔ Accept a one-on-one meal.
- ✔ Accept such freebies as a round of golf or hunting or fishing trips.

Staff also cannot accept meals. For example, an association is not allowed to buy pizzas for congressional staff members when they're working late. The staffers must reimburse the association.

Keeping the Pressure On

Nothing ever comes easily in life and certainly nothing ever comes easily in Congress. If you're serious about your cause and your mission, you must remain attentive and active throughout the legislative process, testifying, pushing, arguing, and lobbying in favor of your cause. At no point can you afford to sit back and allow events take their course, otherwise members will lose interest in your cause and your opponents will rally and kill your legislation.

Having said that, there are certain pressure points where your intervention as an individual citizen can make the most difference. You can contact your senators and representatives at any time, but letters, phone calls, and personal contacts at key moments have greater impact. Figure 12-1 shows the key points where you can have the greatest impact.

Your input can make the greatest difference at the very beginning of the process when ideas for new legislation are taking shape and the Dear Colleague is being written and then circulated. When the Dear Colleague is issued, lobby members to sign it and to sign on to the legislation as sponsors. All this work needs to be done even before the legislation is introduced.

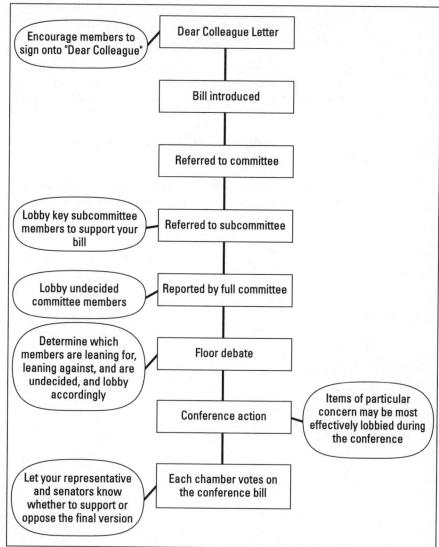

Figure 12-1:
Key lobbying points in the legislative process.

When the legislation is introduced, you can be most effective by lobbying members to sign on as co-sponsors. (See Chapter 5 for the differences between a sponsor and a co-sponsor.) The numbers of co-sponsors show the support for the legislation and can intimidate potential opposition, smoothing its way to passage.

During the committee process, lobby members of the committee or subcommittee to report the bill out favorably. If any committee members raise objections, speak to them and see if you can overcome their objections.

Assuming the bill is reported out of committee favorably, you then have to keep track of amendments and potential amendments. By this time you won't have much impact in shaping the text of the bill — that was largely done in committee — but you need to track the amendments and their impact.

When you have an acceptable bill that reaches the floor, you need to lobby members to vote for it.

When the bill goes to conference you need to lobby the House and Senate conferees to keep it intact and stick to the intent of the legislation.

Chapter 13

Getting the Job Done: Congressional Staff

In This Chapter

▶ Understanding the role of congressional staff

▶ Meeting the different types of staff

▶ Piecing together the structure of congressional offices

▶ Receiving support from other institutions

Staffing is extremely important on Capitol Hill. Members ultimately must cast the votes, bear responsibility for their decisions, and run for reelection, but when it comes to the day-to-day business of government, the huge corps of assistants and experts that inhabit the Capitol campus are the ones who shape legislation and policy, negotiate with all the interested parties, keep the members informed, recommend courses of action, and simply keep government running.

When lobbying for your cause, you'll be dealing extensively with staff members. They're the first people you'll talk to when you want an appointment, and they'll handle your bill as it makes its way through the legislative process. Their recommendations are crucial and can make or break your cause at any point during the process.

Making Contact

REMEMBER

There's no such thing as an unimportant person — whether member or staff — in a congressional office!

When you enter a member's office, you don't know whether the intern, the secretary, the legislative correspondent, or the administrative assistant will be the one to say the word that determines whether the member supports or opposes your bill. So, you can't afford to alienate anyone.

Gatekeepers, or people who provide you with access to the person you need to see, are crucial personnel. In a congressional office, like most offices, key gatekeepers are receptionists and personal secretaries. Be sure to treat these people with special care.

Your first contacts are likely be with staff rather than directly with the member, which is a good thing, because it helps you refine your argument and hone your presentation before you actually meet with the representative or senator. Furthermore, staff questions can reveal the member's likely concerns (or even demeanor) when you discuss your issue directly.

Even members sometimes become exasperated with the growth of staff, as Senator Alan Simpson (R-Wyo. 1979–97) revealed in 1988:

> . . . *(T)he point is we are elected senators and we should try to do our business, occasionally, with ourselves and among ourselves and between ourselves. Even though the staff is critically important, it is also a critical burden upon us in many situations. . . . You cannot live with them and you cannot live without them.*

Surveying Congressional Staff

As you gain experience working with Congress, you must know the basic structures of congressional staffing to be effective in dealing with them.

The types of congressional staff and how they function are:

- **Personal staff** (also known as office or members' staff) works directly for individual representatives and senators. You're most likely to work with personal staffers when you contact your representative or senator.

- **Committee staff** works directly for committees. Committee staffers usually are experts in particular fields of government, although individuals can serve, or be shared, with personal staffs.

- **Leadership staff** works for the leaders of the House and Senate, the majority leaders, whips, and conference and caucus chairmen.

- **Officer staff** works for institutional offices such as the Clerk of the House, the Secretary of the Senate, the sergeants-at-arms, and other congressional officers. These staffers work for Congress as a whole.

> ✔ **Support staff** works for Congress's supporting institutions, known as the *arms* of Congress — the General Accounting Office, the Library of Congress, the Architect of the Capitol, and the Congressional Research Service. It's doubtful that you'll ever have any direct contact with any of these people when you do your lobbying.

Personal staff

A member's personal staff is comprised of some of the first people you'll encounter when you begin lobbying for your cause, contacting a member, or seeking congressional services.

The average representative has 14 staff members, eight in Washington and six in the district. The average Senate office has 34 staff members, 22 in Washington and 12 in the state.

Staff positions

Members have considerable latitude in setting up their offices the way they want. Nonetheless, although titles of the people in congressional offices vary from office to office, the roles they play are common throughout the House and Senate. The roles and how they function include

---

A brief history of staffing in Congress

Congressional staffing began when John Beckley was elected Clerk of the House on April 1, 1789. Throughout the nineteenth century congressional staffs remained extremely small, at most one clerk to a member, and many members didn't even have that. Members' children sometimes served as unpaid clerks. That began to change in the 1890s, but not until the 1930s did members begin thinking that they needed larger staffs to keep pace with the growth of the executive branch. Congressional staffing was reorganized in 1946, but it didn't reach its current levels until 1970. Since then, staff growth has slowed and, in some cases, even declined.

Decrying the growth of congressional staff and government in general is fashionable. Historians and government critics are fond of comparing the one- or two-person staffs of the past with the roughly 17,000 staff members on Capitol Hill today (as of May 2001 that came to 6,464 Senate staff members and 10,660 House staff members). However, the comparison is utter nonsense. Today, the country has 280 million inhabitants and is a world power. Similarly, Congress is doing an immensely complex job at a tremendously fast pace. Of course congressional staff is going to expand!

- **Administrative assistant (AA) or chief of staff (CoS):** The AA runs the office — often hiring everyone else — and makes sure things get done. The AA serves as the member's alter ego, viewing events through the member's eyes, anticipating her needs, seeing potential pitfalls, and analyzing the political implications of different courses of action. One of the AA's top priorities is providing a smoothly functioning office. This position is extremely sensitive and usually given to someone with experience in politics and management on Capitol Hill.

- **Legislative assistant (LA):** This person analyzes legislation and its implications and recommends to the member whether to support or oppose it. The LA must share ideological interests with the member and understand the needs and demands of the member's constituents, district, and state. Members usually work with several LAs, whose responsibilities usually mirror the member's committee assignments; however, issues may be divided up any number of ways.

- **Legislative director (LD), also known as senior legislative assistant or legislative coordinator:** When an office deploys several LAs, an LD coordinates and directs their work.

- **Press secretary or communications director:** This person handles media relations but often serves in a great many other capacities. The press secretary is in charge of the member's relations with the media at large, writing press releases announcing the member's actions and ensuring that they're distributed, and penning speeches for the member to deliver on the floor of the chamber or at meetings back home. The press secretary also is in charge of staying in touch with constituents through newsletters that the member periodically sends out to the state or district and monitoring media coverage of the member at the state, district, and national levels.

- **Appointment secretary or scheduler:** This person is in charge of scheduling the member's activities, and given the number of demands placed on members, it can be a full-time job. In some offices, however, this task may fall upon the AA or the member's personal secretary. Scheduling includes the member's attendance at congressional hearings, press conferences, media interviews, lunches, dinners, rallies, speeches, town meetings, ribbon-cuttings, factory tours, and meetings with constituents. When you arrange a meeting with a member, the scheduler tells you when and for how long. The scheduler does more than merely fill in blank pages in an appointment book. The scheduler must also be politically sensitive to the relative importance of the events in the schedule and diplomatically able to turn people away who make unwarranted demands on the member's time.

The scheduler types up the member's daily schedule on a little card. You often see busy members consulting these cards trying to figure out where to go next.

✔ **Personal assistant, secretary, or executive secretary:** This person handles the member's clerical needs, working closely with the member. The person in this role often is someone who has been with the member for a long time and may have a great deal of influence on the member's thinking.

✔ **Caseworker or constituent services representative:** This person handles the needs and concerns of individual constituents. Caseworkers are often active in the Washington and district offices.

✔ **Legislative correspondent:** This person answers correspondence that comes into the office, either on paper or electronically, although other staffers often pitch in with correspondence.

✔ **Office manager:** This person handles office functions, but without the level of political insight provided by the AA.

✔ **Systems administrator:** This person is responsible for office technology, network administration, and correspondence (digital and paper).

✔ **District director:** This person is in charge of all activities outside Washington, D.C.

✔ **Field representative:** This person represents the member in the district to constituents and helps with casework or other chores when the member isn't able to be present.

✔ **Receptionist or staff assistant:** This position is much more important than the title suggests. The receptionist is the first contact that many constituents, other members, and executive branch officials have with the member's office.

Staff principles

Whatever their precise title or function, staff are driven by several overall, guiding principles, which include:

✔ **Getting the member reelected:** That means doing everything that helps the member with constituents. However, congressional staff members are strictly prohibited from conducting outright campaign work on congressional premises.

✔ **Protecting the member:** Staff members need to shield the member from embarrassment, pitfalls, public gaffes, critics, bad decisions, hostile media, political opponents, and her own stupid comments or self-destructive behavior.

✔ **Promoting the member:** Staff members, especially the press secretary, do everything they can to promote the member's agenda and obtain favorable publicity in the home state, the district, and in Congress.

> ✔ **Staying behind the scenes:** As important as staffers are to the overall legislative process, the member always needs to be the one in the limelight. Whenever a staff member gets publicity, it's usually for the wrong reasons.

Office structure

Every office is organized differently, based upon the preferences of the congressional member. Knowing how the office is structured and how authority is distributed can help you as you work with the member. It tells you how authority flows and whether the right staff member is attending to your needs.

The vast majority of congressional offices, 64 percent of House offices and 83 percent of Senate offices, are centrally structured, as shown in Figure 13-1, with authority administered in a straight line from the member to the AA and downward. That means the member doesn't involve himself in the lower-level activities but relies principally on his AA and LA to run the administrative and legislative affairs of the Washington and district offices and report developments to her.

Applying for a staff position

Think you have what it takes to work for Congress? Applying for a staff job with Congress is easy. You can do it either by mail, online, or in person.

You can apply by mail by sending your resume and a cover letter to the representative or senator of your choice.

To apply by phone:

✔ Dial the House of Representatives Job Line at 202-225-2450; press option 4, and then press option 2.

✔ Dial the Senate Job Line (which is recording of Senate Employment Bulletin) at 202-228-5627.

To apply online:

✔ Go to the House Web site: www.house. gov.

✔ Click on "Employment Opportunities" link.

✔ At the employment site you can post your resume and see what vacancies are open.

The Senate does not have a comparable online employment page.

To apply in person:

✔ Human Resources Vacancy Announcement Books are available at 263 Cannon House Office Building.

✔ The Senate Placement Office is in Room SH-142 of the Hart Senate Office Building, phone 202-224-9167.

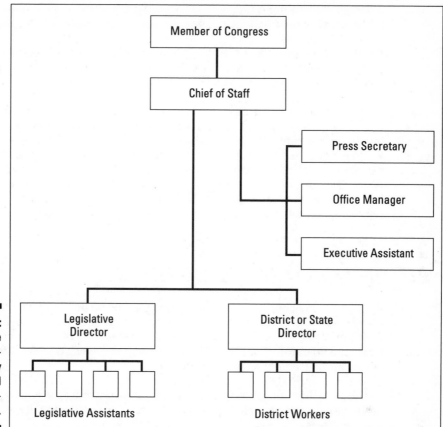

Figure 13-1:
An example
of the typi-
cal, centrally
structured
congres-
sional office.

Other office arrangements are used: Members can put equal emphasis on their Washington and district offices, or they can get very involved in every office function and essentially have everyone in the office reporting directly to them — but these arrangements are so inefficient that they're far less often used.

When you're lobbying an office, assuming that the titles reflect the functions of the office staff is best. True of any office, variations may be evident. For example, a personal secretary may have more clout with a member than the official AA. Nevertheless, assuming that what you see is what you get is best . . . just don't step on any toes in the process.

When you're discussing a piece of legislation, you'll more than likely deal with the LA. The LA is interested in details and policy implications of the legislation, and you need to tailor your discussions accordingly. When you win over the LA, the LA may introduce you to the AA or lobby the AA or member on your behalf.

When you talk to the AA, you'll have to explain political implications for the member, especially if he champions your cause or signs onto your bill.

You may develop a good relationship with a staff member only to be distressed to find that person moving on to a different office. Get used to it — many staff members move from one office to another on Capitol Hill.

Staff turnover can be as high as 50 percent during the first six months of a freshman representative's term. That's because freshman members usually hire friends or campaign workers or return political favors with appointments and don't realize the big difference between running a campaign and running a congressional office. Many of these initial hires find that they don't like Washington or that they're a poor fit for the job they have and move on. Later on, the staff stabilizes, but the first six months of a freshman representative's term are a bad time for getting anything done.

Getting Down to Personalities

Walk into many congressional offices and you're startled by the fact that many staffers, especially on the House side, are young and have been hired right out of college. Many tend to be former presidents of student councils, campaign volunteers, or idealists, all with a strong sense of commitment who want to use politics to do good works.

Unlike many first jobs, however, these people are running the country. They're given enormous responsibility, and they must learn on the job. It's exhilarating and yet stressful.

You may find yourself explaining a piece of legislation that can make or break your company or community to someone who looks like he's 12 years old and who has no experience of the world. Don't ever condescend or become impatient; no one in any office likes that and, besides, this person has the potential to wield considerable power.

On the other hand, you're also going to find older staffers who have more institutional memory than many members.

You want to be as helpful to as many members of the staff as you possibly can, and you must lobby staff just as much as you lobby members. Half your battle with a member may be won if you can win over the staff.

Many congressional staffers eventually run for office on their own. When you build a good relationship with the staff, you may be building a relationship with a future representative, senator, or governor.

And don't ever forget that regardless of the person's title, you never know how much clout that person has in the office.

Whenever you plan to be lobbying for a cause for a long time, you can try to place your friends and supporters in strategic staff positions, especially during the first days after an election. Many long-term, permanent lobbies work that way, acting as quasi personnel offices for key members important to their causes. You can do the same by making sure that your supporter applies for a job and thereafter sending a letter recommending that individual to the member's office. When that person is hired, you'll have a friend in a high place. This tactic is more effective between the election in November and the official January swearing-in, when the member is just putting together a staff, facing many demands, and not thinking too clearly about hiring. The time frame can, however, sometimes extend as far as March and beyond.

An entire culture of permanent staff people work on Capitol Hill. Many of these people have no relationship with a member's state or district but are capable and grasp local issues quickly. In fact, in some instances, staff people have never been to the districts their boss represents.

Acknowledging Committee Staff

The staff that serves congressional committees tends to be older, more experienced than the personal staff, and is comprised of people who thoroughly know issues that come before the committees. Many have served through numerous congresses and began their careers working on a member's personal staff, so they know the personal and committee sides of the institution.

Each committee staff is divvied up by political party; the majority party has more staff members. The number of staff and the types of positions vary widely from committee to committee. Additionally, staff people are assigned to different subcommittees.

Committee staffers serve more masters than do members of personal staffs. Although they directly serve the chairman or ranking member, they also serve all the members of their respective parties who serve on the committee, so they must tread diplomatically among many different bosses with different political priorities and policy agendas. Staff members usually are hired — or at least approved — by the committee chairman or the ranking member and serve the majority or minority party.

Committee staff titles differ slightly from personal staff titles.

- **Staff director:** This person directs the committee staff and runs the office.

- **Communications director:** This person handles media and publicity for the committee and often coordinates communications among the members.

- **Professional staff member:** These people do the work of the committee, but the "professional" in the name is important. Although they serve politicians of different parties, committee staff members tend to stay on the committee through numerous congresses and changes in power. They take pride in their professionalism, viewing their roles as providing objective, unbiased analysis. They usually know well the subject matter of the committee and are experts in their fields.

- **Counsel:** These lawyers serve the committee from the different parties and analyze the legal implications of legislation.

- **Legislative assistant:** This person handles legislation being considered by the committee, helping to draft, analyze, and revise it.

In addition, these positions have their own assistants and deputies (deputy staff director, deputy communications director, assistant counsel, and so on), and you'll see *majority* or *minority* in front of some titles (for example, majority counsel or minority counsel), which indicates whether they serve the party in power or the minority party.

Committee staff

You'll start dealing with committee and subcommittee staff members after your bill has been introduced and referred to the appropriate committees.

After a referral is made, you'll want to find out who on the committee staff is handling your issue. You can do this by simply calling the committee and asking around until you find the right person. Be sure to provide the bill name and number when you call.

When you find the right person, follow up with a letter introducing yourself and your issue and offering to provide the committee staff any assistance it may need, for example, additional information, names of experts in the subject area, or supporting documentation like books or articles. Whenever you don't know the particular staff member handling the issue send the letter to the committee staff director. That way the director can pass the letter onto the appropriate staffer. If the issue ever is handed off to a different staffer, your letter can then be handed off too.

After you make initial contact with staff, you probably ought to back off, because bothering the committee staff or being overly persistent only alienates them. Let them do their jobs and get in touch with you.

When you're lobbying with a group or organization, send the committee staff people who really know the issue, who deal with the substance. Frequently, lobbyists work in teams: One person who may know members well opens the doors, but that person may not be as familiar with the substance of the issue as someone who really is the expert on the issue but doesn't work Capitol Hill. When it comes to dealing with the committee, don't ever bring the door opener. Committee staffers want to deal only with experts.

Leadership staff

Leadership staff serves the leadership of the House and Senate and the party organizations. Their titles are much the same as the committee staff, but almost all their work is done at the direction of the highest-ranking congressional officials like the Speaker of the House or the Senate Majority Leader and relates mainly to the rank and file members.

Finding key staff

Three guides can help you locate staff and other essential numbers for Congress. These guides are

✔ **The Congressional Staff Directory,** is published three times per year by Congressional Quarterly (CQ) Press, Washington, D.C., and contains 1,500 pages of names, phone numbers, and other information about all members and staff, including member and staff bios. An annual subscription costs $329; a single copy costs $209. Subscriptions can be obtained by calling 800-638-1710 or going to the CQ Web site at www.cqpress.com.

✔ **The Congressional Yellow Book,** is published by Leadership Directories, Inc., in New York and Washington. It contains 1,200 pages of the names, phone numbers, and other information about members and

staff and is published four times per year. An annual subscription is $340, with each additional subscription priced at $226. It can be ordered by phone at 212-627-4140 in New York, or 202-347-7757 in Washington, D.C., or online at www.leadershipdirectories.com.

✔ **The Almanac of the Unelected,** is published annually by Bernan Press, Lanham, Md. This book profiles 500 staffers and analyzes their impact on legislation. The roughly 600-page hardcover book is listed at $275 and can be ordered online at www.bernan.com or by phone at 800-416-4374.

All three companies publish a variety of other directories and books that cover other branches of government. The *Congressional Staff Directory* and the *Congressional Yellow Book* feature Web-based updates.

The work of the leadership staff tends to be internal to the Congress and you're not likely to have much interaction with them. However, if you can persuade a leadership staff member to your point of view, you'll have a powerful ally.

Leadership work is mostly political: Many of these staffers serve the party whips who maintain party discipline. (See Chapter 5 on congressional officers.)

Leadership staffers are well informed, knowledgeable about what's happening in each chamber. Their jobs require them to know the strengths, weaknesses, and desires of each member, and they have an institutional overview that personal or committee staff members often lack.

Perhaps the most famous leadership staffer to date was George Stephanopoulus who served Rep. Richard Gephardt (D-Mo.) when Gephardt was House majority leader. Stephanopoulus became a campaign operative for a then obscure Arkansas governor named Bill Clinton.

Recognizing Auxiliary Support Staff

In addition to the basic elements of Congress involving representation and legislation, Congress relies on the services of ancillary and supporting institutions like the ones I describe in this section. Each has its own staff. These support services are not necessarily political, but they play important roles in the way Congress functions. Each hires its own staff, rather than going through members. Although your chance of ever lobbying these people is doubtful, you may, nevertheless, encounter them as you pursue your cause.

Congressional Budget Office

Congress created the Congressional Budget Office (CBO) in 1974 to "provide the Congress with the objective, timely, nonpartisan analyses needed for economic and budget decisions and with the information and estimates required for the Congressional budget process."

The duties of the CBO are

- Helping Congress plan the national budget
- Analyzing and forecasting the economy
- Analyzing the economic impact of the president's annual budget proposal

  ✔ Looking at long-term budget pressures

  ✔ Helping Congress stay within its own national budget

  ✔ Analyzing the budget impact of legislation and government programs

  ✔ Helping Congress consider economic and budgetary issues

The CBO primarily answers to the House and Senate budget committees, followed by the appropriations committees, the House Ways and Means Committee, the Senate Finance Committee, and then the rest of the congressional committees. The CBO is professional, independent, and nonpartisan. Seventy percent of its staff consists of economists with advanced degrees. The CBO doesn't formulate policy or practice party politics. CBO economic projections often are controversial because they can be at odds with presidential analyses — or desires.

Given their lofty reputation, cherished integrity, and objectivity, CBO reports are widely considered economically authoritative and carry great weight during policy debates. A CBO analysis finding that proposed legislation will have a negative budgetary impact can be a crippling blow to the legislation and therefore can require additional work to address the economic concerns that CBO raises.

The CBO Web site can be accessed at www.CBO.gov.

General Accounting Office

The General Accounting Office (GAO) is the investigative arm of Congress. Because Congress raises taxes and appropriates public funds, the GAO's core mission is financial: finding out how taxpayer money is being spent and trying to make those expenditures more efficient and less wasteful.

The GAO was founded in 1921 to reorganize government finances after World War I. It has grown in the years since. By 2000, the GAO had 3,275 employees — actually down from its all-time high of 15,000 in 1945 when it reviewed every government voucher. Today it concentrates on broad management and financial issues.

However, the GAO's activities go well beyond those of financial audits. It also:

  ✔ Evaluates federal programs and activities

  ✔ Provides analyses, options, and recommendations to Congress

  ✔ Investigates allegations of wrongdoing

  ✔ Issues legal decisions and opinions

The GAO is independent and nonpartisan. Any congressional member can order a GAO audit of any subject, and GAO auditors have done some extraordinary work, parachuting into war zones (see the "Jumping to push a pencil" sidebar nearby), uncovering a variety of nefarious dealings, and making recommendations that have saved the government billions of dollars.

When an audit of government spending is completed, a GAO analysis is provided to the member who commissioned it. The member, in turn, is then free to make it public. GAO audits can be powerful ammunition for different sides in a controversy, and they're often extensively covered in the media.

In the past, the GAO faced charges that its audits were politicized or that members crafted the GAO audits to produce specific results, but the GAO itself fiercely defends its independence and objectivity.

The GAO reports can also expose situations or problems that may call for legislation or changes in legislation. Because GAO audits are congressional products, with government resources and the power of Congress behind them, they usually are treated as authoritative pronouncements on given subjects.

Although it can't be lobbied directly, whenever the GAO is looking into a situation or issue that affects your cause, you can provide background information to GAO auditors. Your representative or senator should be able to tell you whether an audit has been commissioned and provide the means of getting in touch with the GAO. And, whenever a situation needs to be brought to light, you can talk to your representative, senator, or congressional champion about commissioning a GAO audit. If the results are favorable, they can be powerful lobbying tools to back up your arguments. But of course, you always run the risk that the audit will be unfavorable, and the resulting publicity and ammunition in the hands of your opponents can be devastating.

Jumping to push a pencil

One of the great, untold GAO stories is that accountants from the General Accounting Office actually parachuted into El Salvador and Honduras in the 1980s to ensure that funds Congress had prohibited from being spent on the Nicaraguan Contras weren't spent illegally against Congress's wishes.

There was no other way to get to the camps where the contras were training and, yes, the accountants would parachute in and check the books! Discrepancies ultimately led to the Contra-gate of the mid-1980s.

When researching for your lobbying campaign, be sure to check with the GAO for useful audits and reports. The GAO Web site can be accessed at www.gao.gov.

Library of Congress and the Congressional Research Service

Founded April 24, 1800, when President John Adams approved a $5,000 appropriation for "such books as may be necessary for the use of Congress," the Library of Congress (LOC) has grown into one of the world's greatest repositories of knowledge.

The LOC has four priorities:

- ✔ Making knowledge and creativity available to Congress so that it can knowledgeably legislate.

- ✔ Acquiring, organizing, preserving, securing, and sustaining a comprehensive record of American history and creativity and a universal record of human knowledge for the use of Congress and the nation.

- ✔ Making its collections as available as possible to Congress, the rest of the government, and the public.

- ✔ Adding interpretive and educational value to its resources.

Today the LOC is the largest library in the world, with, according to its own statistics, 120 million items on approximately 530 miles of bookshelves, including more than 18 million books, 2.5 million recordings, 12 million photographs, 4.5 million maps, and 54 million manuscripts. The world's oldest known example of printing (a Buddhist sutra from 770 A.D.) and a Gutenberg Bible are part of the storied collection.

The LOC relies on enormous numbers of programs and staff to implement its mission. It maintains some of the world's greatest collections of books, recordings, and maps, assists numerous scholars with their work, and makes its records and collections available to the general public.

Within the LOC, the Congressional Research Service (CRS) serves as the public policy research arm of Congress. CRS researchers, who are experts in a wide variety of government-related areas, assist members with formulating legislation, and provide objective, nonpartisan information to them on a confidential basis.

CRS reports are for members only, but members sometimes make them available to the public, and they can be invaluable in researching and providing an understanding of public policy topics.

Unfortunately, finding CRS reports online requires some determined sleuthing, because the CRS doesn't post them in a single location. However, information about the CRS and its employment opportunities can be accessed at the CRS home page, www.loc.gov/crsinfo. For access to information about the Library of Congress in general, go to its home page at www.loc.gov.

Other support staff and services

In addition to the CBO, GAO, and LOC, Congress is supported by the following institutions:

- ✔ **Advisory Committee on the Records of Congress** — A committee headed by the Clerk of the House of Representatives that advises Congress on the handling of its records.

- ✔ **U.S. Capitol Preservation Commission** — A commission headed by the Speaker of the House and made up of House members, the commission deals with questions related to preserving the Capitol building.

- ✔ **Office of Compliance** — An office created in 1995 to ensure that labor laws applying to the rest of government also apply to congressional employees. Its Web site can be accessed at www.compliance.gov.

- ✔ **Government Printing Office** — The office in charge of printing all government documents, not only from Congress but also from the entire government. Its Web site can be accessed at www.gpo.gov.

- ✔ **Medicare Payment Advisory Commission** — A commission that advises Congress on Medicare issues. Its Web site can be accessed at www.medpac.gov.

- ✔ **Office of the Attending Physician** — The doctors and nurses who attend to congressional health matters including the healthfulness of congressional working conditions. This office played a major role during the anthrax attack in October 2001.

- ✔ **Office of Official Reporters** — The office provides reporters and transcribers for congressional hearings and proceedings.

✔ **Office of Senate Official Reporters of Debates** — The Senate's office for recording debates and proceedings.

✔ **Page Schools** — These schools are for congressional pages. For more about the page program, see Chapter 16.

✔ **Press Galleries** — These galleries serve members of the media who cover Congress, overseeing the credentialing of journalists and providing a place to work and access to the floor and hearings (see Chapter 14).

Chapter 14

Making the Most of the Media

. . . .

In This Chapter

▶ Defining the media-Congress relationship

▶ Developing your story

▶ Dealing with journalists

▶ Getting your message out

▶ Handling different kinds of media

▶ Using celebrities

▶ Organizing demonstrations

. . . .

*U*nder the Constitution, Congress legislates, the executive branch administrates, and the judiciary interprets, but without the media, how would anyone know whether any of it ever happened? The media often are called the fourth branch of government and serve as a critical element in how Congress functions.

Were it left to me to decide whether we should have a government without newspapers, or newspapers without a government, I should not hesitate a moment to prefer the latter.

— Thomas Jefferson, "Letter to Col. Edward Carrington," January 16, 1787

Understanding the Relationship between Congress and the Media

The relationship between Congress and the media is a complex one. It's like a marriage of strong-willed partners, with elements of seduction, charm, camaraderie, friendship, love, pride — and the not infrequent screaming, hair-pulling, all-stops-out fight. Sometimes it's contentious, sometimes it's adversarial, sometimes it's cozy — but it's always symbiotic.

Media are crucial in Congress for a variety of reasons, because they:

- ✔ Report to voters what Congress as a whole and its individual members are doing

- ✔ Influence the national agenda by determining the relative importance of different news events

- ✔ Focus attention on specific issues or legislation

- ✔ Reveal wrongdoing and bring to light abuses that require government action

- ✔ Mobilize forces for or against legislation or various government policies

- ✔ Interpret actions of political leaders to their political followers and the public as a whole

- ✔ Are a powerful means for members to communicate with constituents and vice versa

- ✔ Are the means by which political figures communicate with each other, especially across political divides

- ✔ Help Democrats communicate with Republicans, executive branch officials communicate with Congress, low-level officials communicate with their superiors, and opposing camps on different issues find common ground or, in a sense at least, talk to each other through the media

- ✔ Shape public perception of political figures, organizations, and movements, which makes implementing their political agendas easier or harder, depending on the circumstances

Discussing *the media* as a single body is inaccurate and unjust, because the media are composed of broad and diverse forms of communication, competing organizations and individuals, varying political agendas, wildly divergent degrees of skill and competence, and different levels of quality.

If Congress seems unruly and undisciplined, the media seem absolutely chaotic. Thanks to the Constitution's guarantee of freedom of the press and speech, no central government media authority or censorship exists. Anyone can be an editor, publisher, or reporter — and frequently is. As a result, the media are a wonderful, rough-and-tumble combination of marketplace, forum, and boxing ring, full of lights, color, and hoopla, where ideas and personalities choose sides against each other and, presumably, the best ideas and the most talented practitioners win. Yet for all disagreements government or Congress may have with the media, or the *press,* as the Constitution refers to it, media freedom and freedom of speech were considered so important that they were embodied in the very first amendment to the Constitution along with freedoms of religion and assembly and the right to petition government.

Finding reporters in the woodwork

Congressional relations with the media were contentious from the beginning. Only one newspaper regularly sent a reporter to the first congressional meetings. The reporter worked at a small table in the back of the House chamber. That reporter's attacks on Treasury Secretary Alexander Hamilton were so scathing that after Rep. Theodore Sedgwick (Federalist, 1789–1801) became Speaker in 1799, he ordered the table removed and the reporter kept out of the chamber. The resourceful reporter, undeterred, took his table upstairs and reported from the back of the gallery where Sedgwick couldn't see him. Infuriated by uninterrupted disparaging articles, Sedgwick discovered the deception and ordered the reporter out of the building.

The reporter then began relying on congressional sources and did such a good job that he was able to file full daily reports about balloting of the states in the hotly contested election of 1800, when the House elected Thomas Jefferson president. Sedgwick, despite his best efforts, never was able to shut down the reporter's sources.

Sadly, in those days reporters didn't use bylines, so I don't know the reporter's name. But the media's desire to know and Congress's desire to conceal haven't changed a bit since.

Congress shall make no law respecting an establishment of religion, or prohibiting the free exercise thereof; or abridging the freedom of speech, or of the press, or the right of the people peaceably to assemble, and to petition the Government for a redress of grievances.

— Article I, the Bill of Rights, United States Constitution

Getting Your Story Straight

As an advocate, you tend to concentrate on the substance of your issue and what you must do to implement what you want to do. Your head, without a doubt, is full of facts and figures about your cause.

But when it comes to dealing with the media, you must think in a different way. You have to think in terms of telling *stories*. Regardless of the medium, regardless of whether they're working on a two-year investigative report or writing two-minutes before their deadlines, all journalists look for good *stories*. Doing so is their stock in trade and what they pursue day after day.

One good story always trumps ten tons of statistics when you're trying to get your point across in the media.

As is true of any kind of story, from a child's fairy tale to the latest Hollywood blockbuster, good stories always have:

- ✔ A hero
- ✔ A villain
- ✔ A struggle or quest that the hero must encounter to achieve a goal
- ✔ Uncertainty and conflict
- ✔ Drama
- ✔ A buildup, climax, and conclusion

When you start your lobbying campaign, think about what you're trying to do and then put it into story form, incorporating these classic story elements. The hero doesn't have to be an individual, it can be an organization or a movement — or even a country or a people. Often the story sounds something like: You discovered a terrible abuse or wrong and set out to make it right. After overcoming terrible obstacles, you're bringing your plan for justice to Congress and counting on the members to address the situation.

You must tell your basic story again and again, and it may develop and change over time. But whenever you issue a press release, conduct a press conference, or put forward an argument to the media, try putting the facts and arguments of your issue within the terms and parameters of stories you're telling.

Some of America's more effective presidents are known for being great story-tellers. Abraham Lincoln was renowned for his constant stream of stories and homilies. Two presidents who best communicated through the modern media also are among the country's better storytellers. Franklin Delano Roosevelt used storytelling in an immensely effective way, selling his New Deal to the American people. Perhaps the most famous use of a story by FDR to make his point was his speech of September 23, 1944, after Republicans accused him of sending a destroyer to pick up his Scottish Terrier, Fala, from an Aleutian island. Roosevelt turned the tables and with a devastatingly funny response, saying that although he and the family weren't bothered by the accusations, Fala's "Scotch soul" was outraged. Another great storyteller was President Ronald Reagan, who always tried to illustrate abstract ideas with concrete metaphors. Partially because of this ability and because of his own smooth delivery, Reagan became known as "The Great Communicator."

Seeing the shades of gray

While working on your cause, you'll have a tendency to view all media coverage through a filter of your issue. You also may judge one journalist as friendly to your cause and another as hostile. You'll look at media coverage the way you look at everything else in the political spectrum, asking yourself: Are they for me or against me? You'll read an item in a newspaper or view it on television and wonder: What's that reporter's agenda? What's he trying to accomplish by reporting that particular item? Why did he take that particular approach? Why is this news item appearing at this time?

As a journalist, I've seen politicians read some truly bizarre interpretations into otherwise straightforward reporting driven simply by deadlines and the demands of newspaper and broadcast reporting. Reporters are required to produce articles or news broadcasts that are as accurate, complete, and fair as possible while working against a deadline that's always looming. Moreover, they must do this within the limited space allotted to them on a printed page or within a very brief time period when they're doing a broadcast.

Yes, sometimes reporters have agendas that they pursue to the detriment of straight, objective reporting. However, they frequently may simply be covering their beats — assigned areas of coverage — trying to come up with good stories, and telling their readers or viewers what's going on. In fact, a journalist may be dealing with so many different topics that your cause is barely a blip on his radar screen, and he has no attitude toward your position at all.

So, what's good versus bad reporting? From a journalist's standpoint, good reporting is:

Accurate	Objective
Balanced	Thorough
Complete	Well-written or well-produced
Fair	

As an advocate, of course, you want your cause presented to the world in the most favorable light possible. You'll do whatever you can to put a positive spin — or viewpoint — on your coverage, impressing on journalists your version of events and view of the situation. However, when the coverage you receive meets the criteria for good journalistic coverage you'll be doing well.

Do you want to compliment a journalist when you think he's done a good job? Don't tell the journalist the story was "good" or "favorable." That makes him think that he's leaning too far in your direction. The highest journalistic compliment you can offer is that a story was "accurate."

Working the congressional beat

Probably the two most important media components to a member of Congress are his hometown media outlets and his press secretary. These sections tell you how to make use of both.

Notifying the folks back home

In dealing with Congress, remember that the media most crucial to members are the ones back in their home states or districts. Getting national coverage is a thrill and makes a big difference to your cause, but getting coverage in a member's hometown newspaper or on his local TV station is especially important because that's where coverage can have a tremendous impact and actually sway some votes.

Accordingly, you can reward members who assist you with favorable publicity in their home states and districts. Whenever a member helps your cause, send out a press release to local newspapers and broadcast stations saying what he did. Conversely, whenever a member obstructs your progress, you can complain to the hometown media.

Utilizing the media in this way is especially effective at key points during the legislative process. For example, when a committee chairman blocks your legislation or you need to sway the vote of a particular member, the way to complain is through the hometown media of that member.

Describing a press secretary's job

Congressional press secretaries do far more than simply issue press releases. They also write speeches, monitor media coverage of their bosses, and return calls from reporters. Often, press secretaries also have input in policy decisions.

The press secretary's primary job is ensuring that his boss receives favorable coverage, and bosses on Capitol Hill can be very demanding. As one representative once told me, "A day without publicity is a day without sunshine." The press secretary must massage or head off unfavorable coverage, seek favorable coverage, and be responsive to the entire spectrum of media that cover Congress.

A press secretary's frame of mind can go from boredom to terror in a matter of minutes. In the morning, a press secretary may not be able to interest any newspaper in the opinion piece his boss wrote, but by afternoon, he can be besieged by reporters seeking the member's comment about some new scandal, especially if the member is directly involved in the scandal.

You can become doubly effective if you develop contacts with people in the member's state or district who are willing to influence the local media for you. These contacts can be prominent local politicians, businesspeople, and political contributors to the member's campaign. Contacts with local editors, publishers, producers, and media owners also are helpful.

The member who's steering your legislation through Congress should be a good source of advice about which media and reporters to approach and to help you decide on which members of Congress you need to focus your media campaign.

Helping a press secretary, aiding your cause

The more work you do for a press secretary or a congressional office, the more likely you are to receive good publicity for your cause (see the "Describing a press secretary's job" sidebar). For example, if you want to issue a press release that says the member has signed on as a cosponsor of your bill, write the press release yourself but have the member's press secretary issue it. The press secretary may tinker with some of the wording, but you'd be astonished by how much goes sailing through as written.

You can draft an opinion piece supporting your cause and submit it to the press secretary, who, in turn, after approval from the member, releases a final version to appropriate newspapers.

Curry favor by putting a press secretary in touch with reporters who may give his boss favorable publicity or by introducing him to hometown editors.

Press releases and opinion pieces that are sent out over a member's signature must be unique to that member. You never want two members, or even a member and an organization, saying exactly the same things.

A friend who is a press secretary achieved what has to be the ultimate level of public-relations nirvana. He persuaded a reporter to become interested in his boss and arranged an interview. To help, he prepared a list of suggested questions for the reporter to ask. To prepare his boss, he provided a list of answers to those likely questions. When the two sat down together, the reporter asked questions the press secretary had written, and the boss replied with the press secretary's answers. "It was wonderful," the press secretary said. "I'd never written a play before."

Making the News

To this day, no one has come up with a completely satisfying or comprehensive explanation of what constitutes *news*. News, for what it's worth, is anything that's new. And, if it's unusual, different, exotic, or interesting, then news is so much the better. Although most reporters and editors may have a hard time defining it, they know news when they see it.

You must make your cause newsworthy and your story worthy of coverage to further your cause. Not only must your cause be newsworthy, but how you present it and how and when it progresses also must attract attention, especially when dealing with Congress. Each time you take a step forward, each vote that goes in your favor, and each endorsement your cause receives from a member is newsworthy.

Fortunately for you, the media make up a vast, ravenous beast with an endless appetite for news. So many news outlets serve so many audiences on such a constant basis that getting some news outlet interested in your information shouldn't be that difficult. As a news source, your job is helping to feed the beast.

Lobbying the Media

Lobbying the media is different than lobbying Congress. When you lobby the media, you're preparing the ground for specific events and developments that you want publicized. This form of lobbying is a long-term effort that goes well beyond daily headlines.

You essentially want the media to be familiar with you, your cause, and what you're trying to do. For this kind of familiarity, face-to-face contact is best.

Working with editors and producers

Remembering that reporters are not the sum total of the media machine is important. They may report the basic facts, but in print media, the editors shape the story into its final form and decide on its placement. In broadcast media, producers and news directors play the editor's role.

At the outset of your media campaign, call the offices of the media you want to influence in the list below and ask for a meeting with:

> ✔ **Print:** The editorial board, or the editor or managing editor. Publications have a *masthead,* or listing of the editors in order of seniority. This is usually published on the editorial page of newspapers or in the front few pages of magazines. It's always best to start at the top of the hierarchy and work your way downward until you find someone willing to meet with you.

✔ **Television or radio:** The news editor, assignment editor, or the news director. You can usually find out the hierarchy at a television or radio station simply by calling and asking for the news editor, assignment editor, or news director. Many television stations run the names of the people in charge once a week, usually Fridays, at the end of the evening news broadcast.

Explain that you want to introduce yourself and explain your cause. Suggest a meeting time and location. You can meet in an office or offer to take the person to lunch Be sure to provide an estimate of how long the meeting will take, bearing in mind that taking less time usually is better. I suggest nothing longer than a half-hour for an in-office meeting, although nothing is wrong with lingering when you're both having a pleasant meal.

Making the editor or producer aware of your issue and of you as a potential news source in the future is the point of an initial meeting. You're also laying the groundwork for when reporters turn in stories about your cause. You want editors to be equipped with some background about your issue so they connect those stories with you. One simple truth is that a media decision maker who is familiar with an issue is more likely to give it more time or space.

Media outlets don't become successful by walling themselves off from potential sources, so you're likely to experience at least a degree of success in arranging meetings, but large and high-profile organizations are less likely to have time or inclination to meet with you. The same rules apply to media meetings as do with congressional meetings. Know your material, be well organized, make your presentation straightforward and businesslike, and check out the meeting tips in Chapter 12.

The best times for meeting with the media are during quieter times when no one is under deadline pressure. Before your meeting, familiarize yourself with the work and schedules of the particular media outlet, its editors, and its reporters. Research any previous reporting journals or broadcast media have done about your issue or others related to it. You'll make a particularly strong impression if you can cite specific stories the media outlet has published or broadcast on your cause or topic.

Working with reporters

A reporter is the basis cog in the media machine. The reporters churn out the basic element that keeps publications and broadcast news outlets running — the story. Reporters are interested in stories and interesting information they can take back and file or broadcast.

The whole point of a reporter's life is to be accessible to potential news sources. When you see one reporter's *byline* — or name — over articles covering your topic or one broadcast reporter who consistently covers your topic, and you have information to impart or a story to tell, simply call that reporter. Many newspapers now include reporters' e-mail addresses in their articles, so you can reach them that way. Local television stations also broadcast telephone numbers to receive news tips from viewers.

Reporters take their stories to the editors who fine-tune them and then place them either in a publication or in the newscast.

You want to establish yourself as that most valued of media assets, a *reliable source,* especially regarding your cause. That means you consistently must be:

- ✔ **Accurate:** Your information is always good.
- ✔ **Authoritative:** You really know the subject.
- ✔ **Available:** The reporter can reach you when needed and you always get back to the reporter in time for deadline.
- ✔ **Informed:** You really know what's going on at the moment.
- ✔ **Responsive:** You try to help the reporter as much as possible.

However, your most valuable asset as a reliable source is your willingness to give a reporter information that's available to no other news outlet. Whenever a reporter whose reporting you respect is particularly helpful to your cause or a media outlet is particularly important to your cause, you may want take the initiative in feeding that reporter or outlet exclusive information. Remember: Whenever you provide exclusive information, you risk alienating other journalists who may be interested in the same story. Always weigh the benefits of giving a really good story to one reporter or another, and realize beforehand that the most important criteria for exclusives ultimately is the degree to which the appearance of an article or report advances your cause.

Know too that giving exclusive information to only a few sources can alienate all the other reporters covering the topic. Never tell more than one reporter that the information you're giving him is exclusive. Either the information is exclusive or it isn't, but if you're caught lying, you'll be savaged by everyone you thought you deceived — and that kind of maneuver can't be kept secret for long in the very public world of the media.

When you want to reach many news outlets with the same information, disseminating your information widely and not providing exclusives is best. However, you may encounter times when you have a particularly useful piece of information that is best placed with one particular news outlet.

Talking on and off the record

In dealing with the media, the most important things that you need to know are the degrees of confidentiality used in imparting information. Misunderstandings about these terms and conditions are the greatest cause of friction between sources and journalists.

The commonly accepted terms are:

✔ **On the record:** Anything you say is fit to print or broadcast and attribute to you.

✔ **Off the record:** You can tell a reporter something in strict confidence, but it is not to appear in any form.

✔ **On background** and **Not for attribution:** The material can be used, but you can't be identified as the source.

Going *off the record* or *on background* implies a contract between the source and the reporter. The source trusts the reporter not to reveal his identity so he can reveal more information, and the reporter pledges to keep the identity of the source a secret — even to the point of going to jail, if necessary. Breaking the contract is considered a serious breach of trust and is grounds for permanently terminating the relationship.

By the same token, one common cause of misunderstanding is the use of background material. Just because you've given a reporter background material that won't be attributed to you, doesn't mean that the reporter can't take that information to other sources who can confirm it, and then publish it. *Background* and *not for attribution* means the information is usable; it just means that you won't be identified as its source.

When people give interviews, they frequently switch from *on the record* to *off the record* and then back *on the record,* but they often do so without clearly identifying when they stopped speaking *off the record.* **Always make clear when you're changing the ground rules and when you're changing back again.**

Whenever you give an interview and want to go *off the record* or *on background,* clearly identify when you go *off the record* and when you go back *on the record.* Otherwise, reporters won't know when you're off or on the record. That's how things you thought were off the record appear in print or on the airwaves.

Whenever you conduct a press conference, you are assumed to be *on the record* unless you specify otherwise. Never call a press conference or lead reporters to believe they're going to get a publishable story and then suddenly declare the event *off the record.* If you want to stage an event to provide *on-background* material, call it a *background briefing,* and you must tell people the ground rules when you invite them and right at the beginning of the event. Similarly, an event to which TV reporters are invited that is not intended for broadcast is called a *pen and pad.*

Don't ever play games with being on or off the record. You're not likely to win any deceptions, and you can make enemies who will plague you for a very long time. Similarly, whenever you feel a reporter has violated an understanding with you, feel free to complain to his editor — and not deal with that reporter again. It's the one journalistic sin that justifies excommunication.

A discussion of exclusive stories also raises the issue of *leaks* — providing the media with information that is supposed to be kept secret or confidential.

Washington is famous as a town full of leaks and leakers. When people don't like some public policy or a particular individual, they leak information that damages the policy or puts their enemies in a bad light. Indeed, President Richard Nixon was so infuriated in 1972 by damaging leaks about his foreign policy that a group of political operatives nicknamed "Plumbers" was formed to find the source of the leaks — ultimately leading to the Watergate break-in.

Leaking information is a very delicate activity. Leaks of officially classified information that a person has sworn to keep secret can lead to a prison sentence for the leaker. A leaker must have absolute confidence that the reporter won't betray his identity. Even when a leak is made, no guarantees can be given that it will appear in the media or have the desired effect. Nonetheless, leaks, both deliberate and inadvertent, occur all the time in Washington.

No one rule of thumb exists for using leaks to advance a cause. Each case is different, and leaks sometimes can have the desired effect. The law, however, is very clear: Leaks of officially classified information are illegal.

Your basic interaction with reporters takes place in the form of an *interview* — a meeting with a reporter in which you respond to his questions. Interviews can be formal meetings set up long in advance or brief encounters — these kinds of interviews happen all the time with members of Congress.

When you do an interview, clarify the ground rules at its outset. After all, an interview isn't merely a casual conversation, it's a serious working event. Sacrificing a little cordiality and having a clear understanding is better than having a bitter dispute after the information appears in public. (See the "Talking on and off the record" sidebar for information about degrees of confidentiality.)

One of my most valuable sources as a reporter was a corporate public-relations person who always helped me out. He was proactive in calling me when he had a tip. He always was present at crucial meetings, so he knew what was going on, always tried to answer me fully when I called, always had reliable information, and always was prompt in getting back to me. I used to call him just to verify information I'd heard that didn't relate to his company. Whenever he couldn't comment, he always had a great — and usually nasty — newsworthy story about the competition. That's a great source.

Writing and Distributing Press Releases

The basic currency of public relations is the *press release,* which is an article written to publicize something. You send out press releases to as many media outlets as you can and hope they use it.

Thousands of press releases are issued every day on Capitol Hill. Members issue them to generate news, establish positions, comment on events, and take credit for achievements. Committees issue them to keep everyone apprised of their work. Lobbies issue them to comment on what members do and establish their positions on various issues. Executive agencies issue them to announce new developments.

Speaking as an editor, attracting someone's attention with a press release is difficult. You may send out a thousand press releases and never get a single response. Nonetheless, they're an effort you must make and an effort for which there really is no alternative. Then again, every so often a press release will be picked up and published or used. It's like planting seeds: You put them in the ground, pray for rain, and hope they grow. One thing is certain, however, if you don't send out any press releases, no one will *ever* hear of you.

Writing a good press release

Like any newspaper or magazine article, a good press release tells a story or informs readers about a new development to an existing story.

By and large, press releases need to be well written, because they are intended for a professional audience of editors and producers who spend their days evaluating what other people write. Indeed, press releases need to be *better* written than any article appearing in a newspaper or magazine.

Effective press releases have the following elements:

- **A great headline:** Many editors won't read beyond a headline before deciding whether to toss the release into the circular file or act on it. Your headline must be catchy, clever, and capable of inducing the editor or reporter to continue reading. When you're sending out a press release as an e-mail, the subject line substitutes for the headline. Headlines need to be brief but intriguing.

- **A good lead paragraph:** The first paragraph must inform the reader about the new development, preferably in an enticing way that induces him to read on.

  Write clearly and simply in newspaper style and answer journalism's traditional "five w's and an h" questions: who, what, when, where, why, and how.

- **A good second paragraph:** This paragraph sometimes is called a *nut graph* in journalism because it gives the reader something substantial to chew on, like a squirrel chomping on a nut. It needs to tell the reader why he should care about what you're announcing.

✔ **Contact information:** Always be sure to put a contact name, phone number, e-mail address, mailing address, and fax number on the release so that anyone who's interested can get additional information or verify the information in the press release.

The body of the story — and it should be a story (go back to the "Getting Your Story Straight" section earlier in the chapter for a list of story elements) — should tell the reader why your announcement is newsworthy. What's the significance of this particular development? If you're announcing an event, tell the reader why the event is significant.

Make sure, be certain, and then double-check that all facts and spellings in your press release are accurate.

People trying to publicize legislation frequently concentrate on the legislation itself when issuing press releases. A much better story, however, is the effect the legislation will have. For example, instead of saying, "Rep. John Doe's bill, HR 123, requires the government to place a chicken in every pot," try saying, "Every American will have a chicken in his pot, if Rep. John Doe's bill, HR 123, passes Congress." Concentrating on the consequences always makes a better story.

Distributing a press release

Distribution of your press release depends on the media you're trying to reach. You need to send it to the major publications and broadcast news outlets, but sending it to the specific media you're trying to influence also is important, so don't forget trade publications or members' local media. For different kinds of media, see Chapter 15.

Compiling distribution lists

Putting together a distribution list and regularly updating it is one of the more tedious chores of lobbying and public relations, and if you don't want to do it yourself, it can be expensive. A distribution list contains the names, phone numbers, addresses, fax numbers, and e-mail addresses of journalists you need to reach. When your issue affects the entire country, your list may run to thousands of names.

Whenever you're working with an established lobby or public relations firm, the firm likely will have a list. As time passes, however, you may develop your own list of journalists whom you believe should receive your releases.

Many companies offer media lists. Two good media directories are:

✔ The *News Media Yellow Book* by Leadership Directories, New York, N.Y., and Washington, D.C., is published quarterly. An annual subscription is

$340. It can be ordered through the Leadership Directories Web site, www.leadershipdirectories.com, or by writing to Leadership Directories, 1001 G St. NW, Washington, DC 20001, phone 202-347-7757; or 104 5th Ave., New York, NY 10011, phone 212-627-4140.

✔ The *Directory of Membership and News Sources* published by the National Press Club of Washington in Washington, D.C. The directory is available only to members of the National Press Club. An active membership in the club for a professional journalist costs $463 a year with a $150 initiation fee. An associate membership for someone who works regularly with members of the media costs $593 a year with a $175 initiation fee. The Club's Web site can be accessed at npc.press.org or by calling 202-662-7500.

Members of Congress keep lists that usually include all the reporters covering Congress in Washington and key media outlets. Ask the member championing your issue for access to his list. You also can ask your political allies for their lists whenever you're all supporting a common cause.

Deciding on delivery methods

To ensure complete coverage, send out your release by fax and e-mail to the journalists on your list when it's urgent and time-sensitive, or by regular mail when it isn't. Remember to post the release to your cause's Web site, if you have one.

Media outlets increasingly favor e-mail, because material can be pasted easily into stories or publishable formats. The problem with e-mail, however, is that most releases become lost in the deluge, which is one reason that a great headline or subject line is so very important (see the "Writing a good press release" section earlier in this chapter).

Traditional mail has fallen out of favor as a means of distribution, because it's slow and takes more effort on the part of editors and production departments converting the material they receive into publishable shape. But, not having to prepare snail mail isn't a bad thing for you because mailing is the most expensive delivery method.

Distributing your material across all media is very important, so you must send e-mail messages *and* faxes *and* post the information on the Web and not use just one or the other of those methods.

If you have the resources and capabilities, you can send out audio and video press releases. The problem a broadcast station has with airing an electronic press release, however, is that it takes up valuable on-air time that the station can otherwise use for paid commercials or staff-generated material. This type of press release also falls into a gray zone between public service announcements and commercials and it limits the broadcast station's effectiveness.

Following up on your press release

Speaking as a managing editor, the most annoying phone calls are from public relations people and press secretaries asking me whether I received their press releases. I get dozens of these calls during the course of a day — so many that I tell people in my recorded answering message that I can't confirm receipt of releases. Still, I understand why people make these calls and would think them pretty foolish if they didn't make them.

I'm going to regret writing this, and all the other journalists I know will hate me, but it's true: Follow up your press releases with a phone call. Don't call just to see whether the journalist received the release — offer to provide additional information or answer any questions. Be sure to leave your name and contact number even when you don't talk directly to the journalist.

Another follow-up method is to monitor whether and how your release is used. Subscribing to particular publications enables you to determine whether your release was used there. Otherwise, you may need to retain a clipping service, which scans a wide variety of publications and media outlets, alerting you to when and in what media your material is used. You also must frequently search the Internet for mentions of you, your organization, and your issue, particularly after you put out a release.

If you see that one particular media outlet or a certain reporter is especially receptive to your material, concentrate your efforts on that outlet and that reporter.

When you can draw a direct correlation between your release and specific actions or results, especially in Congress — an extremely difficult thing to do — you've attained the highest level of the public relations craft.

Organizing a Press Conference

If the press release is the basic form of currency on Capitol Hill, think of the press conference as taking a trip to the to the bank. Press conferences are the way members, organizations, and individuals distribute their currency by making announcements and putting a human face on their organizations and issues. A press conference is an event where you bring reporters together with sources in person to generate news and coverage of your cause or topic.

When you're planning to bring members and media together, the best way to conduct a press conference is by having a member who's preferably your champion sponsor it and serve as the main speaker. A member of Congress holding a press conference automatically has access to the House and Senate press and to TV/radio galleries. A member serving as the main speaker also ensures at least some media attendance, because the congressional media are ever present in the press galleries. Furthermore, when a member sponsors the press conference, the member's press secretary, who is experienced in obtaining coverage for his boss, handles most of the logistics.

Booking a venue

When it comes to reaching Congress, proximity is everything. Members and the media who cover them don't want to stray too far from Capitol Hill for fear of missing important news or votes when Congress is in session.

Members of Congress constantly hold press conferences, and in good weather, they have specific places they like to do it. Representatives used to meet with the press in a place called the House Triangle, a little triangle of grass outside the House wing of the Capitol that was paved over during Capitol construction of the Capitol Visitor Center (see Chapter 17). It is unclear whether representatives will regain an outdoor venue for press conferences. Senators, on the other hand, hold theirs in a place dubbed the Senate Swamp, an area across from the Senate wing of the Capitol. When the weather is bad, press conferences are held in whatever rooms are available at the Capitol or congressional office buildings. The member's staff must book those rooms.

When you can't get a member to book a venue, or if your organization wants to make a point without a member, the next best place is the National Press Club in downtown Washington, D.C. Many media outlets have their Washington offices in that building or nearby, and the Club is accustomed to accommodating press conferences and other events. The National Press Club can be reached at National Press Club, 529 14th St. NW, 13th Floor, Washington, D.C. 20045; phone 202-662-7500. Its Web site address is: `http://npc.press.org`. Click on the "Book your event" link you can get details about available rooms and make reservations online.

Otherwise, Washington is full of hotels and restaurants that can play host to press conferences, but you're likely to have more success in attracting a larger Congress-related attendance the closer to Capitol Hill you set it up. All you need to do is call one of these hotels or restaurants and tell them when you want a room and how many people you expect.

Organizing the event

For most people, orchestrating a wedding is the biggest and most complex event they ever have to worry about. Organizing a press conference is much like planning a wedding. To organize a press conference or a wedding, you must:

- ✔ Send out invitations to speakers and the media
- ✔ Book a venue and provide an estimate of the number you expect to attend
- ✔ Publicize the event and provide a reason for invitees/journalists to attend
- ✔ Take care of the logistics
- ✔ Provide for food, snacks, and refreshments
- ✔ Pray for good weather if it's outside

When you plan a press conference, you always risk being overshadowed by other events — something may happen on the day of your event that draws away all the journalists.

The Press Galleries

Congressional media are organized into seven press galleries with rooms in the Capitol Building. They are:

- ✔ **The House and Senate daily galleries:** These galleries are where daily reporters have their desks and can cover floor events in both chambers.

- ✔ **The House and Senate periodical galleries:** These are offices for magazine, newsletter, and, more recently, Internet reporters.

- ✔ **The House and Senate TV-Radio galleries:** Facilities for radio and TV reporters are set up in these areas for recording and broadcasting.

- ✔ **The Senate Press Photographers' gallery:** Photographers covering the House and Senate belong to this gallery.

All the galleries include professional staff and are governed by boards elected from among the reporter-members. A journalist joins a gallery based upon his or her respective medium and is accredited by the galleries so he can enter the Capitol and the congressional office buildings.

The galleries play a useful role in determining legitimate media (while weeding out lobbyists trying to pose as journalists), establishing common rules for media behavior, and simply giving journalists a location to work. They're also useful for providing a single place for members to conduct press conferences. After passage of a bill or any significant event, members frequently will go promptly to the galleries for an impromptu press conference with the journalists.

Press Gallery: Congress and the Washington Correspondents by Donald A. Ritchie, Harvard University Press, 1992, is a very readable and lively history of congressional-media relations.

Be that as it may, you must plan so that you can have a successful press conference. Use these tips for spreading the word about your conference:

- ✔ Give the media at least a week's notice. The exception is when you have an emergency situation that requires an immediate announcement.

- ✔ Notify the daily congressional media compilations, such as the Associated Press Daybook, the bible of daily Washington events. Fax information about your event to 202-736-9699.

- ✔ A day or two before the event, make sure you follow up invitations with phone calls to people you particularly want to attend.

- ✔ Book a newsworthy speaker whenever possible. The speaker will be a big attraction.

- ✔ Place the press conference in context with a story. Journalists want to know what kind of a story they'll take away from it. When you invite them, give them a sense of the story's larger significance. Don't just say that someone prominent is speaking, or that you're unveiling a new technology, or that you've done a new study. Instead, you must give the journalist a reason to attend and a way of selling it to his editors as page-one material.

When the time comes for the actual conference, encourage favorable coverage by:

- ✔ Making the press conference as visual as possible so that it's rewarding for television journalists. Charts, graphs, or demonstrations, anything that looks good on television, help you receive broadcast exposure.

- ✔ Preparing enough packets of printed materials so that every attendee takes away at least a packet with:

    - • A press release

    - • Biographies of all the speakers (with their names correctly spelled)

    - • Background explanations of the issue at hand and whatever other information a journalist may need to write a story

    - • A fact sheet listing the important facts that you want them to remember

    - • A list of contacts for future related stories

- ✔ Having someone clearly in charge of the event, someone to serve as moderator, host, and timekeeper.

Don't go too far past the point of diminishing returns. At some point, every press conference passes its peak. When questions become repetitious or trivial, when little real information is being generated, or when reporters start leaving for other appointments, the person in charge of the press conference needs to say, "We'll take one or two more questions," thus bringing the event to a close. Press conferences usually run no longer than a half-hour.

✔ **Managing speakers effectively.** Keep speakers' opening statements as short and to the point as possible. The most rewarding part of a press conference for journalists is the question-and-answer period.

Before the press conference, the person in charge gives speakers a fixed amount of time for an opening statement and makes sure that they stay within that timeframe. Few things are more tortuous or torturous than a press conference that drags pointlessly on.

Make sure that speakers are available after the press conference to talk with reporters. These are interviews where reporters can obtain exclusive information or ask speakers about other stories they're pursuing.

✔ **Providing (whenever possible)** what's called a *mult box,* or a device into which television and radio reporters can plug their cables so they can record from a single microphone on the podium. Most hotels and regular press conference venues provide mult boxes, podiums, and microphones.

If you don't have a mult box, each reporter must individually attach his microphone to the podium. That's when you end up with a forest of microphones (replete with network and station insignia and call letters) bristling in the face of the speaker. When that happens, some microphones don't record as well as others, you may not have enough space on the podium for all the microphones that journalists need to place, and microphones sometimes fall off.

✔ **Offering food whenever possible.** The best way to a front-page story is through a journalist's stomach. And whenever you hold a morning press conference at some ungodly hour, take pity on your long-suffering author and try to be more creative than the standard Danish and bagels.

A press conference is like an airport: Jokes about bombs are likely to go off in your face. At your press conference, use humor sparingly, carefully, or not at all. Avoid sarcasm or personal comments about people, because you never know what offhand remark might be picked up and broadcast around the world.

Every microphone is a *live* microphone. Never say anything around a microphone — *any* microphone — that you can't stand having broadcast on the evening news.

Working with Television

Despite the fragmentation of network and cable channels, television remains the single most powerful medium in the modern world. A single report broadcast on an evening newscast reaches millions of people. A single image can become part of the national consciousness.

Two attributes of television that you have to take into account as you work with this medium are that it is visual and it is symbolic.

When a TV cameraman brings his tape back to the studio, editors look it over for strong visual elements. Does it show action? Are the images emotional, or compelling, or riveting? Is it unusual? Images for which the answers to these questions are yes are called *good visuals.*

No one way or right method exists for producing good visuals or effectively using symbols. Doing so is dependent upon your ingenuity, creativity, and the situation of the moment. But when you want television coverage for your cause, you must think visually and symbolically if you're truly expecting to get it.

In many ways, Congress doesn't lend itself to good visuals, because it's entirely composed of what are known as *talking heads,* or pundits and experts who appear on the screen and just yak.

To get television airtime, you need to turn your cause or your argument into good visuals, and the best way to do that is by using symbols. Whenever you stage a press conference to unveil a new study of a terrible problem that needs to be corrected, the sight of you standing at a podium waving a sheaf of papers is not a good visual. Showing off a stack of statistics may prove your case in court, but if you can produce a person with the terrible problem you're addressing or show in a concrete way how a policy is having a bad effect, you're more likely to get television coverage.

Some examples of using strong visual symbols include:

✔ Sen. Tom Daschle (D-S.D.) and Rep. Dick Gephardt (D-Mo.) bringing a Lexus and a muffler to the Capitol grounds and making their case in a very visual way in 2001 that Republican-proposed tax cuts wouldn't benefit American workers but would be of disproportionate benefit to the rich. Suiting action to the concept, they argued that rich Americans would get tax breaks equivalent to the cost of a Lexus, while working-class Americans would get only the equivalent of a muffler.

✔ Human rights activists bringing children whose hands and feet had been cut off to a congressional hearing so they could focus attention on the mutilation of children by rebels in the African country of Sierre Leone in 2001. The images of those children were more powerful than any testimony an American activist could have delivered.

✔ Rep. Newt Gingrich (R-Ga. 1979–99) having all Republican congressional candidates come to Washington and, in a grand ceremony, sitting down and signing the Contract with America. The idea was to show that they were dedicating and committing themselves to a common set of principles in a very visual and symbolic way.

From a logistical standpoint, TV is especially suited to very formal or ceremonial events that are scheduled long in advance. Despite the use of *minicams* — small, lightweight cameras — TV production by and large remains an elaborate and cumbersome process.

When working with television, giving TV reporters as much advance notice as possible of your event is especially important. An assignment editor has to fit your event into the daily news schedule, and TV crews require an especially long time to set up cameras and lighting.

Broadcasting on Radio

In 1987, the Federal Communications Commission repealed what was known as the *Fairness Doctrine,* a rule that required that both sides in a political debate be given exactly equal time on air. Suddenly, radio station owners no longer had to precisely measure political talk on the airwaves. The first broadcaster to take advantage of this was Rush Limbaugh who set the prototype for the conservative radio commentator. Limbaugh's commercial success encouraged not only political radio, it helped lead an expansion of all-talk radio in general. In 1987, only about 100 all-talk radio stations were on the air in the United States. Today about 1,400 such stations exist. Not all of them are all politics, all the time, but many have a proportion of political shows.

Given the number of stations and hosts, the demand for guests and topics also has risen, and as a result, you have a better chance of getting your message out through this medium.

To obtain a booking as a guest, you or someone from your organization simply calls the radio station and tells the station manager or producer:

- ✔ Who you are
- ✔ Who you represent
- ✔ The nature of your cause (put it in terms of the story you want to tell)
- ✔ Why you would make a good guest
- ✔ Why it would be advantageous for the station to book you

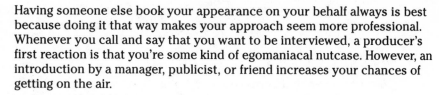

Having someone else book your appearance on your behalf always is best because doing it that way makes your approach seem more professional. Whenever you call and say that you want to be interviewed, a producer's first reaction is that you're some kind of egomaniacal nutcase. However, an introduction by a manager, publicist, or friend increases your chances of getting on the air.

Talk radio primarily exists to entertain, not enlighten.

Don't expect to have a serious, sober discussion of the intricacies of your issue on most radio programs. Stations book you if they think you'll be entertaining, and the job of the host is to keep the conversation moving and lively. Expect a host's questions to be provocative, extremely opinionated, and sometimes even hostile, mostly to get you to say provocative and opinionated things.

In this circumstance your story becomes important. It has to enlighten and entertain the audience. Select one or two points that you want the audience to take away from the conversation and repeat them several times during the course of your interview.

When you're talking with morning disk jockeys or general-interest programs, you're not likely to get any more than 2 to 5 minutes of airtime and most of that will be taken up by the host. Make your points clearly and repeatedly as early in the interview as you can.

Most talk radio hosts scan newspapers for material and build their shows from that. They're not experts in any particular subject, and they're always dealing with a broad spectrum of topics. You'll be helping them and yourself when you bring a list of questions that you'd like them to ask you. Likewise, you'll find them surprisingly appreciative if you make the effort.

You can make your effort more effective by booking your appearances on radio stations in the districts of key members you're trying to influence. You can have a much greater impact in Congress through one small station in a rural district represented by a key member at a critical time in the legislative process than by appearing on a national show.

You don't have to be physically present to participate in radio interviews. Many talk stations do *phoners,* or call-in interviews. You can influence events on the other side of the country from the comfort of your home phone.

Some radio interview shows seriously delve into topics and actually provide sufficient time to do it. Most of them, however, are on noncommercial stations. These programs are useful in reaching opinion leaders and others who may influence other, commercial media. For these kinds of programs, you simply must be articulate, authoritative, and knowledgeable. By the same token, however, the competition for booking on these shows in greater.

Beyond talk radio, radio news reporters always are seeking good audio in much the same way that television reporters seek good visuals. If you can provide sound that illustrates your points — *actuality*, as it's known in the trade, you have a much better chance of having your story broadcast. But doing so is very difficult in most situations. Thus, most common actualities are sound bites of interviews. If you're going to do more, you have to be creative.

Browsing through Internet Media

These days, if your cause doesn't have a Web site it might as well not exist. Web sites are so easy to create, simple to maintain, and inexpensive to establish that you have no excuse not to set one up at the outset of your lobbying campaign. (Check out *Creating Web Pages For Dummies,* 6th Edition, written by Bud Smith and Arthur Bebak and published in 2002 by Wiley, or *Building a Web Site For Dummies,* written by David Crowder and Rhonda Crowder and published in 2000 by Wiley.)

The great advantage of having a Web site from an advocacy standpoint is that your cause always is on display, accessible, and providing great support for your followers, the media, and congressional members and staff.

Because so many factors can affect how you set up a Web site, I'm not going to go into them all here.

Nevertheless every advocacy Web site needs to include:

- ✔ Contact information for the organization, its officers, and staff.
- ✔ A statement of the organization's purpose.
- ✔ Biographies of the leadership of the organization.
- ✔ A fact sheet about the issue and organization.
- ✔ Background on the issue.
- ✔ A brief history of the movement, cause, or organization.
- ✔ All the organization's press releases. Having a link for members of the media is especially effective. Many Web sites call this the *pressroom.*
- ✔ A *frequently asked questions* (FAQs) page.

In addition to the Web site, you need to create an electronic newsletter so you can inform your followers and members of the media about new and breaking developments.

Paying for Space

The great thing about paid advertising is that you completely control the content. The problem is that you have to pay for it.

That said, paid advertising, or in this instance what's called *advocacy advertising,* whether print or broadcast, can have a significant impact on members of Congress either directly or by stirring up grass-roots pressure on members.

At this point I have to insert a personal disclaimer: I'm the managing editor of *The Hill,* a weekly newspaper that makes most of its money from advocacy advertising. Advocacy ads pay my salary.

Having said that, I think that advertising is a perfectly good way — and at times the most effective way — to influence congressional events and positions.

Attractive, professional ads placed in key media at key times help you communicate your position to lawmakers without the filter of reporters, editors, or producers. Furthermore, you can emphasize the points that are most important to you and do it in an arresting and graphic way. A sustained ad campaign can keep your cause or organization in the eye of Congress (and the public) continuously for a long period of time.

Paid advertising is best handled by professional public relations firms or advertising agencies, particularly those with political experience. The people who work for these firms know what works in different media, how to calibrate the effects, and where and when to place ads for the maximum impact. They work with production departments and creative directors who can fully utilize different techniques and media to achieve the results you want.

An outside agency also can maintain a bit of professional distance from your issue, giving it perspective that you may lack. Advocates frequently are so immersed in the specifics of an issue that they can lose sight of the overall impact of an ad, which has its greatest effect when it's simple and direct. As long as you have a good relationship with an ad agency or PR firm, you can educate them in the subtleties of the issue, and they can best craft and implement an ad campaign.

However, if you want, you can produce your own ads, or the media outlets where you want to place ads will create them for you.

Perhaps the most effective paid advocacy ad campaign in recent years was the one that came to be referred to as "Harry and Louise," named after the two main characters in the TV commercials in 1993 and 1994. They were two middle-class, middle-aged people discussing President Bill Clinton's healthcare plan in their home and pointing out its flaws. Perhaps it was their ordinariness, but millions of Americans identified with them and flooded Congress with expressions of opposition to the plan. The plan ultimately died as a result of many factors, not the least of which was congressional opposition. However, the Harry and Louise campaign was an exceedingly effective use of paid advocacy advertising.

Using Celebrities

Witnessing the commotion that can be created in the halls of the Capitol of the United States by someone who warbles for a living or whose chief claim to fame is that she takes on other identities is absolutely astonishing. Singers, actors, athletes, and celebrities of all kinds can have a galvanizing effect on the media, and even the most powerful representatives and senators can turn to mush in their presence. Celebrities bring an incredible amount of publicity to your cause and, when used properly, can be effective. However, they also can bring with them major problems and complications.

In Congress and in Washington, people generally are so immersed in politics and government that Hollywood names may not have much meaning. A story — probably fictitious — circulates around Washington that when actor Robert Redford stopped by a senator's office to lobby, a secretary breathlessly ran into her boss's office and shouted, "Robert Redford is in the waiting room!" "Redford?" asked the senator. "Redford? What group does he represent?" In my own case, my newspaper was collaborating in a TV production involving actress Mercedes Ruehl. People in the office kept talking about "Mercedes Rule," and I kept wondering, "Mercedes' Rule? Is that like Megan's Law?"

Delineating the types of celebrities

Most Hollywood celebrities come to Washington to "raise awareness" of health conditions or diseases or to lobby for medical research funding, which are popular forms of political participation in Hollywood, because they don't involve any controversy. After all, everyone's against diseases and disabilities. (I have yet to hear a celebrity testify in favor of a disease.)

However, a celebrity may genuinely want to assist you in furthering your cause. If that is the case, you want the celebrity to make the points that you need to make according to your agenda.

Academic celebrities can be headstrong, but they're also knowledgeable and articulate and usually only a secretary sits between you and the celebrity. You can contact authors through the publicity departments of their publishers.

The two types of celebrities are

- **Academic celebrities:** These people are high-profile authors, academics, and experts. You need to use these people to impart the gravity of your cause, so that it is taken seriously. Respected retired public officials and former members of Congress fall into this category. They are the kind of people whose presence opens doors for you in Congress and in the executive branch and gains you publicity among the elite media. When they write newspaper essays or op-eds on your behalf, the likelihood is higher that they will be published. For more about op-eds check out Chapter 15.

- **Hollywood celebrities:** These are the actors, actresses, athletes, singers, and entertainers who attract popular media coverage and can help you gain mass publicity for your cause or issue. A hot Hollywood celebrity testifying on your behalf at a hearing or speaking at a rally can guarantee that you receive at least some media attention. However, as much as these celebrities attract attention from members, they carry little weight when it comes to policymaking. You must be the one to supply the facts, figures, and political muscle once you've gained the publicity.

The Motion Picture Association of America (MPAA) is famous for using celebrities and private screenings as lobbying tools. The MPAA often arranges for Hollywood celebrities to lobby on behalf of its positions and is widely regarded as one of the more effective lobbies in Washington.

As the person leading the fight for your cause, your chief concern with celebrities is making sure they're always assets and never liabilities.

Preparing your celebrity

When working with Hollywood celebrities, the substance of your work is with the celebrity's publicist, who plays an important role in deciding whether identifying with your cause is in the celebrity's better interest. When it is and when the celebrity's willing to become involved, you and the publicist must work out the details of the celebrity's involvement.

Getting in touch with a Hollywood celebrity means looking up the celebrity on a Web site or finding a press release about the celebrity and contacting the person responsible for the Web site or the person whose name is on the release. You can usually find the publicist by typing the celebrity's name into an Internet search engine and going through the entries that pop up. Some celebrities identified with particular causes are widely known and can be contacted through the organizations they support, or an organization working with you may have lists of celebrities and their publicists. Some paid services also say that they can provide introductions to celebrities, but I'd suggest being very careful about using any of them. These services usually provide celebrities for commercial purposes and require payment to act as agents. If you're a nonprofit or political organization, you shouldn't have to use them.

Hollywood celebrities frequently change publicists, so the name on the release may be old; however, that person may refer you to the latest publicist.

Whenever a celebrity is testifying on your behalf at a congressional hearing or making any kind of speech, give the celebrity's publicist a draft of the testimony you want the celebrity to deliver.

Keeping your celebrity on a tight leash

Most members of Congress realize celebrities are present mainly to attract media coverage but not necessarily to deliver substantial testimony. They usually go easy on celebrities in hearings and so does the media.

The danger presented when using celebrities of any stripe as a lobbying tool is that they can and do stray from your script, making unauthorized pronouncements on behalf of you or your cause or organization that gain unfavorable publicity and end up putting your cause in a bad light or committing you to a policy that you don't accept.

The celebrity's job is to be glamorous, cultivate people, sign autographs, and attract attention to the cause. You and the publicist need to make clear to the celebrity that off-the-cuff remarks are greatly discouraged. Usually you receive cooperation: After all, the celebrity does this in large part to advance his own career and/or support the cause. Looking stupid in front of the United States Congress and the national media isn't the best means of achieving those ends. Whenever a celebrity says or does something that hurts your cause, all you can do is minimize the damage and set the record straight about your true aims. A celebrity goof is exactly that — a goof — and must be seen as such.

Conducting a Demonstration

If you think organizing a wedding is hard or if you think organizing a press conference is harder, multiply every kind of difficulty you can imagine times ten, and you have an idea about what it takes to organize a demonstration.

Nonetheless, demonstrations are a tool that must be included in your advocacy toolkit.

The uses of demonstrations

Some people think of demonstrations as a form of lobbying, but they're not. They're media events and pep rallies.

Demonstrations exist to:

- ✔ Prove that your cause has a devoted following
- ✔ Invigorate your followers
- ✔ Impress the public with the popularity of your cause
- ✔ Give your followers a sense of participation
- ✔ Attract media attention
- ✔ Reward members of Congress for supporting your cause (by giving them media exposure and allowing them to speak)
- ✔ Rally your allies
- ✔ Vent frustration
- ✔ Drive home your message to the faithful

A successful, well-orchestrated demonstration can propel your cause into the stratosphere and can even make it a national movement.

Marching on the Capitol

Demonstrating as a means of influencing Congress goes back to Jacob Coxey, an Ohio businessman who in the midst of a depression in 1894 led a march of protesters to the Capitol demanding relief programs of the sort that were later implemented in the New Deal in the 1930s. About 500 strong upon their arrival in Washington in May, the protestors were driven from the Capitol lawn, and Coxey was arrested when he tried to read a statement on the Capitol steps. He later ran for the House of Representatives but lost. The march of *Coxey's Army* was one of the great newspaper stories of its day, and it certainly brought attention to the plight of the unemployed.

Another famous march on Congress was the Bonus March of 1932. In the midst of the Great Depression, World War I veterans marched on Washington seeking immediate payment of a bonus they'd been promised for fighting in the war. Some 20,000 men camped in Washington during June and July of that year, hoping Congress would grant the bonus. However, after Congress adjourned in July without passing the bill, tensions rose and the encampment was dispersed by Army troops.

A bad demonstration can sink a movement. Demonstrations are hard to control and can become unruly and violent. The rhetoric can become strident. As a result, the entire affair can put a cause or movement in an extremely bad light, turning even sympathetic lawmakers against it. Almost as bad, when a demonstration fails to meet its expectations, when crowds are small or fervor is lacking or when it is badly organized or poorly conducted, it can do substantial harm to your cause.

Demonstrations must be used with extreme care, a great deal of thought, and sparingly.

Planning a demonstration

Demonstrations vary from a lone protester carrying a single sign to crowds approaching a million people. Nonetheless, as an organizer you must determine at the outset:

- ✔ The purpose of the demonstration.
- ✔ The theme of the demonstration.
- ✔ Your measure of success. (Does success mean getting a million people or just making your concerns known?)
- ✔ Your preferred site for the demonstration.
- ✔ The duration of the demonstration.
- ✔ The date and time of the demonstration.
- ✔ An estimate of the number of people you expect to attend.

Dreaming with Dr. King

One of the most effective demonstrations ever held in Washington, D.C., was the civil rights march of August 28, 1963, when the Rev. Martin Luther King, Jr., gave his famous "I have a dream" speech. That was about as perfect a demonstration as is possible to conduct: Some 250,000 people showed up, making it the largest demonstration to date and exceeding expectations.

The rally was peaceful, the setting was magnificent, and the rhetoric was elevated, raising the civil rights movement into the national consciousness. People who attended left the event with a feeling of their own power and a renewed dedication to their cause. The demonstration lasted only a single day in perfect weather, but it gave the civil rights movement a sense of strength and inspiration that propelled it for years to come.

After you make these determinations, you then must organize and motivate your followers to attend.

The complexity of demonstrations can vary widely, but from a purely logistical standpoint, to conduct a demonstration, you must consider:

- ✔ Funding
- ✔ Transportation
- ✔ Housing
- ✔ Food
- ✔ Medical facilities
- ✔ Sanitary facilities
- ✔ Speakers
- ✔ A stage of some sort
- ✔ Entertainment (many rallies and demonstrations feature some songs or performances)
- ✔ Marshals or appropriate security (to keep order in addition to police)
- ✔ Permits
- ✔ Electrical power
- ✔ Sound and light systems
- ✔ Signs, posters, flags, and visual elements
- ✔ Media coverage
- ✔ Breakdown and cleanup

Demonstrations can be extremely expensive, depending on their size and scope, and although each is different, demonstrations directed specifically at Congress need to:

- ✔ **Accommodate the media:** Make media coverage as easy as possible. Try to work with media in advance of the demonstration to determine their needs, whether it's for viewing platforms or electrical power or lighting. In the case of a big demonstration, meeting to work out logistics with representatives of media outlets well in advance of the demonstration is a good idea.

- ✔ **Always be orderly and law-abiding:** Civil disobedience may sometimes make a point — indeed, members of Congress have been arrested in principled acts of civil disobedience — but a disorderly, chaotic, or destructive demonstration hurts your cause with members more than it helps.

✔ **Be well organized:** You don't want your demonstration dragging on too long or becoming boring at any point. People will start to leave, and the media will lose interest. Make up a schedule, stick to it, and make sure your speakers stick to it. Have a clear chain of command and an acknowledged director.

✔ **Include discussions with members of Congress in addition to the demonstration itself:** Demonstrators may wave signs, shout, and chant, but a Capitol demonstration also is a useful opportunity for those who attend to visit their senators and representatives and seriously lobby them. During these visits, which need to be arranged in advance of the demonstration, lobbyists must:

  • **Have plenty of background material:** Background material is important for the media. You need to distribute the same packet for media at demonstrations that you distribute at a press conference. It needs to contain bios, background, talking points, fact sheets, and contacts.

  • **Keep expectations low:** If you raise expectations of huge turnouts, you're bound to be embarrassed if the numbers you've led the media to expect don't show up. Make sure that your measures of success go beyond mere numbers of people attending, because anticipating a specific number attendees — say a million — is a bad idea.

  • **Provide as much advance notice as possible:** Some demonstrations are annual affairs, so everyone knows a year in advance that they're going to take place. Big demonstrations pegged to certain events, such as specific government or international meetings, are publicized months in advance. The more time you can give yourself for organization, publicity, and planning, the more likely your demonstration will be a success.

✔ **Reward allies in Congress:** Invite friendly members to speak and reward them with favorable publicity.

✔ **Pray for good weather:** Few things are worse than a cold, soggy demonstration.

Obtaining permits and permissions

To hold a demonstration of more than 20 people on the Capitol grounds, you need a permit from the U.S. Capitol Police (USCP). A form for a demonstration or special event can be obtained by writing to the USCP Special Events unit at 119 D St. NE, Washington, D.C. 20510, faxing a request for the form to 202-228-2429, or calling 202-224-8891.

The simple, one-page form asks for information the date, time, duration, and nature of the event, because permits are required not only for demonstrations but also for benefits, performances, receptions, and other activities. Any additional material — podiums, risers, sound systems, and the other accoutrements of an event — must be listed with an estimated number of participants and buses (you have to get them to the show somehow). In addition, the form asks whether anyone is likely to disrupt your activity.

Regulations governing demonstrations and special events prohibit anything that might interfere with congressional business or obstruct access to or egress from the Capitol building. Demonstrations of any kind are prohibited inside the building. Literature can be distributed outside, but never inside. Nothing can be offered for sale, and money cannot be solicited on Capitol grounds. All demonstrations on the steps of the east front of the Capitol require permits. No activity can run for more than 24 consecutive hours including setup and takedown. Permits cover a maximum of seven consecutive days. No sleeping or camping out is permitted. Signs and placards must meet specifications that prevent them from being used as weapons.

Only specific areas some distance from the Capitol building itself are available for demonstrations. Since September 11, 2001, security in those areas has been very tight.

For demonstrations that include more than the Capitol grounds, you need to contact the Washington, D.C. Metropolitan Police. Their Web site can be accessed at http://mpdc.dc.gov/main.shtm, and it has a link to a "Special Events" section that provides all the necessary information for conducting a demonstration or special event. You can also write to the metro police at: John A. Wilson Building, 1350 Pennsylvania Ave. NW, Washington, D.C. 20004; phone 202-727-1000.

Chapter 15

Working with Various Media

In This Chapter

▶ Reviewing different media outlets

▶ Determining the influence of media outlets in Congress

*W*hen pursuing your cause, you'll find that some media outlets are more important to you than others: Some may be more sympathetic, others may give you better or more complete coverage, and still others may have a greater understanding of your issue. You'll also find that some media outlets are more influential and, therefore, more useful in pursuing your goals with Congress than others are.

The media establishment is a vast enterprise employing millions of people at thousands of outlets for news. Cataloging all the sources of information about Congress, politics, or current events is difficult — although presumably not impossible. This list goes over some of the highlights and some of the most prominent news outlets.

Scientific surveys purportedly reveal the degree of influence specific media have with Congress, but in many cases those surveys are proprietary or commissioned by the media outlets to gain advertising. I regard them very warily.

The survey of the media that I provide in this chapter is neither scientific nor comprehensive, but it is based on personal observations I've made over a long period of time, conversations I've had with members and staff, discussions with journalistic colleagues, information gleaned from a variety of sources, and my own personal judgment. In the interests of fairness, bear in mind that I'm managing editor of *The Hill,* a media outlet that covers Congress exclusively and one of the competitors included on this list. That said, I strive for accuracy and the greatest degree of objectivity that I can, without sacrificing the usefulness of my analysis. Any opinions expressed here are entirely mine.

In this chapter, I review a variety of media outlets, provide some useful information about each of them, and provide insight into their degree of influence on Congress. Giving you a useful base of information for approaching different media as you pursue your cause is the point of this chapter.

Delineating Daily Print Media

The daily print media are divided into newspapers that have national scope and impact and those that have local scope. In different ways, each has a role to play in Congress.

The big-three national dailies

Three essential newspapers in Washington that are read by all decision makers and members of Congress — or at least received in each of their offices — are *The Washington Post, The New York Times,* and *The Wall Street Journal.* I call them *the big three.*

People in politics read all sorts of ideological meanings into the coverage of these newspapers. Political conservatives often accuse *The Washington Post* and *The New York Times* of being too liberal, and such large institutions naturally attract numerous complaints about everything from inaccuracies in specific stories to slanting the news for the sake of a political agenda. For the record, newspapers maintain that their reporting is objective and non-ideological, and they keep their opinions on the editorial pages where they belong. Personally, my beef is that they pass Pulitzer prizes around among the three of them, giving other newspapers no realistic shot at the award. But that's just me.

Ideological accusations aside, the big three dominate print coverage of Congress, and as institutions, they are forces to be reckoned with on Capitol Hill.

The Washington Post

The Washington Post is the local daily newspaper of Washington, D.C., but its scope and impact are national. Its most famous scoop was its ongoing exposure of wrongdoing by President Richard Nixon and White House officials following the 1972 break-in at the Democratic National Committee headquarters in the Watergate apartment/office building. The reporting by Carl Bernstein and Bob Woodward resulted in a book, *All the President's Men,* published by Simon & Schuster in 1974, and a 1976 movie of the same name starring Robert Redford and Dustin Hoffman. The Watergate affair put *The Post* on the map as one of the world's most important and influential newspapers.

Opining about op-eds

Most newspapers provide a page for outside opinions and essays that usually is called the *op-ed* page, meaning opposite the editorial page. When promoting your cause, the op-ed pages of newspapers are the most straightforward places to do so.

Op-eds are usually about 750 words long. Editors prefer that they be submitted exclusively to their own newspaper. An op-ed piece written in any one of the big-three newspapers can be influential nationally and with Congress. However, because of their international reputations, the big three receive such a large volume of op-ed submissions that getting one published in any of them is extremely difficult. If getting an op-ed published in a newspaper is important to you, ghostwrite it and then submit it under the byline of a prominent individual (with that person's permission of course). The member who's championing your issue is a good candidate, or you can ask a current or former member of Congress or a present or former high administration official to submit it under his or her name. Furthermore, ask the person submitting the article to contact the op-ed page editor, alerting her to expect its arrival.

Don't overlook the power of a published op-ed in a local newspaper. These newspapers are often more receptive to outside submissions than the big three. An op-ed article in a local paper can have an impact on a representative or senator. When it's published, be sure to send a copy to the office of the member you're trying to influence.

Precisely timing the publication of an article in a newspaper is almost impossible, because so many factors go into editors' choices of which op-eds to publish. Don't think that you can time an op-ed with a specific vote or event in Congress. Op-eds can address broad themes and comprehensive ideas that are more appropriate for longer periods of time than for breaking events.

Although it no longer owns an ironclad monopoly in Washington, *The Post* nonetheless enjoys overwhelming dominance in the nation's capital. Its circulation is about 800,000 on weekdays and about a million on Sundays. Articles appearing in *The Post* are seen by virtually all government decision makers.

The Post has an unquestionable impact on Congress because its presence is pervasive and inescapable. Op-eds and articles in *The Post* can significantly sway members, particularly when they're written by other influential figures.

You can access the Post's Web at www.washingtonpost.com.

The New York Times

Nicknamed "The Great Gray Lady" by journalists for the grayness of its appearance and the somberness of its prose, *The New York Times* strives to be the newspaper of record for the United States, thoroughly and meticulously recording all significant events.

The New York Times has a circulation of 1 million on weekdays and 1.7 million on Sundays.

Without a doubt, *The New York Times* reporting, editorials, and op-eds have an impact nationally and on Congress. The *Times* is known for exhaustive, thorough, and comprehensive reporting. *New York Times* editorials carry real weight, and *New York Times* op-eds frequently are the means by which political leaders float new ideas and express their concerns to each other.

The New York Times Web site is accessible at `www.NYT.com`.

The Wall Street Journal

Reporters and editors at *The Wall Street Journal* like to believe that their newspaper is everyone's *second read* — the newspaper that you read after you've gone through your hometown daily. People read *The Wall Street Journal* to get business and financial news.

Technically, *The Wall Street Journal* isn't a daily newspaper, because it publishes only when the stock exchanges are open, so it isn't published on holidays or weekends.

The Wall Street Journal is a rigorously written and edited newspaper with a high reputation for quality and accuracy. In an April 2002 redesign, it significantly downgraded its political reporting, reducing its role as a Washington player. Its political and policy reporting was moved from its former prominent place on the back page of its front section, and its Friday feature, "Washington Wire," a column of brief items dealing with Washington, was removed from the front page to the middle of the front section.

Politically, *The Wall Street Journal*'s greatest congressional impact comes from its editorial and opinion pages. The editorial page editors strive for — and largely succeed — in making these pages the showcases for politically conservative orthodoxy. A *Wall Street Journal* editorial can set the ideological line for conservative members of Congress, and *WSJ* editorial support or opposition to specific bills can make them or break them.

The Wall Street Journal has a circulation of about 1.7 million readers. Its Web site is available at `www.WSJ.com`.

USA Today and The Washington Times

The daily newspaper *USA Today* falls into a category of its own somewhere between the big three and local dailies. The newspaper, which does not publish on weekends, is widely distributed throughout the country, and items appearing in it can attract extensive readership. Distributed in hotels and airports, it claims a weekday readership of 9.2 million, but that figure includes nonsubscribers.

Despite its wide circulation, *USA Today* doesn't carry the political or intellectual weight in Congress that the big three do. *USA Today* editorials and op-eds may sway popular opinion, but they have little impact in Congress, partially because of the brevity of the articles.

USA Today can be accessed at `www.USAToday.com`.

Washington's other daily newspaper is *The Washington Times,* a newspaper first founded in 1982 by the Unification Church led by the Rev. Sun Myung Moon. The paper has worked hard establishing itself as an independent, credible source of news. It has a conservative political viewpoint and publishes an extensive daily opinion section that has influence with conservative members of Congress. Circulation figures are not available.

The Washington Times is accessible at `www.washtimes.com`.

Local dailies

Too many advocates believe that the big three daily newspapers are the sum total of the printed universe. They're not. In fact, in many ways, you can be much more effective working with local dailies than you can with the big three. Local dailies offer distinct advantages, because

- ✔ They're more accessible to you for op-eds and meetings with the editors
- ✔ Their reporters always are looking for local angles to national stories
- ✔ Their reporters don't have the same kind of access to policy makers, tips, and leaks that the big three reporters do, so they're more receptive to other sources
- ✔ They carry more weight with individual representatives and senators because they directly reach constituents

Most major local dailies have bureaus in Washington, D.C., so when you're working in Washington, you can easily reach reporters for these newspapers. Of course, stories always can be phoned in to the newsrooms regardless of where they're located.

Almost all local dailies today are morning newspapers, giving you the opportunity to influence events at the top of the day. An op-ed published in the morning allows lawmakers to take action during the day, generating more headlines for the following day.

Cozying Up to Columnists

A *columnist* is a journalist who writes a column of opinion, analysis, or commentary on a regular basis. A *syndicated columnist* is one whose work is sent to many different newspapers or print outlets through a syndicate that sells and distributes the columns. Columnists are paid to write their opinions, and they perform the function of putting the news into perspective and giving it a context.

At one time, syndicated columnists carried considerable political weight, because their words reached enormous numbers of readers. People like Walter Lippman in the 1930s or Joseph and Stewart Alsop in the 1950s were extremely influential in government circles and had a direct impact on national and international policy. Political columnists today chiefly are known for their ideological perspectives, giving an openly liberal or conservative gloss to events.

Columnists can help a cause with favorable publicity or an ideological blessing. But be aware, when approaching columnists, you may also be giving them fodder for criticism of your cause.

Columnists can be approached through the syndicates that distribute their work. At the bottom of a syndicated newspaper column is the name of the distributing syndicate. Search the Internet to find the contact information for the syndicate. The syndicate usually has a means of contacting the columnist. You can also write to the columnist in care of your local newspaper, but be aware that the newspaper must then pass the letter on to the syndicate, and the amount of time it takes for your letter to reach the columnist may be considerable — if it reaches the columnist at all.

Making the Most of Magazines and Periodicals

A *periodical* is any publication that is published periodically — usually once a week or once a month. Although the term applies to any kind of publication, it usually refers to a magazine.

Innumerable periodicals impact members of Congress, but not all periodicals are equal. When analyzed for their political influence, they fall into the three categories I cover here.

Newsweek has a feature called "My Turn" that runs essays from readers, and you can submit an essay in support of your cause. You can also submit letters to the editor in support of your cause to any periodical.

The newsweeklies

Precisely what impact newsweeklies have on members of Congress is difficult to say, but clearly, whenever one of them does a story about a member, that member pays close attention. Otherwise, the voice of the newsweeklies tends to be lost in the dull roar that always is directed at Congress.

The newsweeklies, particularly *Time,* excel at what *The New York Times* refers to as a *tick-tock,* or a minute-by-minute description of an event. In the case of Congress, tick-tocks tend to address important or highly contested votes. Newsweekly reporters spend a great deal of time with members or politicians on the condition that they hold off their reports until after the event has taken place. This technique is especially useful in political campaigns and was pioneered by the famous journalist Theodore White, who used it to write his series of books called *The Making of the President.*

The granddaddies of periodical news media are the weeklies *Time* and *Newsweek.* (*Time* has a circulation of 4 million; *Newsweek*'s is 3.1 million. The *Time* Web site is at www.time.com, and *Newsweek* is at www.newsweek.com.) Henry Luce and Briton Hadden founded *Time* in 1922. It set the standard for newsweeklies. Partially to provide a different perspective, Thomas J.C. Martyn founded *Newsweek* in 1933. *Newsweek* always has been the more liberal of the two publications. In 1961, *Newsweek* was purchased by The Washington Post Company.

Time and *Newsweek* once were extremely influential periodicals, but with the onset of more immediate electronic media, they've lost a great deal of their impact.

A third newsweekly, *U.S. News & World Report,* also has gone through turmoil in recent years, and at this time, seems unsure of its mission or purpose. It's the only newsweekly based in Washington, D.C. (*Time* and *Newsweek* are headquartered in New York.) Its most famous feature about Congress and Washington is "Washington Whispers," short items about doings in government and politics. *U.S. News & World Report* has a circulation of 2 million. Its Web site is at www.usnews.com.

Ideological periodicals

In recent years, periodicals with ideological points of view have proliferated in Washington. These magazines are known primarily for their analysis, commentary, and quality of writing. They can have an impact on members who adhere to their ideological lines by generating ideas and providing arguments. They also can set the tone and terms of congressional debate.

These periodicals do their best work when they're in opposition to the current occupant of the White House or the majority party in Congress, providing the ideas and arguments for the advancement of their particular ideologies and attacking the other side.

The founding father of these magazines is *The New Republic,* which was founded in 1914. With a circulation estimated at 100,000, *The New Republic* is generally regarded as the voice of moderate liberalism.

Another periodical, which isn't overtly ideological but nevertheless is as liberal, is *The Washington Monthly,* a monthly magazine known for its muckraking and investigative reports.

The Nation, founded in 1865, is more left wing than *The New Republic.* It's supported by 17,000 subscribers, which it refers to as donors.

The conservative counterpart to *The New Republic* is the *National Review,* founded in 1955 by William F. Buckley.

The 1980s and 1990s saw the founding of two new conservative periodicals: *The American Spectator,* a monthly, and *The Weekly Standard.*

An ideological endorsement from either liberal or conservative media, particularly the side that controls the most seats in Congress, can be a powerful boost — just remember that it carries opposition with it from the other side of the political spectrum.

If a particularly partisan member of Congress is championing your cause, have that member introduce you to writers and editors of the ideological periodicals. Giving you access to these people helps you gain publicity in those publications.

Regional and city periodicals

Statewide or regional periodicals may not have a huge impact on members and government officials as a whole, but they can be extremely important to individual senators or representatives, especially around election time when they tend to do personality profiles.

Some of the better-known regional periodicals include *New York* magazine, *Texas Monthly,* and *Washingtonian.* Usually, these publications concentrate on food, fashion, and style (which generates their advertising), but when they turn to politics and Congress, some do an excellent job of reporting.

Courting Capitol Hill Media

An entire publishing industry is based on Congress and serves the entire congressional community, including members, lobbyists, and staff. The Capitol Hill media are important to you as you track your issue's progress through Congress, and they're essential as you evaluate the effectiveness of your lobbying.

These media are very important to a congressional advocate on two levels:

- ✔ They provide the specialized, detailed reporting of issues, bills and politics that are essential to staying fully informed of congressional developments.
- ✔ They're closely read in Congress so they're a focused means of informing and influencing members and staff.

If you're trying to reach members with your message, op-eds, letters to the editor, advertisements, and articles about your cause can have a big impact if they appear in these publications.

When it comes to Congress, you can never have too many sources of information.

Newspapers

Two newspapers that focus exclusively on Capitol Hill goings-on are *The Hill* and *Roll Call.*

The Hill is a colorful tabloid weekly with a circulation of 22,000 that was founded in 1994. It features investigative reporting, coverage of Congress, and a variety of features. It appears on newsstands every Wednesday. *The Hill*'s Web site is www.thehill.com. *The Hill* also has a free e-newsletter called "The Hill E-News" and "Omens & Portents," which are brief looks at trends and developments in Congress. Subscriptions to "The Hill E-News" are free and can be obtained through the Web site. I confess, I'm the managing editor.

Roll Call is a twice-weekly newspaper that appears on newsstands Mondays and Thursdays. It has a circulation of 17,800. Founded in 1955, *Roll Call* covers congressional news, and one of its best-read features is a column called "Heard on the Hill," which consists of brief congressional items. It also has a daily online version, *Roll Call Daily,* which can be accessed through its Web site at www.rollcall.com. A subscription to *Roll Call Daily* costs $265 per year.

Both Capitol Hill newspapers are closely read by members of Congress, and each features special reports about specific policy issues.

Congressional Quarterly

Congressional Quarterly was founded in 1945. It was a quarterly magazine for a single year before it started meeting demand for more frequent updates. Today, Congressional Quarterly publishes

- *Congressional Quarterly,* a weekly magazine about Congress.
- *Congressional Daily Monitor,* a daily newsletter with information about congressional schedules, wrap-ups of the previous day's events, and features about congressional activity and people.
- *CQ.com On Congress,* an online report about Congress on Congressional Quarterly's Web site at www.cq.com.
- *House Action Reports,* online analyses of bills scheduled for floor consideration, descriptions of amendments, and updates on changes to bills (also at www.cq.com).

Congressional Quarterly Press has the most extensive listing of books that exclusively cover Congress. Many of these are invaluable for research, historical background, and understanding the institution. They include:

- *Congressional Procedures and the Policy Process:* Written by Walter Oleszek, this book is the standard work on procedures and process. It graces many congressional desks. The fifth edition was published in October 2000.
- *Congressional Staff Directory:* A comprehensive listing of staff members and how to contact them.
- *CQ Almanac:* A compendium of the year's doings in Congress and the legislation passed. A very useful historical reference work.

- *Directory of Congressional Voting Scores and Interest Group Ratings:* If you want to know how different interest groups rate members, this work is the most comprehensive listing.

- *How Congress Works:* One of the best overall explanations of Congress and how it functions. The most recent edition was published in 1998.

- *Politics in America:* A standard reference work updated biennially featuring every member's biography and a brief description of each congressional district and state.

National Journal

The National Journal Group publishes a variety of products on paper and online, specifically covering Congress and congressional action. Included are:

- *National Journal,* a weekly magazine covering Congress and politics

- *The Hotline,* a daily, online, password-accessible compendium of political news from the country's media

- *Congress Daily,* a twice-daily news service covering Capitol Hill

- *Government Executive,* a monthly magazine for federal government managers

- *American Health Line,* a daily briefing on healthcare politics, policy, and the healthcare industry

- *Technology Daily,* a daily glimpse of technology-related issues in Congress

Additionally, National Journal Group issues books and directories, including:

- *The Almanac of American Politics,* a biennial review of all the members of Congress, their districts, and political issues

- *The Capital Source,* a directory of 6,500 people and organizations in Washington

- *The Federal Technology Source,* a directory of people and organizations handling government technology

Burning Up the Wire Services

A *wire service* provides information to subscribing news outlets, which then publish the information in their own publications. Many local newspapers receive the bulk of their national and international reporting from wire services, so items carried by these services can receive tremendous coverage across the country. Some major newspapers also sell their own reporting through their own wire services.

Most local newspapers receive their reporting from Washington and around the globe from these wire services, so an article about a cause or development from a wire service can appear in thousands of newspapers and influence millions of readers.

National services

Wire service reporting is immediate and up to the moment. Members of Congress look to this media for breaking news but rarely for ideas or opinions. As an advocate, you want wire service coverage of any events, press conferences, or demonstrations that you may be holding.

The biggest wire services are

- ✔ The Associated Press
- ✔ Reuters
- ✔ United Press International
- ✔ The New York Times News Service and Syndicate
- ✔ The Los Angeles Times-Washington Post News Service

A unique wire service that focuses almost exclusively on congressional action is States News Service, which covers the impact of Washington decision making and policy on the 50 states. States News Service watches state congressional delegations and covers the actions of lawmakers for the newspapers and media outlets back home. Its Web site can be accessed at www.statesnews.com.

Founded in 1975, States News Service always has operated on a shoestring. And yet, it has been a launching pad for numerous Washington journalists and is a great way to start a Washington journalism career.

As an advocate, when you want to send a message to a member's hometown media, States News Service can provide you with an easy shortcut.

Specialized, industry, and trade media

The large publications that cover a broad spectrum of events usually are known as *consumer publications,* because they're directed at general consumers.

However, an enormous universe of media focus on specific issues and industries. These outlets usually are called *specialized* or *trade publications*. Much of the reporting in this branch of the media is of high quality, and the reporters and editors generally have a deep understanding of their respective areas of coverage. Members of Congress and especially staff dealing with a specific issue often look to these media outlets for important information and coverage, and they can be influential in a very focused way.

These publications cover topics like defense, technology, healthcare, housing, and just about every area that government touches.

Trumpeting Broadcast and Cable Television

Of all the media, televised media are the most powerful and pervasive. They reach the most people and can have a tremendous impact, whether used for selling toothpaste or political candidates.

Politically, televised media

- ✔ Influence public opinion by deciding which stories to cover and in what order.
- ✔ Determine which events are of national significance by deciding which ones to cover.
- ✔ *Frame* issues — put them in context — by telling people what arguments are being made by both sides and covering the issues' most important elements.
- ✔ Raise political figures to national prominence.

The broadcast networks

The world of television has what I call the *big-five* broadcast networks:

- ✔ ABC (American Broadcasting Company)
- ✔ NBC (National Broadcasting Company)
- ✔ CBS (Columbia Broadcasting Service)
- ✔ Fox Broadcasting Company
- ✔ PBS (Public Broadcasting Service)

CBS, ABC, and NBC are the original broadcast networks, and they still maintain the lion's share of the television audience. As a result, their news reports and programs reach millions of people.

In recent years, the three original networks have given up some of their political influence in congressional circles, because they've reduced their emphasis on news and public affairs programming and their investments in their news operations. Fox still is developing its place in the media universe. Nonetheless, thanks to the number of their viewers, network reports can have an impact on members of Congress.

PBS consistently maintains a high standing with members of Congress in large part because of its nightly news program, the *MacNeil/Lehrer Report,* which became *The NewsHour with Jim Lehrer.* The *NewsHour* is a full hour of news and commentary that usually delves into three topics in great depth. This format makes possible a genuine discussion of a topic. Furthermore, the *NewsHour* consistently features high-ranking government officials and members of Congress, so in times of crisis and uncertainty, members look to the *NewsHour* for policy pronouncements, insights into high-level thinking, and serious examinations of issues.

One measure of the high esteem provided the *NewsHour* is the fact that its host, Jim Lehrer, consistently is chosen by Republicans and Democrats to moderate presidential debates.

The cable networks

The arrival of hundreds of television channels in peoples' homes through cable broadcasting also opens up hundreds of possibilities for public affairs and political programming. Over the years, some cable networks have emerged as news and opinion leaders on Capitol Hill.

Focusing on Congress: C-SPAN

C-SPAN was created by a consortium of cable television companies that banded together in 1979 to provide congressional coverage as a public service. C-SPAN 1, C-SPAN 2, and, more recently, C-SPAN 3 provide unedited, live coverage of House and Senate floor debates, committee hearings, and other public affairs programming. C-SPAN is continuously on the television sets in just about every congressional office and the press galleries.

Eyeing the influential: CNN

In Washington, D.C., the world of cable television news is dominated by CNN (Cable News Network), a 24-hour-a-day, seven-day-a-week, all-news network.

CNN often is on the TVs continuously in congressional offices, in newsrooms, and on executive branch desks — not to mention in Washington, D.C., gyms and sports clubs.

CNN has a reputation as a serious, reliable source of breaking news that's especially valuable during events of great drama like the Gulf War of 1990–1991 and the terrorist attacks of September 11, 2001. CNN takes Congress seriously and gives it consistent, high-quality coverage.

Evaluating the relative newbies

Fox News Network was launched in 1996 as a competitor to CNN. It maintains that it strives for "fair and balanced" coverage of events, but it's still too new to determine what impact it has on Congress.

Other cable news networks include MSNBC and CNBC, but these outlets are more oriented toward business news, and nothing that I've heard indicates they're widely viewed in Congress.

Talk shows

Sundays are devoted to public affairs programming on broadcast and cable channels. TV moderators interview executive branch officials, members of Congress, and sometimes even foreign heads of state.

Depending on the stature of the guests and the topics being covered, these shows can be important to members of Congress. Although only a hard-core political junky can sit glued to the tube for all these shows, sometimes such vigilance pays off when an administration official clarifies policy, a senator makes an announcement about a campaign, or anyone utters a sound bite that's replayed on network news. Furthermore, these shows are opportunities for executive branch officials to defend administration policy and for members of Congress to stake political positions.

Meet the Press (NBC) started on television in 1947. It was a radio program for two years before that. *Face the Nation* (CBS) started in 1954. They are the two oldest political shows. ABC has *This Week*. CNN plays host to *Late Edition*, and Fox has *Fox News Sunday*. On weeknights, CNN airs *Inside Politics*.

In addition to these programs, numerous current-events programs are aired. Most of them feature discussions among journalists. The oldest, *Washington Week in Review* on PBS, started in 1967, and the loudest is the McLaughlin Group, which was the first public affairs roundtable discussion to receive a widespread, commercial following. After McLaughlin paved the way, numerous imitators have followed, each seeking to be louder and more entertaining than the last. Although they occasionally produce arguments about issues that members can use, these shows need to be regarded as entertainment rather than serious political discussions.

As an advocate, being invited to appear on a show is fairly difficult unless you're already famous or your issue is a hot topic. In that case, the shows will seek you out. Your best chance of getting publicity on one of these shows is when your champion is a guest and mentions your cause in the course of her interview.

Tuning in to Radio

The most highly regarded radio program in Washington, D.C., is *All Things Considered,* which is aired by National Public Radio (NPR), a nonprofit public corporation. This program and its morning version, *Morning Edition,* feature consistently excellent political coverage. NPR also is the only broadcast outlet that features regular, serious coverage of the judicial branch and legal issues, thanks to correspondent Nina Totenberg, who repeatedly breaks important stories about judicial nominees. Stories reported by NPR receive attention in both chambers and congressional members and staff frequently listen to the network's programs.

Another radio program that's highly regarded in the congressional community is the Diane Rehm Show, an extended-interview program broadcast by WAMU-FM, a local Washington public broadcast station. The show features interviews with political figures and officials and in-depth examinations of current political issues.

During the Clinton administration, conservative radio talk-show host Rush Limbaugh became a political force thanks to his popularity outside Washington. He is influential among conservative members of Congress who look to him to set the standard of conservative thinking, knowing their constituents are listening to him. Limbaugh's influence seemed to wane after President Clinton left office, but his legacy continued in a widespread network of conservative talk show hosts. For a discussion of dealing with talk radio, see Chapter 14.

Another political broadcaster is Don Imus, whose radio talk show is currently heard in 90 markets. Imus interviews political figures and does public affairs commentary.

Bear in mind that local radio stations in key members' districts can be as powerful as national media — indeed, more so — in influencing that member and her constituents. In launching a media campaign, always be aware of the radio stations within members' districts and states.

Investigating Internet Media

The Drudge Report (www.Drudgereport.com) is the Internet site that no one in Washington admits to reading yet everyone does. Created in 1994, it set the pattern for news Web sites by featuring dozens of links to other news sites along with catchy headlines. It presents a great deal of information but does the work of sorting through it and highlighting particular items. Of course, the person who decides a news items' importance is Matt Drudge. He favors the most sensational and sometimes bizarre news items. Drudge wields influence in Congress because his is the most recognizable and frequently accessed Web site that carries political news.

Drudge first achieved fame by breaking the news that *Newsweek* had suppressed information about a relationship between President Clinton and intern Monica Lewinsky. As the scandal developed, Drudge remained consistently ahead of the rest of the media, breaking new developments in the case. Despite being maligned and denigrated by the mainstream media, all Drudge's scoops checked out except for one about White House aide Sidney Blumenthal, who sued Drudge for what turned out to be an incorrect report. Drudge apologized when he realized it was an error, and the suit ultimately was dropped.

Despite complaints about Drudge not checking his facts and that he has no editors, his site still is one of the best for breaking news items, political and nonpolitical. It's an excellent place to find links to other media Web sites.

A mention in the Drudge Report also can be a powerful source of recognition around the world. Drudge provides a means of sending e-mail news items to him, and much of his early fame came from e-mail tips. However, Drudge receives so many e-mails that sending him one can be like throwing a message in a bottle into the sea.

When it comes to breaking election news over the Internet, the best site is CNN.com. For the 2000 election, CNN invested heavily in equipment and infrastructure, producing up-to-the-minute election results. Its site never crashed despite heavy use.

During the 2000 presidential election, a flood of political Web sites appeared on the Internet. Some of them were lavishly funded: Politics.com, Voter.com, Grassroots.com, Freedomchannel.com, Democracy.net, Politicsonline.com, Web White and Blue (www.webwhiteblue.org), and on and on. All offered links to other Web sites, wire service reports, and ways to contact representatives and senators. With the bursting of the dot-com bubble, most have disappeared.

One political Web site that survived the crash is FastPolitics.com (www.fastpolitics.com), which features an enormous number of links to a wide variety of politically useful information. Another site is Vote.com (www.vote.com), created by former Clinton advisor Dick Morris. Vote.com conducts continuous online polling about a variety of subjects.

Going Abroad with Foreign Media

An enormous number of foreign correspondents work out of Washington, and whenever your issue has international implications, you may want to contact them. Many of the bureaus of foreign media outlets are headquartered in the National Press Building.

If your issue is international — for example, if it involves foreign trade or diplomatic relations — you may want to get your message out overseas by using the foreign media. You may find foreign correspondents receptive to meeting with you and using you as a source.

The most influential foreign publication in Washington is *The Economist,* a weekly magazine published in London. The Economist Group also owns the biweekly Capitol Hill newspaper, *Roll Call. The Economist* is known for its analysis and commentary, which also colors its reporting. It often reports about matters and issues overlooked by the American media, and it reaches an influential and elite audience.

Analyzing the media

Through the years, some excellent books covering specific media outlets have been published. I list a few of them here:

✔ *The Powers that Be,* by David Halberstam, published by Knopf in 1979, exhaustively traces the histories of *The Washington Post, The Los Angeles Times, Time* magazine, and CBS in an insightful and penetrating way.

✔ *The Kingdom and the Power* by Gay Talese, published by World Pub Co. in 1969, is a thorough account of *The New York Times* and the people who have run it through the years.

✔ *All the President's Men* by Bob Woodward and Carl Bernstein, published by Simon &

Schuster in 1974, is a classic tale of political skullduggery uncovered by investigative reporting.

✔ A good, handy guide to media relations is the book, *Media Isn't a Four Letter Word: A Guide to Effective Encounters with the Members of the Fourth Estate,* written by David J. Shea and John F. Gulick and published by the Aerospace Industries Association (AIA), Washington, DC, 2002. The book can be ordered from the AIA web site, www.aia-aerospace.org/pubs/books/media_isnt.cfm.

Part V
Putting the Practical Side to Use

The 5th Wave   By Rich Tennant

Consider yourself lucky. Not everyone gets to meet the national bird when they come to Washington, D.C.

In this part . . .

From checking out the Capitol itself to getting an appointment to West Point, these chapters cover some of the more immediate and practical matters associated with Congress.

Chapter 16

Making Use of Congressional Services

In This Chapter

▶ Using members' connections in Washington

▶ Looking into local issues

▶ Recommending and nominating

*I*n addition to doing the nation's business, members of Congress can take care of some business for you, too. Congressional offices provide *constituent services* to assist you in your dealings with the federal government, getting you any government benefits you're owed, helping with nominations to the military service academies and congressional institutions, and providing internships. Some representatives view constituent services, or *casework* as it's known on Capitol Hill, as the most rewarding aspect of their job, and members who do it well are often rewarded at election time.

Both senators and representatives work on behalf of constituents, but individuals usually turn to their representatives first because they're responsible for a smaller area than a senator, are usually personally in contact with more people than a senator, and are much more oriented toward constituent service. Nonetheless, when seeking assistance, it's often a good idea to contact your representative and both your senators. Or, if you're writing to a representative, send copies of your message to both of your senators, also.

Helping Out with the Feds

Acting on your behalf with a federal agency is one of the most important ways a member can help his constituents. Dealing with the federal bureaucracy can be one of life's great frustrations as people confront a bewildering array of forms, offices, and officials in trying to get something done. A member has more clout with a federal agency, and a call from a staff member asking about an issue or problem can do wonders in cutting through red tape on your behalf.

Intervening with federal agencies

Try to resolve any difficulties with a federal agency yourself before going to your member. All the federal agencies have Web sites that can provide assistance, usually with a page with frequently asked questions (FAQs) that may cover your issue. A single government Web site that links to all other government sites and can search across agencies and departments is www.FirstGov.gov. Federal agencies have become more sensitive to dealing with taxpayers as customers and make great efforts to assist people.

But, if your efforts to resolve a problem meet a roadblock, your member can present your case to agencies including Medicaid, Medicare, and Social Security, the Immigration and Naturalization Service and the Internal Revenue Service. Some of the more common ways members help are by:

- Making sure that constituents receive full Medicare and Medicaid benefits as well as any other health benefits the federal government offers

- Assisting constituents with:

    - Citizenship applications and dealing with the Immigration and Naturalization Service

    - Issues with the Internal Revenue Service

- Helping seniors get the full range of benefits available to them, including Social Security

- Encouraging businesses to take advantage of federal assistance and intercede in dealings with the federal government

- Ensuring that federal workers are treated fairly and receive their full retirement benefits from the government

- Helping veterans receive their full benefits including health, pay, and retirement, loans and mortgages

A member cannot act as a private attorney or provide private legal services. However, a member can send letters to the federal agency inquiring about your case or your issue and argue on your behalf to the agency.

When you write to your representative or senator, be sure to:

✔ Explain the situation clearly

✔ Be clear about what assistance you're seeking

✔ Enclose copies of any documentation or correspondence with the agency

Expediting your passport

One of the most common congressional services offered to constituents is assistance with getting a passport quickly.

To get a passport, you normally apply to the Department of State, either through their passport Web site at `http://travel.state.gov/passport_services.html` or by applying at certain post office branches.

Under ordinary circumstances it takes about six weeks to receive the passport. If you need it more quickly, the State Department will expedite the process if you show them your travel tickets and pay an additional $35 fee. However, even this quicker procedure takes about two weeks.

Your representative can usually get you a passport more quickly if necessary. Contact your representative or senator, and follow the directions from staff.

Intervening in Local Issues

Members of Congress are major political figures in their states and districts, and they have to get reelected, so naturally, they're intimately involved in local politics. They can endorse local candidates for other offices, weigh in on local issues, and intervene with the local party, especially if they think doing so helps their reelection prospects. Furthermore, they're the interface between the local and national government, so, for example, if the local government is looking for a federal grant, the member is the person who must get it.

You always have the opportunity to contact your senator or representative about a local issue. Whether he gets involved depends on whether there's a federal role to play, whether it's advantageous politically, and the member's degree of interest. Nonetheless, calling on a federal representative or senator is certainly a recourse you have as a citizen.

Getting a flag

You can purchase a flag flown over the Capitol through your senators or representative. It's a small but much-used service, and the flags make great gifts. The cost depends on the flag's size and whether it's made of nylon or cotton, but prices run from $16.50 to $25.25. The flag, which must be made in the United States, comes with a certificate saying that it was flown over the Capitol and the date it was flown. Furthermore, you can request that it be flown on a certain date like a birthday or anniversary.

After you make the purchase, the flag literally is run up a flagpole atop the Capitol.

Since September 11, 2001, demand for flags has been extremely heavy and at one point Congress ran out of flags. It's difficult to say if the delivery time will ever return to the previous wait of four to six weeks. Go to your representative or senator's Web site to check on the waiting period for flag delivery.

In the House, the address is: www.House.gov, and in the Senate, it's www.Senate.gov. When you go to your representative or senator's site, go to "Services" or "Constituent services." Most members have a link marked "Flags," where sizes are listed. Some members have an online form to fill out; others need to be contacted by phone, e-mail, or fax.

Even when the member feels that his intervention is inappropriate or unwarranted, he can refer you to the proper official or provide an introduction to people who can address your issue.

Putting in a Good Word

Members have a crucial role to play in helping young people achieve their ambitions whether in the military, in politics, or in government service. By nominating people as candidates for the military service academies, by getting them appointed as congressional pages, or by sponsoring them as interns in their offices, members help shape the next generation.

Getting an academy nomination

The United States government always needs trained professionals in critical areas like defense and transportation, and it has set up specialized academies to provide the education required. The government welcomes applicants from all walks of life between the ages of 18 and 23.

Congress has an important role to play in these institutions because members nominate applicants to the schools. Four government-run service academies take congressional nominations:

✔ The U.S. Military Academy at West Point, New York, trains Army officers and is run by the U.S. Army (www.usma.edu). You can contact it by writing to: U.S. Military Academy, West Point, NY 10996. The telephone number is 845-938-4011.

✔ The U.S. Naval Academy at Annapolis, Maryland, trains Navy and Marine Corps officers and is run by the U.S. Navy (www.usna.edu). It can be contacted by writing to: U.S. Naval Academy, 121 Blake Rd., Annapolis, MD 21402-5000.

✔ The U.S. Air Force Academy at Colorado Springs, Colorado, trains Air Force officers and is run by the U.S. Air Force (www.usafa.af.mil). It can be contacted by writing to: United States Air Force Academy, HQ. USAFA, Colorado Springs, CO 80840; phone 719-333-3813.

✔ The U.S. Merchant Marine Academy at Kings Point, New York, trains merchant marine officers and is run by the U.S. Department of Transportation (www.usmma.edu). It can be contacted by writing to: USMMA, 300 Steamboat Rd., Kings Point, NY 11024; phone 516-773-5000.

✔ The U.S. Coast Guard Academy at New London, Connecticut, trains Coast Guard officers but does not take congressional nominations. Its Web site is www.cga.edu. It can be contacted by writing to: U.S. Coast Guard Academy, 15 Mohegan Avenue, New London, CT 06320. Its telephone number is 860- 444-8444.

These academies charge no tuition, and all the usual expenses — room, board, books — are covered by the government. However, admission is very competitive and having received an education there, a graduate is required to serve five years in the sponsoring service branch.

The nomination process

A nomination by your representative or senator is the first step toward attending a service academy. Each member of Congress is allowed ten nominations to each academy every year. However, only five of a member's nominees can be in the same class in each academy — meaning that if a member nominates the full slate allowed, at least half won't be admitted.

In addition to the members of Congress, the three military academies (Army, Navy, and Air Force) take nominations from the Vice President who can also nominate five candidates from the country at large.

Representatives nominate candidates from their home districts and senators from their home state. The member can handle the nominees in several different ways:

✔ Simply send all ten nominees to the academies and allow the academies to select among them.

✔ Select one nominee as the *principal nominee* — the person the member would most like to attend or believes is best qualified — and rank the rest in order of preference.

✔ Select a principal nominee and then allow the academy to select from the rest.

Some members conduct interviews with applicants before forwarding their applications or consult with former academy graduates about the qualifications of the applicants and whether they are likely to succeed at the academy.

After selections are made, candidates who aren't selected immediately are put on a national waiting list. Several hundred of these wait-listed applicants usually receive their appointments after the initial selections.

How to be considered

To be considered for a nomination to a service academy, write to your representative or senator and request a nomination to one of the academies. All the academies are looking for applicants who:

✔ Are citizens of the United States

✔ Are between 17 and 23 years of age by July 31 of the year they're admitted

✔ Are single, with no dependents and not pregnant

✔ Have at least a 3.0 grade-point average and a high school diploma

✔ Engaged in extracurricular activities while in school

✔ Have a strong interest in science or engineering

✔ Are of good moral character

✔ Are physically fit and athletic

✔ Show leadership abilities and can take responsibility

The members' nominations are due to the academies by January 31 of the year of admission, but every congressional office has different deadlines and requirements for nominees, so it's very important that you contact your representative or senators' offices individually to find out their deadlines. Some may set the deadline as early as October in the year prior to admission. Apply in the spring of your junior year of high school or spring of the year prior to the year you want to be admitted.

Make sure to write separate letters to your representative, both senators, and — if you're applying to a military academy — the vice president. The vice president can be contacted at: Vice President, The Old Executive Office Building, Room 490, Washington, DC 20501. For contact information for members, see the Cheat Sheet at the front of the book.

Serving Congress as a page

Congress has a terrific program for high school students — having them to serve as *pages,* assistants to the members. Being a page is a wonderful opportunity to get to know the institution up close. Many pages have been elected to serve in Congress and others return as congressional officials and officers. One page who didn't return to government but nonetheless achieved a certain prominence was a student named Bill Gates.

Pages serve as couriers, answer telephones, do research for members, and prepare the chamber floors for sessions, distributing legislation and papers. The duties rotate so pages have a chance to serve all functions.

The House and Senate each have their own programs with a few common requirements: Pages must be high school juniors and at least 16 years old when they start their duties with at least a 3.0 grade-point average. Beyond, that, however, requirements for nominations vary from office to office.

Appointments are very competitive: Although not all representatives or senators can nominate pages every semester, more than 400 representatives nominate pages for just 66 House slots each semester, and the majority of senators nominate for 30 slots. Check with your representative or senator to see if he's eligible to nominate that year. If your representative is ineligible, try your senator; if your senator is ineligible, try your representative.

To apply, send a letter to your representative or senator with the following information:

- Full name
- Date of birth
- Social Security number
- Home address and phone number
- Name of parent or guardian
- School name, address, and phone number
- Any honors or accomplishments

- ✔ Extracurricular activities
- ✔ Certified copy of school transcripts
- ✔ Grade-point average
- ✔ Semesters you'd like to attend. Pages can serve longer than a single semester as long as they're 16 years old.

Pages are employees of Congress and are paid a salary from which room and board are deducted. In the House, the salary comes to $13,405 per year at a gross monthly salary of $1,115 per month, with deductions made for taxes, Social Security, and $300 per month for room and board. In the Senate, pages are paid $14,500 per year but also have higher room and board fees: $450 per month.

Pages are expected to serve at least a full semester but can serve as long as a year, but they serve at will and can be dismissed at any time. Pages also have to be covered by medical insurance — most have family policies, but if they don't, they can obtain coverage from the Federal Employees Health Benefits Program which requires payment of a premium.

The House page program

The page program operates in two academic semesters and at least one summer semester — or possibly two if the House remains in session. Pages don't work for individual members, but for the House as a whole.

Not all representatives can recommend pages. Which ones are permitted to do so is a political decision made by the party caucuses. Check with your representative's office or Web site to see whether he is eligible to recommend pages. If he can't nominate pages, try your senators.

A majority chief page and a minority chief page supervise the pages and manage their work responsibilities. The pages report to one or the other depending on which member sponsored them and whether that member belongs to the party with the most seats in the House or to the minority party.

The overall program is overseen by a Page Board made up of two majority party members selected by the Speaker, one member from the minority party selected by the minority leader, the Clerk of the House and the Sergeant-at-Arms of the House. The board makes the final decision on which pages to accept.

The board was partially a response to allegations that surfaced in 1982 that two members had sexual relations with pages. Since then, the pages are more stringently monitored and supervised.

Pages live on the Capitol campus in a restored nurses' dormitory. They share rooms, and the living arrangements are similar to any college or boarding school dormitory. An adult director and five assistants, all of whom reside in the hall, supervise them.

The academic semesters

The academic semesters are for the fall and spring.

The pages attend the U.S. House of Representatives Page School in the Jefferson Building of the Library of Congress and take a high-school junior-year college-prep curriculum including math, English, social studies, science, French, Spanish, and computer technology. They also go on field trips and hear guest speakers.

A big difference between page school and regular high school is evident in its hours. Classes start at 6:45 a.m., and the pages usually start working in the Capitol around 9:00 a.m. They continue working until 5:00 p.m. or until the House adjourns. If the House keeps working past 10:00 p.m., classes are postponed for the next day. At the completion of the semester they should be able to return to their home high schools and be up to speed academically.

The pages have a strict dress code that calls for short hair for the men. White shirts, blue blazers, gray slacks, and black shoes are required for the men, and the same goes for the women with the exception that women can wear a knee-length, nonslit, gray skirt. Both the men and women wear ties supplied by the page program.

The summer semesters

The summer semester begins the second week of June and ends when Congress adjourns for its August recess, usually at the end of July. The congressional workload also determines whether there will be a second summer semester through August.

Everything is more relaxed during the summer: No classes are in session, and pages can live off the Capitol campus and commute to work. The dress code also is relaxed. Pages don't have to wear jackets except when they're working on the House floor.

For two testimonials about the page experience access: www.house.gov/petri/tracey_r.htm or www.house.gov/petri/kelly_l.htm. Rep. Tom Petri (R-Wis.) sponsored both of these pages.

The Senate page program

Not all senators can recommend pages. Which senators have the privilege is a political decision made by the respective party caucuses. You should check your senators' Web sites to see whether they're eligible to recommend pages, and if not, try your representative.

The Senate page program is very similar to the House program. Pages must also be 16 and in their junior year of high school. The Senate pages, however, live four or six to a room in Daniel Webster Hall, about two blocks from the Hart Senate Office Building. Their classes start at 6:15 a.m. and usually go to 9:30 a.m. or one hour before the Senate convenes. The Senate Sergeant-at-Arms administers the Senate page program and the school is run by the Secretary of the Senate.

Like the House pages, Senate pages serve during two academic semesters and may have one or two summer semesters depending on the Senate workload.

Interning in the Capitol

Washington is full of internships — during the academic year and during the summer. Members, congressional committees, the congressional leadership, federal agencies, lobbies, trade associations, newspapers — like *The Hill* — all have internship programs. Most congressional internships are available starting in a student's junior year of college, although some interns may be taken earlier.

Internships are an invaluable way to learn about Congress and government, and a Washington internship is especially exciting because it takes the intern into the heart of power and teaches lessons that simply can't be conveyed in a classroom. Congressional internships can add special prestige to a résumé and may lead to full-time Capitol Hill jobs.

As a result, Washington internships — and especially congressional internships — are highly prized and fiercely sought.

Most interns do basic work in congressional offices: Opening mail, attending to office chores, answering telephones, and doing research. At the same time, congressional internships offer the opportunity to meet other politically active interns, come into contact with members of Congress and high government officials, see how things really work, and be at the center of power and great events.

Washington also presents an abundance of social opportunities, especially during the summer when the town is full of interns. There are numerous social events, receptions, fundraisers, parties, and galas put on by different associations and lobbying groups. Think tanks hold seminars, debates, and lectures often featuring renowned experts in their fields. There are also celebrities passing through and the occasional movie premier to create excitement.

Every congressional office has its own internship program so you need to contact your representative or senator directly to find out what internships are available. The best way to start out is to go to the member's Web site and look under "internships" or "constituent services." That should give you the basic rules and procedures for applying.

Some universities and colleges have internship programs that help place interested students in congressional internships. Check with your school to see what's available.

Representatives are always looking for interns from their home districts. Senate internships may have more competition since the senator is drawing on applicants from the entire state.

Intern scandals

In recent years a number of scandals have involved Washington interns. The most infamous was the one involving Monica Lewinsky who served as a White House intern during the administration of President Bill Clinton and whose relationship with the president led to his impeachment.

Chandra Levy, an intern at the Federal Bureau of Prisons had an affair with Rep. Gary Condit (D-Calif.) and mysteriously disappeared in the spring of 2001. Her remains were discovered in Washington in May 2002.

Magazine articles also have been written about interns having relationships with members of Congress or behaving wildly during their time in Washington.

The institution of internship survives despite the scandals. There's a reason for this — internships are invaluable for the institution offering them and for the interns who take advantage of them.

People who deal with internship programs on a long-term basis know that these scandals are extremely rare. The level of social activity among interns in Washington is about equivalent to that of a college campus. Thousands of interns come to Washington every year and the vast majority of interns attracted to congressional or government service are serious about learning from their experiences and making a contribution to their country.

There's no doubt that the Monica Lewinsky and Chandra Levy scandals hurt the reputation of Washington internships in general. But the most remarkable thing coming out of the scandals is that they didn't put a dent in the desire of institutions to sponsor internships or the number of applicants seeking them.

At the end of the day an internship is what you make of it — and you get out of it what you put into it.

Chapter 17

Visiting Congress

· ·

In This Chapter

▶ Exploring the Capitol and surrounding buildings

▶ Understanding the features of the House and Senate sides

▶ Entertaining in the Capitol

▶ Eating on the Hill

· ·

*T*here's something thrilling and awe inspiring about approaching the Capitol building, the home of Congress (see Figure 17-1). The Dome perched regally over the landscape and topped by the Statue of Freedom gleams against the sky. Many people who work there, some who've spent their entire careers within its walls, say they're still inspired every morning when they approach it.

Visiting the nation's capital is something every American needs to do at least once. Regardless of whether you come to sightsee or seriously lobby the members of Congress, seeing the places where decisions are made and power is wielded and knowing that all that power is derived from your vote and your participation is thrilling.

Washington, D.C., has numerous attractions: historic sites, the Smithsonian, museums, monuments, and memorials. You can spend years in the area and still not see all the sights. Indeed, you can spend weeks exploring just the Capitol and its environs. Plenty of guidebooks are available to walk you through the attractions, not least of which is *Washington, D.C. For Dummies*, by Beth Rubin, published in 2001 by Wiley.

Visiting the Capitol Campus

The Capitol building sits amid a complex of 283 acres that contain parks, gardens, office buildings, and support structures. The Supreme Court building is included in the United States Capitol Complex and so are the three large buildings that make up the Library of Congress.

The House and Senate have separate office buildings to the north and south of the Capitol. When your visit includes conducting business with Congress, meeting with your representative or senator, or attending hearings, you're likely to spend time in these office buildings.

The Capitol building, shown in Figure 17-1, dominates the entire complex.

Figure 17-1:
An angle on
the Capitol
building.

The Capitol sits atop a modest hill — hence the term *Capitol Hill* — that rises 88 feet above the level of the Potomac River, which flows through the nation's capital. Although it isn't an overwhelming elevation, you can really feel every inch of it when you're running uphill on a hot day, trying to arrive promptly for an appointment.

Finding out what's where

When it first was created, the Capitol building held both houses of Congress, the Supreme Court, all congressional offices, and the Library of Congress. As the country has expanded, so has Congress's working quarters.

You can view a good brief history of the Capitol at the Architect of the Capitol's Web site, www.aoc.gov/homepage.htm. A beautiful book on the Capitol and its history is *History of the United States Capitol* by William C. Allen, an architectural historian in the Architect's office. The book was published in 2001 by the U.S. Government Printing Office, Washington, D.C.

The Capitol has no back. Instead, it has two fronts — an East Front and a West Front. The East Front overlooks a parking lot and lawns to the Supreme Court and the Library of Congress's Thomas Jefferson Building. The East Front has the magnificent steps that visitors use to enter the building. The West Front consists of terraces and steps and looks toward the Washington Monument, the Lincoln Memorial, Pennsylvania Avenue, and the Potomac. The West Front is where Fourth of July concerts, inaugural addresses, and big rallies take place — it's the side you see in the news.

The building has five levels:

- ✔ The basement contains machinery rooms, custodial rooms, and tunnels to the House and Senate office buildings. From the basement, people in the building also can take subways for quick rides to the nearby office buildings. If you have business in the complex and need to travel quickly from one end of the building to the other, or to the office buildings, using these tunnels is best.

- ✔ The first floor includes the public entrance, offices for the officers of the House and Senate, a House dining room, and some committee rooms. Public areas include the Hall of Columns on the House side, the Brumidi Corridors on the Senate side, the Old Supreme Court Chambers, and the Crypt, a round open area beneath the dome, halfway between the House and Senate.

- ✔ The second floor is where House and Senate chambers are located and congressional leaders maintain their offices. Most of these areas are closed to the public, but three major public areas are located on the second floor: The enormous Rotunda under the dome is exactly halfway between the House and Senate. National Statuary Hall on the House side is where the House of Representatives used to meet, but now it features sculptures from different states. And the Old Senate Chamber is where the Senate met until 1859, when it moved to the current Senate wing.

- ✔ The third floor contains public galleries above the House and Senate chambers, offices, committee rooms, and press galleries. This area is where the public is directed to view congressional proceedings.

- ✔ The fourth floor is not open to the public, but it contains additional offices and hearing rooms.

Elevators are located throughout the building, but some are marked for members only and others are designated for the press. When members must quickly move to the floor of their chambers so they can cast votes, some elevators that ordinarily are open to the public are designated for members only.

Buying or selling is expressly forbidden in the Capitol and the congressional office buildings.

Touring the Capitol

All you need to do to take a guided tour of the Capitol is obtain a free ticket at the East Front Screening Facility, which is located near the fountains on the East Front plaza of the Capitol. The tickets are distributed on a first-come, first-served basis. Visitors are screened at this facility and then escorted by a Capitol Police officer and a guide from the Capitol Guide Service to the Rotunda where the tour begins. The maximum number of people on a tour is 40 people.

Members can arrange special tours through the Capitol Guide Service. Call your representative or senator to arrange this kind of tour.

If you can't get to the Capitol, there's a wonderful Web site that allows you to take a virtual tour of the building. Various hot spots in the views of the Capitol room allow you to click and get more information about the room and the objects in it. The effect is remarkably like being in the room — you can look up, down, or to either side. The site is: www.senate.gov/vtour/index.html.

Prior to September 11, 2001, the Capitol was open to all visitors. People simply came in, passed through a metal detector, and were free to go anywhere open to the public. Immediately after September 11, 2001, the Capitol was closed to the public. Although it reopened on December 8, 2001, restrictions are now in place.

The Capitol Architect and police

The Capitol building and the entire United States Capitol Complex are overseen by the Architect of the Capitol. The Architect is appointed by the president and confirmed by the Senate and serves a ten-year term. Once confirmed, the Architect becomes a congressional employee. The Architect's office is staffed by architects, engineers, and historians. A Capitol maintenance and custodial staff sees to building operations.

In addition to the Architect's office, the campus has its own police force, the U.S. Capitol Police, consisting of approximately 1,000 personnel who guard the buildings. A board consisting of the Architect, and the sergeants-at-arms of the House and Senate oversees the force.

A whole lotta building

According to official statistics, the Capitol takes up 175,170 square feet, or about 4 acres, and has floor space the equivalent of approximately 16½ acres or 775,000 square feet. It's 751 feet, 4 inches long from north to south. If outside steps are included, it's 350 feet wide at its widest. It's 288 feet high from its base to the top of the Statue of Freedom. It has approximately 540 rooms, 658 windows — including 108 in the dome that light the Rotunda — and 850 doorways. In short, it's massive. It also was one of America's architectural wonders when it was completed in its current form in 1863.

Three ways that you can to tour the Capitol include:

- The Capitol Guide Service (CGS) conducts tours from 9:00 a.m. until 4:30 p.m. Monday through Saturday. Visitors must get tickets for these tours, and tickets are given away free, one per person, on a first-come, first-served basis at the Capitol Guide Service kiosk near the intersection of First Street SW and Independence Avenue. The CGS recommends that people line up no later than 7:30 a.m. for that day's tickets. Ticket distribution begins at 8:15 a.m., and all tickets are usually distributed very quickly. Tour groups can be up to 40 people. Other than Sundays, the Capitol is closed to tours only on Thanksgiving and Christmas.

- Personal staff can conduct tour groups of up to 15 people.

- Members can conduct tours in person. These tours are not limited in size.

The number of public visitors declined drastically after September 11 but is beginning to rebound. As of July 2002, the number of visitors was running at about 9,000 a day, half of previous totals.

Adhering to security restrictions

Even before 2001, security measures were added to restrict access to the building. After the United States declared war on Germany in 1917, heavy iron gates were erected at all the Capitol's doors. During World War II, however, the only Capitol security measures added were fake machine guns placed on the roof. Following a bomb explosion in 1983, some entrances were designated for visitors and others were marked for only members, press, and staff. (See the "Surviving various attacks" sidebar in this chapter.)

After the events of September 11, 2001, security measures became much more strict. All visitors are screened through metal detectors. Items that cannot be brought into the Capitol are:

- ✔ Aerosol and nonaerosol sprays, including mace and pepper spray
- ✔ Cans and bottles
- ✔ Unusually large suitcases, duffel bags, and large backpacks
- ✔ Knives of any length, razors, and box cutters
- ✔ Guns and explosives

Visiting the Capitol Visitor Center

To ease the wear and tear on the Capitol building, an underground Capitol Visitor Center (CVC) is scheduled for completion in 2005. The CVC was necessary because the number of visitors to the Capitol — sometimes as many as 18,000 on a single day — was putting a strain on the building despite repeated restorations. Additionally, exhibits about the building are scattered throughout its corridors, sometimes in unpredictable places, such as the Crypt beneath the Rotunda.

In the mid-1970s, the Architect of the Capitol began formulating a master plan for the future of the building. The plan went through successive revisions throughout the 1990s and emerged with the CVC as its centerpiece. Ground was broken June 8, 2000.

The new center is a massive project, requiring a 196,000-square-foot excavation. However, when it's complete, its three levels will provide 580,000 square feet of space and be capable of handling 5,000 people at a time.

The center is intended to provide many things, not least of which is security. When it's done, a visit to the Capitol will be much more enjoyable than in the past. The CVC will feature more room for exhibits, two orientation theaters, an auditorium, food service, gift shops, and restrooms, and it'll be connected to the other buildings in the complex and to the utility tunnels.

Meanwhile, however, the Capitol campus is a construction site, full of building materials, earth-moving equipment, dirt, and fences. Historic trees are being moved, and parking is at a premium.

You can see weekly updates on the progress of the Visitor Center at www. aoc.gov/cvc/cvc_updates.htm.

Surviving various attacks

The Capitol has survived a great number of incidents since it first was occupied in 1800. The British burned the original building in 1814, although a rainstorm saved it from total ruin. After being rebuilt, it suffered another fire in 1851 that burned the Library of Congress, which then was housed in the building.

In the early days of the Civil War, 4,000 federal soldiers camped out in the building, spreading their bedrolls on the floor of the House of Representatives, lighting cooking fires in the Rotunda, and baking bread in ovens in the basement.

On November 6, 1898, a natural gas explosion and fire severely damaged the Senate wing. Fortunately, it occurred on a Sunday and no one was injured. Although Spanish agents were suspected of planting a bomb that caused the explosion after the Spanish-American War, that proved not to be the case. A faulty gas meter leaked fumes into a basement room, and when they reached a hanging lamp, they exploded.

Bombs have gone off in the Capitol three times. The worst in terms of damage occurred on July 2, 1915. Erich Muenter, a professor of German at Harvard University, protested American support for the British war effort in what would be known as World War I by successfully blowing up the Capitol switchboard shortly before midnight. Muenter also shot financier J.P. Morgan, but the wound was only superficial. Muenter was caught, incarcerated for both crimes, and committed suicide in prison.

In the early hours of March 1, 1971, the Weather Underground, protesting American involvement in Laos, exploded a bomb hidden in a restroom on the Senate side.

On November 7, 1983, a bomb exploded in a Senate corridor late at night. A group expressing solidarity with Grenada and Lebanon claimed responsibility.

All of these bombs were deliberately timed to go off when no one was present. They were intended to make political points, not kill people. But that wasn't the case during the worst act of violence by terrorists inside the Capitol, which occurred March 1, 1954, when three Puerto Ricans seeking independence for the island began firing on the House floor from the visitors' gallery. They fired 30 shots and wounded five representatives. After this incident, Capitol Police restricted access to the visitors galleries and started a credentials system. Bullet holes from the incident remain in some of the desks and legend has it that sticking your finger in one of them means you'll have good luck.

On July 24, 1998, a deranged gunman who forced his way into the building killed two Capitol police officers, Jacob Chestnut and John Gibson, as they protected House offices.

On September 11, 2001, the Capitol and the congressional office buildings were evacuated when reports reached Washington that in addition to three planes that crashed into the World Trade Center towers and the Pentagon, a fourth aircraft had been hijacked and was headed to an unknown destination. The passengers on that plane fought the hijackers, and the plane crashed in a field near Shanksville, Pennsylvania.

Making Your Way to the House Side

Just as the Framers intended the House and Senate to be separate and distinct parts of the legislature, the House and Senate sides of the Capitol building and the Capitol complex are two distinct worlds. People usually refer to these as the House and Senate *sides*.

Figure 17-2 is a mini map of the area around the Capitol and shows the location of the House and Senate office buildings.

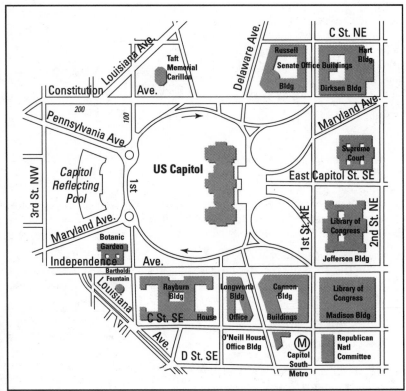

Figure 17-2:
A map of the Capitol area.

In a moment of high drama, ceremony, and symbolism in 1999, members of the House Judiciary Committee walked through the House wing and met the Senate Sergeant-at-Arms in the center of the Rotunda. He escorted them to the Senate to present evidence against President Bill Clinton. Circumstances were rare in that instance with members of the House paying a visit to the Senate in person (rather than just sending legislation). That scene had only been played out once before in 1868, during the impeachment of President Andrew Johnson.

Distinguishing the House office buildings

The House side has five office buildings outside the Capitol building itself. Those buildings contain personal offices of members, offices of committees, and hearing rooms. Freshman members receive their room assignments by a lottery conducted at the beginning of the Congress. Senior members receive highly coveted private offices known as *hideaways* in various parts of the buildings, in addition to their public offices.

You can see where your representative is located by looking on his Web site. The buildings also have directories in their lobbies, and guards can direct you to offices. Addresses are also in some of the Capitol guidebooks (see Chapter 6). Although you must go through a security screening to enter these buildings, you don't have to be in a tour group. The House office buildings include:

- ✔ **The Cannon House Office Building,** First Street and Independence Avenue SE, is the oldest House building. It opened in 1908 and is named for Speaker Joe Cannon (R-Ind., 1873–1923, with interruptions). You know an office is located in Cannon if its number has three digits.

- ✔ **The Longworth House Office Building,** Independence and New Jersey Avenues SE, opened in 1933 and is named for Speaker Nicholas Longworth (R-Ohio, 1903–1931, with interruptions). Its office numbers have four digits that start with "1."

- ✔ **The Rayburn House Office Building,** Independence Avenue and South Capitol Street SW, was opened in 1965 and is the largest of the office buildings. It's named for Speaker Sam Rayburn (D-Texas, 1913–1961). Its office numbers have four digits that start with "2." The Rayburn Building is home to many of the House committee offices and some of the larger, more impressive hearing rooms.

- ✔ **The O'Neill House Office Building,** formerly the Congressional Hotel, was acquired in 1972. It's located at New Jersey Avenue and C Street SE and is named for Speaker Tip O'Neill (D-Mass., 1953–1987). It's in terrible shape and slated for demolition in 2002 and replacement thereafter. Many subcommittees have offices here.

- ✔ **The Ford House Office Building** is some distance from the main Capitol complex at 300 D Street SW and is named for former Minority Leader (and later president) Gerald Ford (R-Mich., 1949–1973). It housed the Federal Bureau of Investigation (FBI) until that agency moved to new quarters, and Congress acquired it in 1975. It houses many of Congress's support offices.

Whenever you're conducting business with members or attending a hearing, the overwhelming likelihood is that you'll be going to one of these office buildings.

Making the most of other features

In addition to office buildings, the House side features the U.S. Botanic Gardens Conservatory, open free of charge to the public from 10 a.m. to 5 p.m. every day. Congress established the conservatory, which is located at Maryland Avenue and First Street SW, in 1820. Its most recent renovation was completed in 2001. It features a variety of plants and programs and is sometimes host to special functions. Information about the conservatory and its calendar of events can be found on its Web site at www.aoc.gov/USBG/usbg_overview.htm.

Plans have been drawn for a National Garden on three acres adjacent to the conservatory, and funds now are being raised to create it. For more information, check out its Web site at www.aoc.gov/projects/usbg_ng/ng_overview.htm.

Across from the conservatory is Bartholdi Park, where varieties of landscaping and plants are displayed. It's named after Frederic Auguste Bartholdi, the sculptor who created the fountain located at its center.

The Capitol Power Plant has provided heat and utilities to the Capitol complex since 1910.

Seeing the Senate Side

Because the Senate has fewer senators than the House has representatives, the offices on the Senate side tend to be more spacious and, in some cases, more grandiose than those on the House side.

The three office buildings that serve the Senate are

- **The Russell Senate Office Building,** First Street and Constitution Avenue NE (East corner), is the oldest Senate office building. It opened in 1909 and is named for Sen. Richard Russell (D-Ga., 1933–1971). The Russell Building has a large, imposing caucus room used for some of the more high-profile hearings.

- **The Dirksen Senate Office Building,** First Street and Constitution Avenue NE (West corner), was opened in 1958 and is named for Sen. Everett Dirksen (R-Ill., 1951–1969).

> ✔ **The Hart Senate Office Building,** Second and C Streets NE, opened in 1982 and is named for Sen. Philip Hart (D-Mich., 1959–1976). This building was affected by the anthrax attacks of October 2001. The building features a large, modern hearing room designed to accommodate television and other media. It's frequently the site of the most crowded and high-profile events and hearings.

The bells and lights of the Capitol

Members of Congress now wear pagers to receive notices about votes, and they carry handheld devices that provide wireless access to e-mail so they can stay in touch with their offices. Nevertheless, the Capitol campus retains an old system of bells, buzzers, and lights that alert members to actions occurring on the floor. These bells and lights also go off in the congressional office buildings. Naturally, the House and Senate have different bell systems.

For the Senate:

✔ One ring means a yea or nay vote is being held.

✔ Two rings means a quorum call is being conducted.

✔ Three rings calls for absentees.

✔ Four rings means the end of the daily session.

✔ Five rings means that the time for a yea or nay vote is half over and only seven and a half minutes remain.

✔ Six rings means the end of the morning session if the lights go off. If they stay on, it means a recess during the day.

For the House:

✔ One long ring followed by three rings means the start or continuation of a quorum call.

✔ One long ring means the end of a quorum call.

✔ Two rings means an electronically recorded vote.

✔ Two rings followed by two more rings means a roll-call vote.

✔ Two rings followed by five rings means a first vote under suspension of the rules — meaning that regular parliamentary rules are suspended to quickly complete non-controversial business.

✔ Three rings means a quorum call, and rings are repeated every 5 minutes until 15 minutes elapse, enabling members to get to the floor to be counted.

✔ Three rings followed by five rings means a quorum call in the Committee of the Whole, when the House forms itself into one big committee, enabling it to do business with fewer rules and restrictions.

✔ Four rings means the daily adjournment.

✔ Five rings means a five-minute electronically recorded vote.

✔ Six rings means a recess.

In addition to the bells, the lights that shine in the Capitol can tell you if Congress is in session or not. While the Capitol is always bathed in light, if a light is on in the *Tholus,* the cylindrical area directly below the Statue of Freedom atop the dome, it means one or both of the houses are in session. You can determine which body by the flag flying over its chamber. The respective flags fly when each chamber is in session.

An interesting feature on the western side of the Capitol grounds, on the Senate side, is the brick Summerhouse, which was completed in 1880. Designed by the famous landscape architect Frederick Law Olmsted, it's also known as the grotto or the resting court. A dark, cool retreat covered with ivy, it features cold-water fountains to refresh senators and visitors on hot days.

Holding a Function at the Capitol

The Capitol, congressional office buildings, and Library of Congress have numerous rooms and venues available for private functions like receptions or meetings.

If you do stage an event in a room, the member who makes the reservation must attend — and attend for the entire event, no ducking his head in and then leaving. You'll have to pay rent for the room, and you must use the official caterer, Guest Services Inc., or one of its subcontractors, Uptown Caterers or Ridgwells.

Special events must be booked through a member of Congress, but depending on which side of the complex you want to conduct your meeting or function, you need to contact either your representative or your senator. The member then contacts the special events office of his chamber's sergeant-at-arms.

On the Senate side, special events are administered through the Senate Rules and Administration Committee. Different rooms fall under different jurisdictions. For example, on the House side, some rooms are controlled by the Office of the Speaker, the Architect of the Capitol, or the Chief Administrative Officer. The special events office coordinates the rooms.

The advantage of staging an event in the Capitol complex is simply that it's convenient for members, and they're more likely to attend the event, especially during busy sessions when they must be close to the floor for votes.

Dining on Capitol Hill

As one might expect, numerous restaurants are convenient to Capitol Hill workers. Cafeterias also serve congressional members and staff, but they're also open to the public during certain hours.

In the Capitol building is a members' dining room on the House side, just off the Hall of Columns shortly after you come in the entrance. It consists of two rooms, one for members only and their guests and one for the public, although members receive preferential seating on crowded days. The dining room is closed when Congress is not in session.

Cafeterias also are located in the Longworth, Rayburn, and Ford buildings on the House side, and in the Dirksen Building on the Senate side. Additionally, small coffee shops, carryout eateries, and snack bars are situated in the Cannon and Hart buildings.

On the House side small commercial strips feature restaurants and bars along First Street SE and Pennsylvania Avenue SE. On the Senate side, Union Station, magnificently restored in 1988 as an urban shopping mall, has numerous restaurants and shops including a large food court for fast dining. It also houses Amtrak, Marc, and Metro train stations. Additionally, other restaurants are easily accessible to Capitol Hill workers along North Capitol Street and Massachusetts Avenue NW.

Part VI
The Part of Tens

The 5th Wave   By Rich Tennant

In this part . . .

In these short and sweet chapters, I gather tips to help you lobby, meet with a member, and handle a journalist. I also offer my own modest suggestions for ways to improve the great institution that is the U.S. Congress

Chapter 18

Ten Tips for Conducting a Lobbying Campaign

●●●

In This Chapter

▶ Establishing your bottom line

▶ Pursuing clear objectives

▶ Achieving your lobbying goals

●●●

*L*obbying is salesmanship, and if you can sell anything, you can sell your idea, your cause, or your bill. The American political system is extraordinarily flexible and responsive to voters, but nothing in life is easy, and getting legislation enacted is one of the most difficult tasks of all. Nonetheless, adhering to certain principles will see you through not only the political process but also through life.

Knowing Your Core Issues

Before anyone can help you or ally with you, you have to be clear about what's important to you in your own mind. Having a clear understanding isn't necessarily the same as knowing what you're trying to achieve (see next section). *Core issues* are set principles that you hold dear. *Achievements* are what you're trying to accomplish in pursuit of those core issues.

As you make your way through the congressional process, you'll be buffeted by opposition, dilemmas, distractions, diversions, and compromises. Unless you're extremely clear about the principles that guide your actions, you'll never be able to achieve anything legislatively or politically. Reaching a political goal is like walking through a storm: The wind may buffet you, but if your feet are firmly planted in your beliefs, you'll never be blown off course. You don't have to be fanatical about attaining your political goals, but you do have to know where you're headed.

Knowing What You're Trying to Achieve

When you start a lobbying campaign, be very clear about what you're trying to do. Are you trying to pass a particular piece of legislation? Get a congressional resolution? Bring a particular cause to public attention? The ends you seek determine your means, and if you're clear about your goals, you're bound to operate with clarity, precision, and effectiveness.

Knowing your goals doesn't mean that you'll necessarily pursue a straight path toward your objectives. For that matter, you may not even have well-defined objectives when you start lobbying Congress on a particular issue. Frequently a particular bill is absorbed by a different piece of legislation and you may discover yourself supporting legislation or a proposition that you never imagined you'd be concerned about to achieve a higher end. Nonetheless, the clearer your aims, the more likely you are to achieve them.

Assessing Your Assets and Liabilities

Sit down and think through the assets and liabilities you're bringing to your campaign. Assess your strengths and those of your likely opponents. Know what cards you have to play, and if you don't have as many cards as you'd like, think about how you can develop more of them. For a fuller discussion of potential assets and liabilities, go to Chapter 12.

Knowing Whereof You Speak

You need to be thoroughly versed in your issue: That means having a command of the facts, the issue's history, and the positions of your opposition. When meeting members of Congress, you need to know who they are, their backgrounds, their states or districts, and determine their attitudes toward your issue as best you can.

In short, you need to be informed. Being informed means knowing the current state of your issue. You must absorb everything being said about your issue every day regardless of whether it's in the halls of Congress or in the media. You need to read everything you can get your hands on and listen to broadcast reports about your issue. Hiring a professional clipping service to track coverage of your issue may be worthwhile, especially when you're going to be working on your issue for a long time. You can also subscribe to online information services such as Lexis-Nexis (www.Lexisnexis.com) or Dow Jones' Factiva (www.factiva.com) service. You certainly need to do frequent Internet searches on your issue and related topics.

Building Coalitions and Alliances

Persuade as many people and organizations as you can to take your side. When it comes to politics, more is better. The bigger and more powerful the forces you command, the more likely that you'll achieve your goals. You must find like-minded people wherever you can when seeking out potential allies. Try determining which individuals, groups, or organizations have interests similar to yours and whether they'd be served by your success, and then try building alliances with them by:

- Treating every relationship as a long-term one regardless of whether it's with interns, staffers, members, or anyone with whom you deal. You never know where these people will turn up in the future.

- Thinking through every imaginable implication of your legislation no matter how peripheral it may seem and then approaching groups that have an interest in any of those areas.

- Sitting down and putting yourself in the position of one of your opponents and trying to come up with every possible argument against your position and then thinking through your responses to those arguments. You never know, you just may change an opponent's mind.

Helping Your Friends and Frustrating Your Enemies

Members of Congress who help you will seek out your help in return, either in getting reelected or achieving other goals. Give it to them. If you want reliable friends, you must also be a reliable friend. Sometimes that means overlooking much that you might otherwise consider distasteful. You may have to remain silent when you disagree with the member on other issues. Just remember why you're lobbying and your ultimate goal.

Remember, too, that opponents must suffer a penalty for opposing you and members need to know about it. Use whatever leverage you can — within the bounds of law — to achieve your goals. By the same token, burn as few bridges as possible. Today's opponent may be tomorrow's ally. You need all the allies you can get.

Friends and enemies must know what they must do to be either your friend or your opponent. They must know clearly and unambiguously what you expect of them and — equally important — what you don't want them to do. Your job is making those factors clear to them.

Keep detailed records of how members behave toward your issue, the statements they make, the votes they cast, and whether they're supportive. You can then use these records for guiding your own actions toward the members and motivating your allies for or against them. These records are the material that you'll use whenever you decide to issue a scorecard.

Being Open to Compromise

Although you need to be determined in achieving your ends, you need to know your goals, you need to understand your capabilities, and you also must be open to a certain amount of compromise.

In a system of government that encompasses all points of view and tries to accommodate differing interests, what you seek inevitably entails a certain amount of compromise. What you compromise on and to what degree you compromise depends on individual circumstances. That's why knowing your core issues and your ultimate goal are so important. When you know your final destination, you also know how much you can give up to get there.

Compromising often takes on a negative connotation, because it inevitably means surrendering some ideals and accommodating other, opposing points of view. But one of the great geniuses of the American system is the willingness of its statesmen to find common ground despite vastly different perspectives and interests. Different parties have almost always given up some of their goals in recognition of a larger good. Political compromises have been very successful: The most outstanding was one that balanced the needs of smaller states with that of the larger ones to create a House of Representatives and a Senate. That compromise has endured and worked well since 1789.

Only once have different American interests been so divergent that no compromise of any kind was possible — and the result was a civil war. As terrible as that episode was, the United States suffered less than many countries endure in multiple civil wars over their political differences. The secret to that success is the general willingness of Americans to seek out common ground and forge mutually acceptable compromises among differing parties.

As you pursue your goals, you must remember that making compromises is not the same as defeat or humiliation. Compromises are part of a tradition and a way of doing business that has served the country well.

Not Expecting Quick Results

Remember that Congress works very, very slowly. Budget and appropriations legislation takes first priority and must be passed every year. So, if your cause doesn't result in appropriations-related legislation, it may be shunted to the side. Additionally, a representative system of government is designed to ensure that everyone has a say in what's passed and that everyone's concerns, interests, and objections are incorporated into its actions. All this takes time, so you must think in terms of years.

Nonetheless, whenever your cause is worth pursuing, it's worth pursuing over a long period of time. Commit for the long haul.

Finding a Champion

You don't just need friends or a member to sponsor legislation, you need a champion, someone in Congress who takes up your cause and pursues your issue. A champion is a member who can maneuver through Congress for you and can push your cause with the same vigor as you. (Chapter 11 gives you tips on finding and dealing with congressional champions.)

Being Patient, Persistent, and Persevering

When you try a means of accomplishing something, and it fails, try something else. Somewhere, somehow you'll find a solution to the obstacles you face and a way around the barriers in your path. Believing that your efforts make a difference and that extra effort can produce extra results is essential. Success never is guaranteed, but if you don't try, failure *is* guaranteed.

Tom Paine's words to a weary Continental Army are worth remembering: "That which we achieve too easily, we esteem too lightly." If what you're trying to achieve were easily done, then it more than likely already would have been done. Otherwise, there's a reason it hasn't been done, and it's then up to you to make it happen.

Chapter 19

The Ten Commandments for Dealing with Congressional Staff

In This Chapter

▶ Meeting a member or a member's staff

▶ Making your visit effective and memorable

▶ Following up on your visit and working with members and their staffs

*V*isiting a member or a member's staff is when you get to make your pitch for your cause in person. Your visit is the most important kind of lobbying you can do.

Remember, when you visit a member or staff, or anyone for that matter, you're conveying an impression not only of yourself but also of the cause or constituents you represent. As the old saying goes: "You only get one chance to make a first impression." And, first impressions can be lasting.

Being Prompt

Remember that time is of the essence in Congress. Always be punctual to a scheduled meeting and remember that the member is very pressed for time. Members can forgive political opposition, but wasting their time is unforgivable.

Knowing the Goal of the Meeting

Why are you having this meeting, and what do you want to come out of it? You need to have a clear idea of why you want to meet face-to-face with the member. Set goals for the meeting. Do you want to emerge with a letter of support or a commitment from the member to vote a certain way on a piece of legislation? Be clear about your purposes and your criteria for success.

Preparing the Ground

By the time you have a face-to-face meeting, the member should know about your issue and the purpose of your visit, because you've already communicated with the member or her staff through e-mail, a letter, and by phone. Driving home your concerns in a personal way and discussing concerns of the member and staffers are the purposes of the meeting.

You shouldn't walk into a meeting with strangers. The member and staffers need to feel as though you're an old friend. The staff needs to be familiar with you and your cause. If you've established a paper trail and prepared the ground, you'll encounter familiar and knowledgeable people.

Doing Your Homework

Find out everything that you can about the member before your meeting. At a minimum, you need to know her state, district, and party affiliation. Knowing her previous votes on your issue, her public statements, what the local and/or national media are saying about her, what political pressures she's subjected to, her standing with her party leadership, the state of her campaign finances, and her political situation regarding her reelection bid is preferable. You can never know too much. (See Chapters 2 and 3 about learning about your representative and senators.)

Being Courteous and Calm

Courtesy toward members of Congress is essential. In an institution full of constant conflict and outwardly exhibited political passions, courtesy is the lubricant that helps get things done and keeps differences from getting too personal. You're part of that system. You don't need to fawn or abase yourself before a member or staff, but neither should you be rude or insulting. The member is an important part of the national government and represents the hopes and interests of a significant number of people. She is due the respect that position commands.

Remember to remain calm and rational regardless of provocations or frustrations you may face. Just because the righteousness of your cause is blindingly obvious to you doesn't mean that it's equally obvious to members or staffers who are dealing with an enormous range of issues and constituents. Emotion isn't going to win you any battles; logic will take you much further.

Courtesy also extends to dress and grooming. Walking in casually as a tourist to get tickets to the Capitol gallery is one thing, but when you're having a business meeting, you need to dress for business. Attending a scheduled meeting with a member or staff dressed as though you're on a weekend outing is insulting to the member and won't help your cause. When you're serious about what you're trying to accomplish, your appearance needs to reflect the care and consideration you give to your issue.

Commanding the Facts

You have absolutely no excuse for not knowing everything you need to know about your issue. To discuss a particular piece of legislation, you must, at a minimum, know its number, title, and sponsors. You must be conversant about its substance, and knowing the exact legislative language is a major plus. Vagueness, ambiguity, or ignorance about your issue when you've requested a member's valuable time to discuss it is unforgivable.

Respecting the Staff

Staffers play major roles in shaping and passing legislation. Everyone in a congressional office is a potential ally, including the interns. Furthermore, regardless of a staffer's job title, you never know who in the office is most influential with the member. Treat staff with the same courtesy and respect as the members. Remember that lobbying the staff the way you lobby a member never hurts. Chapter 13 provides details about congressional staffs.

Being Ready to Offer Assistance

A member may ask you for assistance for a particular cause — something that may have nothing to do with yours. Be prepared for such requests and know how far you're willing to go and how much you can offer. At moments like these, being clear about your core issues and your goals is particularly important.

Giving them Something to Remember You By

Leaving some kind of artifact of your visit always is a good idea. Remember that members and staff are inundated with visitors pushing different agendas. You need something that makes your visit memorable.

When you're thanking a member or wanting to praise her for past actions, a plaque or framed certificate from your organization is a very good memento. Other mementos can include pens, mugs, caps or T-shirts. Remember mementos cannot exceed the $10 gift limit.

Regardless of whether you provide an object of some kind, leaving a packet of information is best. It needs to include:

✔ An introductory letter

✔ Talking points

✔ A copy of the bill already introduced or a draft of the bill you'd like to see passed

✔ A one-minute speech

✔ A long speech

✔ Background material

✔ A press release

For a detailed description of the packet and the items in it, see Chapter 10.

If the member or staff agrees (and you need to clear this factor in advance), you may want to bring a photographer to record your visit. If you do, make sure that you send the member a copy of the photograph.

Always Following Up

Always follow up on every interaction with a member of Congress. After you meet, be sure to send a thank-you note. Whenever you and a member reach an understanding on an issue, a letter clarifying your understanding of your agreement prevents future disputes. If a conversation is significant — and even if it isn't — write a memorandum of the conversation for your own records. Never let an interaction with a member occur without it being part of your overall lobbying campaign.

Chapter 20

Ten Tips for Dealing with Journalists

- -

In This Chapter

▶ Seeking truth and accuracy

▶ Making comments in the public eye

▶ Exercising care in dealing with the media

- -

*W*henever you do any kind of advocacy work, you need to deal with journalists to get your message out. Dealing effectively with these members of the media is extremely important if you're ever going to convince Congress to see things your way.

Much of the wisdom you'll need when dealing with the media comes only through experience — often harsh experience. However, following the basic principles that I outline in this chapter can assist you in your media dealings.

Assume the Best

Assume neither that the media is against you nor that it automatically favors you. Assume, instead, that journalists are trying to pursue the highest ideals of their profession. Over time, you'll discover which reporters are consistently accurate, which ones understand your cause, which ones to trust, and which ones to avoid.

Journalists come in all persuasions and perceptions, and they're highly individualistic. Sometimes they run in a pack, but never assume that they all have preconceived notions.

Don't take anything personally. You'll encounter plenty of honest and dishonest glitches, mistakes, betrayals, miscommunications, and misunderstandings.

Remember that dealing with the media has little to do with you as a person. Bad things are often just part of doing business.

Strive for Accuracy

You must strive for absolute accuracy in every press release or public pronouncement you make, because you're an official source. Journalists may forgive one or two honest slip-ups, but if you develop a reputation for sloppiness or inaccuracy or — worst of all — deception, you and your cause will be toast, and your credibility will be shot.

If you discover that you've made an honest mistake, correct it immediately.

Don't Pick a Fight with Anyone who Buys Ink by the Barrel

You'll naturally respect some journalists more than others. With some, you'll even develop a personal affinity. And, of course, you'll find still other reporters you distrust, or just plain don't like, or both. But regardless of how you feel about individual reporters, don't get into a fight with any of the institutions they serve. Media institutions are bigger, more powerful, and have longer memories than you can ever hope to have or even imagine.

You can't bar a journalist from your press conferences or treat him unfairly, regardless of the temptation. You may not want to give an exclusive story or leak information to a particular journalist, but don't exclude or be rude to him, either.

Remember that individual journalists are part of a larger institution and that everything in journalism is driven by deadlines, time, and available space. You have to accommodate the strictures and structures of the media process whether the medium is print, broadcast, or the Internet. Find out what the process is and respond accordingly.

Whenever you see or hear a media report that you don't like, remember that someone other than the journalist with whom you're dealing may have added the message to which you're objecting. Stories pass through many hands before they're printed or broadcast, and someone with whom you've never spoken may have inserted some of the things you don't like. Reporters always blame editors, and editors always think that reporters haven't done their jobs as well as they should.

Don't blame a reporter for the headline you don't like or the photograph you find unflattering. The reporter rarely has any say regarding the placement, layout, or headline of a story.

Realize that the Only Bad Question is the One that Isn't Asked

Don't be offended by any question asked by a journalist regardless of how absurd, insulting, outlandish, irrelevant, or inane it may seem. Journalists are trying to obtain whatever information they can, and asking questions is the only way to do it. The presumption among journalists is that they control the questions, and the subject controls the answers, and that gives the subject the stronger position.

Journalists are in the business of asking questions, and they don't think any question is unfair when the person they're interviewing is a public figure. Never tell a journalist that he isn't allowed to ask a question. (I once had a huge fight with a lobbyist who put a topic out of bounds at a press conference.)

Likewise, never be condescending or assume knowledge. You're likely to be working with numerous journalists with various levels of understanding. You may thoroughly know your topic, but that doesn't mean the journalist knows anything at all about it. You'll have to explain the same basic facts again and again, and you'll probably get sick of it, but if you're going to succeed, you must impart that information nicely each and every time.

You Don't Have to Comment but Never Stonewall

At times, saying nothing may be your best course of action. Just because you're asked a question doesn't mean you have to answer it. You can refuse to answer in several ways:

- You can politely and simply say, "I don't have any comment on that."
- When you're asked about something you don't feel confident discussing, you can simply say that you don't know enough about the subject to comment.

> ✔ When you're asked about information that isn't public, you can simply say, "I'm sorry, that's classified (or proprietary or not public), and I can't discuss it."
>
> ✔ When you don't have the information on hand to provide an answer, you can promise to get back to the journalist later — and then do so promptly.

Not commenting isn't the same as *stonewalling,* a term used by President Richard Nixon during the Watergate investigation to mean cutting off all communication or information. Not commenting is one thing, but concealing information is another. Nothing whets the appetites of journalists like the thought that you're hiding something important. Sooner or later journalists will discover what they're after and when they do it's unlikely to be the story you want to tell.

If you can't reveal facts or respond to a question, be honest when explaining why.

And yet, don't let attacks in the media go unanswered. If your opponents attack you in the media, you need to respond immediately. Some people believe that responding is beneath them. Others say that they don't want to "stoop to their level," or they wait until they can draft a comprehensive answer and have it approved by superiors. Unanswered attacks, however, demoralize your friends and allies, demonstrate weakness on your part, and indicate (regardless of whether it's true) that you have something to hide. By getting some kind of response out there immediately, you can then elaborate on the issue as time permits.

Understand the "Public" in Public Figure

A public podium is no place for shrinking violets. When you're dealing with the media you must be knowledgeable, fast on your feet, and have a thick skin. Without those attributes, you need to defer to someone who has them. If you're working with Congress and trying to get something done in the political arena, you're automatically a public figure because you're trying to affect public policy. When you become a public figure in serving your cause, remember that you also must give up some of your privacy.

Avoid Source Remorse

Remember that you can't take back the things that you've said. If you said it, it becomes part of the public record. Saying too little is better than saying too much and then regretting it.

Keep Things in Perspective — They'll Wrap Fish in It Tomorrow

No one wraps fish in newspapers anymore, but the concept remains: News is here for today, not tomorrow. Bad publicity or coverage can be damaging, but it tends to be ephemeral and fleeting — people forget quickly.

If President Bill Clinton could put his affair with Monica Lewinsky behind him and continue to function, and even regain public approval, anything is possible. Whenever you receive bad publicity, don't cave in or resign yourself to it, work to improve your image. And remember — another edition comes out tomorrow.

Don't Fall for "Trust Me, I'm a Journalist"

No matter how friendly you become with a journalist, remember that journalists are *always* on the job and that they're professional news gatherers, not personal friends.

Never fall for the ploy TV journalist Connie Chung used when she asked Rep. Newt Gingrich's mother to whisper something in her ear in confidence. Ms. Chung then broadcast the "secret" to the world.

Because journalists always are working, you have to be on your toes, too.

Return Journalists' Phone Calls First

This one's my favorite! A journalist may call for your comment on a story that is important to you or to pass along valuable information. Even if you aren't prepared to comment, you nevertheless need to find out what's going on right away.

Keep in mind that the media machine grinds on regardless of your schedule or priorities, and if you're going to get your side into a story, you have to respond in a timely fashion.

Chapter 21

Not Even Ten Suggestions for Improving Congress

In This Chapter

▶ Go online and toll-free

▶ Preserve House history

Throughout this book, I've tried to be very objective and not to preach. Okay, so I preached in a few spots, but basically the book accepts the way things stand today. However, you can't write a book about Congress and citizen participation and not notice a few things that would make Congress more responsive, more accessible, and more open. And since I have this bully pulpit, I can't resist making a few suggestions.

Get a Toll-Free Number

It seems incredible in this day and age, but there's no toll-free way for a constituent to call her representative or senator. You can call 202-224-3121 and be connected to a member of Congress, but you have to pay for the call. And, though it may not seem like a big expense to some people, if you're a constituent with limited means in Alaska or Hawaii or Guam that call can be a pretty big expense — especially if you want to discuss something at length.

Some people may say that a constituent can call a state or district office, but what if the constituent needs to talk to the member immediately to register an opinion or discuss a case?

It doesn't seem an insuperable technological difficulty for Congress to open a toll-free phone number for the public.

Gather Voting Records Online

In 2001, a group of 10 congressional interns formed the Congressional Voting Record Project when they realized that members' voting records weren't posted on the Internet or on Thomas, the online legislative search engine. There's no simple, single, convenient place online to see members' complete voting records.

They wrote to members encouraging them to post their voting records on their individual web sites and visited offices to lobby for their idea. According to a Jan. 18, 2002, op-ed in *The Washington Post* by Nickolas Rodriguez, a public policy student at Stanford University who interned for Sen. Dianne Feinstein (D-Calif.), the interns were met with hostility and indifference. Members and staff argued that the information is already posted, that posting it would be inconvenient, that posting it was unnecessary, and that the public might not understand some of the more technical votes, making members vulnerable to criticism.

The objections are nonsense, and the interns are right: Votes are the public positions that members take on all questions before the body. Whether they're great or small, technical or titanic, there should be a searchable, online database of votes by members that can be broken down by member and vote.

Making voting records available online is something that Congress should do as an institution.

Post Appropriations Online in a Timely Fashion — Like Immediately

Under the current system, appropriations are made and approved and then shoved in front of the chamber and passed before anyone can delve into them in depth. Furthermore, the appropriations bill and conference report with all the appropriations aren't released to the public until they're typeset, proofread, and bound, usually months after they're approved.

What's going on is clear: appropriators are moving their decisions through the system as quickly as they can before anyone can examine them in depth. There's a certain efficiency to this way of doing things: Too much democracy could slow down the unavoidably messy and cumbersome appropriations process. It also might stop some people in positions of seniority and power from ladling out the pork they seek for their friends and constituents.

But, in the digital age, there's no technological reason why appropriations can't be posted on the Internet as they're finished, or certainly no later than the time it takes to send them to a server. And let's not have any baloney about needing six months to proofread or check for accuracy. This stuff should be posted the morning after a committee or conference vote is taken. It would serve the members, it would serve the public, and it would serve the country.

Hire a Historian for the House

In researching this book, I spent a great deal of time delving into House and Senate archives, Web sites, and histories, and after that immersion, I can say without qualification that the House suffers greatly for lack of an official Historian.

The House had a historian in the past, but following a controversial appointment by Speaker Newt Gingrich, the position was abandoned.

The lack of an official historian cripples the House's standing with the public and jeopardizes the information the House puts forward for public consumption, the usefulness of its archives and records for researchers, academics, political scientists, and historians.

I invite comparison with the Senate historian's superb work, particularly in popularizing and explaining that body and its history.

There simply has to be a professional staff and director tracking the House, its works, and its actions. As George Orwell put it so tellingly in his novel 1984: "He who controls the present controls the past and he who controls the past controls the future." It's time the United States House of Representatives took control of its past, present, and future.

Upgrade the House Web Site

The House web site is serviceable and has evolved over time, but it can do much more to educate, enlighten, and inform the public. Comparison with the Senate Web site is invited. The House search function is clunky and cumbersome and needs to be streamlined and improved.

Particularly dismaying is the site's lack of accessibility and information for younger students and children. The existing educational function is unattractive and easy to overlook. Furthermore, the House's basic information, like the legislative process, is less accessible than it could be. Links are convoluted and poorly conceived and labeled.

The House Web site needs to be upgraded and redesigned with the public in mind.

Part VII
The Appendixes

The 5th Wave — By Rich Tennant

A pie factory is no place to find out you're not a political animal, Brad.

In this part . . .

The first appendix is a glossary that, even if I do say so myself, is as complete a list of congressional terms as I've seen anywhere. Check here if you forget what a term means, or just read through these pages to become familiar with congressional lingo.

Appendix B lists current congressional committees.

Appendix A

Glossary of Congressional and Political Terms

• •

*T*here's nothing like vocabulary for making what should be a straightforward and transparent institution obscure and opaque, but somehow it's too often done. The legislative, political, and budgetary processes all have their own special terms to provide verbal shortcuts for insiders and keep outsiders out. I remember how strange and confusing some of this language seemed when I first arrived in Washington.

To the best of my knowledge, this is the most complete and comprehensive glossary of the best-known terms you may encounter when dealing with Congress, congressional politics, budgets and appropriations, lobbying, and campaign finance. I even include slang terms known and beloved of insiders. Sources for these terms are largely congressional documents and Web sites, although some are simply based on common usage.

501(c)(3): A nonprofit educational organization exempt from the Internal Revenue Code under Section 501(c)(3). Many 501(c)(3)s produce educational programs and studies directed at Congress.

Act: A law.

Actuality: In a media context, a bit of sound from an actual, live event. *See sound bite.*

Adjourn/adjournment: The end of a legislative session when work ends, either at the end of each day or at the end of the session. The act of ending the session. Neither body can adjourn for more than three days without the approval of the other.

Adjournment sine die: The end of a session (see *sine die* later in the list).

Adjournment to a day and time certain: Adjournment to a specific time and day.

Conditional adjournment: An adjournment for longer than three days, but with the provision that the leadership of either body can call the chamber back into session if necessary.

Administrative assistant (AA): The staff assistant in congressional offices who oversees their functioning and internal processes; he or she usually handles political matters for the member.

Advocacy: The act of arguing in favor of a particular point of view or action.

Advocacy group: An organization arguing in favor of a particular point of view or political agenda.

Advocate: Someone who argues in favor of a particular course of action or set of beliefs.

Agency: An executive branch body — either a commission, board, or bureau.

Agenda: A set of priorities.

Amendment: A change in a bill or document that adds, subtracts, or alters parts of it. There are three kinds of amendments:

Amendment in the nature of a substitute: An amendment that removes or *strikes* the entire contents of a bill and puts in completely new language. An amendment that does this is called a *substitute amendment* as opposed to a *perfecting amendment* (see below).

Amendments also are distinguished by their origins:

Committee amendment: An amendment offered during committee consideration of a bill.

Floor amendment: An amendment offered on the floor of a chamber.

Perfecting amendment: An amendment that alters or perfects a bill but doesn't change all the language in it.

Pro forma amendment: This is just a way for a member to get five minutes to speak on the floor when the House is meeting as a *Committee of the Whole.* The member moves to "strike the last word" and gets five minutes to speak. It doesn't change the legislation or require a vote, and the amendment is dropped after the five minutes.

Amendment tree: A diagram of the kinds of amendments and the order in which they are considered.

Apportionment: The process of determining the number of House seats each state will get based on the census results.

Appropriate: To spend money for a particular purpose.

Appropriations: The funds designated for a particular purpose.

Appropriations act: A law allowing the spending of government money for a particular purpose.

Architect of the Capitol: The individual and office responsible for maintenance and upkeep of the Capitol building and all congressional structures and grounds.

Association: A group of companies, an industry, or individuals who band together to lobby on behalf of their interests.

At-large: A House seat that represents an entire state.

Authorizing: Providing authority, giving permission.

Authorizing committee: A committee that has authority over executive branch programs and authorizes them.

Authorizing legislation: Legislation that permits the continued operation of an executive branch program or office.

Beat: In a media context, an area or topic assigned to a reporter for coverage.

Bicameral: Pertaining to a two-chamber legislature.

Bill: A legislative proposal; legislation.

Borrowing authority: Permission to borrow money.

Briefing: An informational session. The term is derived from the military.

Budget: A master spending plan.

Budget authority: Congressional permission to spend money by an executive agency, similar to the limit on a credit card.

Budget baseline: Projected spending on the assumption that all other factors (policies, revenues, deficits) will remain the same.

Budget deficit: Occurs when the government spends more than it's expected to take in; technically, when total outlays exceed projected revenues.

Budget resolution: Congress's budget, passed in the form of House and Senate concurrent resolutions. These resolutions aren't signed by the president, aren't considered laws, and apply only within Congress.

Budget surplus: When more money is taken in than is expected to be spent; technically, when revenues exceed outlays.

Bundling: Putting many campaign contributions together into a single package.

By request: The phrase used by a member when a bill is introduced at the request of an executive branch official or agency.

Cabinet: The executive branch department heads who advise the president and run the executive branch.

Calendar: In the congressional context, a calendar is the schedule under which legislation will be considered. The House operates under five calendars:

Correction calendar: Created in 1995, this calendar deals with measures that are so noncontroversial that no debate about them is required. In the beginning, it was also intended to correct flaws in previously passed legislation. Prior to 1995, it was known as the *Consent Calendar.* Held on the second and fourth Tuesdays of each month.

Discharge calendar: Discharge petitions that call for releasing legislation from committee consideration are considered under this calendar. It's very rarely used and, in fact, often consists of a restatement of the rule creating it and a blank page. It's scheduled for the second and fourth Mondays of each month, but it's really used only when a discharge petition is being considered.

The Senate also has a calendar of legislative business:

Executive calendar: A calendar in the Senate to consider treaties and executive branch nominations.

House calendar: The calendar for resolutions dealing with internal House matters that have no impact on government spending.

Private calendar: The agenda of private bills, considered on the first and third Tuesdays of each month.

Union calendar: The regular calendar of bills.

Calendar day: A normal, commonly used 24-hour day, including weekends; as opposed to *working days,* which include only Mondays through Fridays, or *legislative days* when Congress is in session and voting.

Calendar year: The 12 months commonly used to designate a year, as opposed to the fiscal year.

Capital budget: The budget for land, structures, equipment, and intellectual property owned and used by the federal government that will be used for more than two years.

Capitol: The main building housing both houses of Congress.

Casework: Work for individual constituents or district problems.

Caucus: An informal gathering of members. The biggest caucuses are the Democratic and Republican caucuses. Other caucuses are based on ethnicity, interests, common positions, businesses, and industries.

Chairman: The leader of a committee or subcommittee.

Chairman's mark: The final version of a bill that has been edited by a committee; a committee chairman's version of a bill.

Champion: As used in this book, a member who takes a particular interest in or "champions" a bill or cause.

"Christmas tree" bill: Slang for a bill that's attracted so many unrelated amendments and riders that it looks like a Christmas tree hung with ornaments.

Classified: Secret.

"Clean" bill: Slang for a bill without amendments or extraneous riders; often a substitute for a bill that was mangled beyond recognition.

Clerk of the House: The officer overseeing the administrative functions in the House of Representatives. A Secretary serves the same function in the Senate.

Client: In a lobbying context, the person or organization hiring a professional lobbyist.

Cloakroom: Rooms off the House and Senate floors where members of the same party gather to relax or talk. Many deals are worked out in the cloakrooms.

Closed/Closed session: For members only, not open to the public, secret.

Closed rule: In the House, a bill that can't be amended; based on a ruling by the House Rules Committee.

Cloture: A Senate rule to limit debate, ending a filibuster. It enables the Senate to limit consideration of a pending matter to 30 additional hours, but it requires three-fifths of the Senate to approve it, normally 60 votes.

Codel: Short for *congressional delegation;* a group of members traveling on official business.

Commit: To send a bill to a committee for consideration.

Committee: A group of people who meet for a specific purpose, usually to consider, investigate, or take action on legislative matters.

Committee of the Whole: A House term. The House may declare that it is meeting as one big committee. This declaration enables it to suspend some of its rules so that it can dispatch business more efficiently. It also lowers the quorum from 218 to 100, meaning that more business can be done with fewer people.

Committee staff: Staff serving a committee; as opposed to *personal staff* serving an individual member.

Concurrent resolution: A resolution generally used to express the feelings of the House and Senate. Concurrent resolutions don't make law and aren't submitted to the president. They're designated *H.Con.Res.* or *S.Con.Res.,* depending on where they are introduced.

Conferees: Members meeting to reconcile House-Senate differences in a bill being considered by a conference committee.

Conference: A meeting between members of the House and Senate to reconcile differences to each chamber's version of piece of legislation.

Congress: A *Congress* is the two-year term of the House of Representatives. *Congresses* are numbered beginning with the first one in 1789. When you hear people discuss the activities of a number, like "the 106th" or "the 107th," they're referring to a specific two-year term of the House of Representatives.

Congressional Record: The official record of House and Senate debates and proceedings published daily, although not a transcript.

Constituents: The people served by a representative or senator.

Constitution: The basic document establishing the United States government and its functions.

Continuing resolution: A resolution passed by Congress that continues funding for the federal government at current levels; almost always used when Congress fails to pass all its appropriations bills by October 1, the start of the fiscal year. Technically, it provides temporary budget authority to federal agencies for the specified period. It's a joint resolution.

Controlled time: A block of floor time held by a bill's floor manager. He can yield the time to members on his side of the issue, enabling them to speak on the matter.

Core issue: A matter of deep concern central to an individual, group, or organization.

Cosponsor: A member who signs on to a bill after it's been introduced but before it's reported out of committee.

Credit authority: Permission to borrow money.

Current services budget: The level of spending or taxes that occur when all programs and policies continue unchanged; similar to a baseline. A section of the president's annual budget must have a current services budget under the Budget Act. It gives Congress the opportunity to compare new spending against current spending.

Dear colleague: A letter from one member to the rest of the House or Senate. Dear colleagues are usually used to solicit support for a pending bill or a member's initiative.

Debt: Money owed.

Debt ceiling: The congressionally established limit of debt the country can incur.

Deficit: The amount by which spending exceeds income.

Delegate: A representative of one of the U.S. territories or the District of Columbia. Delegates have votes in committees but not on the floor.

Direct spending: Money that must be spent; mandatory spending, usually for entitlement programs.

Discharge petition: A petition signed by a simple majority of the House (218 members) that takes a bill from a committee's control and submits to the full chamber. Used to free legislation from committees that won't consider the measure.

Discretionary spending: Money that doesn't have to be spent for an already-designated purpose.

District: The geographic area served by a member of the House of Representatives.

En bloc amendment: A group of amendments considered together.

Enabling clause: The clause or sentence in a bill that provides the authority to the appropriate officials to enforce or execute the bill's provisions.

Enacted: When a bill has become law; at this point, it ceases being called a bill and begins to be called an act.

Enacting clause: The sentence in every bill that states: *Be it enacted by the Senate and House of Representatives of the United States of America in Congress assembled . . .* This clause is required by an 1871 law and must be included in every bill whether it originates in the House or Senate.

Engrossed: An official copy of a passed bill or resolution by the House or Senate. Named for the 18th-century practice of providing a formal copy of a document written in calligraphy. The well-known copies of the original Declaration of Independence and the Constitution are engrossed.

Enrolled: The final copy of a bill passed by both chambers and submitted to the president for signature. This is an elaborate, formal document on parchment signed by the leaders of both chambers.

Entitlements: Programs to which people or businesses are entitled because they meet the eligibility criteria. For example, any citizen who is 65 years of age or older and who has paid Social Security taxes is entitled to Social Security payments upon retirement.

Emergency spending: Money that must be spent immediately for an emergency. Many of the normal budget rules are suspended in this case.

Ex officio: Latin for "by virtue of one's office." Certain officials are *ex officio* members of all committees, or committee chairmen are *ex officio* members of all subcommittees, although *ex officio* members usually don't cast votes on the committees or subcommittees.

Executive/Executive branch: The branch of government that executes policy; the president and the government bodies under his control.

Executive business: Business from the president or the executive branch.

Executive order: A presidential decision or order.

Executive session: A session to consider executive business.

Expenditure: Spending; a purchase.

Filibuster: A Senate practice in which a member holds up any further proceedings by speaking continuously, introducing time-consuming procedural motions, or delaying or obstructing any other business. It can be overcome by a *cloture* vote.

Final passage: Adoption of a bill after all the amendments are incorporated.

Fiscal: Pertaining to finances.

Fiscal year: An accounting period of 12 months. The U.S. federal fiscal year goes from October 1 through September 30.

Five-minute rule: A rule allowing representatives to propose an amendment and debate it for five minutes.

Floor: The entire chamber. Having the floor means that the member is the only person allowed to speak unless the speaker chooses to yield time to other members.

Floor amendment: An amendment offered from the floor; as opposed to a *committee amendment,* which is one offered in committee.

Floor leaders: The majority and minority leaders. They get priority consideration to speak on the floor.

Floor manager: The member who manages a bill through the amendment process to a vote.

Foreign agent: In a lobbying context, a lobbyist hired by a foreign organization, corporation, or country to lobby Congress; technically, an individual or organization receiving funds from a foreign principal to represent his interests. Foreign agents must register as such.

Frank/franking: A member's official signature, used instead of a stamp for official correspondence, mailings, and communications with constituents; (*verb*) the act of mailing out material to constituents under a member's frank.

Function: Purpose; in budgetary terms, one of the government's activities.

General consent: A unanimous, silent vote, usually for routine business. If the chair hears no objections, he usually says, "If no objections, so ordered."

Germane: Relevant. When applied to bills, an amendment that has some relationship to the content of the bill. In the House, amendments must be germane; Senate rules are far less strict. An amendment that has little to do with a bill's substance is said to be *nongermane*.

Gerrymander: To draw the lines of a congressional district to achieve a certain political outcome. Named after Massachusetts governor Elbridge Gerry.

Grass roots: Slang for average citizens.

Grass tops: Local opinion leaders or activists.

Gucci gulch: Slang for hallways outside appropriations rooms where highly paid lobbyists congregate to press their cases. Derived from a high-priced shoe brand.

Hard money: Campaign contributions regulated by the Federal Election Commission that go to particular candidates' campaigns.

Hearing: A session, usually of a committee or subcommittee, to gather information and hear testimony.

Hold: A Senate practice in which a senator requests that a floor leader stop a measure from reaching the floor; a frequent practice when senators oppose executive branch or judicial nominations.

Hopper: The box on the desk of the Clerk of the House into which members drop bills. Origin of the phrase, "Dropping in a bill."

Horse: Archaic slang for a member who champions a bill or cause, as in a horse pulling a cart. In this book, the term *champion* has been substituted.

Hour rule: Giving members a full hour to debate each amendment to a bill. This rule applies only when the House is meeting in full session.

Hustings: The campaign trail; campaigning.

Ideology/Ideological: Following a particular point of view or belief system; for example, liberal or conservative.

Impeachment: To try a high government official for high crimes and misdemeanors. Impeachment is simply the act of trying the individual; it doesn't necessarily result in removal from office. Under the Constitution, the House acts as a grand jury and indicts the individual and the Senate serves as a jury, presided over by the Chief Justice of the Supreme Court if the trial is of the president. Otherwise the vice president presides.

Impoundment: Holding money or, technically, precluding the obligation or expenditure of budget authority.

Imputation: The practice of estimating the number of individuals in a given area that weren't reached by census takers.

In session: Congress is meeting.

Independent agency: An executive branch board, commission, or bureau that isn't part of a cabinet department.

Independent/Independent expenditure: In a campaign context, an organization unconnected to any particular candidate's campaign and political spending not directed by any candidate.

Industry: A particular area of manufacturing or production.

Inside the Beltway: Parochial to Washington, D.C. Something of interest only to Washington or Washington insiders. Derived from Interstate 495, the Beltway, the highway that surrounds Washington, D.C.

Interest: A share or stake in something; a common concern.

Intern: A person gaining experience by temporarily working at a job.

Introducing: Submitting a bill for consideration.

Issue: A point of disagreement; a matter of particular concern to an individual, group, or organization.

Joint: Referring to both chambers.

Joint committee: A committee with members from the House and Senate.

Joint resolution: A resolution with a preamble, often used to amend existing legislation, and the vehicle for a constitutional amendment.

Journal: The record of proceedings for the House and Senate. Each chamber has its own journal. Not the same as the *Congressional Record.*

Jurisdiction: The realm or extent of authority of an individual, committee, or government body.

K Street: The main commercial thoroughfare in Washington where many lobbyists have their offices; used to refer to the lobbying community as a whole.

Key vote: An important vote that demonstrates a lawmaker's position on an issue. Also informally called a *litmus test* based on the test to determine a chemical's composition and now defined as any test in which a single factor determines the finding (a litmus test for political candidates).

King-of-the-hill: A parliamentary procedure under which a number of amendments are voted upon, and the last one to pass is enacted.

Lame duck: Slang for an elected official who has lost an election or announced a retirement but is continuing to serve while waiting for a replacement to be sworn in. This term also applies to entire congressional sessions, which take place after elections but before a new Congress takes office.

Language: In the congressional context, the text of a bill or other document.

Layover: A period of time required by a rule before a measure can be considered. Usually one or two days.

Leader/leadership: The leaders in either chamber. In the House, that includes the Speaker, Majority Leader, and Majority Whip. In the Senate, it's the Majority Leader and Majority Whip. The minority party has similar leaders.

Leader time: Time given to the majority and minority leaders at the beginning of the day to organize the chamber's business.

Legislate: To make laws.

Legislation: Any product of the legislative process.

Legislative assistant (LA): The staff assistant handling the details of legislation.

Legislative day: A day of legislative activity; as opposed to a calendar day.

Legislative session: A time when legislative work is being considered by a chamber; as opposed to executive session.

Line item: An individual item, or line, in the budget or other budget or appropriations document.

Line-item veto: The ability of an executive to veto individual items in a budget. Ruled unconstitutional on a federal level in 1998, but used by governors in some states.

Litmus test: *See key vote.*

Logrolling: Slang for members helping each other pass legislation.

Lobby: (*noun*) An interest group or any group outside Congress that tries to influence congressional or government action. (*verb*) Trying to influence or convince a lawmaker to take a specific action.

Majority party: The political party holding the most seats in a chamber.

Mandatory: Compelled or commanded, obligatory.

Mandatory spending: Money that must be spent for a specific purpose, usually to fulfill an entitlement.

Mark-up: (*noun*) A bill that's been edited by a committee; the session at which a bill is edited. (*verb*) Going through a bill line by line (this takes place in congressional committees).

Measure: Legislation; a bill or resolution.

Member: An elected member of the House or Senate (usually used to denote a member of the House).

Member management: Staff slang for protecting a member; convincing a member to take a particular action; saving a member from himself despite foolish remarks or ill-considered actions.

Minority party: The political party with fewer seats in a chamber.

Monetary policy: The executive branch's policies on the money supply.

Morning business: Routine business attended to at the start of every legislative day.

Motion: A proposal for a certain action to be taken.

"Must pass" bill: Slang for a bill that's so important that it absolutely must pass.

NGO: Nongovernment organization; usually a charitable or humanitarian organization working overseas in disaster areas.

Nominee: A person put forward for consideration for a particular office.

Nonpartisan: Not having a party loyalty or point of view; neutral, objective.

Nonprofit: An incorporated organization that doesn't seek profits. Many of these groups lobby Congress and seek to influence legislation.

Not for attribution: *See on background.*

Objection: An objection to an action on the floor; more specifically, a challenge to a unanimous consent request.

Obligation: A contractual commitment to pay for a good or service.

Off the record: Remarks that are for the listener's information only, not to be used publicly in any context, and the source's identity is to be kept secret.

Off-budget federal entity: A federal body whose income and expenditures aren't included in the president's budget; for example, Social Security trust funds.

Offset/offsetting collections and/or receipts: Money the government takes in from the sale of goods and services like postage stamps, the radio spectrum, surplus equipment, and other businesslike activities.

Omnibus bill/legislation: A single piece of legislation that combines many disparate elements.

On background: Information that's not to be attributed to the speaker but may be verified by other sources and used for publication or broadcast. The same as *not for attribution.*

On the record: Remarks that are public and attributable to the speaker.

One minutes: Speeches that are one minute long given by representatives on any topic at the beginning of the legislative day in the House.

Open rule: A bill that can be amended subject to a ruling by the House Rules Committee.

Other body: The means of referring to the other chamber.

Outlays: Money actually spent; expenditures.

Outlay rates: The rate of expenditures and their ratio to the amount of money taken in.

Override: To overturn a presidential veto. Overrides require two-thirds votes in each chamber.

Oversight/oversee: To monitor a federal agency or program usually by a committee or subcommittee with jurisdiction.

PAC: Political Action Committee.

Page: A member of the House or Senate page program working as a courier or assistant for a semester. Must be 16 years old.

Parliamentarian: The person overseeing rules and procedures.

Parliamentary inquiry: A challenge to current proceedings to ensure that they conform to the rules.

Partisan: Committed to a single party, an advocate.

Pass/Passed: Approved or approving legislation

Passage: The process of moving legislation through the legislative process and getting it approved.

Pay-as-you-go: A budgetary technique to ensure budgetary discipline; any money spent must be offset by an equal amount of revenue.

Pen pal: Staff slang for a constituent who writes again and again, engaging in a long and pointless dialogue.

Pending amendment: An amendment under consideration.

Permanent: In a congressional context, a regular or standing committee. In a budgetary context, budget authority available as a result of a previous appropriation; as opposed to a *current* appropriation enacted in the current session of Congress.

Personal staff: The staff serving an individual member of Congress.

Petition: A plea; in the congressional context, a request to consider legislation; a signed document requesting a particular action.

Pocket veto: A presidential means of vetoing a bill without taking action. If the president fails to sign legislation within ten days, it becomes law; however, if Congress adjourns during those ten days, the bill dies if it isn't signed.

Point of order: An objection to a procedure because a member believes that it violates a rule.

Policy: A direction for government; a master plan.

Pork: Slang for wasteful or unnecessary spending.

Pork barrel bill: Slang for a bill full of pork.

President of the Senate: The vice president.

President pro tempore: The senator who presides over the Senate in the vice president's absence; usually the most senior senator in the majority party.

President's budget: The president's budget request to Congress.

Presiding officer: Whoever presides over a chamber; usually a representative or senator designated to serve in the absence of the Speaker of the House, or the vice president in the Senate.

Press secretary: The staff assistant who handles press and media questions and puts out information about the member or committee.

Press the flesh: Slang for shaking hands, usually on a mass basis during campaigning.

Previous question: A way to end debate and get on with a vote. If a member makes a previous question motion and it's approved, no more talking or amending is allowed, and a vote is taken. However, if a previous question motion is defeated, the other side's floor manager gets another hour for debate.

Private bill: A bill affecting an individual rather than public law or the country as a whole.

Pro forma session: In Latin, "for form"; usually a session that's held purely to satisfy a constitutional or legal requirement but where no real business is conducted.

Proxy: A vote on behalf of someone else.

Public law: A law applying to the entire country (as opposed to a private bill), numbered by the Congress and a sequential number; for example, PL 107-1.

Question of privilege: A question that affects the safety, dignity, or integrity of the chamber. These questions are brought by the majority or minority leaders and take priority over all other business.

Quorum: The minimum number of members required to conduct a vote. Quorums are one more than half the members in each chamber (51 in the Senate, 218 in the House). Generally, the presiding officer presumes that there's a quorum unless a member challenges that by saying: "I suggest the lack of a quorum."

Quorum call: The act of suggesting the lack of a quorum and demanding that the roll be called. This tactic is often used to stop proceedings and do a little extra lobbying or conferring among members.

Ranking member: The most senior and highest ranking member of the minority party.

Reading: Literally, reading the bill or amendment so that all members know what's in it. Bills get three readings before coming to a vote. Readings are frequently waived because they're time consuming and everyone has a copy anyway.

Receipts: Collected revenues.

Recess: A period when Congress isn't meeting but will meet again. Recesses usually fall around major holidays and all of August. Lately, Congress hasn't liked the implication that members are just goofing off during recess, so they've started calling these periods "district work periods," meaning that the members have returned home and are doing their work back in the district rather than in Washington. There's some validity to this because members are never truly off duty. They're always meeting people, working the grass roots, or giving speeches.

Recognition: Being given permission to speak by the presiding officer.

Recommit: Sending a bill back to committee.

Reconciliation: The process of working out the differences between House and Senate bills.

Reconciliation instructions: The instructions each chamber gives to its conferees when they go into negotiations with members of the other chamber; these instructions tell conferees what points may be compromised and what cannot.

Reconsideration: A motion to reconsider what has just occurred, usually a vote.

Recuse/Recusal: To withdraw oneself from considering an official matter because of a personal interest or involvement.

Redistricting: The process by which congressional districts are redrawn every ten years to reflect population changes recorded by the census.

Referral: Assigning a bill to a committee.

Concurrent referral: Assigning the bill to two committees at the same time.

Sequential referral: Assigning the bill first to one committee then another.

Simple referral: Assigning the bill to a single committee.

Split referral: Assigning part of the bill to one committee and another part to a different committee.

Registered lobbyist: A professional lobbyist who's registered as such with Congress.

Regulation: A rule issued by an executive branch agency; as opposed to a *law,* passed by Congress and signed by the president.

Representative: A member of the House of Representatives.

Rescission: To remove or rescind; in a budget context, to cancel or remove budget authority; to stop spending on a specific item or program. Under current procedures, Congress must enact the rescission.

Reserve fund: A provision in a budget resolution that enables the chairman of the Budget Committee to make some changes in the budget resolution if certain conditions are met.

Resident Commissioner: The title of the person representing Puerto Rico. The only member of the House to serve a four-year term.

Resolution: A bill dealing with the position of the House or Senate that doesn't have the force of law; usually deals with a chamber's internal affairs.

Resolving clause: The sentence in joint resolutions that states: *Resolved by the Senate and House of Representatives of the United States of America in Congress assembled . . . .*

Rider: An amendment to a bill that doesn't relate directly to the bill's content. Riders are much more common in the Senate than in the House.

Roll: The list of all the members of the House or Senate.

Roll-call vote: A vote in which the roll is called and every member of the body responds individually, "Yea," "Nay," or "Present."

Rule: In a legislative context, the terms of debate as determined by the House Rules Committee. A bill awaiting a decision by the committee is said to be *subject to a rule.*

Scorecard: A list of members' votes and ratings of their standings on a particular issue. Also called a *rating.*

Scoring/Scorekeeping: In a budgetary context, tracking the impact of congressional budget actions. If an expenditure is *scored* against a budget, revenues to support the expenditure must be found, or another expenditure must be canceled or scaled back to accommodate it.

Select committee: A committee that doesn't pass legislation. A select committee may be formed to oversee one particular subject and be dissolved after a short period of time.

Senator: A member of the U.S. Senate.

Seniority: The status and rank accorded members due to their length of service.

Sequester: To withdraw or set apart; in a budget context, to hold back funds.

Sergeant-at-arms: The officers in the House and Senate responsible for security and order.

Session: Each year of a Congress is a *session.* The first year of a Congress is the "first session;" the second year is the "second session." So, if you hear someone say, "That bill passed in the first session of the 105th," you know that he's discussing a particular instance when a bill passed.

Sine die: At the end of a Congress, the Speaker bangs his gavel and announces "This Congress is adjourned, sine die," which is Latin for "without day;" in other words, without a specific day to reconvene. It signifies the final adjournment of the Congress, but that a new Congress will indeed meet again.

Soft money: Contributions to organizations unconnected with a particular campaign and not subject to campaign finance regulations.

Sound bite: A brief quote used in a broadcast news report.

Speaker of the House: The presiding official of the House elected by the members of the House at the beginning of the Congress.

Special interests: Individuals, groups, or organizations with particular points of view or seeking particular goals. In a *derogatory sense* groups more committed to their own goals than to the good of the country as a whole.

Special orders: Speeches in the House of up to an hour in length at the end of the legislative day. Members may speak on any topic. They often address an empty chamber, but this provision enables them to put their thoughts on the record and before the public.

Spending limits: Limits on political campaign contributions.

Spin: In a media context, putting a particular light or perspective on events or trying to convince someone to see things in a particular way.

Sponsor: The member or members who introduce a bill. The number of sponsors has no limitations.

Staffer: Slang for someone serving on a congressional staff.

Standing committee: A permanent committee that considers bills and can make law.

Statutes at large: The list of laws enacted each Congress.

Stump/Stumping/Stump speech/On the stump: Political campaigning, derived from the days when candidates would stand on a nearby tree stump to deliver a speech; (*verb*) to speak or campaign. A *stump speech* is a standard speech delivered again and again with little or no variation. To be *on the stump* is to be campaigning.

Subcommittee: A subunit of a committee, usually specializing in a particular area of the committee's jurisdiction.

Supplemental: An appropriation requested outside the regular appropriations process; usually when the government faces an emergency need or discovers that it didn't request sufficient funds in its initial budget.

Suspension of the rules: A House procedure to expedite consideration of legislation, usually of an uncontroversial nature. Under suspension of the rules, floor debate is limited to 40 minutes, floor amendments are prohibited, and a two-thirds vote is required for final passage.

Tabling: Putting a bill or motion aside for later consideration. In Congress, this action is tantamount to killing the proposal. (The United States differs from most other English-speaking parliamentary governments where "tabling" a bill means introducing it.)

Talking heads: In a media context, a broadcast program or report that only makes use of individuals speaking without any other visual elements or action; (*singular*) a broadcast commentator.

Talking points: Brief arguments that can be used when discussing an issue.

Tax expenditures: Revenue losses caused by tax breaks, such as special exclusions, exemptions, credits, rates changes, or deferrals.

Testimony: Information given to Congress by a sworn witness, usually, although not necessarily, at a hearing.

Unanimous consent: General agreement; a procedure under which all the members agree to a measure as long as no one objects.

Unanimous consent request: A request that everyone agree to something rather than go through the time-consuming procedure of a roll-call vote. In response to the request, the presiding officer usually responds, "If there is no objection, so ordered."

Unfunded mandates: A federal provision that requires a local, state, or lower government to spend money without reimbursement from the federal government.

Unlimited debate: In the Senate, the right of any senator to speak as long as desired on a measure during a debate.

Up or down vote: Common phrase for a pass or fail vote.

Vehicle: A piece of legislation moving through the legislative process. Usually used in a Senate context where amendments and riders can be attached.

Veto: From the Latin, "I refuse." The president's power to stop legislation passed by Congress. A presidential veto can be overridden by a two-thirds vote in both houses.

Visuals: In a media context, graphic elements, the eye-catching qualities of a photograph or videotape.

Voice vote: A vote under which all the members vote orally together rather than individually.

Vote: (*noun*) A ballot. (*verb*) The act of expressing an opinion, approval, or disapproval through a formal mechanism.

Well: The place in the House or Senate directly in front of the presiding officer's platform. In the House, members address the chamber from two lecterns in the Well. In the Senate, members speak from their desks.

Whip: The person in both parties and both chambers who ensures that members toe the party line and vote the way the leadership requires.

Whip count: The Whip's count of which members are for a bill, against a bill, leaning for it, leaning against it, and undecided. Although anyone can count noses, the Whip's count is usually the most authoritative because the Whip is most closely in touch with all the members. The Whip count is usually kept secret.

Wonk: Slang for someone immersed in the minutiae of legislation, policy, or process.

Yea and nay vote: More than a voice vote but less than a roll call. Each member registers his or her vote without going in order. Doing so allows a record to be kept of how each individual voted, as opposed to a **voice vote** where everyone votes orally at the same time.

Yield: The practice of giving up time, or the right to speak, to allow another member to make a comment.

Appendix B
Committees of the 107th Congress

House Standing Committees

Administration

Agriculture Appropriations

Armed Services

Budget

Education and the Workforce

Energy and Commerce

Financial Services

Government Reform

International Relations

Judiciary

Permanent Select Intelligence

Resources

Rules

Science

Small Business

Standards of Official Conduct

Transportation and Infrastructure

Veterans Affairs

Ways and Means

Senate Standing Committees

Agriculture, Nutrition, and Forestry

Appropriations

Armed Services

Banking, Housing, and Urban Affairs
Pensions

Budget

Finance

Foreign Relations

Governmental Affairs

Health, Education, Labor, and

Judiciary

Commerce, Science, and Transportation

Energy and Natural Resources

Environment and Public Works

Rules and Administration

Small Business

Veterans' Affairs

Senate Select and Special Committees

Special on Aging

Select on Ethics

Select on Indian Affairs

Select on Intelligence

Joint Committees

Joint Economic Committee

Joint Printing

Joint Taxation

Index

• A •

AARP (American Association of Retired Persons), 163
ABC (American Broadcasting Company), 263–264
academic celebrities, 243
academy nominations, 274, 276–277
ACLU (American Civil Liberties Union), 162
act, defined, 321
actuality, defined, 321
Adams, Charles, *For Good and Evil: The Impact of Taxes on the Course of Civilization, 2nd edition,* 117
adjournment, defined, 321
adjournment *sine die,* defined, 321
administrative assistant (AA), 202, 321
advertising a cause, 241–242
Advisory Committee on the Records of Congress, 214
advocacy advertising, 241–242
advocacy, defined, 321
advocacy group, defined, 321
AFSCME (American Federation of State, County, and Municipal Employees), 162
agency, defined, 321
agenda, defined, 321
AIPAC (American Israel Public Affairs Committee), 193
All the President's Men, Carl Bernstein and Bob Woodward, 252, 268
All Things Considered (radio program), 266
Allen, William C., *History of the United States Capitol,* 285
Almanac of American Politics, 261
Almanac of the Unelected, directory of staffers, 209
Alsop, Joseph and Stewart (political columnists), 256
amendments
  amendment in the nature of a substitute, 97, 321–322
  amendment tree, 98, 322
  committee amendment, 322
  Constitution, 15

definition, 321
  en bloc amendment, 97, 324
  floor amendment, 322, 325
  king-of-the-hill, 327
  pending amendment, 328
  perfecting amendment, 322
  pro forma amendment, 322
  substitute amendment, 97, 321–322
  types, 97–98
American Association of Retired Persons (AARP), 163
American Broadcasting Company (ABC), 263–264
American Civil Liberties Union (ACLU), 162
American Conservative Union, 162
American Federation of State, County, and Municipal Employees (AFSCME), 162
American Israel Public Affairs Committee (AIPAC), 193
The American Spectator, 258
Americans for Democratic Action, 162
Ames, Fisher, Rep. (Mass., 1789–1797), 55
anthrax attacks, 31, 43, 181–183
applying for staff positions, 204
appointment secretary, 202
apportionment, defined, 322
appropriate, defined, 322
appropriations bills, 120, 132–133, 135–136, 322
appropriations (budget), 129, 131–132, 316–317, 322
appropriations committees, 126, 129–132, 137
appropriations subcommittees, 130
Architect of the Capitol, 285–286, 288, 322
Articles of Confederation, 11
Ashcroft, John, Sen. (R-Mo., 1995–2001), 51
Associated Press, 262
association, defined, 322
at-large seat (House), 26, 322
attacks on the Capitol, 289
authorization act, 128
authorizing the budget, 128, 322
authorizing committees, 126, 128, 322
authorizing legislation, defined, 322

• B •

Baker, Richard, *Senate Historical Minutes,* 45
Barone, Michael, *National Journal's Almanac of American Politics*, 34
Bartholdi Park, 292
BCRA (Bipartisan Campaign Reform Act of 2002), 142–143, 148
bean soup (on dining room menus), 18
beats (media coverage), 222, 322
Bebak, Arthur, *Creating Web Pages For Dummies, 6th Edition,* 240
Beckley, John (first Clerk of the House), 201
bell systems (voting), 293
Bernstein, Carl, *All the President's Men,* 252, 268
bi-cameral legislature, defined, 322
Bill of Rights, 15
bills
    appropriations bills, 120, 132–133, 135–136, 322
    chairman's mark, 71, 323
    challenging, 108–109
    "Christmas tree" bill, 323
    "clean" bill, 323
    closed rule, 323
    committing, 323
    conferences, 101–104
    cosponsors, 64, 67, 324
    Dear colleague letter, 64, 67, 324
    definition, 58–59, 322
    discharge petition, 69, 324
    enabling clause, 325
    enacted bills, 325
    enacting clause, 325
    engrossed, 325
    enrolled bills, 325
    final passage, 325
    germane, 97, 326
    hearings, 69–71
    hopper, 326
    introducing, 59, 62–65, 90–91, 326
    language, 327
    logrolling, 327
    markup, 71, 327
    "must pass" bill, 328
    name, 63–64
    number, 63
    omnibus bill, 328
    open rule, 328
    passage, 328
    passing, 67–73
    president's role, 105–107
    president's signature, 105, 108
    private bill, 61–62, 329
    protecting, 109–110
    readings, 92, 329
    recommitting, 330
    referral process, 68–69
    referrals, 330
    reporting out, 72
    by request, 322
    rider, 47–48, 131, 330
    sponsor, 63–66, 331
    tabling, 331
    title, 63
    vehicle, 332
    writing, 59
Bipartisan Campaign Reform Act of 2002 (BCRA), 142–143, 148
Blue Dogs caucus, 81–82
Boller, Paul F., *Congressional Anecdotes,* 91
Bonus March of 1932, 245
borrowing authority, defined, 322
branches of government. *See also* House of Representatives; president of the United States; Senate; Supreme Court
    checks and balances, 12
    congressional branch, 12–13
    executive branch, 14, 325
    judicial branch, 15
bribes, 142
briefing, defined, 322
broadcast faxes, 186
broadcast networks, 236–237, 263–264
Broderick, David, Sen. (D-Calif., 1857–1859), 99
Brooks, Preston, Rep. (D-S.C., 1853–1857), 99
budget
    allocations, 125–127
    appropriations, 129, 131–132, 317, 322, 331
    appropriations bills, 120, 132–133, 135–136, 322
    appropriations committees, 129–132, 137
    appropriations subcommittees, 130
    authorization act, 128
    authorizing committees, 126, 128

baseline, 322
biennial budget, 120
budget authority, 125, 322
calendar year, 121–122, 124
capital budget, 323
Congressional Budget and Impoundment
　Control Act of 1974, 124
Congressional Budget Office (CBO), 124,
　210–211
continuing resolution, 133
current services budget, 324
debt, 324
debt ceiling, 324
deficit spending, 128, 322, 324
definition, 322
diagram of the process, 123
discretionary spending, 125, 324
earmarks, 133–134, 136
emergency spending, 325
expenditures, 325
fiscal year, 121, 325
functions, 125–126, 325
funding requests, 136–137
impoundments, 124, 326
limitations, 134
line items, 327
mandatory (direct) spending, 125,
　324, 327
Office of Management and Budget (OMB),
　121, 124
offset collections, 328
omnibus continuing resolution, 133
outlays, 125, 328
pay-as-you-go, 127, 328
pork, 135, 329
posting appropriations online, 316
president's role, 121, 329
procedural restraints, 127
reconciliation legislation, 122
rescissions, 330
reserve fund, 330
resolutions, 322
sequestering funds, 330
State of the Union address, 121
statutory restraints, 127
supplemental appropriation, 128
surpluses, 128, 322
timetable, 121–122, 124
top line, 125
unfunded mandates, 332

Building a Web Site For Dummies, David
　Crowder and Rhonda Crowder, 240
Bumpers, Dale, Sen. (D-Ark., 1975–1999), 95
bundling campaign contributions, 322
*Bushmanders & Bullwinkles: How Politicians
　Manipulate Electronic Maps And Census
　Data To Win Elections,* Mark Monmonier,
　27
Butler, Andrew, Sen. (D-S.C., 1846–1857), 99
by request, defined, 322
Byrd, Robert, Sen. (D-W.Va.), 44, 95, 129

● *C* ●

Cabinet, 14, 322
cable networks, 236–237, 263–265
Cable News Network (CNN), 264–265
calendars
　budget, 121–122, 124
　calendar year, 323
　correction calendar, 323
　definition, 322
　discharge calendar, 323
　executive calendar, 323
　House, 83–87, 323
　private calendar, 323
　Senate, 87–88
　union calendar, 323
campaign finance
　Bipartisan Campaign Reform Act of 2002
　　(BCRA), 142–143, 148
　bribes, 142
　bundling contributions, 322
　campaign finance laws, 147–149
　donations to pay for campaigns, 141
　election cycle, 142
　Federal Election Campaign Act
　　(FECA), 144
　Federal Election Commission (FEC),
　　141, 153
　fundraising, 149–152
　hard money, 147, 326
　independent expenditure, 326
　individual contributions, 140–143
　limits on contributions, 142–143
　nonmonetary contributions, 153
　PAC contributions, 144–147
　soft money, 147–148, 331
　spending limits, 331
　spending records, 139

Campaign Finance Institute (CFI), 143, 153
Campbell, Ben Nighthorse, Sen.
    (R-Colo.), 187
Cannon House Office Building, 291
Cannon, Joe, Rep. (R-Ill., 1893–1923), 16
capital budget, defined, 323
Capital Source, directory of people and
    organizations in Washington, D.C., 261
Capitol Advantage Publishing, 91
Capitol Complex
  Architect of the Capitol, 286, 288, 322
  attacks, 289
  Bartholdi Park, 292
  campus, 283–284
  Capitol building, 283–287, 290–291,
    293, 323
  Capitol Hill, 284
  Capitol Power Plant, 292
  Capitol Visitor Center (CVC), 288
  dining options, 294–295
  flags, purchasing, 274
  history, 284–285
  House of Representatives, 291–292
  Library of Congress, 284
  lights, 293
  map, 290
  National Garden, 292
  private functions, 294
  renovations, 3, 288
  security restrictions, 287–288
  Senate, 292–294
  special events, 294
  Summerhouse, 294
  Supreme Court, 283
  tours, 286–287
  U.S. Botanic Gardens Conservatory, 292
Capitol Guide Service (CGS), 287
Capitol Hill media
  Congressional Daily Monitor
    newsletter, 260
  Congressional Quarterly, 260
  The Hill, 251, 259–260
  National Journal, 261
  Roll Call, 259–260, 268
Capitol Police, 286
Capitol switchboard, 30, 42
Capitol Visitor Center (CVC), 288
Caraway, Hattie, Sen. (D-Ark.), 42
cardinals, 129
Caro, Robert A., *The Years of Lyndon Johnson:
    Master of the Senate,* 45

casework
  academy nominations, 274–277
  definition, 323
  expediting a passport, 273
  House of Representatives, 37
  internships, 280–281
  local political issues, 273–274
  pages, 277–280
  purpose of, 271
  resolving difficulties with federal agencies,
    272–273
  Senate, 39
caseworker, 203
caucuses, 80–82, 323
cause
  achievements, 299–300
  advertising, 241–242
  alliances, 301
  assets, 173–174, 300
  celebrity endorsements, 242–244
  champions, 177–178, 303, 323
  coalition-building, 175–178, 301
  compromise, 171, 302
  core issues, 171, 299, 324
  demonstrations, 244–249
  discussing with a representative or senator
    in person, 186–190
  enemies, 301–302
  follow-up, 190
  friends, 301–302
  information packets, 174–175, 308
  leaks, 227–228
  liabilities, 173–174, 300
  lobbying days, 191
  media relations, 219–228
  negative pressure, 191–193
  persistence required, 196–198, 302–303
  press conferences, 232–236
  press releases, 228–232
  radio programs, 238–240
  researching and communicating, 170–173,
    190–191, 300
  testifying before Congress, 178–180
  TV coverage, 236–238
  Web site, 240
  writing about to a representative or senator,
    182–183, 185–186
CBO (Congressional Budget Office), 124,
    210–211
CBS (Columbia Broadcasting Service),
    263–264

celebrity endorsement of a cause, 242–244
census, 26–27
Center for Responsive Politics, 153
Centrist Coalition, 82
CFI (Campaign Finance Institute), 143, 153
CGS (Capitol Guide Service), 287
chairman, defined, 323
chairman's mark (bill), 71, 323
Chamber of Commerce, 162
champions of a cause, 177–178, 303, 323
chaplain in House and Senate, 57
checks and balances, 12
Chief Administrative Officer (House of
　Representatives), 57
chief of staff (CoS), 202
Christian Coalition, 162
"Christmas tree" bill, defined, 323
civil rights, 46, 246
classified, defined, 323
"clean" bill, defined, 323
Clerk of the House, 32, 57, 201, 323
client, defined, 323
Clinton, Bill
　budget crisis, 120
　Contract with America, 88
　impeachment, 18, 49, 95, 183
　Monica Lewinsky scandal, 281
cloakrooms, defined, 323
closed rule, defined, 323
closed sessions, defined, 323
cloture vote, 47, 323
CNBC, 265
CNN (Cable News Network), 264–265
codel, definition, 323
Columbia Broadcasting Service (CBS), 263–264
columnists, 256
commit a bill, defined, 323
committee amendment, defined, 322
committee assignments, 57–58
Committee on Official Standards of Conduct,
　193–194
committee staff, 200, 207–209, 324
Committee of the Whole, 24, 324
committees
　Advisory Committee on the Records of
　　Congress, 214
　appropriations committees, 126,
　　129–132, 137
　authorizing committees, 126, 128, 322
　bill referral, 68–69
　chairman's power, 58

chairman's role, 58
Committee on Official Standards of
　Conduct, 193–194
definition, 323–324
discharge petition, 69
House Budget Committee, 127
House Committee on Standards of Official
　Conduct, 25
House Rules Committee, 92–94
House Ways and Means Committee, 115
joint committees, 68, 326, 334
Joint Taxation Committee, 116
number of, 67
ranking member, 58, 329
rules committees, 92–94
select committees, 68, 330, 334
Senate Finance Committee, 115–116
Senate Rules and Administration
　Committee, 92–93, 194
special committees, 68, 334
standing committees, 68, 331, 333–334
subcommittees, 331
communications director, 202
Concord Coalition, 162
concurrent resolution, 60–61, 324
Condit, Gary, Rep. (D-Calif.), 281
conditional adjournment, defined, 321
conferees, defined, 324
Conference Chairmen (Senate), 78–79
conferences, 101–104, 324
Congress. *See also* House of Representatives;
　Senate
　beginnings, 12
　definition, 324
　online biographical service, 4
　powers, 12–14
Congress at Your Fingertips, guide to
　Congress, 91
Congressional Anecdotes, Paul F. Boller, 91
Congressional Budget and Impoundment
　Control Act of 1974, 124
Congressional Budget Office (CBO), 124,
　210–211
congressional calendars
　calendar year, 323
　correction calendar, 323
　definition, 322
　discharge calendar, 323
　executive calendar, 323
　House of Representatives, 83–87, 323

congressional calendars *(continued)*
  private calendar, 323
  Senate, 87–88
  union calendar, 323
Congressional Daily Monitor newsletter, 260
congressional districts, 24, 26–30, 324
Congressional Procedures and the Policy Process, Walter Oleszek, 260
Congressional Progressive Caucus, 82
Congressional Quarterly magazine, 260
Congressional Quarterly Press
  Congressional Procedures and the Policy Process, 260
  Congressional Staff Directory, 81, 260
  CQ Almanac, 260
  Directory of Congressional Voting Scores and Interest Group Ratings, 261
  How Congress Works, 72, 261
  Politics in America, 34, 261
Congressional Record, 324
congressional redistricting, 26–29
congressional relationships
  with constituents, 18–19
  with executive branch, 17–18
  between House and Senate, 16
  with media, 217–219
Congressional Research Service (CRS), 213–214
Congressional Staff Directory, directory of Congress, 81, 209, 260
congressional staffers. *See* staffers
Congressional Voting Record Project, 316
Congressional Yellow Book, directory of Congress, 81, 209
constituent services
  academy nominations, 274–277
  Capitol flags, purchasing, 274
  definition, 324
  expediting a passport, 273
  internships, 280–281, 326
  local political issues, 273–274
  pages, 277–280
  purpose of, 271
  resolving difficulties with federal agencies, 272–273
  suggested improvements, 315–317
constituent services representative, 203
Constitution
  amendments, 15
  Article I, 12–13
  Article II, 14
  Article III, 15
  Bill of Rights, 15
  definition, 324
  first amendment, 218–219
  history, 11
Continental Congress, 11
continuing resolution, 133, 324
Contract with America, 88
controlled time (debate), defined, 324
correction calendar, defined, 323
Corzine, Jon, Sen. (D-N.J.), 139
cosponsor (bill), 64, 67, 324
Coxey, Jacob (protestor), 245
CQ Almanac, 260
CQ.com On Congress Web site, 260
CRS (Congressional Research Service), 213–214
Creating Web Pages For Dummies, 6th Edition, Bud Smith and Arthur Bebak, 240
credit authority, defined, 324
Crowder, David and Rhonda, *Building a Web Site For Dummies,* 240
C-SPAN, 73, 89, 264
current services budget, defined, 324
CVC (Capitol Visitor Center), 288

• D •

Daschle, Tom, Sen. (D-S.D.), 181, 237
DCCC (Democratic Congressional Campaign Committee), 152
Dear colleague letter, 64, 67, 324
debate
  amendments, 97–98
  cloture vote, 323
  controlled time, 324
  definition, 90
  filibustering, 47, 325
  five-minute rule, 325
  hold, 326
  hour rule, 326
  introduction of bills, 90–92
  objection, 328
  parliamentary procedure, 94
  previous question, 329
  reality versus movie depiction, 89
  recognition, 329
  rules of decorum, 95–96
  rules for legislation, 92–94
  seating systems, 100
  Senate, 45–47

timing, 96–97
unlimited debate, 332
violence, 99
voting, 98, 100–101
waiting period, 90
yield, 332
debt ceiling (budget), 324
debt, defined, 324
deficit spending, 128, 322, 324
DeLaney, Ann, *Politics For Dummies,* 2nd
    Edition, 22
DeLay, Tom, Rep. (R-Texas), 77
delegates (House), 24, 324
delegations, 80, 83
Democratic Caucus Chairman, 78
Democratic Congressional Campaign
    Committee (DCCC), 152
Democratic National Committee (DNC), 152
Democratic Senate Campaign Committee
    (DSCC), 152
Democratic-Republican party, 28
demonstrations, 244–249
Diane Rehm Show (radio program), 266
direct spending, 125, 324
*Directory of Congressional Voting Scores and
    Interest Group Ratings,* 261
Directory of Membership and News Sources,
    media directory, 231
Dirksen Senate Office Building, 292
discharge calendar, defined, 323
discharge petition, 69, 324
discretionary spending, 125, 324
distributing press releases, 230–231
district director, 203
districts, 24, 26–30, 324
DNC (Democratic National Committee), 152
Douglas, Stephen, Sen. (D-Ill., 1847–1861), 99
Dow Jones' Factiva, 300
Drudge, Matt (journalist), 267
Drudge Report, 267
DSOC (Democratic Senate Campaign
    Committee), 152
Dubois, Fred, Sen. (R-Idaho, 1891–1907), 16

• *E* •

earmarks (budget), 133–134, 136
The Economist, 268
editors, meeting, 224
election cycle, 142
elections, 20–21

e-mail addresses
    representatives, 31
    senators, 43
e-mailing
    letter to a representative or senator,
        183–185
    press releases, 231
emergency spending, defined, 325
EMILY's List (PAC), 143
en bloc amendment, 97, 324
enacted bills, defined, 325
engrossed bills, defined, 325
enrolled bills, defined, 325
entertainment perks, 195–196
entitlements, defined, 325
ethics, 25, 193–194
ex officio, defined, 325
executive branch
    agencies, 14
    bureaus, 14
    Cabinet, 14, 322
    commissions, 14
    definition, 325
    monetary policy, 327
    nomination approvals, 50–51
    powers, 14
    relationship with Congress, 17–18
    size, 14
executive business, defined, 325
executive calendar, defined, 323
executive order, defined, 325
executive session, defined, 325
expenditure, defined, 325

• *F* •

Face the Nation (television show), 265
factions, 160
Factiva, 300
FastPolitics.com Web site, 268
faxing
    letter to a representative or senator, 186
    press releases, 231
FEC (Federal Election Commission), 141, 153
FECA (Federal Election Campaign Act), 144
federal agencies
    resolving difficulties with, 272–273
    Web sites, 272
Federal Election Campaign Act (FECA), 144
Federal Election Commission (FEC), 141, 153

Federal Technology Source, directory of people and organizations in government technology, 261

Feingold, Russ, Sen. (D-Wis.), 148

Feinstein, Dianne, Sen. (D-Calif.), 316

field representative, 203

filibustering, 47, 325

final passage of a bill, defined, 325

Finance Committee, 115–116

First Session, 24, 84–85

fiscal, defined, 325

fiscal year, 121, 325

Fitzgerald, Ruth Coder (activist), 187

five-minute rule, defined, 325

501(c)(3)s, defined, 321

flags, purchasing a Capitol flag, 274

floor amendment, defined, 322, 325

floor debate. *See* debate

floor, defined, 325

floor leaders, defined, 325

floor manager, defined, 325

For Good and Evil: The Impact of Taxes on the Course of Civilization, 2nd edition, Charles Adams, 117

Ford House Office Building, 291

foreign agents, defined, 325

foreign media, 268

Fox Broadcasting Company, 263

Fox News Sunday (television show), 265

franking privileges, 37, 325

functions (budget), 125–126, 325

fundraisers, 149–152

Fundraising For Dummies, Katherine Murray and John Mutz, 153

• G •

Gallegly, Elton, Rep. (R-Calif.), 187

gatekeepers, 200

General Accounting Office (GAO), 211–213

general consent, defined, 326

Gephardt, Dick, Rep. (D-Mo.), 237

germane (bills), 97, 326

Gerry, Elbridge (Massachusettes governor), 28

gerrymandering, 28, 326

Gibbons, Sam, Rep. (D-Fla., 1963–1997), 99

gift-giving, 193, 195, 308

Gingrich, Newt, Rep. (R-Ga., 1979–1999), 88, 237–238

Glass Houses: Congressional Ethics and the Politics of Venom, Martin and Sue Tolchin, 25

Golden Fleece Award, 135

Government Printing Office, 214

Grant, Ulysses S., 159

grass roots, 158, 326

grass tops, defined, 326

Great Compromise, 13

Gucci gulch, defined, 326

guided tours of the Capitol, 286–287

• H •

Hagel, Chuck, Sen. (R-Neb.), 97

Halberstam, David, *The Powers That Be,* 268

hard money, 147, 326

Hart, Philip, Sen. (D-Mich., 1959–1976), 293

Hart Senate Office Building, 293

Hastert, Dennis, Speaker of the House (R-Ill.), 148

hearings, 69–71, 178–180, 326

The Hill, (newspaper), 251, 259–260

hiring a lobbyist, 163–167

historians (official), 317

History of the United States Capitol, William C. Allen, 285

hold, defined, 326

Hollywood celebrities, 243

hopper, defined, 326

horse, defined, 326

hour rule, defined, 326

House Action Reports Web site, 260

House Budget Committee, 127

House Committee on Standards of Official Conduct, 25

House of Representatives
  amendments, 97–98
  appropriations bills, 132–133
  at-large seat, 26, 322
  bell system, 293
  calendar, 83–87, 323
  Capitol Complex, 290–292
  casework, 37
  chaplain, 57
  Chief Administrative Officer, 57
  Clerk of the House, 32, 57, 201, 323
  committee assignments, 57–58
  Committee of the Whole, 24, 324
  committees (listing of), 333
  congressional districts, 24, 26–30, 324

constituent relations, 23
contacting members, 31
debates, 89–100
delegates, 24, 324
Democratic Caucus Chairman, 78
ethics manual, 25
finding members, 29–30
first female member, 42
floor activity, 89–90
franking privileges, 37
Great Compromise, 13
historian, 317
internships, 281
leadership, 76–78
legislation, 36–37
Majority Leader, 77
majority rule, 24–25
Majority Whip, 77
meeting members, 161
Minority Leader, 77
Minority Whip, 77
number of members, 24
page program, 278–279
parliamentarian, 57
postmaster, 57
qualifications of members, 25
House Rules Committee, 92–94
House Ways and Means Committee, 115
House-Senate relations, 16
How Congress Works, Congressional
    Quarterly, 72, 261
hustings, defined, 326

● *I* ●

IDEA (Individuals with Disabilities Education
    Act), 172
ideological publications, 258
ideology, defined, 326
Immigration and Naturalization Service
    (INS), 272
impeachment process, 44, 48–49, 326
impoundments, 124, 326
imputation, defined, 326
Imus, Don (radio talk-show host), 266
in session, defined, 326
independent agent, defined, 326
independent expenditure, defined, 326
Individuals with Disabilities Education Act
    (IDEA), 172
industry caucuses, 82

industry, defined, 326
information packets for a cause, 174–175, 308
Information Technology Industry Council, 162
inside the Beltway, defined, 326
Inside Politics (television show), 265
interest, defined, 326
intern scandals, 281
Internal Revenue Service (IRS), 117, 272
Internet media, 240–241, 267–268
internships, 280–281, 326
introducing a bill, 59, 62–65, 90–91, 326
investigative hearings, 70
IRS (Internal Revenue Service), 117, 272
issue, defined, 326

● *J* ●

Jeffords, Jim, Sen. (I-Vermont), 80, 172
Johnson, Andrew, 17, 49
Johnson, Lyndon, 45–46, 128
joint committees, 68, 326, 334
joint, defined, 326
joint resolution, 60, 326
Joint Taxation Committee, 116
journal, defined, 327
journalists. *See* media
judicial branch
    nomination approvals, 50–51
    powers, 15
jurisdiction, defined, 327

● *K* ●

K Street, defined, 327
Kefauver, Estes, Sen. (D-Tenn., 1948–1963), 71
Kennedy, Caroline, *Profiles in Courage for Our
    Time,* 45
Kennedy, John F. (D-Mass., 1953–1961), 45
key vote, 162, 327
King, Rev. Martin Luther, Jr., 246
The Kingdom and the Power, Gay
    Talese, 268
king-of-the-hill, defined, 327

● *L* ●

La Follette, Robert, Sen. (R-Wis.,
    1906–1925), 135
lame duck, defined, 327
language of a bill, defined, 327

Late Edition (television show), 265
laws. *See also* legislation
  campaign finance laws, 147–148
  implementing, 110
  loopholes, 110
  public laws, 329
  statutes at large, 331
layover, defined, 327
leader time, defined, 327
leadership
  definition, 327
  House, 76–78
  political parties, 76
  Senate, 78–79
leadership staff, 200, 209–210
League of Conservation Voters, 162
League of Nations, 18
leaks to the media, 227–228
legislate, defined, 327
legislation
  authorizing legislation, 322
  bill, 59
  chairman's mark, 71
  challenging, 108–109
  concurrent resolution, 60–61
  conferences, 101–104
  cosponsors, 64, 67, 324
  Dear colleague letter, 64, 67, 324
  definition, 327
  descriptions of the legislative process,
    72–73
  diagram of legislative process, 65
  discharge petition, 69, 324
  final passage, 325
  germane, 97, 326
  hearings, 69–71
  hopper, 326
  House, 36–37
  introducing, 59, 62–65, 90–91, 326
  joint resolution, 60
  language, 327
  logrolling, 327
  markup, 71, 327
  media coverage, 90
  "must pass" legislation, 328
  names, 63–64
  omnibus legislation, 328
  open rule, 328
  passage, 328
  passing, 67–73
  president's role, 105–107

president's signature, 105, 108
private bill, 61–62, 329
protecting, 109–110
readings, 92, 329
recommitting, 330
reconciliation legislation, 122
referral process, 68–69, 330
reporting out, 72
by request, 322
resolution, 59–60
Senate, 39, 44–48
sponsor, 65–66, 331
tabling, 331
tax legislation, 114–117
Thomas Web site, 170
vehicle, 332
legislative assistant (LA), 202, 327
legislative correspondent, 203
legislative day, defined, 327
legislative director (LD), 202
legislative hearings, 70
legislative session, defined, 327
Lehrer, Jim (journalist), 264
Levy, Chandra (Congressional intern), 281
Lewinsky, Monica (White House
    intern), 281
Lexis-Nexis, 300
Library of Congress, 91, 213–214, 284
lights in Capitol building, 293
Limbaugh, Rush (radio talk-show
    host), 266
limitations (budget), 134
Lincoln, Abraham, 17, 220
line items (budget), defined, 327
line-item veto, 327
Lippman, Walter (political columnist), 256
lobbying
  assets, 173–174
  associations, 158
  campaigns, 158
  champions, 177–178
  client, 323
  coalition building, 175–176
  coalitions, 158
  compromises, 171–172
  corporations, 158
  definition, 157, 327
  entertainment perks, 195–196
  follow-up, 190
  gift-giving, 193–195
  grass roots, 158, 326

grass tops, 326
Gucci gulch, 326
history, 159
individuals, 158
key votes, 162
liabilities, 174
media, 224–227
Memory Plaque Project, 187
negative pressure, 191–193
nonprofits, 158
opportunities, 197–198
packets of information, 174–175, 308
persistence required, 196–198
planning process, 170–174
research, 172–173
research and communication, 190–191
scorecards, 162–163
special interests, 159–160
testifying before Congress, 178–180
travel perks, 193–195
lobbying days, 191
lobbyists
developing a plan of action, 167
evaluating, 167–168
fees, 165
foreign agents, 325
hiring, 163–167
K Street, 327
professionals, 163–167
qualifications, 166–167
registration, 160, 165, 330
types, 158–159
local daily newspapers, 222–223, 255–256
Lodge, Henry Cabot, Sen. (R-Mass.,
1893–1924), 18
Log Cabin Republicans, 82
logrolling, definition, 327
Long, Huey, Sen. (D-La., 1932–1935), 47
Longworth House Office Building, 291
loopholes in laws, 110
The Los Angeles Times-Washington Post
News Service, 262

• *M* •

MacNeil/Lehrer Report, 264
magazines
The American Spectator, 258
Congressional Quarterly, 260
The Economist, 268
ideological magazines, 258
National Journal, 261
National Review, 258
The New Republic, 258
Newsweek, 257
newsweeklies, 257
publication frequency, 256
regional and city magazines, 258–259
Time, 257
U.S. News & World Report, 257
The Washington Monthly, 258
The Weekly Standard, 258
Majority Leader
House, 77
Senate, 78
majority party, definition, 327
majority secretary (Senate), 57
Majority Whip
House, 77
Senate, 78
mandatory, defined, 327
mandatory (direct) spending, 125, 324, 327
Marbury *vs.* Madison, 15
marching on Capitol Hill, 245
markup (bill), 71, 327
Marshall, John, Chief Justice of the U.S.
Supreme Court, (1801–1835), 15, 113
Mazzoli, Romano L., Rep. (D-Ky., 1971–1995),
33
McCain, John, Sen. (R-Ariz.), 97, 135, 147–148
McCarthy, Joseph, Sen. (R-Wis.,
1947–1957), 71
McLaughlin Group (television show), 265–266
measure, defined, 327
media
beats, 222, 322
coverage of legislation, 90
demonstrations, 247
directories, 230–231
first amendment, 218–219
importance of, 218
leaks, 227–228
lobbying, 224–227
meetings with, 224–227, 309–313
news, 223–224
pitching stories to, 219–223
press conferences, 232–236
press galleries, 215, 234
press releases, 228–232
relationship with Congress, 217–219
sound bites, 265, 331

media *(continued)*
  talking heads, 331
  tips for working with, 309–313
  visuals, 237–238, 332
media outlets
  broadcast networks, 236–237, 263–264
  cable networks, 236–237, 263–265
  Capitol Hill media, 251, 259–260
  columnists, 256
  determining importance of, 251
  foreign media, 268
  ideological publications, 258
  influence of, 251
  Internet media, 240–241, 267–268
  local dailies, 222–223, 255–256
  magazines, 256–257
  National Journal, 261
  New York Daily News, 256
  New York Post, 256
  The New York Times, 252–254
  newsweeklies, 257
  op-eds, 253
  radio programs, 238–240, 266
  regional and city periodicals, 258–259
  specialized publications, 263
  syndicated columnists, 256
  talk shows, 265–266
  trade publications, 263
  USA Today, 254–255
  The Wall Street Journal, 252, 254
  The Washington Post, 252–253
  The Washington Times, 255
  wire services, 261–262
Medicaid, 272
Medicare, 272
Medicare Payment Advisory Commission, 214
Meehan, Martin, Rep. (D-Mass.), 148
Meet the Press (television show), 265
meetings
  with editors or producers, 224–225
  with reporters, 225–226, 309–313
  with representatives or senators, 161,
    186–190
  with staffers, 305–308
member of Congress, defined, 327
member management, defined, 327
Memory Plaque Project, 187
military academy nominations, 274–277
Minority Leader
  House, 77
  Senate, 78

minority party, defined, 327
minority secretary (Senate), 57
Minority Whip
  House, 77
  Senate, 78
monetary policy, defined, 327
Monmonier, Mark, *Bushmanders &*
    Bullwinkles: How Politicians Manipulate
    Electronic Maps And Census Data To Win
    Elections, 27
morning business, 327
Morning Edition (radio program), 266
motion, defined, 327
Motion Picture Association of America
    (MPAA), 243
MSNBC, 265
Murray, Katherine, *Fundraising For Dummies,*
    153
"must pass" bill, defined, 328
Mutz, John, *Fundraising For Dummies,* 153
My Declaration of Independence, Jim
    Jeffords, 80

• *N* •

National Broadcasting Company (NBC),
    263–264
national debt ceiling, 115
National Garden, 292
National Journal Group, 261
National Journal magazine, 261
National Journal's Almanac of American
    Politics, Michael Barone and Grant
    Ujifusa, 34
National Press Building, 268
National Press Club, 233
National Public Radio (NPR), 266
National Republican Campaign Committee
    (NRCC), 152
National Republican Senatorial Committee
    (NRSC), 152
National Review, 258
National Rifle Association (NRA), 193
National Tax-Limitation Committee, 162
National Taxpayers Union, 162
NBC (National Broadcasting Company),
    263–264
Nelson, Knute, Sen. (R-Minn.,
    1895–1923), 16
New Deal, 18
The New Republic, 258
New York Daily News, 256

New York magazine, 259
New York Post, 256
The New York Times, 252–254
The New York Times News Service and
    Syndicate, 262
news, 223–224
News Media Yellow Book, media directory,
    230–231
The NewsHour with Jim Lehrer, 264
newspapers
    columnists, 256
    The Hill, 251, 259–260
    local dailies, 255–256
    New York Daily News, 256
    New York Post, 256
    The New York Times, 252–254
    op-eds, 253
    Roll Call, 259–260, 268
    syndicated columnists, 256
    USA Today, 254–255
    The Wall Street Journal, 252, 254
    The Washington Post, 252–253
    The Washington Times, 255
newsweeklies, 257
NGO (nongovernment organization),
    defined, 328
Nixon, Richard, 49, 124, 144, 228, 252
nominations
    executive and judicial appointments, 50–51
    military academies, 274–277
nominee, defined, 328
nonpartisan, defined, 328
nonprofit, defined, 328
NPR (National Public Radio), 266
NRA (National Rifle Association), 193
NRCC (National Republican Campaign
    Committee), 152
NRSC (National Republican Senatorial
    Committee), 152
Nutting, Brian, *Congressional Quarterly's
    Politics in America,* 34, 261

• O •

Obey, David, Rep. (D-Wis.), 136
objection, defined, 328
obligation, defined, 328
off the record, 227, 328
off-budget federal entity, defined, 328
Office of the Attending Physician, 214
Office of Compliance, 214

Office of Management and Budget (OMB),
    121, 124
office manager, 203
Office of Official Reporters, 214
Office of Senate Official Reporters of
    Debates, 215
officer staff, 200
offset collections, defined, 328
Oleszek, Walter, *Congressional Procedures and
    the Policy Process,* 260
OMB (Office of Management and Budget),
    121, 124
omnibus bill, defined, 328
omnibus continuing resolution, 133
on background, 227, 328
on the record, 227, 328
one minutes, defined, 328
O'Neill House Office Building, 291
op-eds, 253
open rule, defined, 328
organizing a demonstration, 246–249
organizing a press conference, 232–236
other body, defined, 328
outlay rates, defined, 328
outlays, defined, 328
overriding a veto, 108, 328
oversight hearings, 70, 328

• P •

packets of information for lobbying a cause,
    174–175, 308
PACs (political action committees)
    contribution limits, 147
    corporate PACs, 146
    definition, 328
    EMILY's List, 143
    influence of, 144
    membership, 147
    names, 145
    nonconnected committees, 145–146
    registering, 145
    separate segregated funds, 145–146
page schools, 215, 279–280
pages, 277–280, 328
paid advertising, 241–242
Pallone, Frank, Rep. (D-N.J.), 37
parliamentarian, 57, 328
parliamentary inquiry, defined, 328
parliamentary procedure, 94
participation of citizens, 19–22

partisan, defined, 328
party leaders, 76
party secretaries (Senate), 57
passage, defined, 328
passport services, 273
pay-as-you-go (budget), 127, 328
PBS (Public Broadcasting Service), 263–264
Pelosi, Nancy, Rep. (D-Cal.), 77
pending amendment, defined, 328
perfecting amendment, defined, 322
periodicals
    The American Spectator, 258
    Congressional Quarterly, 260
    The Economist, 268
    ideological periodicals, 258
    National Review, 258
    The New Republic, 258
    Newsweek, 257
    newsweeklies, 257
    publication frequency, 256
    regional and city periodicals, 258–259
    Time, 257
    U.S. News & World Report, 257
    The Washington Monthly, 258
    The Weekly Standard, 258
permanent, defined, 328
permits for demonstrations, 249
personal assistant, 203
personal staff, 200–207, 328
petition, defined, 328
pitching stories to the media, 219–223
pocket veto, 107–108, 329
point of order, defined, 329
Policy Committee Chairmen (Senate), 79
policy, defined, 329
political action committees (PACs)
    contribution limits, 147
    corporate PACs, 146
    definition, 328
    EMILY's List, 143
    influence of, 144
    membership, 147
    names, 145
    nonconnected committees, 145–146
    registering, 145
    separate segregated funds, 145–146
political campaigns
    Bipartisan Campaign Reform Act of 2002
      (BCRA), 142–143, 148
    bribes, 142
    bundling contributions, 322

campaign finance laws, 147–149
    donations to pay for campaigns, 141
    election cycle, 142
    Federal Election Campaign Act
      (FECA), 144
    Federal Election Commission (FEC),
      141, 153
    fundraising, 149–152
    hard money, 147, 326
    independent expenditure, 326
    individual contributions, 140–143
    limits on contributions, 142–143
    nonmonetary contributions, 153
    PAC contributions, 144–147
    soft money, 147–148, 331
    spending limits, 331
    spending records, 139
political contributions. *See* political
    campaigns
political parties
    abbreviations, 4
    caucuses, 81–82
    Conference Chairmen, 78–79
    Democratic Caucus Chairman, 78
    Democratic Congressional Campaign
      Committee (DCCC), 152
    Democratic National Committee
      (DNC), 152
    Democratic Senate Campaign Committee
      (DSCC), 152
    Democratic-Republican party, 28
    fundraising, 152
    leadership, 76
    majority party, 327
    minority party, 327
    National Republican Campaign Committee
      (NRCC), 152
    National Republican Senatorial Committee
      (NRSC), 152
    Policy Committee Chairmen, 79
    Republican Conference Chairman, 77
    Republican National Committee (RNC), 152
Politics in America, Brian Nutting and H. Amy
    Stern (editors), 34, 261
Politics For Dummies, 2nd Edition, Ann
    DeLaney, 22
pork, 135, 329
postmaster, 57
The Powers That Be, David Halberstam, 268
president pro tempore (Senate), 78, 329
president of the Senate, 78, 329

President of the United States
  agenda, 88
  budget, 121, 329
  cabinet, 14
  executive order, 325
  impeachment process, 44, 48–49
  lobbying tactics, 105–106
  Office of Management and Budget (OMB),
    121, 124
  powers, 14
  relationship with Congress, 17–18
  role in legislation, 105, 108
  State of the Union address, 121
  veto power, 105, 107–108
presidents
  Clinton, Bill, 18, 49, 88, 120, 183, 281
  Grant, Ulysses S., 159
  Johnson, Andrew, 17, 49
  Johnson, Lyndon, 45, 128
  Lincoln, Abraham, 17, 220
  Nixon, Richard, 49, 124, 144, 228, 252
  Reagan, Ronald, 106, 220
  Roosevelt, Franklin Delano, 18, 88, 220
  Truman, Harry, 107
  Wilson, Woodrow, 17
presiding officer, defined, 329
press. *See* media
press conference
  announcing, 235
  media coverage, 235–236
  organizing, 232–236
  venue, 233
press the flesh, defined, 329
press galleries, 215, 234
*Press Gallery: Congress and the Washington
  Correspondents,* Donald A. Ritchie, 234
press releases
  distributing, 230–231
  following up, 232
  proliferation of, 229
  purpose of, 228
  writing, 229–230
press secretary, 202, 222–223, 329
previous question, defined, 329
private bill, 61–62, 329
private calendar, defined, 323
pro forma amendment, 322
pro forma session, defined, 329
producers, meeting, 225
professional political fundraisers, 151–152
Profiles in Courage, John F. Kennedy, 45

Profiles in Courage for Our Time, Caroline
  Kennedy, 45
Proxmire, William, Sen. (D-Wis.,
  1957–1989), 135
proxy vote, defined, 329
Public Broadcasting Service (PBS), 263–264
public law, defined, 329

question of privilege, defined, 329
quorum, 100–101, 329
quorum call, defined, 329

radio programs, 238–240, 266
Rankin, Jeannette, Rep. (R-Mont.,
  (1916–1918)), 42
ranking member (committees), 58, 329
Rayburn House Office Building, 291
Rayburn, Sam, House Speaker, (D-Texas,
  1940–1961), 76
readings of a bill, 92, 329
Reagan, Ronald, 106, 220
receipts, defined, 329
receptionist, 203
recess, defined, 329
recognition, defined, 329
recommitting a bill, defined, 330
reconciliation legislation, 122, 330
reconsideration, defined, 330
recuse, defined, 330
redistricting, 26–29, 330
referral of bills, 68–69, 330
registering
  lobbyists, 160, 165
  political action committees (PACs), 145
regulation, defined, 330
Rehm, Diane (radio talk-show host), 266
reporters, tips for working with, 225–227,
  309–313
reporting out a bill, 72
representatives
  career courses, 33–34
  definition, 330
  e-mail addresses, 31
  e-mailing, 183–185
  finding, 29–30
  meeting, 161, 186–188
  qualifications, 25

representatives *(continued)*
  relationship with Senate, 16
  Republican Conference Chairman, 77
  resident commissioner, 24, 330
  roles, 32–33
  rules and regulations, 25, 93–94
  seating systems, 100
  seniority system, 79–80
  Sense of the House resolutions, 36
  sergeant-at-arms, 57, 330
  sessions, 84–86
  Speaker of the House, 24, 77, 331
  staffers, 57
  suspension of the rules, 331
  taxes, 36
  term of members, 24
  term of office, 24
  timeframes, 34
  voting, 98, 100–101
  Web sites, 29–32, 317
  workweek, 35
  writing letters to, 181–183, 185–186
  ZIP code, 31, 186
representatives (by name)
  Ames, Fisher (Mass., 1789–1797), 55
  Brooks, Preston (D-S.C., 1853–1857), 99
  Cannon, Joe (R-Ill., 1893–1923), 16
  Condit, Gary (D-Calif.), 281
  DeLay, Tom (R-Texas), 77
  Gallegly, Elton (R-Calif.), 187
  Gephardt, Dick (D-Mo.), 237
  Gibbons, Sam (D-Fla., 1963–1997), 99
  Gingrich, Newt (R-Ga., 1979–1999), 88,
    237–238
  Hastert, Dennis, Speaker of the House
    (R-Ill.), 148
  Mazzoli, Romano L. (D-Ky., 1971–1995), 33
  Meehan, Martin (D-Mass.), 148
  Obey, David (D-Wis.), 136
  Pallone, Frank (D-N.J.), 37
  Pelosi, Nancy (D-Cal.), 77
  Rankin, Jeannette (R-Mont., (1916–1918)), 42
  Rayburn, Sam (D-Texas, 1940–1961), 76
  Sedgwick, Theodore (Federalist,
    1789–1801), 219
  Shays, Chris (R-Conn.), 148
  Thomas, Bill (R-Calif.), 17, 99
Republican Conference Chairman, 77
Republican National Committee (RNC), 152
rescission, defined, 330
reserve fund, defined, 330

resident commissioner, 24, 330
resolution, 59–60, 322, 324, 326, 330
return veto, 107
Reuters, 262
revenue
  General Accounting Office (GAO), 211–213
  Internal Revenue Service (IRS), 117
  sources, 113–114
  taxes, 114–117
rice pudding (on dining room menus), 17
rider (bill), 47–48, 131, 330
Ritchie, Donald A., *Press Gallery: Congress
    and the Washington Correspondents,* 234
RNC (Republican National Committee), 152
Rohde, Stephen F., *Webster's New World
    American Words of Freedom,* 15
Roll Call, 259, 268
roll-call vote, 101, 330
Roosevelt, Franklin Delano, 18, 88, 220
Rules Committee, 194
rules committees, 92–94
Russell Senate Office Building, 292

• *S* •

Santorum, Rick, Sen. (R-Pa.), 17
scheduler, 202
scorecards, 162–163, 330
seating systems, 100
"The Second Reply to Haynes," speech by
    Daniel Webster, 95
Second Session, 24, 85–86
Secretary of the Senate, 57
security restrictions in Capitol building,
    287–288
Sedgwick, Theodore, Rep. (Federalist,
    1789–1801), 219
select committees, 68, 330, 334
Senate
  advice and consent, 49–51
  amendments, 97–98
  appropriations bills, 132–133
  balance of power, 80
  bell system, 293
  calendar, 87–88
  Capitol Complex, 290, 292–294
  casework, 39
  chaplain, 57
  cloture vote, 47, 323
  committee assignments, 57–58
  committees (listing of), 333–334

Conference Chairmen, 78–79
contacting members, 42–43
debates, 45–47, 89–100
duties, 42, 44
filibustering, 47, 325
finding members, 42
first female member, 42
floor activity, 89–90
Great Compromise, 13
historian, 45
history, 44–45
House-Senate relations, 16
impeachment powers, 44, 48–49
internships, 281
leadership, 78–79
legislation, 39, 44–48
Majority Leader, 78
Majority Whip, 78
Minority Leader, 78
Minority Whip, 78
nominations (of executive and judicial
    appointments), 50–51
number of members, 40
page program, 279–280
parliamentarian, 57
party secretaries, 57
Policy Committee Chairmen, 79
president of the Senate, 78, 329
president pro tempore, 78, 329
qualifications of members, 41
role, 13, 40
seating systems, 100
Secretary of the Senate, 57
seniority system, 79–80
sergeant-at-arms, 57, 330
staffers, 57
state offices, 43
states rights, 41
term of members, 41
treaties, 49–50
voting, 98, 100–101
Web site, 43, 45
ZIP code, 43, 186
Senate Finance Committee, 115–116
Senate Historical Minutes, essays by
    Richard Baker, 45
Senate Rules and Administration Committee,
    92–93
senators
  contacting, 42–43
  definition, 330

duties, 42, 44
e-mail addresses, 43
e-mailing, 183–185
faxing, 186
finding, 42
first female senator, 42
meeting, 161, 186–188
qualifications, 41
state offices, 43
term of office, 41
writing letters to, 181–183, 185–186
senators (by name)
  Ashcroft, John, Sen. (R-Mo.,
      1995–2001), 51
  Broderick, David (D-Calif., 1857–1859), 99
  Bumpers, Dale (D-Ark., 1975–1999), 95
  Butler, Andrew (D-S.C., 1846–1857), 99
  Byrd, Robert (D-W.Va.), 44, 95, 129
  Campbell, Ben Nighthorse (R-Colo.), 187
  Caraway, Hattie (D-Ark., 1932–1945), 42
  Corzine, Jon (D-N.J.), 139
  Daschle, Tom (D-S.D.), 181, 237
  Douglas, Stephen (D-Ill., 1847–1861), 99
  Dubois, Fred (R-Idaho, 1891–1907), 16
  Feingold, Russ (D-Wis.), 148
  Feinstein, Dianne (D-Calif.), 316
  Hagel, Chuck (R-Neb.), 97
  Hart, Philip (D-Mich., 1959–1976), 293
  Jeffords, Jim (I-Vermont), 80, 172
  Johnson, Lyndon (D-Texas,
      1949–1961), 46
  Kefauver, Estes (D-Tenn., 1948–1963), 71
  Kennedy, John F. (D-Mass., 1953–1961), 45
  La Follette, Robert (R-Wis., 1906–1925), 135
  Lodge, Henry Cabot (R-Mass., 1893–1924), 18
  Long, Huey (D-La., 1932–1935), 47
  McCain, John (R-Ariz.), 97, 135, 147–148
  McCarthy, Joseph (R-Wis., 1947–1957), 71
  Nelson, Knute (R-Minn., 1895–1923), 16
  Proxmire, William (D-Wis., 1957–1989), 135
  Santorum, Rick (R-Pa.), 17
  Simpson, Alan (R-Wyo., 1979-1997), 200
  Sumner, Charles (R-Mass., 1851–1874), 99
  Thurmond, Strom (R-S.C.), 47
  Tower, John (R-Texas, 1961–1985), 51
  Webster, Daniel (Whig-Mass., 1827–1841),
      46, 95
seniority system, 79–80, 330
Sense of the House resolutions, 36
sequester, defined, 330
sergeant-at-arms, 57, 330

service academy nominations, 274–277
session
  closed session, 323
  definition, 331
  executive session, 325
  First Session, 24, 84–85
  legislative session, 327
  pro forma session, 329
  Second Session, 24, 85–86
Shays, Chris, Rep. (R-Conn.), 148
silly season, 86
Silverman, David, *Taxes For Dummies,* 117
Simpson, Alan, Sen. (R-Wyo., 1979-1997), 200
sine die, defined, 331
Smith, Bud, *Creating Web Pages For Dummies,*
  6th Edition, 240
Social Security agency, 272
soft money, 147–148, 331
sound bite, 265, 331
Speaker of the House, 24, 77, 331
special committees, 68, 334
special interests, 159–160, 331
special orders, defined, 331
specialized publications, 263
spending limits (defined), 331
spin, 221, 331
sponsors (bills), 331
staffers
  administrative assistant (AA), 202, 321
  applying for a staff position, 204
  appointment secretary, 202
  caseworker, 203
  chief of staff (CoS), 202
  committee staffers, 200, 207–209, 324
  communications director, 202
  constituent services representative, 203
  contacting, 199–200
  definition, 331
  district director, 203
  e-mail processing, 184–185
  field representative, 203
  finding, 209
  gatekeepers, 200
  guiding principles, 203–204
  House of Representatives, 57
  leadership staffers, 200, 209–210
  legislative assistant (LA), 202, 327
  legislative correspondent, 203
  legislative director (LD), 202
  meeting, 305–308
  office manager, 203

office structure, 204–206
officer staffers, 200
personal assistant, 203
personal staffers, 200–207, 328
personalities, 206–207
press secretary, 202, 329
receptionist, 203
roles, 57
scheduler, 202
Senate, 57
support staffers, 201, 210–215
systems administrator, 203
turnover, 206
staffing history, 201
standing committees, 68, 331, 333–334
State Department, 273
State of the Union address, 121
States News Service, 262
states rights, 41
statutes at large, defined, 331
Stern, H. Amy, *Congressional Quarterly's
  Politics in America*, 34, 261
stumping, defined, 331
subcommittees, 331
substitute amendment, 97, 321–322
Summerhouse, 294
Sumner, Charles, Sen. (R-Mass.,
  1851–1874), 99
supplemental appropriations, defined, 331
support staff, 201, 210–215
Supreme Court, 15, 283
suspension of the rules, defined, 331
syndicated columnists, 256
systems administrator, 203

• T •

tabling a bill, defined, 331
Talese, Gay, *The Kingdom and the Power,* 268
talk shows, 265–266
talking heads, defined, 331
talking points, defined, 331
tax expenditures, defined, 331
taxes
  committees, 115–116
  creation of new taxes, 36
  General Accounting Office (GAO), 211–213
  Internal Revenue Service (IRS), 117, 272
  legislation, 114–117
  purpose of, 114
  regulations, 117

tax credits, 114
tax cuts, 114
Whiskey Rebellion, 36
Taxes For Dummies, Eric Tyson and David Silverman, 117
television networks, 236–237, 263–265
Terry, David, California Chief Justice, 99
testifying before Congress, 178–180, 331
Texas Monthly magazine, 259
This Week (television show), 265
Thomas, Bill, Rep. (R-Calif.), 17, 99
Thomas, Clarence, Supreme Court Justice, 51
Thomas Web site, 91, 170
Thurmond, Strom, Sen. (R-S.C.), 47
Time, 257
Tolchin, Martin and Sue, *Glass Houses: Congressional Ethics and the Politics of Venom,* 25
toll-free number for Congress, 315
touring the Capitol, 286–287
Tower, John, Sen. (R-Texas, 1961–1985), 51
trade publications, 263
travel perks, 193–195
treaties, 49–50
Truman, Harry, 107
turnover of congressional staffs, 206
TV coverage, 236–238
TV networks, 236–237, 263–265
Tyson, Eric, *Taxes For Dummies,* 117

• *U* •

Ujifusa, Grant, *National Journal's Almanac of American Politics,* 34
unanimous consent, defined, 331
unanimous consent request, defined, 332
unfunded mandates, 332
union calendar, defined, 323
United Press International, 262
unlimited debate, defined, 332
up or down vote, 101, 332
U.S. Air Force Academy, 275
USA Today, 254–255
U.S. Botanic Gardens Conservatory, 292
U.S. Capitol Police, 249, 286
U.S. Capitol Preservation Commission, 214
U.S. Coast Guard Academy, 275
U.S. Congress Handbook, guide to Congress, 91
U.S. Merchant Marine Academy, 275
U.S. Military Academy, 275

U.S. Naval Academy, 275
U.S. News & World Report, 257
U.S. territories, representation in House, 24

• *V* •

vehicle, defined, 332
veto
  definition, 332
  line-item veto, 327
  overriding, 108, 328
  pocket veto, 107–108, 329
  purpose of, 105, 107–108
  return veto, 107
vice president of the United States
  academy nominations, 277
  role in Senate, 78
violence during floor debates, 99
visuals, 237–238, 332
voice vote, 101, 332
vote, defined, 332
Vote.com Web site, 268
Votenet Solutions, 91
voting for Congress, 20–21, 84
voting in Congress
  bell systems, 293
  House of Representatives, 101
  influence and power of party leaders, 76
  key votes, 162, 327
  online voting records, 316
  proxy vote, 329
  quorum, 100–101, 329
  roll-call vote, 98, 100–101, 330
  scorecards, 162–163, 330
  Senate, 101
  up or down vote, 101, 332
  voice vote, 101, 332
  yea and nay vote, 101, 332

• *W* •

The Wall Street Journal, 252, 254
The Washington Monthly, 258
The Washington Post, 253
The Washington Times, 255
Washington Week in Review (television show), 265
Washingtonian magazine, 259
Watergate, 144, 252
Ways and Means Committee, 115

Web sites
American Civil Liberties Union, 162
American Conservative Union, 162
American Federation of State, County, and
Municipal Employees
(AFSCME), 162
Americans for Democratic Action, 162
Architect of the Capitol, 285
Campaign Finance Institute (CFI), 143, 153
Center for Responsive Politics, 153
Chamber of Commerce, 162
Christian Coalition, 162
Clerk of the House, 32
Concord Coalition, 162
Congressional Budget Office (CBO), 211
Congressional Quarterly, 260
CQ.com On Congress, 260
creating, 240–241
C-SPAN, 73
Dow Jones' Factiva, 300
Drudge Report, 267
FastPolitics.com, 268
federal agencies, 272
Federal Election Commission (FEC),
141, 153
General Accounting Office (GAO), 213
Government Printing Office, 214
The Hill, 259–260
House Action Reports, 260
House of Representatives, 29–30, 32, 317
Information Technology Industry
Council, 162
League of Conservation Voters, 162
Lexis-Nexis, 300
Library of Congress, 91
National Tax-Limitation Committee, 162
National Taxpayers Union, 162
The New York Times, 254
Newsweek, 257
Office of Compliance, 214
representatives' individual sites, 30–31

Roll Call, 260
Senate, 43, 45
States News Service, 262
Thomas, 91, 170
Time, 257
USA Today, 255
U.S. News & World Report, 257
Vote.com, 268
The Wall Street Journal, 254
The Washington Post, 253
The Washington Times, 255
Webster, Daniel, Sen. (Whig-Mass.,
1827–1841), 46, 95
*Webster's New World American Words of
Freedom,* Stephen F. Rohde, 15
The Weekly Standard, 258
well, 96, 100, 332
whip, 77–78, 332
whip count, defined, 332
whip notices, 90
Whiskey Rebellion, 36
Willard Hotel, 159
Wilson, Woodrow, 17
wire services, 261–262
women in Congress, 42
wonk, defined, 332
Woodward, Bob, *All the President's Men,* 252,
268
writing
bills, 59
letters to a representative or senator,
181–183, 185–186
press releases, 229–230

• *X-Y-Z* •

yea and nay vote, 101, 332
*The Years of Lyndon Johnson: Master of the
Senate,* Robert A. Caro, 45
yield (debate), defined, 332

FOR DUMMIES®

The easy way to get more done and have more fun

PERSONAL FINANCE & BUSINESS

Investing
0-7645-2431-3

Home Buying
0-7645-5331-3

Grant Writing
0-7645-5307-0

Also available:

Accounting For Dummies
(0-7645-5314-3)

Business Plans Kit For Dummies
(0-7645-5365-8)

Managing For Dummies
(1-5688-4858-7)

Mutual Funds For Dummies
(0-7645-5329-1)

QuickBooks All-in-One Desk Reference For Dummies
(0-7645-1963-8)

Resumes For Dummies
(0-7645-5471-9)

Small Business Kit For Dummies
(0-7645-5093-4)

Starting an eBay Business For Dummies
(0-7645-1547-0)

Taxes For Dummies 2003
(0-7645-5475-1)

HOME, GARDEN, FOOD & WINE

Feng Shui
0-7645-5295-3

Gardening
0-7645-5130-2

Cooking
0-7645-5250-3

Also available:

Bartending For Dummies
(0-7645-5051-9)

Christmas Cooking For Dummies
(0-7645-5407-7)

Cookies For Dummies
(0-7645-5390-9)

Diabetes Cookbook For Dummies
(0-7645-5230-9)

Grilling For Dummies
(0-7645-5076-4)

Home Maintenance For Dummies
(0-7645-5215-5)

Slow Cookers For Dummies
(0-7645-5240-6)

Wine For Dummies
(0-7645-5114-0)

FITNESS, SPORTS, HOBBIES & PETS

Fitness
0-7645-5167-1

Golf
0-7645-5146-9

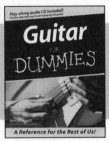

Guitar
0-7645-5106-X

Also available:

Cats For Dummies
(0-7645-5275-9)

Chess For Dummies
(0-7645-5003-9)

Dog Training For Dummies
(0-7645-5286-4)

Labrador Retrievers For Dummies
(0-7645-5281-3)

Martial Arts For Dummies
(0-7645-5358-5)

Piano For Dummies
(0-7645-5105-1)

Pilates For Dummies
(0-7645-5397-6)

Power Yoga For Dummies
(0-7645-5342-9)

Puppies For Dummies
(0-7645-5255-4)

Quilting For Dummies
(0-7645-5118-3)

Rock Guitar For Dummies
(0-7645-5356-9)

Weight Training For Dummies
(0-7645-5168-X)

Available wherever books are sold.
Go to www.dummies.com or call 1-877-762-2974 to order direct

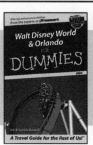

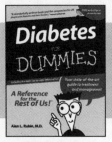

FOR DUMMIES®

Helping you expand your horizons and realize your potential

GRAPHICS & WEB SITE DEVELOPMENT

0-7645-1651-5

Creating Web Pages

0-7645-1643-4

Macromedia Flash MX

0-7645-0895-4

PROGRAMMING & DATABASES

0-7645-0746-X

Visual Studio .NET

0-7645-1626-4

XML

0-7645-1657-4

LINUX, NETWORKING & CERTIFICATION

0-7645-1545-4

TCP/IP

0-7645-1760-0

Networking

0-7645-0772-9

Available wherever books are sold.
Go to www.dummies.com or call 1-877-762-2974 to order direct